CW00539214

ARCHITECTURE NOW!

HOUSES

2

IMPRINT

PROJECT MANAGEMENT
Florian Kobler, Cologne

COLLABORATION
Harriet Graham, Turin

PRODUCTION
Ute Wachendorf, Cologne

DESIGN
Sense/Net, Andy Disl and Birgit Eichwede, Cologne

GERMAN TRANSLATION
Kristina Brigitta Köper, Berlin

FRENCH TRANSLATION
Jacques Bosser, Paris

PRINTED IN ITALY
ISBN 978-3-8365-1973-1

Hohenzollernring 53
D-50672 Cologne
www.taschen.com

ARCHITECTURE NOW!

HOUSES

Architektur heute! HÄUSER

L'architecture d'aujourd'hui! MAISONS

Philip Jodidio

2

CONTENTS

INTRODUCTION

HOUSES ON THE EDGE

A book about houses is interesting for all kinds of reasons, some avowed, and others less worthy of praise. There is always a bit of voyeurism in the urge to see someone else's interior. How do the rich live? What is it like to have a fabulous beachside house in Bahia, Brazil? In fact, the JZ House (Camaçari, Bahia, Brazil, 2006–08, page 75) by the architects Bernardes + Jacobsen is, at 1850 square meters, the largest house published in this second volume of *Architecture Now! Houses*. And a very beautiful house it is. But what of houses of more "normal" dimensions? Those are present here, too, and in great number. The brutal economic slowdown experienced in the housing market in the United States or in Spain, for example, has already taken part of its toll in this selection. There are fewer completely extravagant houses like the 3000-square-meter YTL Residence published in the first volume of *Architecture Now! Houses* (Kuala Lumpur, Malaysia, 2004–08, Jouin Manku architects). On the other hand, there are surely more very small houses, often built with limited means. Thus, at just 6.5 square meters, the Watershed (Willamette Valley, Oregon, USA, 2006–07, page 145) holds the record in this book for the smallest usable floor area. Casey Brown's Permanent Camping residence (Mudgee, NSW, Australia, 2007, page 89) weighs in at a mere 18 square meters, while Sou Fujimoto's Final Wooden House (Kumamura, Kumamoto, Japan, 2007–08, page 164) has 22 square meters of usable space perched in unexpected locations. For those who have written in the press that books such as the Taschen *Architecture Now!* series will have less to focus on in the midst of economic downturn, this book is a first response. Architects are nothing if not adaptable, and when clients ask for smaller, cheaper houses, they will have to satisfy that demand. There is something, too, to be said for the inevitable pressure to be inventive posed by economic constraints. A number of houses in this book demonstrate precisely that truth, and confirm that new houses have not gone the way of Bernie Madoff and other "stars" of economic collapse.

HOW MUCH DOES IT COST?

Another, sometimes unstated question concerning houses designed by architects is how much they cost. The answer is, usually a bit more than the equivalent size house by a less talented designer. Unfortunately, although we systematically ask the architects present in these books how much a published house cost to build, they frequently decline to divulge this information, usually to ensure the privacy of their clients. For those who hesitate to call on an architect because of cost considerations, the current climate should encourage them to be demanding and to set precise limits in their own budget. With somewhat less work, even well-known architects may well be game to take on the challenge of cheaper creativity.

Environmental concerns are clearly more present than they were even in the recent past. Many architects make use of "passive" strategies that may involve the orientation of a house or the nature of its glazing. The notion of thermal mass associated with substantial concrete elements is also cited regularly as a way to reduce energy consumption. To put things clearly, a large stone (i.e. concrete) mass preserves coolness in summer and radiates daylight heat slowly at night when it is cool. These strategies do not logically add a great deal to construction costs, whereas other methods, ranging from solar panels to heat pumps can, indeed, create an initial extra expense, presumably compensated over time by lower electricity bills.

1
Olson Kundig Architects, Rolling Huts, Mazama, Washington, USA, 2007

1

CHEAP THRILLS

On occasion, concerns for both ecology and economy are combined in a single house. The Watershed designed by Erin Moore of FLOAT (Willamette Valley, Oregon, USA, 2006–07, page 145) has minimal poured-in-place concrete foundation piers, while a steel frame allows cedar planks to be bolted on (or off) with ease. Encouraging awareness of the natural setting in the watershed of the Marys River is one objective of this tiny structure, but it is clearly also a rather inexpensive venture. The Watershed can be compared to Casey Brown's Permanent Camping structure in Australia (2007, page 89), half a world away. Set in a mountainous terrain, the house is clad in copper and can be closed entirely to protect it from frequent bush fires near its isolated site. Prefabricated in Sydney and transported to Mudgee, Permanent Camping makes use of roof water-collectors, and a wood-fired stove. With a nine-square-meter footprint, this house would not make much of an impact on its environment in any case, but the architects have emphasized both its economic and ecological aspects in using recycled ironbark (eucalyptus) inside, for example. Permanent Camping sits lightly on the ground and looks as though it could be hauled away as easily as it was transported to the site. The concept of sitting above the ground, as though accepting the transient nature of both human occupation of a structure and indeed architecture itself, is a relatively frequent element of Australian contemporary architecture, carried in this instance to its logical extreme. Although the Watershed is in a more willful mode of environmental observation and respect, both of these tiny wilderness houses could be seen as responses to the degradation of urban and suburban living environments and their attendant wave of pollutants and waste.

Rolling Huts (Mazama, Washington, USA, 2007, page 298) designed by the noted architect Tom Kundig, Principal of Olson Kundig Architects, are guest houses located on a former camping site. Their wheeled design is meant to preserve the mountain meadow where they are located, but then, too, the steel box and wood platform design speaks of a return to fundamental values, which more than anything else may characterize the spirit of the moment in house design. Tom Kundig states: "The huts evoke Thoreau's simple cabin in the woods; the structures take second place to nature."

Concerns of economy are expressed in many houses in this volume, but architects do not always point them out. The New York architect Thomas Phifer built his Salt Point House (Salt Point, New York, USA, 2006–07, page 19) in the Hudson River Valley. At 204 square meters, this house is much larger than the more experimental wilderness houses of Erin Moore or Casey Brown, and yet, from its passive energy schemes (natural ventilation, etc.) to its use of materials, the Salt Point House might also be termed appropriate for today's more cautious climate, even though it was completed in 2007. "All of the building and finish materials were carefully selected for function, durability, and especially economy. In the interior, the walls, floors, and ceilings are all clad in economical and durable maple plywood. Custom furniture pieces and interior cabinetry are constructed of the same plywood," state the architects.

TESTING THE LIMITS

Whatever the economic climate, house projects are often an occasion for architects to test limits—be these the limits of what the climate will accept or those of local authorities. The point is rarely one of simply making a spectacular gesture—it is more often a matter of seeing what houses and, indeed, architecture are capable of. Though numerous architects have experimented with moving parts in their

2

2
Sou Fujimoto Architects, N House, Oita Prefecture, Japan, 2007–08

buildings, much as Santiago Calatrava has throughout his career, the London firm dRMM attempted with its Sliding House (Suffolk, UK, 2006–09, page 111) to make a residence that can literally change size and form at will. This feat is accomplished by inserting a 20-ton mobile roof and wall enclosure mounted on rails. Thus the apparently ordinary lines of the house can be stretched, increasing available floor area by as much as 100 square meters.

The Japanese architect Sou Fujimoto is the designer of numerous houses that challenge some of the basic, generally accepted principles of such structures. His N House (Oita Prefecture, Japan, 2007–08, page 159) is made up of a succession of shells that generate ambiguous space, neither fully within the house, nor really outside either. "I have always had doubts about streets and houses being separated by a single wall," says Fujimoto, "and wondered if a gradation of this rich domain accompanied by various senses of distance between streets and houses might be a possibility, such as: a place inside the house that is fairly near the street; a place that is a bit further from the street; and a place as far removed from the street as possible, in secure privacy." When considering houses, particularly urban ones, few architects have ever dared to question the issue of boundaries in this way. In Japan, in particular, land in cities is expensive and rare, and the usual tendency is to squeeze as many square meters of usable space into a plot as zoning regulations allow. Fujimoto takes a step back with his N House to examine the very fundamental relationship between architecture and the city. Another project by this prolific and fascinating architect is the so-called Final Wooden House (Kumamura, Kumamoto, Japan, 2007–08, page 164). Measuring just 22 square meters, the Final Wooden House is the result of a "mindless" stacking of 350-millimeter square pieces of lumber on a tiny, 15-square-meter site. This approach generates a distribution of solids and voids that counters almost all expected norms. This is not a house in the usual sense, but rather more of a spatial experiment. "Rather than just a new architecture," Fujimoto concludes, "this is a new origin, a new existence."

HOUSE BEFORE HOUSE

Sou Fujimoto is one participant in an ambitious project called Sumika (Utsunomiya, Tochigi Prefecture, Japan, 2008, page 216–227), headed by the architect Toyo Ito with Tokyo Gas as the sponsor. The idea of this group of houses, and one pavilion designed by Ito, was to explore the idea of what a "primitive" house might be like in a modern city. In terms of size, and also ideas, this initiative also fits in with the growing perception that living standards and the sort of freedom to pollute that has existed until now are both due to be more strictly controlled. The other participants in the Sumika project were Terunobu Fujimori, a Professor at Tokyo University well-known for his tiny teahouses and residences inspired by Japanese tradition, and Taira Nishizawa, the brother of Ryue Nishizawa of SANAA fame. Sou Fujimoto's project, called House Before House, measures just 61 square meters in usable floor area. "I envisioned creating a place that is suggestive of the primitive future, analogous to being simultaneously new and from the prehistoric age; engendered with unforeseen newness yet subsuming something akin to the unequivocal and archetypical form of a house," declares Fujimoto. He maintains that a house must be almost "indistinguishable" from the city in which it is located, further advancing the ideas behind his N House and other works. Terunobu Fujimori ventured to create a "cavelike" house that in some sense harkens back to the origins of human habitation. Taira Nishizawa's house is built to reconquer the diurnal rhythms often lost in urban circumstances, where day and night can easily be confused. By using ample daylight and natural ventilation, Nishizawa seeks to make modernity aware of basic facts that have been lost from both theory and practice in residential architecture. Toyo Ito's Sumika Pavilion (published in this volume, page 217) is a general meeting place for this group of houses, where treelike forms and ample light also bridge the gap between the distant past and the densely urban present of Japan.

Experimentation of the sort sponsored by Tokyo Gas for the Sumika Project is certainly one way to engage inventive architects on the path to renewing the very idea of the house. Those who know Japan appreciate its unusual blend of extreme modernity and acceptance of tradition. This link between past and present that modern architecture has been seeking to reestablish since the *tabula rasa* of early modernism is perhaps most present and fruitful in Japan. Because houses engage more modest means than public architecture or other large-scale buildings, it is clear that a good part of the most innovative architecture comes to the fore in the area of residential design.

THE MEXICANS ARE COMING

Books about contemporary architecture such as this one are dependent on good sources of information. It may be worth noting that the talented Mexican architect Michael Rojkind was asked if he had designed any houses recently. He responded by saying that although he had not, he had friends who had. Michael Rojkind put us in touch with PRODUCTORA and Celula Arquitectura. PRODUCTORA then gave our address to Studio Gracia. PRODUCTORA is a Mexico City-based office founded in 2006. Its founding members are Abel Perles (born in Argentina in 1972), Carlos Bedoya (born in 1973 in Mexico), Victor Jaime (born in 1978 in Mexico), and Wonne Ickx (born in 1974 in Belgium). Their House in Chihuahua, Mexico (2008, page 325) is a study in white polygons inserted into a desert environment, proof, if need be, that contemporary residential architecture at a high level exists in many places other than Tokyo or Los Angeles. Celula Arquitectura is a "multidisciplinary practice focused on integrating architecture, landscape, and art" also based in Mexico City. Their Clay House (Valle de Bravo, Mexico, 2007–08, page 101) mixes a steel-frame structure with a surprising clay veneer cladding that is inspired by local architecture. This mixture of modernity and old methods updated for current needs shows that architects from many different parts of the world are looking to the past for a certain amount of inspiration without in any way bringing the so-called postmodern pastiche back from its well-deserved place of rest. Jorge Gracia Garcia (Jorge Gracia Studio) is another Mexican architect under 40 years of age (1973), but he is based in San Diego. His house in Todos Santos (Baja California Sur, Mexico, 2006, page 177) was built entirely with local materials and has sand-colored exposed concrete walls that, again, evoke local finishes. Though surely comfortable, this 320-square-meter residence does immediately bring to mind the architect's stated desire to "get back to the basics."

MOUNTAINS AND SEA

Economic concerns are surely rippling through the Latin American housing (and architecture) markets, and yet a number of the houses published here are clear indications that inventiveness or, indeed, astonishing designs are by no means the monopoly of clever Japanese architects. dRN Architects, founded in 2005 by Nicolás del Río (born in 1975) and Max Núñez (born in 1976) in Santiago, can be cited as an example. The pair have designed a number of houses in extreme locations, such as their Mountain Refuge C7 (Portillo, Chile, 2008), built at

3
McBride Charles Ryan,
Letterbox House, Blairgowrie, Victoria, Australia, 2006–08

an altitude of 2870 meters near the Cerro Aconcagua. The architects' Los Canteros Mountain Refuge (Farellones, Chile, 2008, page 117) is located at a "mere" 2000 meters above sea level, and is built to deal with rigorous winter conditions. Double thermal insulation and very limited glazing in the lower levels of the house contrast with the upper story, where spectacular views of the mountain environment are a key feature of the house. While the use of black slate for some exterior cladding is a nod to local stone structures, this house is original in form and spirit. Though it sits on a hillside with other, somewhat less distinguished, residences, it remains proof that good architecture not only stands out, but can also deal with difficult conditions, which here required building in the six-month warmer period.

Another Chilean team under 40—Mauricio Pezo (born in Chile in 1973) and Sofía Von Ellrichshausen (born in Argentina in 1976)—has recently completed two formally similar houses, respectively in San Pedro (Fosc House, Chile, 2008–09, page 315) and in Andalue (Wolf House, Chile, 2006–07, page 21). In relatively simple exterior envelopes, in colored concrete or metal, the architects have inserted large windows that give an unexpected openness to the somewhat irregular but monolithic forms of the houses. These are singular presences, measuring 160 square meters and 136 square meters, respectively, that retain the power both to surprise and to satisfy the needs of the client. Achieving originality within fairly restricted circumstances is no small accomplishment of these young, talented architects.

The JZ House (Bernardes + Jacobsen, Camaçari, Bahia, Brazil, 2008, page 75) has already been referred to as the largest house in this book, at 1850 square meters. In many senses, it is at the opposite end of the spectrum from the high-altitude exercises of dRN, for example. Located not only at the beach side, but literally on a sand dune, this house is the stuff of dreams of the Brazilian paradise. Bernardes + Jacobsen are used to building sumptuous homes, but they have also proven their ability to create sensational temporary architecture, as was the case in their Tim Festival (Rio de Janeiro, 2007), a 40 000-square-meter venue for a two-night music festival that they assembled in one week on a limited budget with 250 six- and twelve-meter shipping containers. The JZ House is partially set up on piloti, and features a "great room" with a sensational view of the ocean and gardens. Local materials, such as eucalyptus trellises and Bahia beige marble for the floors, were used by the architects, but this might not be the most ecologically responsible house published in this volume. Houses published in this book are present for reasons of their formal architectural qualities, and, in this instance, too, their ability to make readers dream of a place where life is somehow better. The familiarity of these Rio architects with their own country, and with a clientele that clearly has the means to build what it wants, allows them to surpass what outsiders might imagine as being possible.

A LETTERBOX AND A BIT OF GREEN

At the opposite end of the world, but also in the Southern Hemisphere, the continuing creativity of architects from Australia and New Zealand is demonstrated by a number of houses in this book. Often, these houses take advantage of spectacular natural settings, as is the case of the Sandy Bay Farm House (Sandy Bay, Tutukaka Coast, New Zealand, 2007–08, page 133) by the Auckland architects Fearon Hay. Here, a modern, single-story structure with a good deal of full-height glazing is set on a ridge on the Tutukaka Coast of the Northland region overlooking the Pacific Ocean in the direction of the Poor Knights Archipelago. This house demonstrates that a part of the talent of architects designing houses is expressed in their ability to find clients with the taste for such a site, and, in this instance, to fit a comfortable house into

4
McBride Charles Ryan,
Klein Bottle House, Rye, Victoria,
Australia, 2005–07

4

an obviously sensitive natural setting. The Australian architect Robert McBride has taken a different approach to originality with the Letterbox House (Blairgowrie, Australia, 2006–08, page 271) and the Klein Bottle House (Rye, Australia, 2005–07, page 276), both published here. "We like buildings that make you smile (not laugh)," says the architect. The first house is imagined as though it might have unfolded from the letterbox that gives it its name, while the second is an "origami version" of a "descriptive model of a surface developed by topological mathematicians" (the Klein bottle). While the interests in these cases appear to be formal, they are nonetheless interesting takes on the kind of shapes that can be generated around a residential project. The McBride houses are certainly surprising and original—in a way precisely the kind of thing many clients hope to get when they call on an inventive architect.

Michael Bellemo (born in 1967 in Melbourne), and Cat Macleod (born in 1963 in Penang, Malaysia), founded Bellemo & Cat in Melbourne in 1992. Their 155-square-meter Polygreen residence (Northcote, Melbourne, Australia, 2007–08, page 69) was built for a low budget of 220 000 euros. They have used a decidedly industrial vocabulary for this structure, located in a service lane for old brick warehouses. Bellemo & Cat are by no means the first architects, nor the last, to use industrial elements in residential architecture—in this instance, they have also added a translucent printed skin that makes the building stand out clearly from its environment despite its adoption of the language of warehouses. The color of the printed skin (and the name of the project) was their somewhat humorous response to a neighbor's request for a bit of green.

BRAD MAKES IT RIGHT

In recent years, there have been a number of ambitious projects involving "star" architects who are called on to design houses within a given site. The houses at Sagaponac in New York, or the Sumika Project are examples of this kind of initiative. Often, the very scale of the projects and the nature of the personalities involved condemn these concepts to a certain degree of failure. Two ongoing and ambitious housing projects published here are Make it Right, an effort to build new houses for people who suffered from Hurricane Katrina in the Lower Ninth Ward of New Orleans, and, in a very different vein, Ordos 100, in Inner Mongolia.

The Lower Ninth Ward was one of the areas most severely damaged by Hurricane Katrina in August 2005. In an initiative curated by the actor Brad Pitt, work was undertaken beginning in 2007 to build 150 homes. The Berlin and Los Angeles-based architects Graft and William McDonough + Partners collaborated with Brad Pitt, Reed Kroloff, and the Lower Ninth Ward Community Coalition to develop a scheme that would eventually call on a total of 13 local, national, and international architects to design low-cost houses for the area. Criteria for the selection were prior interest or involvement in New Orleans, preferably post-Katrina, and/or experience with disaster relief, familiarity and interest in sustainability, experience with residential and multi-family housing, proven skilled innovation on low-budget projects, experience dealing with structures that must successfully address water-based or low-lying environment(s), and a clear respect for design quality. Amongst the architects participating are Graft (Berlin), Trahan Architects (Baton Rouge), Kieran Timberlake (Philadelphia), Morphosis (Los Angeles), Pugh + Scarpa (Santa Monica), Adjaye Associates (London), MVRDV (Rotterdam), and Shigeru Ban (Tokyo). John Williams Architects from New Orleans are serving as executive architects for the project. The first Make it Right House was inaugurated in time for the third anniversary of the storm,

5

5
Graft, Make it Right, New Orleans, Louisiana, USA, 2007–

in 2008, and as this book was going to press, there were eight homes completed (two of which by Graft are featured on page 281). In July 2009, Make it Right announced a new series of 14 duplex houses designed by such architects as Hitoshi Abe, Elemental (Chile), and Gehry Partners. Architects such as Shigeru Ban or Elemental have considerable experience in refugee housing or residences for the disadvantaged, so their presence here is not surprising. What is more intriguing is the way that the star power of Brad Pitt allied with the talents of Graft and others has drawn in a veritable who's-who of contemporary architecture, both in the United States and internationally. Given the usual distance between low-cost initiatives and most contemporary architects who are well known, Make it Right may just have more impact on the profession itself than it does on the Lower Ninth Ward. In any case, this is a laboratory for storm-resistant, inexpensive, responsible housing.

The Ordos 100 project curated by the artist Ai Wei Wei, with an initial selection of participating architects by Herzog & de Meuron and with Jiang Yuan Water Engineering Ltd. as the client, is not really a humanitarian project like Make it Right. The project statement for Ordos 100 reads: "The scope of the project is to develop 100 villas in Ordos, Inner Mongolia, China, for the client, Jiang Yuan Water Engineering Ltd. FAKE Design, Ai Wei Wei studio in Beijing, has developed the master plan for the 100 parcels of land and will curate the project, while Herzog & de Meuron have selected the 100 architects to participate. The collection of 100 architects hails from 27 countries around the globe. The project has been divided into two phases. The first phase is the development of 28 parcels while the second phase will develop the remaining 72. Each architect is responsible for a 1000-square-meter villa." Actually, the project seems to have been divided into a third phase with six houses designed nearby by Ai Wei Wei, EM2N (Zurich), Galli Rudolf (Zurich), EXH from Shanghai, the large international firm Cannon Design, and the Basel team HHF. The Dune House by HHF (Ordos, Inner Mongolia, China, page 200) is nearing completion, and images of this ambitious house are published here, although the residence is not yet complete. The very international aspect of Ordos 100, with its leaders coming from China and Switzerland and participants from all over the rest of the world, is certainly of interest and indicative, again, but for different reasons, of the spreading influence of contemporary architecture of quality, especially where houses, less capital-intensive than larger projects, are concerned. Ordos 100 is certainly to be followed if the enterprise manages to advance beyond these first experimental projects.

METAMORPHOSES

Renovations and extensions have long been a staple of the work of some architects. These are also the kind of projects that can be expected to proliferate in times of economic hardship, since they usually engender lower costs than newly built houses. Two projects of this nature were coincidentally carried out by architects with the kind of broad international background that seems to be more and more common in young firms. The Powerhouse Company was founded in 2005 simultaneously in Rotterdam and Copenhagen by Charles Bessard and Nanne de Ru. Bessard was born in 1971 in France, and Nanne de Ru was born in 1976 in the Netherlands. Their Spiral House (Burgundy, France, 2007–08, page 13) is an extension of an old house. This project is interesting not only for its exterior architecture, but above all for its concept of circulation that the architects term a "programmatic loop." With its sophisticated play on transparency and opacity, this extension is almost a re-creation of a modern house in lieu of the older residence that occupied the large property in the past. Delphine Ding was born in Switzerland in 1978 and graduated from the Federal Polytechnic University of Lausanne (EPFL) in 2005. José Ulloa Davet was born in Chile in

6
Powerhouse Company, Spiral House, Burgundy, France, 2007–08

6

1977. He graduated as an architect from the Universidad Católica de Chile in 2002. Ding and Ulloa Davet have worked together since 2005. Their Metamorphosis House (Casablanca, Tunquén, Chile, 2008, page 397) is a reworking of a 1990 wooden house undertaken for a low budget of $70 000. A "ventilated wooden skin" and terraces give an overall appearance that hardly seems anything else than an entirely new building. In another part of the world, the inventive architect Pei Zhu took on an unexpected project for the artist Cai Guo-Qiang (Cai Guo-Qiang Courtyard House Renovation, Beijing, China, 2007, page 385). A courtyard house is, of course, one of the most frequent designs in Chinese traditional architecture. In this instance, the architect has both renovated existing spaces, such as the old wooden structure, and brought in what he calls "futuristic space" in the southern part of the building. It is interesting to note that Cai Guo-Qiang has made his considerable international reputation through works that often make reference to Chinese art and culture of the past. He frequently uses fireworks, for example. The renovation carried out by Pei Zhu would seem to be very much in the spirit of the work of Cai Guo-Qiang, at once decidedly modern and yet also rooted in the past, the omnipresent tradition of their native China.

The facility with which information about very recent architecture can now be transmitted via Internet may be one reason for which talents from countries not always noted for their contemporary architecture have been coming to the fore. The development of Eastern Europe is one factor in a spreading awareness of the interest of well-designed houses. Born in 1969 in Katowice, Robert Konieczny is the principal of KWK PROMES, a firm that has completed a number of unusual houses. One of these, the 556-square-meter Safe House (Okrzeszyn, Poland, 2005–08, page 257), as its name implies, puts great stock in the safety of its residents. This leads to a closed, bunker-like design, whose almost worrisome aspect is accentuated by its black color. For all its sealed aspect, the Safe House also opens out onto its garden, offering a few rays of sunlight to its well-protected inhabitants. The OUTrial House (Ksiazenice, Poland, 2005–08, page 260) has the same rather blocky, geometric appearance as the Safe House, but it also has a grass-covered roof that somewhat softens its relatively hard lines. These houses may not fit readily into the stereotypes imagined for a book about the latest contemporary architecture, yet they are surprising and, in their own way, inventive.

AMERICA, STILL DREAMING

Because of the high rates of ownership of homes in the United States and its position as one of the centers of creativity of contemporary architecture, the country has long played a central role in the evolution of house design. And yet something of a drought of invention has touched on America in recent years, taken up first in a spiraling race to build increasingly extravagant mansions, and more recently in a reverse spiral of foreclosure and slowing construction. The examples selected in this volume would, however, tend to show that contemporary architecture is, indeed, alive and well in the land of Frank Lloyd Wright. The Red House (Los Angeles, California, USA, 2004–06, page 95) by Padraic Cassidy is an interesting composition realized for the screenwriter Larry Karaszewski. Cassidy, who worked in the offices of Daly Genik and Frank Gehry before creating his own office, has used both color and geometry to enliven this house, which stands out boldly from its eucalyptus forest site. At the opposite end of the country, Kyu Sung Woo, who worked from 1970 to 1974 for José Lluis Sert (Sert, Jackson & Associates), has created his own family vacation house in Putney, Vermont. Split into three elements, this house shows a characteristic that

7

7
Kyu Sung Woo, Putney Mountain House, Putney, Vermont, USA, 2005–07

seems to be more and more frequent in contemporary house design—a basic modernity that is rendered more complex through a sophisticated juxtaposition of elements and forms. Kyu Sung Woo pays careful attention to energy consumption in this design, which confirms its fundamentally contemporary nature.

A final, perhaps more unexpected, example of creativity in contemporary American architecture is proposed here in the form of Michael Jantzen's Homestead House (2009, page 228). Like much of the architect's oeuvre, this house is unbuilt. Using "readily available agricultural building components" for the design, Jantzen is seeking a "prefabricated, modular, high-strength, low-cost, arch building system" that can be assembled using simple tools. Pulped newspaper as insulation, photovoltaic cells, a wind turbine, and passive strategies assure that this house for a new century would indeed be more environmentally responsible than the thousands of suburban houses that dot America's residential areas. Although some may feel that "virtual" architecture has already lived its heyday, Jantzen's Homestead House is proof that some continue to try to improve the life of individuals and the community through architecture.

BACK TO BASICS

Houses can sometimes be assimilated to works of art, in the most positive sense of this analogy. One of the more surprising and inventive houses to have been completed in recent years is Jürgen Mayer-Hermann's (J. Mayer H.) Dupli.Casa (near Ludwigsburg, Germany, 2006–08, page 264). Engaging in a duplication and rotation of the volumes of a family house built on the same site in 1984, the architect constitutes what he calls a "family archeology," at the same time as he creates a lyrical, ebbing and flowing, sculptural, new house. He refers to the existing, older house as a "found object"—an obvious reference to modern art. With its cantilevers and white curves, the Dupli.Casa is not readily comparable to other recent houses, and, as such, it confirms that Germany, too, is a place where the frontiers of contemporary architecture are being redefined. The idea of "archeology" in the case of such a modern residence is one that fits in with worldwide concerns about linking modernity to the roots of culture, of place and making continuity the new rule in place of the *tabula rasa*. This battle is certainly not over—the desire to break with all that is past runs deep in contemporary creativity—but the values that have driven architecture and art for centuries are stronger than superficial change. Economic crisis brings things back into perspective and dictates that basics are again the name of the game. The houses published here may seek to allow unobtrusive observation of an Oregon watershed, or simply to shelter their inhabitants from the storm. Ecology, in the form of lower energy consumption, seems to be here to stay, if only because using less electricity means lower bills. And then, so many of these houses are really points of observation, privileged locations where views of the remaining natural world are framed and cherished. Like Tom Kundig's Rolling Huts, many of these houses admit their fundamentally ephemeral nature. The new rules of ecology dictate that more and more houses can be disassembled, taken away, and perhaps reused, without leaving a trace on the land where they sat. These factors are all relatively new in residential architecture, but they are likely to become more and more present. In many ways, the houses published here are on the edge: partly creations of a new world, and partly anchored in the past.

Though some architects make a substantial effort to interpret the desires of their clients, others clearly attempt to impose their own concept, even their own fantasies, on houses. It is rare that client, architect, and economic interests find the point of equilibrium that makes a

8
J. MAYER H., Dupli.Casa, near Ludwigsburg, Germany, 2006–08

8

contemporary house something of a work of art. When a masterpiece leaks, as did Le Corbusier's Villa Savoye, living in a work of art comes at an unexpected price for the client. Although 2009 may be too early to judge the real fallout of the economic crisis that came to the fore in late 2008, some houses in this volume would already seem to take into account the need for economy or, perhaps more clearly, responsibility that is inevitably being generated by necessity. New houses, or even renovated older ones, will always be needed, and they are a way for architecture to evolve, to change with the times. Because of their rapid construction cycle as compared to larger projects, houses are a veritable barometer of contemporary architecture, or even its future. A modernity that is not reductive, but rather builds on circumstances, sites, conditions, or sometimes just aesthetics is what is driving contemporary architecture today, and these houses demonstrate precisely that point.

Philip Jodidio, Grimentz, Switzerland, August 2009

EINLEITUNG

HÄUSER ZWISCHEN GESTERN UND MORGEN

Ein Buch über Wohnhäuser ist aus den unterschiedlichsten Gründen interessant – aus absolut vertretbaren wie auch aus weniger rühmlichen. Es hat immer auch etwas Voyeuristisches, wenn man sehen will, wie andere Menschen wohnen. Wie leben sie, die Reichen? Wie ist es, ein formidables Anwesen am Strand von Bahia zu besitzen – eines wie die Residência JZ (Camaçari, Bahia, Brasilien, 2006–08, Seite 75) der Architekten Bernardes + Jacobsen? Mit seinen 1850 m² ist es das größte der im vorliegenden zweiten Band von *Architecture Now! Houses* vorgestellen Projekte und schlichtweg schön. Wie aber steht es mit „normal" dimensionierten Häusern? Auch solche sind hier in großer Zahl vertreten. Der gewaltige wirtschaftliche Niedergang des Wohnimmobilienmarktes, sei es in den Vereinigten Staaten oder z. B. in Spanien, hat seinen Niederschlag auch in der vorliegenden Auswahl gefunden: Es gibt weniger übermäßig extravagante Domizile wie die 3000 m² große YTL Residence (Kuala Lumpur, Malaysia, 2004–08, Jouin Manku Architects) aus dem ersten Band von *Architecture Now! Houses*. Stattdessen finden sich diesmal zahlreiche auffallend kleine Häuser, die oftmals mit begrenzten Mitteln entstanden. Den ersten Platz in dieser Hinsicht belegt in diesem Buch das Watershed (Willamette Valley, Oregon, USA, 2006–07, Seite 145), das mit 6,5 m² die kleinste Nutzfläche besitzt. Die von Casey Brown unter dem Namen Permanent Camping entworfene Behausung (Mudgee, NSW, Australien, 2007, Seite 89) wartet mit gerade einmal 18 m² auf, Sou Fujimotos Final Wooden House (Kumamura, Kumamoto, Japan, 2007–08, Seite 164) wiederum mit immerhin 22 m², die sich jedoch auf höchst ungewöhnliche Weise zusammensetzen. Damit sei eine erste Antwort auf Unkenrufe gegeben, wonach in Zeiten einer Rezession der Stoff für Bücher wie die der *Architecture-Now*-Reihe knapp werde. Zu den wichtigsten Eigenschaften eines Architekten gehört seine Anpassungsfähigkeit: Äußern seine Auftraggeber den Wunsch nach kleineren und kostengünstigeren Wohnhäusern, muss er diesem auch entsprechen. Nicht wenige der im Folgenden präsentierten Projekte treten den Beweis an, dass der Innovationszwang, der sich aus ökonomischen Beschränkungen automatisch ergibt, auch einiges für sich hat. Für die jüngere Wohnarchitektur hatte die Finanzkrise jedenfalls keineswegs so negative Auswirkungen wie für Investmenthasardeure wie Bernie Madoff und Konsorten.

WAS SOLL ES KOSTEN?

Eine mitunter vernachlässigte Frage ist die nach den Kosten für den Bau eines Architektenhauses. Die Antwort geht dahin, dass diese für gewöhnlich etwas höher ausfallen als bei einem gleich großen, aber von weniger talentierter Hand entworfenen Eigenheim. Natürlich erkundigen wir uns bei den in unserer Reihe vorgestellten Architekten auch stets nach den Baukosten eines Hauses. Bedauerlicherweise jedoch halten sich die Befragten mit der Preisgabe entsprechender Daten häufig zurück, zumeist um die Privatsphäre ihrer Klienten zu wahren. Wer aus Kostengründen Bedenken hat, die Dienste eines Architekten in Anspruch zu nehmen, der sollte sich vom gegenwärtigen Klima dazu ermuntert fühlen, ein Maximalbudget festzulegen und doch einmal eine Anfrage zu stellen. Angesichts der schlechteren Auftragslage dürften auch bekanntere Architekten dazu bereit sein, die Herausforderung anzunehmen und für weniger Geld kreativ zu werden.

Auch die Berücksichtigung von Umweltaspekten nimmt einen weitaus größeren Raum als noch vor kurzer Zeit ein. Zahlreiche Architekten setzen auf „passive" Strategien wie die Ausrichtung eines Gebäudes oder die Art seiner Verglasung. Auch die Wärmespeicherung durch den Einsatz von Betonelementen gilt als probates Mittel zur Senkung des Energieverbrauchs. Hält doch, konkreter gefasst, großzügig

9
FLOAT, Watershed, Willamette Valley, OR, USA, 2006–07

9

verbauter Stein bzw. Beton im Sommer kühl und strahlt in den kälteren Nachtstunden die tagsüber gespeicherte Wärme wieder ab. Während solche Maßnahmen die Baukosten nicht unbedingt erhöhen, entstehen bei anderen, etwa dem Einbau von Solaranlagen oder Wärmepumpen, anfangs Mehrausgaben, die sich erst im Lauf der Zeit durch niedrigere Stromkosten amortisieren.

KLEINE FREUDEN ZUM KLEINEN PREIS

Bei manchen Häusern greifen ökonomische und ökologische Gesichtspunkte direkt ineinander. Das von Erin Moore, Gründerin und Chefin von FLOAT, entworfene Watershed (Willamette Valley, Oregon, USA, 2006–07, Seite 145) besteht aus minimalen Fundamentpfeilern aus Ortbeton und einem darauf aufsitzenden Stahlrahmen, an den sich Zedernholzbohlen leicht an- und abmontieren lassen. Das kleine Haus will nicht nur die Aufmerksamkeit des Benutzers für die Natur im Einzugsgebiet des Marys River schärfen, sondern ist auch erstaunlich kostengünstig. Ein vergleichbares Projekt ist Casey Browns Permanent Camping (2007, Mudgee, NSW, Australien, Seite 89) auf der anderen Seite der Erdkugel in Australien. Das einsam in einem hügeligen Gelände errichtete Haus wurde mit Kupfer verkleidet und kann vollständig geschlossen werden, um es so vor den in der Umgegend regelmäßig auftretenden Buschfeuern zu schützen. Das in Sydney vorgefertigte und nach Mudgee transportierte Permanent Camping wurde mit Wasserkollektoren auf dem Dach und einem Holzofen ausgestattet. Mit seinen 9 m² Grundfläche sollte das Haus zwar ohnehin keine sonderlichen Auswirkungen auf seine Umwelt haben, doch auch im Innenraum, der mit recyceltem Eukalyptusholz ausgestaltet wurde, setzt sich der ökonomische wie ökologische Anspruch der Architekten fort. Die mit etwas Abstand zum Boden errichtete Konstruktion erweckt den Eindruck, dass sie sich ebenso leicht wieder abtransportieren lasse wie sie hergebracht und aufgebaut worden war. Das Konzept, das Haus nicht komplett auf den Boden aufzusetzen – als würde man sich gleichsam eingestehen, dass die Nutzung durch den Menschen, ja die Architektur selbst nicht von ewiger Dauer sei –, ist in der neueren australischen Architektur verhältnismäßig häufig anzutreffen, wenn auch nicht so extrem umgesetzt wie hier. Während beim Watershed die Naturbeobachtung und der Respekt vor der Umwelt vielleicht noch deutlicher im Vordergrund stehen als bei Casey Browns Entwurf, lassen sich doch beide dieser mitten in der Wildnis aufgestellten Häuser als Gegenentwürfe zu urbanen und suburbanen Lebensräumen mit ihrem Schmutz und Müll begreifen.

Für das Gelände eines ehemaligen Campingplatzes entwarf der renommierte Architekt Tom Kundig, Chefarchitekt des Büros Olson Kundig Architects, seine sogenannten Rolling Huts (Mazama, Washington, USA, 2007, Seite 298). Die Gästehütten wurden mit Rücksicht auf ihren Standort, eine Bergwiese, mit Rädern versehen, aber auch der Stahlrahmen und die Holzterrasse künden von einem wiedererwachten Interesse an einer Rückkehr zu elementaren Werten – ein Kennzeichen der momentan in der Wohnarchitektur vorherrschenden Haltung. Dazu Tom Kundig: „Die Behausungen erinnern an die schlichte Waldhütte Thoreaus; die künstlichen Gebilde lassen der Natur den Vortritt."

Viele Häusern im vorliegenden Band künden von ökonomischen Beschränkungen, auch wenn die Architekten das nicht immer betonen. Das von Thomas Phifer im Hudson River Valley gebaute Salt Point House (Salt Point, New York, USA, 2006–07, Seite 19) ist mit 204 m² Grundfläche deutlich größer als die experimentelleren, in der abgeschiedenen Natur errichteten Häuser Erin Moores oder Casey Browns. Trotzdem kann man dem Gebäude angesichts seiner Passivbauweise (natürliche Belüftung etc.) und der verwendeten Materialien bescheinigen, bereits dem heutigen umsichtigen Geist zu entsprechen, obgleich es schon 2007 fertiggestellt war. Wie die Architekten ausführen, wurden „sämtliche der für Bau und Ausstattung verwendeten Materialien gezielt nach Funktionalität, Haltbarkeit und vor allem Wirtschaftlichkeit ausgewählt. Wände, Böden und Decken im Inneren wurden mit erschwinglichem, dauerhaftem Ahornsperrholz verkleidet, das ebenfalls als Material für das Mobiliar und die festen Einbauten diente."

DIE GRENZEN AUSLOTEN

Unabhängig vom jeweiligen wirtschaftlichen Klima bieten Wohnhausprojekte für Architekten häufig eine Gelegenheit zum Ausloten von Grenzen dar – seien es die Baubestimmungen vor Ort oder die Grenzen dessen, was man der Umwelt zumuten kann. Dabei geht es seltener um ein spektakuläres Zeichen, als vielmehr darum, das Potenzial von Wohnarchitektur – und damit von Architektur als solcher – zu ergründen. Santiago Calatrava etwa experimentiert schon seit langem mit beweglichen Gebäudeteilen. Das Londoner Architekturbüro dRMM hat indes mit seinem Sliding House (Suffolk, Großbritannien, 2006–09, Seite 111) ein Eigenheim entworfen, dessen gesamte Form und Größe beliebig veränderbar sind. Um dieses Kunststück zu vollbringen, wurde ein aus Dach und Wänden bestehendes, 20 t schweres Element auf Schienen gesetzt. Auf diese Weise lässt sich das scheinbar normale Gebäude in die Länge erweitern und seine Grundfläche um mehr als 100 m² vergrößern.

Auch der japanische Architekt Sou Fujimoto hat zahlreiche Gebäude entworfen, die einige anerkannte Grundprinzipien des Wohnhausbaus infrage stellen. Fujimotos Haus N (Präfektur Oita, Japan, 2007–08, Seite 159) besteht aus einer Folge von Gehäusen, die sich zu einem unbestimmten Gesamtraum zusammensetzen, der weder klassischer Innenraum, noch wirklich Außenraum ist. „Es schien mir schon immer zweifelhaft, Straßen und Häuser durch eine einzige Mauer zu trennen", erklärt Fujimoto, „und so fragte ich mich, ob es nicht denkbar sei, eine Abstufung dieser komplexen Zone vorzunehmen, die ein Gefühl für die unterschiedlich großen Entfernungen zwischen Häusern und Straßen vermitteln würde: ein Ort im Haus beispielsweise, der sich recht nah an der Straße befindet, dahinter ein weiterer Ort mit etwas größerem Abstand zur Straße und zuletzt einer, der so weit wie möglich von der Straße entfernt ist und einen abgeschlossenen privaten Bereich bildet." Nur wenige Architekten haben es beim Wohnhausbau, speziell im urbanen Umfeld, bislang gewagt, sich auf diese Weise mit dem Thema Raumbegrenzung auseinanderzusetzen. Gerade in Japan aber ist der Baugrund in den Städten rar und teuer, was im Allgemeinen dazu führt, so viele Quadratmeter an Nutzfläche aus einem Grundstück herauszuholen wie die Baubestimmungen nur irgend erlauben. Mit seinem Haus N geht Fujimoto einen Schritt zurück und untersucht die grundsätzliche Beziehung zwischen Architektur und Großstadt. Ein weiteres Projekt des ebenso faszinierenden wie produktiven Architekten ist sein Final Wooden House (Kumamura, Kumamoto, Japan, 2007–08, Seite 164). Das auf einem nur 15 m² großen Grundstück errichtete Gebilde bietet als Resultat eines „planlosen" Übereinanderstapelns von 350 x 350 mm starken Kanthölzern eine nutzbare Fläche von 22 m². Entstanden ist ein Arrangement aus Massivität und Raum, das im Widerspruch zu praktisch sämtlichen gängigen Normen steht, kein Haus im gewohnten Sinne, eher eine Art Raumexperiment, wie Fujimoto festhält: „Es ist mehr als bloß ein neues Stück Architektur – es ist ein neuer Anfang, eine neue Daseinsweise."

10
Thomas Phifer, Salt Point House, Salt Point, New York, USA, 2006–07

HAUS VOR DEM HAUS

Sou Fujimoto gehört auch zu den Teilnehmern des ambitionierten Sumika-Projekts (Utsunomiya, Präfektur Tochigi, Japan, 2008, Seite 216–227), das der Architekt Toyo Ito mit Unterstützung des Sponsors Tokyo Gas kuratiert hat. Die in diesem Rahmen entstandenen Wohnhäuser und der von Ito entworfene Pavillon befassen sich mit der Frage, wie ein „primitives" Haus in einer modernen Großstadt aussehen könnte. Was den Maßstab und die Zielrichtung betrifft, liegt die Initiative zudem auf einer Linie mit der immer häufiger vertretenen Auffassung, nach der unsere bisherige Lebensweise inklusive der Umweltverschmutzung künftig strenger kontrolliert werden müsse. Die weiteren Teilnehmer des Sumika-Projekts waren Terunobu Fujimori, ein Professor an der Universität von Tokio, der für seine kleinen Tee- und Wohnhausentwürfe im Geist der japanischen Tradition bekannt ist, und Taira Nishizawa, der Bruder des durch SANAA berühmt gewordenen Ryue Nishizawa. Sou Fujimotos Projekt, das den Namen „House Before House" trägt, hat eine Nutzfläche von nur 61 m². „Meine Vorstellung ging dahin, einen Raum wie aus einer primitiven Zukunft zu erschaffen – der gleichzeitig neu ist und auf eine ferne Vorzeit verweist, einen Raum, in dem trotz seiner völligen Neuartigkeit die eindeutige Form des archetypischen Hauses aufscheint", erklärt Fujimoto. Die dem Haus N und anderen seiner Bauten zugrundeliegenden Überlegungen vertiefend, spricht Fujimoto sich dafür aus, dass ein Haus sich so wenig wie möglich von seinem jeweiligen städtischen Umfeld unterscheiden sollte. Terunobu Fujimori wiederum legte den Entwurf eines „höhlenartigen" Gebäudes vor, das in gewisser Weise zu den Ursprüngen der menschlichen Behausung zurückkehrt. Taira Nishizawa ging es bei seinem Haus um die Wiedergewinnung des Tages- und Nachtrhythmus, der unter dem Vorzeichen urbaner Lebensumstände, in denen Tag und Nacht zuweilen miteinander verschwimmen, verloren gegangen ist. Mit der ausgiebigen Berücksichtigung von Tageslicht und natürlicher Belüftung macht Nishizawa auf einige grundlegende Gesichtspunkte aufmerksam, die in der Theorie und Praxis der Wohnarchitektur seit der klassischen Moderne ins Hintertreffen geraten sind. Toyo Itos Sumika-Pavillon (vorgestellt auf Seite 217) bildet innerhalb des Häuserensembles einen Versammlungsort, der mit seinen baumartigen Strukturen und dem großzügig einfallenden natürlichen Licht ebenfalls eine Brücke zwischen der fernen Vergangenheit und der urbanen Dichte des heutigen Japan schlägt.

Experimentierfelder wie das von Tokyo Gas gesponserte Sumika-Projekt sind eine Möglichkeit, innovative Architekten dafür zu gewinnen, die Grundidee des Wohnhauses neu zu überdenken. Wer Japan kennt, schätzt seine ungewöhnliche Mischung aus extremer Modernität und Rücksichtnahme auf die Tradition. Das in der heutigen Architektur festzustellende Anliegen, nach der Tabula rasa der klassischen Moderne die Verbindung zwischen Vergangenheit und Gegenwart wiederherzustellen, trägt vielleicht nirgends so reiche und sichtbare Früchte wie in Japan. Dass gerade die Wohnarchitektur besonders innovativ ist, muss nicht verwundern, lassen sich Wohnhäuser doch mit weitaus bescheideneren Mitteln realisieren als öffentliche Bauten oder sonstige Großprojekte.

DIE MEXIKANER KOMMEN

Bücher über aktuelle Architektur, wie das vorliegende, sind auf gute Informationsquellen angewiesen. Insofern erscheint es erwähnenswert, dass wir u. a. den talentierten mexikanischen Architekten Michael Rojkind gefragt haben, ob er in jüngerer Zeit auch Wohnhäuser entworfen habe – Rojkind verneinte zwar, vermittelte uns aber an Freunde, die unlängst auf dem Gebiet aktiv waren, nämlich an PRODUCTORA

11

11
PRODUCTORA, House in Chihuahua, Chihuahua, Mexico, 2008

und Celula Arquitectura; erstere wiederum reichten unsere Kontaktdaten weiter an das Studio Gracia. PRODUCTORA wurde 2006 von Abel Perles (geboren 1972 in Argentinien), Carlos Bedoya (geboren 1973 in Mexiko), Victor Jaime (geboren 1978 in Mexiko) und Wonne Ickx (geboren 1974 in Belgien) mit Sitz in Mexiko-Stadt gegründet. In der Halbwüste des mexikanischen Bundesstaats Chihuahua hat PRODUCTORA ein ganz aus weißen Polygonen komponiertes Haus (2008, Seite 325) realisiert, das den Beweis antritt (wenn es denn überhaupt eines Beweises bedarf), dass anspruchsvolle zeitgenössische Wohnarchitektur keineswegs nur an Orten wie Tokio oder Los Angeles entsteht. Celula Arquitectura, ebenfalls mit Sitz in Mexiko-Stadt, beschreibt sich als „multidisziplinäres Team, das sich darauf spezialisiert hat, Architektur, Landschaft und Kunst miteinander zu verbinden". Im Falle ihrer Casa en el Bosque (Valle de Bravo, Mexiko, 2007–08, Seite 101) versahen die Architekten eine Stahlrahmenkonstruktion mit einer ungewöhnlichen Lehmziegelverkleidung, die von der regionalen Architektur inspiriert ist. Diese Verbindung von klassischer Moderne und althergebrachten, aber an heutige Bedürfnisse angepasste Baumethoden zeigt, dass sich Architekten aus ganz verschiedenen Teilen der Welt in der Vergangenheit nach Anregungen umschauen, ohne dabei zwangsläufig den Mischmasch der architektonischen Postmoderne aus seinem wohlverdienten Ruhestand zu holen. Ein weiterer Vertreter der mexikanischen Architektengeneration unter 40 ist der 1973 geborene Jorge Gracia Garcia, der in San Diego lebt. Garcias Haus im niederkalifonischen Todos Santos (Baja California Sur, Mexiko, 2006, Seite 177) besteht ausschließlich aus vor Ort verfügbaren Materialien und bezieht sich auch mit seinen sandfarbenen Sichtbetonwänden auf das typische Aussehen der Häuser, die man in dieser Gegend findet. Bei aller Komfortabilität ist das 320 m² große Wohnhaus zugleich Manifestation des vom Architekten formulierten Anliegens, „zum Wesentlichen zurückzukehren".

BERGE UND MEER

Die wirtschaftlichen Entwicklungen haben natürlich auch die lateinamerikanische Immobilien- und Bauwirtschaft nicht unberührt gelassen; gleichwohl lassen viele der hier vorgestellten Häuser keinen Zweifel daran, dass Erfindungsreichtum und eindrucksvolle Entwürfe kein Monopol findiger Architekten aus Japan sind. Ein gutes Beispiel ist das 2005 von Nicolás del Río (geboren 1975) und Max Núñez (geboren 1976) in Santiago gegründete Büro dRN Arquitectos. Das Architektengespann hat eine Reihe von Häusern an extremen Orten entworfen, z. B. das Refugio C7 (Portillo, Chile, 2008), das unweit des Cerro Aconcagua in einer Höhe von 2870 m errichtet wurde. Auch das Refugio Los Canteros (Farellones, Chile, 2008, Seite 117), das zwar „nur" auf 2000 m Höhe liegt, ist gebaut, um einem harschen Winterklima zu trotzen. Der doppelt wärmegedämmte und großenteils mit sehr kleinen Fensteröffnungen versehene Hauptkörper des Gebäudes wird kontrastiert von einem gläsernen Aufsatz, der eine atemberaubende Aussicht auf das umliegende Bergpanorama bietet. Abgesehen von der Verwendung schwarzen Schiefers als Reverenz an die typischen Steinbauten der Gegend zeichnet sich das Haus durch eine hohe formale und ästhetische Originalität aus. Obwohl das Haus neben anderen, weniger herausragenden Wohnbauten steht, bleibt es ein Beweis dafür, dass gute Architektur sich nicht bloß nach Auffälligkeit bemisst, sondern genauso nach dem Meistern schwieriger Standortbedingungen, wie in diesem Fall einer auf die sechs wärmeren Monate des Jahres beschränkten Bauzeit.

Von einem weiteren chilenischen Architektenduo unter 40 – dem 1973 in Chile geborene Mauricio Pezo und der 1976 in Argentinien geborenen Sofía von Ellrichshausen, stammen zwei neuere, in formaler Hinsicht gleichartige Häuser: das eine in San Pedro (Casa Fosc, Chile,

12

*12
Pezo Von Ellrichshausen Architects,
Wolf House, Andalue, Chile, 2006–07*

2008–09, Seite 315), das andere in Andalue (Casa Wolf, Chile, 2006–07, Seite 21). Die relativ schlichten Außenhüllen aus farbigem Beton bzw. Metall haben die Architekten mit großen Fensteröffnungen versehen, die den etwas ungleichmäßigen, aber doch monolithischen Formen der Häuser eine überraschende Offenheit verleihen. Die beiden ungewöhnlichen Bauten, 160 bzw. 136 m² groß, verfügen über die Qualität, zu überraschen und zugleich die Bedürfnisse ihrer Auftraggeber zu erfüllen. Dass sie es auch unter verhältnismäßig beschränkten Rahmenbedingungen nicht an Originalität mangeln lassen, ist für diese jungen, begabten Architekten nicht die schlechteste Leistung.

Die oben bereits angeführte Residência JZ (Bernardes + Jacobsen, Camaçari, Bahia, Brasilien, 2006–08, Seite 75), das mit 1850 m² Grundfläche größte der hier präsentierten Häuser, steht Entwürfen wie den Refugios von dRN in vieler Hinsicht diametral gegenüber. Das nicht nur in Strandnähe, sondern direkt auf einer Sanddüne errichtete Anwesen ist der Stoff, aus dem die Träume vom brasilianischen Paradies sind. Bernardes + Jacobsen sind mit dem Bau von Luxushäusern vertraut, haben sich aber auch als versierte Schöpfer aufsehenerregender temporärer Architektur erwiesen, etwa für das TIM Festival von 2007 (Rio de Janeiro). Trotz eines begrenzten Budgets gelang es ihnen, das 40 000 m² große Gelände für das zweitägige Musikfestival innerhalb von nur einer Woche mit Veranstaltungsbauten aus 250 Frachtcontainern von 6 bzw. 12 m² Größe auszugestalten. Ihre teilweise auf *pilotis* aufgeständerte Residência JZ wartet mit einem „großen Salon" auf, der eine sensationelle Aussicht über Gärten hinweg und hinaus auf den Ozean bietet. Zwar verwendeten die Architekten regionale Baumaterialien wie Eukalyptusholz für das Gitterwerk oder beigefarbenen Bahia-Marmor als Bodenbelag, trotzdem ist die Residência JZ nicht gerade das ökologischste der hier vorgestellten Häuser. Ausschlaggebend für die Auswahl der Projekte waren ihre formalen architektonischen Qualitäten, aber eben auch, wie bei dem vorliegenden Beispiel, ihr Potenzial, den Leser von Orten träumen zu lassen, an denen es sich besser leben lässt. Dank der Vertrautheit mit ihrem Land und mit einer Klientel, die über die Mittel verfügt, sich jeden Bauwunsch erfüllen zu können, sind die von Rio und São Paulo aus operierenden Architekten in der Lage, die gängigen Vorstellungen des Machbaren zu übertreffen.

EIN BRIEFKASTEN UND EIN WENIG GRÜN

Dass es am anderen Ende der Welt in der südlichen Hemisphäre nicht minder kreativ zugeht, bezeugen einige der von uns ausgewählten Häuser australischer und neuseeländischer Architekten. Häufig profitieren diese Entwürfe gezielt von einer imposanten Naturkulisse, so z. B. das Sandy Bay Farm House (Sandy Bay, Tutukaka Coast, Neuseeland, 2007–08, Seite 133) des Architektenbüros Fearon Hay aus Auckland. Das moderne, fast ringsum raumhoch verglaste eingeschossige Bauwerk wurde auf einem Hügelkamm an der Tutukaka-Küste auf der Nordinsel errichtet, mit weitem Blick über den Pazifik in Richtung der Poor Knights Islands. Wie man sieht, gehört zum Talent eines auf Wohnhausentwürfe spezialisierten Architekten auch die Fähigkeit, Auftraggeber mit einem Faible für derartige Orte zu finden; darüber hinaus stellte sich hier die Aufgabe, ein komfortables Wohnhaus in eine offenkundig sensible Naturlandschaft einzubetten. Der australische Architekt Robert McBride wählte mit seinem Letterbox House (Blairgowrie, Australien, 2006–08, Seite 271) und seinem Klein Bottle House (Rye, Australien, 2005–07, Seite 276) einen anderen, aber nicht weniger originellen Ansatz. „Wir mögen Häuser, die einen zum Schmunzeln bringen (nicht zum Lachen)", so McBride. Das erste der beiden Häuser sollte aussehen, als sei es gerade einem Briefkasten entnommen worden – daher sein Name –, während das zweite sich als „Origamiversion" eines „aus der Geometrie entwickelten Modells zur Oberflächenbeschreibung" (der sogenann-

13

13
Bellemo & Cat, Polygreen, Northcote, Melbourne, Australia, 2007–08

ten Klein'schen Flasche) präsentiert. Auch wenn das übergeordnete Interesse in beiden Fällen formaler Natur gewesen sein dürfte, sind es reizvolle Beispiele für die mannigfachen Formen in der Wohnarchitektur. Die Häuser von McBride sind jedenfalls überraschend und originell – womit sie in gewisser Weise genau das bieten, was viele Bauherren von einem innovativen Architekten erwarten.

Michael Bellemo, geboren 1967 in Melbourne, und Cat Macleod, geboren in 1963 im malaysischen Penang, gründeten 1992 in Melbourne ihr Büro Bellemo & Cat. Mit einem Budget von nur 220 000 Euro baute das Duo das 155 m² große Wohnhaus Polygreen (Northcote, Melbourne, Australien, 2007–08, Seite 69) an einer Zufahrtstraße mit alten Backsteinlagerhäusern, für das sie eine industriell geprägte Formensprache wählten. Bellemo & Cat sind weder die ersten noch die letzten Architekten, die im Rahmen von Wohnarchitektur auf Industrieelemente zurückgreifen – in diesem Fall ergänzt um eine bedruckte, durchscheinende Hülle, durch die sich das Gebäude trotz des Lagerhausstils deutlich von seiner Umgebung absetzt. Die Farbe der bedruckten Gebäudehülle (und der Name des Projekts) war Bellemo & Cats augenzwinkernde Antwort auf die Bitte eines Nachbarn um ein wenig Grün.

BRAD MACHT'S RICHTIG

In den vergangenen Jahren gab es viele ehrgeizige Projekte, bei denen „Stararchitekten" um Beiträge für ein bestimmtes Bauareal gebeten wurden. Die Häuser in Sagaponac in New York oder das Sumika-Projekt sind Beispiele für solche Initiativen. Nicht selten allerdings sind solche Projekte aufgrund ihrer schieren Größe und des Wesens der hieran beteiligten Persönlichkeiten mehr oder weniger zum Scheitern verurteilt. Zwei ambitionierte und weiterhin andauernde Wohnbauprojekte, die hier vorgestellt werden, sind die Initiative Make it Right, die sich dem Bau neuer Unterkünfte für die Bewohner des vom Hurrikan Katrina zerstörten Lower Ninth Ward in New Orleans verschrieben hat, und das ganz anders geartete Projekt Ordos 100 in der chinesischen Inneren Mongolei.

Der Lower Ninth Ward war einer jener Stadtbezirke, die der Hurrikan Katrina im August 2005 am meisten zerstörte. 2007 begann die Initiative Make It Right unter Schirmherrschaft des Schauspielers Brad Pitt mit den Planungen für den Bau von 150 Eigenheimen. Zusammen mit Pitt, Reed Kroloff und der Lower Ninth Ward Community Coalition erarbelteten das in Berlin und Los Angeles ansässige Architektenteam Graft und das Büro William McDonough + Partners ein Konzept, auf dessen Grundlage insgesamt 13 Architekturbüros – lokale, nationale und internationale – gebeten wurden, preisgünstige Häuser für dieses Gebiet zu entwerfen. Die Auswahl der Teilnehmer erfolgte anhand bestimmter Kriterien: Vorzuweisen waren eine frühere Beschäftigung mit oder Beteiligung an Aufträgen in New Orleans – vorzugsweise in der Zeit vor Katrina – und/oder Erfahrungen im Bereich der Katastrophenhilfe, das Interesse an bzw. die Vertrautheit mit nachhaltigem Bauen, Erfahrungen mit dem Bau von Mehrfamilienhäusern, Kreativität bei der Umsetzung gering budgetierter Projekte, Erfahrungen mit dem Bauen in Gewässernähe oder unter Wasserspiegelniveau und schließlich eine hohe Entwurfsqualität. Neben Graft (Berlin) gehören zu den beteiligten Architekturbüros Trahan Architects (Baton Rouge), Kieran Timberlake (Philadelphia), Morphosis (Los Angeles), Pugh + Scarpa (Santa Monica), Adjaye Associates (London), MVRDV (Rotterdam) und Shigeru Ban (Tokio). John Williams Architects aus New Orleans fungieren als ausführende Architekten. Das erste Make-it-Right-Haus wurde 2008 zum dritten Jahrestag der Sturmkatastrophe eingeweiht; zum Zeitpunkt der Entstehung des vorliegenden Buchs waren acht Häuser fertiggestellt (darunter die beiden auf Seite 281 vorgestellten Entwürfe von Graft). Im

Juli 2009 kündigte Make it Right eine zweite Serie von 14 Doppelhäusern nach Entwürfen von Architekten wie Hitoshi Abe, Elemental (Chile) oder Gehry Partners an. Dass Architekten wie Elemental oder Shigeru Ban dabei sind, ist insofern nicht überraschend, als diese bereits über umfassende Erfahrungen mit der Realisierung von Behelfsbauten für Flüchtlinge oder Häusern für Notleidende verfügen. Bemerkenswerter erscheint das Phänomen, welches Who's Who der amerikanischen und internationalen Gegenwartsarchitektur sich ein Stelldichein gibt, wenn sich die Strahlkraft eines Brad Pitt mit den Talenten von Graft und Kollegen verbündet. Bedenkt man, wie selten normalerweise bekannte Gegenwartsarchitekten mit niedrig budgetierten Projekten in Berührung kommen, könnte Make it Right eine größere Auswirkung auf den Berufsstand selbst als auf den Lower Ninth Ward haben. In jedem Fall ist die Initiative ein vorbildliches Labor für das verantwortungsbewusste Bauen kostengünstiger, sturmsicherer Häuser.

Bei dem von der Firma Jiang Yuan Water Engineering Ltd. in Auftrag gegebenen Projekt Ordos 100, für das Ai Wei Wei als Kurator auftritt und Herzog & de Meuron eine erste Teilnehmerauswahl getroffen haben, geht es im Gegensatz zu Make it Right weniger um den humanitären Aspekt. In der Selbstdarstellung von Ordos 100 heißt es: „Ziel des Projekts ist die Entwicklung von 100 Villen für den Auftraggeber Jiang Yuan Water Engineering Ltd. in Ordos in der Inneren Mongolei. Der Masterplan für die 100 Grundstücke stammt von FAKE Design, dem Pekinger Atelier Ai Wei Weis, welches das Projekt auch kuratieren wird. Herzog & de Meuron haben die Auswahl der 100 beteiligten Architekturbüros aus 27 Ländern übernommen. Das Projekt ist in zwei Phasen aufgeteilt. Im ersten Abschnitt finden die Planungen für 28 Grundstücksparzellen statt, im zweiten die der übrigen 72 Parzellen. Jeder Architekt ist verantwortlich für ein 1000 m² großes Wohnhaus." Inzwischen hat sich anscheinend eine dritte Phase ergeben, mit sechs Häusern in der näheren Umgebung nach Entwürfen von Ai Wei Wei, EM2N (Zürich), Galli Rudolf (Zürich), EXH (Shanghai), der großen, weltweit aktiven Architekturfirma Cannon Design und dem Baseler Architektenteam HHF. Die Arbeiten an dessen Dune House (Ordos, Innere Mongolei, China, 2008–09, Seite 200) sind zwar noch nicht ganz abgeschlossen, trotzdem stellen wir den ehrgeizigen Entwurf mit einigen Bildern vor. Der internationale Ansatz von Ordos 100 mit Teilnehmern aus aller Welt unter chinesisch-schweizerischer Federführung ist sicherlich nicht ohne Reiz; zugleich verweist er – wie Make it Right, nur eben vor anderem Entstehungshintergrund – auf den wachsenden Einfluss zeitgenössischer Qualitätsarchitektur insbesondere auf dem Gebiet des weniger kapitalintensiven Wohnbaus. Ist das Projekt erst einmal über seine ersten experimentellen Schritte hinausgelangt, könnte Ordos 100 durchaus Schule machen.

METAMORPHOSEN

Renovierungen und Gebäudeerweiterungen waren lange Zeit die Domäne einer überschaubaren Anzahl von Architekten. Andererseits wird es in Zeiten wirtschaftlicher Schwäche vermehrt solche Projekte geben, sind sie doch für gewöhnlich mit geringeren Kosten verbunden als Neubauten. Zwei dieser hier vorgestellten Projekte stammen zufälligerweise von Architekten mit breitem internationalem Background, wie er bei jungen Büros immer häufiger die Regel zu sein scheint. Charles Bessard und Nanne de Ru gründeten 2005 die Powerhouse Company, mit Sitz in Rotterdam und Kopenhagen; Bessard wurde 1971 in Frankreich geboren, de Ru 1976 in den Niederlanden. Ihr Spiralhaus (Burgund, Frankreich, 2007–08, Seite 13) ist aus dem Wunsch hervorgegangen, ein altes Bauernhaus zu erweitern. Interessant an dem Projekt ist

14
HHF, Dune House, Ordos, Inner Mongolia, China, 2008–09

14

nicht allein die äußere Gestalt der Architektur, sondern vor allem die Leitidee des Kreislaufs oder – in den Worten der Architekten – des „programmatischen Loops“. Durch sein ausgeklügeltes Spiel mit Transparenz und Opazität macht der Anbau aus dem älteren, das Grundstück früher allein beherrschenden Anwesen gleichsam ein neues modernes Haus.

Seit 2005 bilden die 1978 geborene Schweizerin Delphine Ding und der 1977 geborene Chilene José Ulloa Davet ein Team; Ding schloss 2005 ihr Studium an der École Polytechnique Fédérale de Lausanne ab, Ulloa Davet erhielt sein Architekturdiplom bereits 2002 an der Universidad Católica de Chile. Ihr Haus Metamorphosis (Casablanca, Tunquén, Chile, 2008, Seite 397) ist die mit 70 000 Dollar bescheiden budgetierte Umgestaltung eines Holzhauses aus dem Jahr 1990. Neu hinzugefügte Terrassen und eine „belüftete Haut aus Holz“ sorgen für eine Gesamterscheinung, die das alte Gebäude praktisch nicht mehr erkennen lässt. In einer völlig anderen Region der Erde führte der innovative Architekt Pei Zhu ein ungewöhnliches Projekt für den Künstler Cai Guo-Qiang aus: die Renovierung und Erweiterung eines Hofhauses (Peking, China, 2007, Seite 385). Solche Hofhäuser sind in der traditionellen chinesischen Architektur sehr häufig. Hier hat der Architekt sowohl die vorhandenen Räume und die alte Holzkonstruktion renoviert als auch den südlichen Teil der Anlage um einen zusätzlichen, so Pei Zhu, „futuristischen Raum“ erweitert. Interessant ist in diesem Zusammenhang, dass Cai Guo-Qiangs internationales Renommee sich auf Kunstwerke gründet, die oftmals auf die Kunst und Kultur der chinesischen Vergangenheit Bezug nehmen; beispielsweise verwendet er häufig Feuerwerkskörper. Insofern ist die von Pei Zhu vorgenommene Modernisierung von einem ganz ähnlichen Geist getragen wie die Arbeiten Cai Guo-Qiangs – sowohl dezidiert modern als auch in der Vergangenheit, der allgegenwärtigen Tradition ihres Heimatlandes China verwurzelt.

Die Leichtigkeit, mit der sich Informationen über das jüngste Architekturgeschehen über das Internet vermitteln lassen, könnte mit ein Grund sein, weshalb heute auch Talenten aus solchen Ländern, die nicht unbedingt für ihre aktuelle Architektur bekannt sind, größere Aufmerksamkeit zuteil wird. Mit der Entwicklung in Osteuropa ist auch das Interesse an anspruchsvoller Architektur gewachsen. Der 1969 in Katowice geborene Robert Konieczny ist der führende Kopf von KWK PROMES, einem Architekturbüro, das einige recht ungewöhnliche Häuser realisiert hat. Eines davon ist das 556 m² umfassende Safe House (Okrzeszyn, Polen, 2005–08, Seite 257), bei dem, wie der Name verrät, besonderes Gewicht auf die Sicherheit seiner Bewohner gelegt wurde. Das führte zu einer abgeschotteten, bunkerartigen Bauweise, deren fast beunruhigende Erscheinung durch schwarze Farbe noch betont wird. Bei aller Abgeschlossenheit öffnet sich das Gebäude zum Garten hin und bietet seinen gut geschützten Nutzern doch ein paar Sonnenstrahlen. Das Haus OUTrial (Ksiazenice, Polen, 2005–08, Seite 260) zeigt ein ähnlich blockhaftes geometrisches Erscheinungsbild wie das Safe House, hat jedoch ein grasbewachsenes Dach, das die relativ harten Linien etwas abmildert. Häuser wie diese mögen nicht den Klischees entsprechen, die man in einem Buch über neueste Architektur erwartet, was die Bauten jedoch nicht weniger eindrucksvoll und auf ihre Weise originell macht.

AMERIKA TRÄUMT WEITER

Weil in den USA so viele Menschen in eigenen Häusern und Wohnungen leben und das Land ein Zentrum kreativer, zeitgenössischer Architektur ist, spielt es seit langem eine wichtige Rolle bei der Entwicklung der Wohnarchitektur. Seit einigen Jahren jedoch ist in Amerika eine gewisse Innovationsflaute zu bemerken, die mit einem rasanten Wettbewerb um den Bau immer extravaganterer Häuser einsetzte, der

15
Ulloa + Ding, Metamorphosis House, Casablanca, Tunquén, Chile, 2008

15

dann in eine rasche Abwärtsspirale mit Zwangsvollstreckungen und ein Abebben der Bautätigkeit umschlug. Die für das vorliegende Buch ausgewählten Beispiele sprechen jedoch dafür, dass es um die zeitgenössische Architektur im Lande Frank Lloyd Wrights keineswegs schlecht bestellt ist. Eine interessante Komposition ist das von Padraic Cassidy für den Drehbuchautor Larry Karaszewski gebaute Red House (Los Angeles, Kalifornien, USA, 2004–06, Seite 95). Cassidy, der vor der Eröffnung seines eigenen Büros für Daly Genik und Frank Gehry arbeitete, hat mittels Farbe und Geometrie ein lebendiges Wohnhaus geschaffen, das munter aus seiner mit Eukalyptusgehölzen bewachsenen Umgebung hervorleuchtet. Am geografisch genau entgegengesetzten Zipfel des Landes, in Putney im Bundesstaat Vermont, hat Kyu Sung Woo, der von 1970 bis 1974 für José Lluis Sert (Sert, Jackson & Associate) tätig war, ein Feriendomizil für seine Familie gebaut (Putney, Vermont, USA, 2005–07, Seite 407). Das in drei Elemente geteilte Haus weist eine Charakteristik auf, die in der zeitgenössischen Wohnhausarchitektur immer beliebter zu werden scheint: eine klassisch-moderne Grundform, die durch die geschickte Gegenüberstellung von Gestaltungs- und Formelementen in ihrer Komplexität gesteigert wird. Daneben hat Kyu Sung Woo bei seinem Ferienhaus besonderen Wert auf einen niedrigen Energieverbrauch gelegt, was den ausgesprochen zeitgemäßen Charakter des Entwurfs unterstreicht.

Als letztes und vielleicht etwas unerwartetes Beispiel für kreative Gegenwartsarchitektur aus den Vereinigten Staaten wollen wir Michael Jantzens Homestead House (2009, Seite 228) vorstellen. Wie der Großteil von Jantzens Œuvre existiert auch dieses Haus bislang nur im Entwurfsstadium. Jantzen will „leicht erhältliche Baukomponenten aus dem landwirtschaftlichen Nutzungsbereich" verwenden und sucht ein „vorgefertigtes, modulares, sehr belastbares, erschwingliches Bogensystem", das sich mit einfachem Werkzeug zusammensetzen lässt. Aus recyceltem Zeitungspapier hergestelltes Dämmmaterial, eine Solar- und eine Windkraftanlage sowie passive Strategien sorgen dafür, dass Jantzens Haus der Zukunft allemal umweltfreundlicher ist als die Tausende von Vorstadthäusern in den amerikanischen Wohngebieten. Wer die Blütezeit der „virtuellen" Architektur bereits für beendet hält, für den tritt Jantzens Haus den Gegenbeweis an, dass es nach wie vor Menschen gibt, die versuchen, das Leben des Einzelnen und der Gemeinschaft durch Architektur zu verbessern.

ZURÜCK ZUM WESENTLICHEN

Von Zeit zu Zeit entstehen Wohnhäuser, die man mit Kunstwerken vergleichen kann – was hier im positiven Sinne gemeint ist. Eines der reizvolleren und originelleren Häuser dieser Art aus jüngerer Zeit ist Dupli.Casa von Jürgen Mayer-Hermann (J. Mayer H., bei Ludwigsburg, Deutschland, 2006–08, Seite 264). Mayer-Hermann orientierte seinen Entwurf bewusst an dem Einfamilienhaus, das 1984 auf dem Grundstück errichtet worden war, indem er dessen einzelne Baukörperteile „duplizierte" und drehte – ein Vorgehen, das der Architekt als „Familienarchäologie" bezeichnet und mittels dessen er ein hoch ästhetisches, vor- und zurückwogendes skulpturales neues Gebäude schuf. Von dem Vorgängerhaus spricht Mayer-Hermann als einem „vorgefundenen Objekt" – und verweist damit direkt auf die moderne Kunst. So wenig sich die Dupli.Casa mit ihren Auskragungen und weißen Kurven mit anderen Wohnhäusern jüngeren Datums vergleichen lässt, so deutlich unterstreicht sie, dass auch in Deutschland die Grenzen der zeitgenössischen Architektur neu definiert werden. Die Vorstellung von „Archäologie" bei einem derart modernen Wohnhaus passt zu den weltweiten Bestrebungen, Modernität mit kulturellen oder regionalen Wurzeln zu verbinden und Kontinuität als neue Regel an die Stelle der Tabula rasa zu setzen. Gewiss ist diese Schlacht noch nicht endgültig geschlagen – der

16

16
Padraic Cassidy, Red House, Los Angeles, California, USA, 2004–06

Wunsch, mit allem Vorangegangenen zu brechen, sitzt auch bei den heutigen Kreativen immer noch tief –, doch die Werte, von denen Kunst und Architektur seit Jahrhunderten getragen werden, sind immer noch stärker als ein oberflächlicher Veränderungswille. Wirtschaftliche Krisensituationen rücken die Dinge wieder die richtige Perspektive und zwingen dazu, sich auf das Wesentliche zu konzentrieren. Mögen einige der hier vorgestellten Häuser auch zur stillen Beobachtung eines Flussgebiets in Oregon gedacht sein oder einfach als Schutz vor Sturm – der ökologische Aspekt, in Form geringen Energieverbrauchs, dürfte künftig nicht mehr wegzudenken sein, und sei es nur deshalb, weil geringerer Verbrauch eine niedrigere Stromrechnung bedeutet. Viele dieser Häuser erweisen sich dank ihrer außergewöhnlichen Lage als veritable Aussichtspunkte, die überwältigende Natureindrücke vermitteln. Und wie Tom Kundigs Rolling Huts machen viele dieser Behausungen gar keinen Hehl daraus, nicht für die Ewigkeit geschaffen zu sein. Die neuen Regeln der Ökologie gebieten, dass immer mehr Häuser demontierbar, transportierbar und an anderer Stelle wieder aufbaubar sein müssen, ohne an ihren Standorten Spuren zu hinterlassen. Solche Eigenschaften sind in der Wohnarchitektur noch relativ neu, doch sie werden immer häufiger. Die hier vorgestellten Häuser befinden sich in vieler Hinsicht in einem Zwischenstadium: teilweise sind sie Schöpfungen einer neuen Welt, teilweise sind sie in der Vergangenheit verankert.

Während manche Architekten sich nach Kräften darum bemühen, den Wünschen ihrer Auftraggeber gerecht zu werden, sind andere vor allem darauf bedacht, ausschließlich die eigenen Konzepte oder gar Fantasien zu verwirklichen. Es ist selten, dass die Vorstellungen des Architekten, die des Auftraggebers und schließlich die Kosten zu einer solchen Balance finden, dass ein zeitgenössisches Haus einem Kunstwerk gleicht. Hat ein Meisterwerk ein undichtes Dach, wie es bei Le Corbusiers Villa Savoye der Fall war, wird für den Auftraggeber das Vergnügen, in einem Kunstwerk zu wohnen, unerwartet kostspielig. Auch wenn es 2009 noch zu früh sein mag, die Auswirkungen der im Herbst 2008 eskalierten Wirtschaftskrise zu beurteilen, hat man den Eindruck, dass einige der Häuser in diesem Buch das Wirtschaftlichkeitsgebot oder, vielleicht besser gesagt, die Verantwortung, die sich in einer Zwangslage stets automatisch stellt, bereits berücksichtigen. Neue Häuser oder aber renovierte ältere Häuser werden immer gebraucht, und dieser Bedarf bringt die Architektur dazu, sich weiterzuentwickeln und mit der Zeit zu verändern. Da die Bauzeit von Wohnhäusern im Vergleich zu größeren Projekten recht kurz ist, sind Häuser vorzügliche „Stimmungsbarometer" der Architektur der Gegenwart – und mitunter sogar der Zukunft. Modernität, die keine Reduktion ist, sondern sich an Gegebenheiten, dem jeweiligen Umfeld, speziellen Vorgaben und auch durchaus an ästhetischen Gesichtspunkten orientiert, bringt die zeitgenössische Architektur heute voran – so wie es die im Folgenden präsentierten Häuser demonstrieren.

Philip Jodidio, Grimentz, Schweiz, August 2009

INTRODUCTION

MAISONS SUR LE FIL

Un livre sur les maisons peut intéresser son lecteur pour toutes sortes de raisons, certaines avouées, d'autres non. N'y a-t-il pas toujours un peu de voyeurisme dans l'envie de découvrir le lieu de vie de quelqu'un d'autre ? Comment vivent les riches ? Est-on heureux dans une fabuleuse maison sur la plage de Bahia ? En fait, avec ses 1850 m², la maison JZ (Residência JZ, Camaçari, Bahia, Brésil, 2006–08, page 75) des architectes Bernardes + Jacobsen est la plus vaste de celles publiées dans ce second volume d'*Architecture Now! Houses*. C'est vraiment une superbe demeure. Mais qu'en est-il de toutes les maisons de dimensions plus « normales » ? Elles sont tout aussi présentes, et même en grand nombre. Le brutal ralentissement économique vécu par le marché de l'immobilier aux États-Unis, en Espagne et ailleurs a déjà mis sa marque sur cette sélection. On y trouve moins de résidences extravagantes comme la résidence YTL de 3000 m² parue dans le premier volume d'*Architecture Now! Houses* (Kuala Lumpur, Malaisie, 2004–08, Jouin Manku), tandis qu'apparaissent beaucoup plus de très petites maisons, souvent bâties avec des moyens limités. Ainsi, la minuscule Watershed de l'agence FLOAT (Willamette Valley, Oregon, États-Unis, 2006–07, page 145) et ses 6,5 m² détient le record de la plus petite surface utile présentée dans ce livre. La résidence de camping permanent de Casey Brown (Permanent Camping Residence, Mudgee, NGS, Australie, 2007, page 89) ne mesure guère plus de 18 m², tandis que la maison de bois définitive de Sou Fujimoto (Final Wooden House, Kumamura, Mumamoto, Japon, 2007–08, page 164), perchée dans un site vraiment bizarre, n'offre que 22 m² tout au plus. Pour ceux qui ont écrit dans la presse que des livres comme la série *Architecture Now!* de Taschen auraient moins de grain à moudre avec le retournement économique, cet ouvrage est une première réponse. Les architectes savent parfaitement s'adapter et sont prêts à répondre à une demande de maisons plus petites et moins chères. Par ailleurs, la contrainte économique peut stimuler l'inventivité comme l'illustrent un certain nombre de réalisations qui confirment que ces nouvelles maisons n'ont pas emprunté les chemins d'un Bernard Madoff et autres « stars » de l'effondrement financier.

COMBIEN ÇA COÛTE?

Une question, souvent non posée, porte sur le prix des maisons conçues par des architectes de talent. La réponse est qu'elles coûtent généralement un peu plus cher qu'une réalisation équivalente signée d'un praticien moins doué ou moins connu. Malheureusement, même si nous leur posons systématiquement cette question, les architectes refusent fréquemment de donner cette information pour des raisons qui tiennent le plus souvent à un devoir de discrétion par rapport à leur client. Pour ceux qui hésitent à faire appel à un architecte pour des raisons budgétaires, le climat actuel devrait les encourager à s'informer et à fixer des limites financières précises à leur projet. Les architectes, même très connus, dont le carnet de commande a baissé, peuvent être tentés par le défi d'une créativité plus soucieuse des réalités économiques.

Les préoccupations environnementales sont certainement plus présentes aujourd'hui que dans un passé récent. Beaucoup d'architectes mettent en œuvre des stratégies « passives » qui peuvent modifier l'orientation ou la nature du vitrage d'une maison. Le principe de masse thermique associé à des éléments substantiels en béton est lui aussi régulièrement cité pour réduire la consommation énergétique. En bref, la masse (par exemple en béton) préserve la fraîcheur de l'intérieur en été, et diffuse doucement la chaleur du jour pendant la nuit plus froide. Ces stratégies ne renchérissent pas vraiment les coûts de construction, alors que d'autres méthodes, des panneaux solaires aux pompes à chaleur, représentent des investissements initiaux qui ne seront compensés qu'avec le temps par la baisse des factures d'électricité.

PETITS PLAISIRS À PETITS PRIX

À l'occasion, les préoccupations écologique et économique peuvent se rejoindre dans un seul projet. Le Watershed, conçu par Erin Moore de l'agence FLOAT (Willamette Valley, Oregon, USA, 2006/07, page 145), possède des piles de fondation en béton coulé en place, qui soutiennent une ossature d'acier sur laquelle des planches de cèdre viennent facilement se boulonner (ou se déboulonner). L'un des objectifs de cette toute petite construction est de profiter du cadre naturel du bassin de la Marys River, mais la volonté de limiter les coûts est tout aussi claire. Elle peut se comparer à la Structure de camping permanent (Permanent Camping Structure) de Casey Brown (2007, Australie, page 89), réalisée de l'autre côté du monde, en Australie. Implantée dans un terrain montagneux, cette maison habillée de cuivre peut se refermer entièrement sur elle-même pour se protéger des incendies du bush qui font de fréquents ravages dans ce site isolé. Préfabriquée à Sidney et transportée à Mudgee, elle récupère les eaux de pluie du toit et se chauffe au bois. Son emprise au sol de 9 m^2 lui assure un impact minimal sur son environnement. Avec cette petite résidence, les architectes se sont particulièrement attachés aux aspects écologique et économique, en utilisant notamment de l'eucalyptus recyclé en intérieur. Cette petite résidence repose à peine sur son terrain, comme si elle pouvait être transportée ailleurs, aussi facilement qu'elle a été livrée. Le concept de constructions légèrement posées sur le sol – comme si elles pensaient à la nature transitoire de la présence humaine et donc de celle de l'architecture – est assez fréquent dans l'architecture contemporaine australienne, mais elle est ici poussée jusqu'à ses extrémités logiques. Si la Watershed manifeste un mode d'observation et de respect de l'environnement plus volontaire, ces deux petites réalisations isolées en pleine nature peuvent être considérées comme des réponses à la dégradation des cadres de vie urbains et suburbains et aux accumulations de polluants et de déchets qu'elle entraîne.

Les Huttes sur roues (Rolling Huts, Mazama, Washington, États-Unis, 2007, page 298), conçues par le remarquable architecte Tom Kundig, dirigeant de l'agence Olson Kundig Architects, sont des maisons d'hôtes édifiées sur un ancien terrain de camping. Leurs roues ont pour but de préserver la prairie dans laquelle elles se trouvent, mais, là encore, la construction à plate-forme de bois et en « boîte » d'acier exprime un intérêt nouveau pour un retour à des valeurs fondamentales, qui, plus que tout, caractérise peut-être l'esprit du moment dans le secteur de la maison. Pour Tom Kundig : « Les huttes évoquent la petite cabane dans les bois de Thoreau ; les structures viennent en second, après la nature. »

Si les préoccupations économiques s'expriment dans de nombreuses maisons présentées dans ce volume, leurs auteurs n'insistent pas toujours sur ce point. L'architecte new-yorkais Thomas Phifer a construit sa maison de Salt Point (Salt Point, New York, 2006–07, page 19) dans la vallée de l'Hudson. Mesurant 204 m^2, elle est beaucoup plus vaste que les maisons expérimentales d'Erin Moore ou de Casey Brown, et, cependant, de sa stratégie d'énergie passive (ventilation naturelle, etc.) au recours à certains matériaux, elle traduit bien le climat

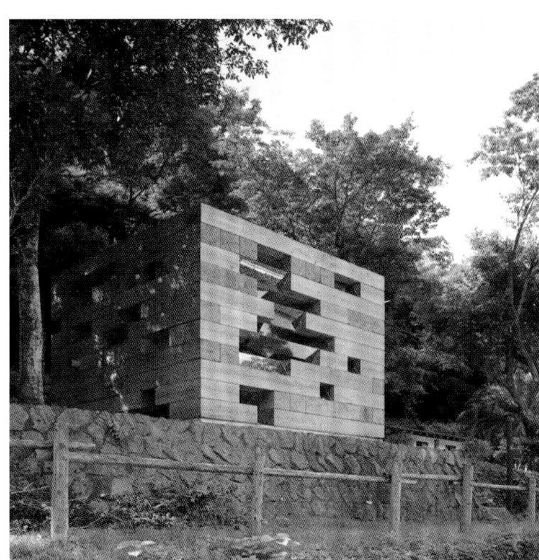

17
Sou Fujimoto, Final Wooden House, Kumamura, Kumamoto, Japan, 2007–08

17

plus prudent qui règne actuellement, même si elle a été achevée en 2007. « Tous les matériaux de construction et de finition ont été soigneusement choisis pour leur fonction, leur durabilité et plus particulièrement leur coût. À l'intérieur, les murs, les sols et les plafonds sont habillés de contreplaqué d'érable, un bois à la fois économique et durable. Le mobilier sur mesure et la menuiserie intérieure sont fabriqués dans le même contreplaqué », précise l'architecte.

TESTER LES LIMITES

Quel que soit l'état de l'économie, les projets résidentiels sont souvent pour un architecte l'occasion de tester tant les limites du climat que celles des autorités locales. Il s'agit donc rarement de simplement faire un geste spectaculaire, mais plutôt de voir de quoi les maisons, et, bien sûr, l'architecture sont capables. Si de nombreux praticiens ont tenté d'introduire des éléments mobiles dans leurs projets, comme Santiago Calatrava tout au long de sa carrière, l'agence londonienne dRMM a tenté avec sa maison coulissante (Sliding House, Suffolk, G.-B., 2006–09, page 111) de réaliser une maison qui change littéralement de dimensions et de formes à volonté. Cet exploit tient à l'insertion d'un toit mobile et à sa structure à murs de vingt tonnes montés sur rails. Le profil apparemment ordinaire de la maison peut ainsi se déployer, et sa surface utile s'accroître jusqu'à 100 m².

L'architecte japonais Sou Fujimoto a conçu de nombreuses maisons qui remettent en cause certains principes de base généralement acceptés pour ce type de constructions. Sa maison N (N House, préfecture d'Oita, Japon, 2007–08, page 159) se compose d'une succession de coques qui créent un espace ambigu, ni vraiment intérieur, ni réellement extérieur. « J'ai toujours eu des interrogations sur les maisons séparées de la rue par un simple mur », explique Fujimoto, « et je me suis demandé s'il n'était pas intéressant d'explorer une certaine gradation dans ce domaine encore inexploré et les différentes perceptions de la distance entre la rue et la maison, par exemple : un lieu assez proche de la rue, un autre un peu plus éloigné, un autre enfin le plus loin possible pour assurer l'intimité. » Peu d'architectes ont osé remettre en question à ce point les enjeux des limites, surtout en ville. Au Japon en particulier, le foncier urbain est cher et rare, et la tendance normale est de concentrer autant de mètres carrés que possible sur une parcelle, tout en respectant la réglementation d'urbanisme. Fujimoto pratique ainsi un retour en arrière pour étudier la relation fondamentale entre l'architecture et la ville. Un autre projet de cet architecte prolifique et fascinant est sa maison de bois définitive (Final Wooden House, Kumamura, Kumamoto, Japon, 2007-08, page 164). Mesurant à peine 22 m², elle est l'aboutissement de l'empilement « décontracté » de grumes de bois de section carrée de 35 cm de côté sur un minuscule terrain de 15 m². Cette approche entraîne une distribution des vides et des pleins qui prend toutes sortes de formes inattendues. Ce n'est pas une maison au sens habituel du terme, mais davantage une expérimentation spatiale. « Plutôt que simplement une nouvelle architecture », conclut Fujimoto, « c'est une nouvelle origine, une nouvelle existence. »

LA MAISON D'AVANT LA MAISON

Sou Fujimoto est l'un des participants à un projet audacieux intitulé Sumika (Utsunomiya, préfecture de Tochigi, Japon, 2008, page 216–217), réalisé par l'architecte Toyo Ito, et sponsorisé par Tokyo Gas. L'idée de ce groupe de maisons et d'un pavillon conçu par Ito était d'explorer le concept d'une maison « primitive » dans une ville moderne. En termes de dimensions mais aussi d'idées, cette initiative s'intègre dans la perception croissante de ce que les conditions de vie et la liberté de polluer, qui ont prévalu jusqu'à présent, doivent être plus strictement contrôlées. Les autres participants à ce projet étaient Terunobu Fujimori, professeur à l'université de Tokyo, célèbre pour ses maisons de thé et ses minuscules résidences inspirées de la tradition japonaise, et Taira Nishizawa, frère de Ryue Nishizawa de SANAA. Le projet de Fujimoto, appelé la maison d'avant la maison (House Before House), mesure tout juste 61 m² de surface utile. « J'ai eu envie de créer un lieu qui suggère un futur primitif, contenant l'idée d'appartenir simultanément au monde contemporain et à celui de l'âge préhistorique ; d'être engendré par un esprit de nouveauté imprévu, mais qui concentre quelque chose de comparable à la forme non équivoque et archétypique d'une maison », a déclaré l'architecte. Il soutient qu'une maison ne doit presque pas se distinguer de la ville dans laquelle elle se situe, et développe ici des idées expérimentées dans sa maison N, et ses autres recherches. Le professeur Fujimori est allé jusqu'à créer une maison « caverne » qui, en un certains sens, renvoie aux origines de l'habitat humain. La maison de Nishizawa est pensée pour tenter de reconquérir les rythmes biologiques qui se désintègrent dans le contexte urbain, lorsque le jour et la nuit se confondent. En utilisant une abondante lumière et une ventilation naturelles, il cherche à rendre la modernité consciente de certains constats évacués de la théorie, mais aussi de la pratique de l'architecture résidentielle. Le pavillon Sumika de Toyo Ito (page 217) est un lieu de réunion commun à ce groupe de maisons. Ses formes arborescentes et l'emploi généreux de la lumière comblent le fossé entre le passé lointain et le présent si fortement urbanisé du Japon actuel.

Ce type d'expérimentation financé par Tokyo Gas est certainement une façon d'encourager des architectes créatifs à renouveler l'idée même de maison. Les connaisseurs du Japon apprécieront ce mélange de modernité extrême et d'acceptation de la tradition. Le lien entre le passé et le présent que l'architecture a tenté de rétablir depuis la *tabula rasa* des débuts du modernisme est peut-être aujourd'hui plus présent et plus fructueux au Japon. Parce que les enjeux financiers de la maison individuelle sont plus modestes que ceux de l'architecture des bâtiments publics ou des immeubles de grandes dimensions, il semble qu'une bonne part de l'innovation architecturale s'exprime dans le domaine de l'habitat résidentiel.

LES MEXICAINS ARRIVENT!

Les ouvrages d'architecture contemporaine du type de celui-ci dépendent de la qualité de leurs sources d'information. Ainsi, le grand architecte mexicain Michael Rojkind avait été contacté pour savoir s'il avait récemment réalisé un projet de maison. Comme ce n'était pas le cas, il nous a conseillé de nous adresser à ses confrères PRODUCTORA et Celula Arquitectura, puis PRODUCTORA a donné notre adresse au Studio Gracia. PRODUCTORA est une agence de Mexico fondée en 2006 par Abel Perles (né en Argentine en 1972), Carlos Bedoya (né au Mexique en 1973), Victor Jaime (né au Mexique en 1978) et Wonne Ickx (née en Belgique en 1974). Leur maison à Chihuahua (2008, page 325) est une recherche menée à partir de polygones blancs insérés dans un environnement désertique, preuve si nécessaire que l'architecture résidentielle contemporaine de haut niveau s'épanouit en de nombreux pays et pas seulement à Tokyo ou Los Angeles. Celula Arquitectura est « une agence multidisciplinaire qui se consacre à l'intégration de l'architecture, du paysage et de l'art », également basée à Mexico.

18

18
Taira Nishizawa, U-tsuno-miya House, Utsunomiya, Tochigi Prefecture, Japan, 2008

Sa maison d'argile (Clay House, Valle de Bravo, Mexique, 2007–08, page 101) combine une ossature en acier à un étonnant habillage en argile inspiré de l'architecture locale. Le mélange de modernité et de méthodes anciennes adaptées aux besoins actuels montre que dans de nombreuses parties du monde, des architectes se penchent vers le passé pour y trouver une inspiration, sans ressusciter pour autant le pastiche postmoderne. Jorge Gracia Garcia (Jorge Gracia Studio) est lui aussi un Mexicain de moins de 40 ans (né en 1973), mais basé à San Diego aux États-Unis. Sa maison à Todos Santos en Basse-Californie-du-Sud (Todos Santos House, Baja California Sur, Mexique, 2006, page 177) a été entièrement construite en matériaux locaux. Ses murs en béton de couleur sable évoquent, là encore, certains types de finitions locales. Bien que certainement confortable, cette résidence de 320 m² renvoie au désir affiché de l'architecte de « revenir aux principes de base ».

MER ET MONTAGNES

Des préoccupations économiques se propagent également sur les marchés du logement (et de l'architecture) sud-américains, et un certain nombre de maisons publiées ici indique clairement que l'inventivité ou l'originalité surprenantes du design ne sont pas le monopole d'architectes japonais intelligents. L'agence dRN Architects, fondée en 2005 par Nicolás del Río (né en 1975) et Max Nuñez (né en 1976) à Santiago du Chili, peut être citée en exemple à cet égard. Ce couple a conçu plusieurs maisons dans des sites « extrêmes », comme leur Refuge de montagne C7 (Refugio C7, Portillo, Chili, 2008) construit à 2870 m d'altitude, près du Cerro Aconcagua. Leur Refuge de montagne Los Canteros (Farellones, Las Condes, Chili, 2008, page 117) est situé à près de 2000 m au-dessus du niveau de la mer, et doit faire face à des conditions hivernales rigoureuses. Une double isolation thermique et la limitation des ouvertures sur une bonne partie des façades contraste avec le premier étage d'où partent des perspectives spectaculaires sur les montagnes environnantes. Si l'utilisation de l'ardoise noire pour une partie de l'habillage extérieur est un hommage en passant aux constructions en pierre de la région, cette maison est aussi originale de forme que d'esprit. Bien qu'elle soit implantée à flanc de colline parmi d'autres résidences un peu moins intéressantes, elle reste la preuve que la bonne architecture ne doit pas forcément se faire remarquer et pouvoir affronter des conditions aussi difficiles qu'en ces lieux où l'on ne peut construire que pendant les six mois de la belle saison.

Une autre équipe chilienne de moins de 40 ans – Maurizio Pezo (né au Chili en 1973) et Sofía von Ellrichshausen (née en Argentine, 1976), a récemment achevé deux maisons formellement similaires : la maison Fosc (Casa Fosc, San Pedro, Chili, 2008–09, page 315) et la maison Wolf (Casa Wolf, Andalue, Chili, 2006–07, page 21). Dans une enveloppe extérieure relativement simple en béton teinté ou métal, les architectes ont inséré de vastes baies qui donnent une ouverture inattendue à des formes monolithiques plutôt irrégulières. Ces maisons à la présence singulière, mesurant respectivement 160 et 136 m², réussissent à la fois à surprendre et à répondre aux besoins des clients. Atteindre à l'originalité dans un contexte assez contraignant n'est pas une mince réussite pour ces jeunes architectes de talent.

La maison JZ de Bernardes + Jacobsen (JZ House, Camaçari, Bahia, Brésil, 2008, page 75) a déjà été présentée comme la plus vaste maison de ce livre : 1850 m². À de nombreux égards, elle est à l'opposé des exercices de haute altitude de dRN. Implantée non seulement au bord d'une plage, mais aussi sur une dune de sable, elle incarne tous les rêves de l'exotisme brésilien. Bernardes et Jacobsen ont l'habitude

19

19
Bernardes + Jacobsen, JH House, São Paulo, Brazil, 2008

de construire des résidences somptueuses, mais savent aussi imaginer des architectures temporaires extraordinaires, comme la structure de 40 000 m² conçue pour les deux journées du Tim Festival (Rio de Janeiro, 2007). Celle-ci fut assemblée en une semaine à partir de 250 conteneurs de transports de 6 x 12 m pour un budget limité. La maison JZ, en partie montée sur piloti, possède une « grande salle » qui jouit d'une vue exceptionnelle sur l'océan et des jardins. Les architectes ont utilisé des matériaux locaux, comme des treillis en eucalyptus et du marbre beige de Bahia pour les sols, mais ce n'est sans doute pas la proposition la plus écologique de cet ouvrage. Son choix tient à ses qualités architecturales formelles et à sa capacité à faire rêver le lecteur d'un lieu où la vie est peut-être meilleure. Les liens étroits que ces architectes de Rio entretiennent avec leur pays, et une clientèle qui entend clairement faire construire ce qu'elle désire, les autorisent à aller au-delà ce qui pourrait être imaginé comme possible, vu de l'extérieur.

UNE BOÎTE À LETTRES ET UN PEU DE VERDURE

À l'autre bout du monde, mais toujours dans l'hémisphère sud, la constance de la créativité architecturale australienne et néo-zélandaise s'illustre dans un certain nombre de réalisations retenues pour ce livre. Elles bénéficient souvent de cadres naturels spectaculaires, comme c'est le cas de la Ferme de Sandy Bay (Sandy Bay Farm House, Tutukaka Coast, Nouvelle-Zélande, 2007–08, page 133) des architectes Fearon Hay d'Auckland. Cette construction d'un seul niveau en grande partie vitrée, qui s'ouvre sur toute sa hauteur, a été comme déposée sur une crête de la côte Pacifique de Tutukaka face à l'archipel des Poor Knights dans la région du Northland. Elle démontre qu'une partie du talent des architectes tient aussi à leur capacité à trouver des clients qui apprécient ce type de site et, dans le cas présent, à insérer une maison confortable dans un cadre naturel très sensible. L'architecte australien Robert McBride a trouvé une approche originale différente pour sa maison boîte aux lettres (Letterbox House, Blairgowrie, Australie, 2006–08, page 271) et sa maison en bouteille de Klein (Klein Bottle House, Rye, Australie, 2005–07, page 276). « Nous aimons les constructions qui font sourire (pas rire) », précise l'architecte. La première maison semble se déplier hors de la boîte aux lettres qui lui donne son nom, tandis que la seconde est une « version origami » d'un « modèle descriptif de surface développé par les mathématiciens spécialisés en topologie (la bouteille de Klein) ». Si l'intérêt de ces projets semble plutôt formel, ils n'en représentent pas moins des visions intéressantes du type de formes que peut générer une réflexion sur un projet résidentiel. Les maisons de McBride sont surprenantes et originales. C'est peut-être exactement le type de proposition que certains clients souhaitent lorsqu'ils font appel à un architecte inventif.

Michael Bellemo, né à Melbourne en 1967, et Cat Macleod, née à Penang en Malaisie en 1963, ont fondé l'agence Bellemo & Cat à Melbourne en 1992. Leur maison de 155 m², appelée Polygreen (Northcote, Melbourne, Australie, 2007–08, page 69), a été construite pour 220 000 euros seulement au bord d'une allée dans une ancienne zone industrielle d'entrepôts en brique. Ils ont fait appel à un vocabulaire résolument technique. Ce ne sont en aucun cas les premiers ni les derniers architectes à utiliser des composants industriels dans le domaine résidentiel, mais ils y ont ajouté une peau translucide imprimée qui distingue la maison de son environnement malgré l'adoption du langage des entrepôts. La couleur de cette peau (et le nom du projet) est une réponse assez humoristique à la demande d'un voisin « d'un peu de verdure ».

20
Fearon Hay, Sandy Bay Road House, Sandy Bay, Tutukaka Coast, New Zealand, 2007–08

20

VINT BRAD

Au cours des années récentes, un certain nombre de projets ambitieux impliquant des architectes « stars » ont été mis sur pied. Les maisons de Sagaponac dans l'État de New York, ou le projet Sumika, illustrent ce type d'initiative. Il arrive souvent que l'échelle même de ces entreprises et le caractère des fortes personnalités concernées les condamnent à un certain échec. Deux projets audacieux de logements en cours publiés dans ces pages sont « Make it Right », une initiative en faveur des victimes de l'ouragan Katrina, dans le quartier du Lower Ninth Ward à la Nouvelle-Orléans, et, dans une veine très différente, Ordos 100 en Mongolie intérieure.

Le Lower Ninth Ward fut l'une des zones urbaines de la Nouvelle-Orléans les plus durement touchées par l'ouragan Katrina en août 2005. Dans le cadre d'une initiative lancée par l'acteur Brad Pitt, les travaux de construction de cent cinquante maisons pour ce quartier éprouvé ont débuté en 2007. Les architectes basés à Berlin et New York, Graft et William McDonough + Partners, ont collaboré avec Brad Pitt, Reed Kroloff et la Lower Ninth Ward Community Coalition pour mettre au point un projet faisant appel à pas moins de treize architectes locaux, nationaux et internationaux afin de concevoir des maisons économiques. Les critères de sélection portaient en premier lieu sur l'intérêt pour la Nouvelle-Orléans ou l'implication en faveur de cette ville, de préférence après le passage du cyclone Katrina, et/ou l'expérience des opérations de secours après une catastrophe ; la connaissance concrète des concepts du développement durable ; l'expérience des logements résidentiels et multifamiliaux ; la compétence prouvée en innovation dans le cadre de budgets limités ; l'expérience réussie de la construction en environnement gorgé d'eau ou sous le niveau des eaux ; l'attachement à la qualité de conception.

Parmi les architectes participant figurent : Graft (Berlin), Trahan Architects (Baton Rouge), Kieran Timberlake (Philadelphie), Morphosis (Los Angeles), Pugh + Scarpa (Santa Monica), Adjaye Associates (Londres), MVRDV (Rotterdam) et Shigeru Ban (Tokyo). L'agence John Williams Architects de la Nouvelle-Orléans était en charge de l'exécution. La première maison Make it Right a été inaugurée à temps pour le troisième anniversaire du passage de l'ouragan en 2008 et, au moment où ce livre a été imprimé, huit autres sont achevées (dont deux par Graft, présentées page 281). En juillet 2009, Make it Right a annoncé la mise en chantier d'une nouvelle série de quatorze maisons en duplex, conçues par Hitoshi Abe, Elemental (Chili) et Gehry Partners. Des architectes comme Shigeru Ban ou Elemental possèdent une expérience confirmée dans le domaine des logements pour réfugiés ou personnes handicapées et leur présence dans ce groupe n'est donc pas surprenante. Plus intriguant est le fait que la puissance médiatique de Brad Pitt alliée aux talents de Graft et d'autres ait pu attirer un véritable *who's-who* de l'architecture contemporaine aussi bien américain qu'international. Quand on connaît le peu de goût de la plupart des architectes contemporains réputés pour les petits budgets, Make it Right aura peut-être en fait plus d'impact sur la profession que sur le Lower Ninth Ward. En tout état de cause, cette initiative aura fait naître un laboratoire de recherche sur les logements résistant aux catastrophes naturelles, peu coûteux et responsables.

Le projet Ordos 100, sous la direction de l'artiste chinois Ai Wei Wei, réalisé par une équipe de participants invités animée par Herzog & de Meuron, n'est pas vraiment un projet humanitaire comme le précédent l'était. Dans sa définition officielle, on peut lire : « L'objectif du projet est de réaliser cent villas à Ordos en Mongolie intérieure (Chine) pour le client Jiang Yuan Water Engineering Ltd. FAKE Design, l'atelier d'Ai Wei à Pékin, a mis au point le plan directeur pour cent parcelles et dirigera le projet. Herzog & de Meuron ont sélectionné cent architec-

21

21
Studio Pei Zhu, Cai Guo-Qiang Courtyard House Renovation, Beijing, China, 2007

tes, choisis parmi vingt-sept pays du monde entier. Le projet se divise en deux phases. La première concerne vingt-huit parcelles, la seconde les soixante-douze restantes. Chaque architecte est responsable d'une villa de 1000 m². » En fait l'opération semble comporter une troisième phase à proximité, comprenant six maisons conçues par Ai Wei Wei, EM2N (Zürich), Galli Rudolf (Zürich), EXH (Shanghaï), la grande agence internationale Cannon Design et l'équipe bâloise de HHF. La maison sur la dune signée HHF (Dune House, Ordos, Mongolie-Intérieure, Chine, 2008–09, page 200) approche de l'achèvement, et les images de cet ambitieux projet en cours sont présentées dans cet ouvrage. L'aspect international d'Ordos 100, dont les animateurs viennent de Pékin et de Bâle et ses participants du reste du monde, est certainement intéressante et témoigne, une fois encore et pour des raisons différentes, de la diffusion de l'influence de l'architecture contemporaine de qualité, en particulier dans le domaine de la maison individuelle, financièrement moins complexe. L'expérience d'Ordos 100 sera certainement à suivre si le projet parvientà dépasser ses premières réalisations expérimentales.

MÉTAMORPHOSES

Rénovations et extensions ont été longtemps l'activité principale de certains architectes. On peut imaginer que ce type de projet prolifère en période de difficultés économiques puisqu'ils sont généralement moins coûteux que la construction à neuf. Coïncidence, deux projets de cette nature ont été menés à bien par ces architectes jeunes et déjà dotés d'une expérience internationale importante, que l'on trouve de plus en plus dans les agences récentes. La Powerhouse Company a été fondée en 2005 simultanément à Rotterdam et Copenhague par Charles Bessard et Nanne de Ru. Bessard est né en 1971 en France et Nanne de Ru en 1976 aux Pays-Bas. Leur maison spirale (Spiral House, Bourgogne, France, 2007–08, page 13) est l'extension d'une maison ancienne sur un vaste terrain. Ce projet est intéressant non seulement pour son architecture extérieure, mais surtout pour son concept de circulation que ses architectes ont appelé « boucle programmatique ». Par son jeu sophistiqué sur la transparence et l'opacité, cette extension aboutit pratiquement à la recréation d'une maison moderne à la place de l'ancienne.

Delphine Ding est née en Suisse en 1978 et a obtenu son diplôme de l'École polytechnique fédérale de Lausanne (EPFL) en 2005. José Ulloa Davet, né au Chili en 1977, est architecte diplômé de l'Université catholique du Chili en 1977. Tous deux travaillent ensemble depuis 2005. Leur maison Metamorphosis (Casablanca, Tunquén, Chili, 2008, page 397) est l'adaptation d'une maison de bois, datant de 1990, qui n'a coûté que 70 000 dollars. « Une peau de bois ventilée » et des terrasses suggèrent en fait une maison entièrement nouvelle. Dans une autre partie du monde, le très inventif architecte Pei Zhu s'est lancé dans un projet inattendu pour l'artiste Cai Guo-Qiang (rénovation de la maison à cour de Cai Guo-Qiang, Pékin, 2007, page 385). Une maison à cour est le type d'habitat le plus fréquent en architecture traditionnelle chinoise. Ici, l'architecte a à la fois rénové les volumes existants, dont la vieille demeure en bois, et fait intervenir ce qu'il appelle « un espace futuriste » dans la partie sud du bâtiment. Il est intéressant de noter que Cai Guo-Qiang est internationalement connu pour des œuvres qui font souvent référence à l'art et à la culture chinois du passé. Il utilise par exemple fréquemment des feux d'artifice. La rénovation de Pei Zhu semble bien dans l'esprit de l'œuvre de son propriétaire, à la fois résolument moderne et enracinée dans le passé, dans la tradition omniprésente de sa Chine natale.

La facilité avec laquelle l'information sur l'architecture la plus récente se transmet aujourd'hui sur Internet est peut-être une des raisons pour lesquelles des talents issus de pays qui ne sont pas toujours réputés pour la qualité de leur architecture contemporaine réussissent à se faire connaître. Le développement que connaît l'Europe de l'Est est un facteur qui explique une nouvelle prise de conscience dans ces pays de la nécessité d'une meilleure conception architecturale. Né en 1969 à Katowice, Robert Konieczny dirige KWK PROMES, une agence qui a réalisé un certain nombre de maisons peu communes. L'une de celles-ci, la maison de sécurité de 556 m² (Safe House, Okrzeszyn, Pologne, 2005–08, page 257), comme son nom l'indique, insiste sur la sécurité de ses résidents. Elle se présente sous la forme d'un volume fermé, style bunker, dont l'aspect presque dérangeant est renforcé par sa couleur noire. Malgré cet aspect renfermé, la maison s'ouvre quand même sur un jardin pour offrir quelques rayons de soleil à ses habitants si bien protégés. La maison OUTrial (OUTrial House, Ksiazenice, Pologne, 2005–08, page 260) possède la même apparence géométrique, mais elle est dotée d'une toiture recouverte d'herbe qui adoucit légèrement ses lignes relativement dures. Ces maisons ne correspondent peut-être pas aux stéréotypes que l'on imagine trouver dans un livre sur l'architecture très contemporaine, mais sont étonnantes et, à leur façon, inventives.

LE RÊVE AMÉRICAIN. TOUJOURS.

Le taux élevé de propriété individuelle aux États-Unis et leur position centrale en matière de créativité architecturale expliquent qu'ils aient longtemps joué un rôle essentiel dans l'évolution de la conception résidentielle. Cependant, un phénomène qui pourrait ressembler à un assèchement de la capacité d'invention semble avoir touché ce pays au cours des dernières années. Il a d'abord été entraîné dans une course vers des résidences de plus en plus extravagantes, et, récemment, dans une spirale inverse sous le signe des saisies et du ralentissement de la construction. Les exemples sélectionnés ici tendent néanmoins à montrer que l'architecture contemporaine se porte encore bien au pays de Frank Lloyd Wright. La maison rouge (Red House, Los Angeles, États-Unis, 2004–06, page 95), par Padraic Cassidy, est une intéressante composition réalisée pour le scénariste Larry Karaszewski. Cassidy, qui a travaillé chez Daly Genik et Frank Gehry avant de créer sa propre agence, s'est servi à la fois de la couleur et de la géométrie pour animer cette maison qui se détache fièrement dans une forêt d'eucalyptus. À l'autre extrémité du pays, Kyu Sung Woo, qui a travaillé de 1970 à 1974 chez José Luis Sert (Sert, Jackson & Associates), a créé sa propre maison de vacances à Putney dans le Vermont. Divisée en trois éléments, elle présente une caractéristique qui semble de plus en plus fréquente dans les maisons contemporaines : une modernité de base, mais rendue complexe par une juxtaposition sophistiquée d'éléments et de formes. L'architecte a porté une grande attention à la consommation d'énergie, ce qui confirme également la nature fondamentalement contemporaine de ce projet.

Peut-être plus inattendu, un dernier exemple de la créativité de l'architecture contemporaine américaine est proposé ici sous la forme de la maison ferme de Michael Jantzen (Homestead House, 2009, page 228). Comme une grande partie du travail de cet architecte, cette maison n'est pas encore construite. Utilisant « des éléments de constructions agricoles facilement disponibles », Jantzen a cherché à créer « un système constructif à base d'arcs préfabriqués, modulaire, hautement résistant et économique », qui s'assemble à l'aide d'outils simples. Une isolation à base de pulpe de papier, des cellules photovoltaïques, une éolienne et diverses stratégies passives font que cette maison du XXIe siècle devrait être plus environnementale que les milliers de maisons de banlieues américaines. Bien que certains pensent que l'architecture « virtuelle » a déjà vécu son apogée, cette « Homestead House » est la preuve que certains continuent à essayer d'améliorer la vie des individus et de la communauté par l'architecture.

RETOUR AUX BASIQUES

Les maisons peuvent parfois être assimilées à des œuvres d'art, au sens le plus positif de cette analogie. L'une des plus étonnantes et des plus inventives achevées récemment est la Dupli.Casa de Jürgen Mayer-Hermann (J. Mayer H., près de Ludwigsburg, Allemagne 2006–08, page 264). Pratiquant une duplication et une rotation des volumes d'une maison familiale édifiée sur le même site en 1984, l'architecte élabore ce qu'il appelle une « archéologie familiale », tout en créant une maison nouvelle, sculpturale, lyrique, faite de flux et reflux. Il part de l'idée de la maison ancienne considérée comme un « objet trouvé », en référence nette à l'art moderne. Par ses porte-à-faux et ses courbes toutes blanches, la Dupli.Casa se distingue radicalement d'autres maisons récentes, et confirme que l'Allemagne est également l'un des lieux où se redéfinissent les frontières de l'architecture contemporaine. L'idée d'une « archéologie » dans le cas d'une maison aussi moderne s'inscrit dans les préoccupations universelles à lier la modernité aux racines de la culture et au lieu. La continuité est une règle nouvelle qui prend la place de la *tabula rasa*. Cette bataille n'est certainement pas encore finie – le désir de rompre avec tout ce qui relève du passé est profondément ancré dans la créativité contemporaine –, mais les valeurs qui animent l'art et l'architecture sont plus fortes que celles du changement superficiel. La crise économique remet les choses en perspective et impose à nouveau une réflexion sur les fondamentaux. Les maisons publiées ici peuvent vouloir offrir une vue illimitée d'un bassin hydrographique dans l'Oregon ou simplement protéger leurs habitants de la tempête. L'approche écologique, sous la forme d'une réduction des consommations d'énergie, semble devoir durer, ne serait-ce que parce qu'elle entraîne la baisse des factures d'énergie. Par ailleurs, beaucoup de ces maisons sont des points d'observation, des lieux privilégiés au sein desquels les vues de ce qui reste du monde naturel sont cadrées pour être mieux appréciées. Comme les « Rolling Huts » de Tom Kundig, beaucoup de ces maisons admettent leur nature éphémère fondamentale. Les nouvelles règles de l'écologie veulent que de plus en plus de maisons puissent se démonter, se transporter et peut-être se réutiliser sans laisser la moindre trace sur le terrain qui les avait accueillies. Ces facteurs sont tous relativement nouveaux en architecture résidentielle, mais seront sans doute de plus en plus présents. À de nombreux égards, les maisons figurant dans ces pages se trouvent sur un fil conceptuel, entre la création d'un monde nouveau et l'ancrage dans le passé.

Si certains architectes s'efforcent d'interpréter les désirs de leurs clients, d'autres tendent clairement à imposer leurs propres concepts, voire leurs fantasmes. Il est rare que le client, l'architecte et les intérêts économiques trouvent le juste d'équilibre qui fera d'une maison contemporaine quelque chose qui se rapproche d'une œuvre d'art. Lorsqu'un chef-d'œuvre apparaît, comme la Villa Savoye de Le Corbusier en son temps, vivre dans une œuvre d'art peut représenter pour le client un prix à payer inattendu. Bien qu'il soit trop tôt (fin 2009) pour juger des conséquences de la crise apparue à l'automne 2008, certaines maisons présentées ici semblent déjà prendre en compte des besoins d'économie ou peut-être plus clairement, manifester un plus grand esprit de responsabilité, généré par la nécessité. Les maisons

22
KWK PROMES, OUTrial House, Ksiazenice, Poland, 2005–08

22

nouvelles, ou les anciennes rénovées, seront toujours en demande. Elles constituent pour l'architecture une façon d'évoluer et de s'adapter à son époque. Du fait de leur cycle de construction rapide, comparé à celui des projets de dimensions plus importantes, les maisons constituent un véritable baromètre de l'architecture contemporaine et même de son futur. Une modernité non réductrice, mais plutôt construite sur des circonstances, des conditions, des sites, ou parfois juste une esthétique, est ce qui anime l'architecture actuelle, comme le démontrent les maisons présentées dans les pages qui suivent.

Philippe Jodidio, Grimentz, Suisse, août 2009

AMARTERRANCE

Amarterrance
Pavillon Meguro 201
1–3–31 Meguro, Meguro-ku
Tokyo 153–0063
Japan

Tel: +81 3 3495 7200
Fax: +81 3 3495 2467
E-mail: info@amarterrance.com
Web: www.amarterrance.com

Hiroshi Marubashi was born in Gunma Prefecture in 1968. He graduated from the Department of Architecture, Musashino Art University in Tokyo (1991), and received his M.Arch degree from Shibaura Institute of Technology in Tokyo (1993). He worked in Tokyo for the offices Archiwerk (1994) and Sasaki Architect (1998), before creating **AMARTERRANCE** with Satoshi Yamaguchi in Tokyo in 2002. Satoshi Yamaguchi was born in Kanagawa Prefecture in 1968. He graduated from the Shibaura Institute Technology in Tokyo (1991), where he received his M.Arch degree in 1993. He worked with Beam Studio in Tokyo (1993) and established in 1997 in Yokohama IQ Architects, before creating Amarterrance. Hiroshi Marubashi explains that the name Amarterrance comes from the name of *Amaterasu Oomikami*, the "most important God and the ancestor of the Japanese empire." *Amaterasu* also means "that the sun shines impartially on all." The firm's work includes a Docomo Shop (Maebashi City, 2003); the Harmonic Club Hotel (Karuizawa, 2004); Abstract Forest (Yamanashi, 2007, published here); and the Miyokawa Restaurant (Kamakura, 2008), all in Japan.

Hiroshi Marubashi wurde 1968 in der Präfektur Gunma geboren. Nach Abschluss seines Architekturstudiums an der Musashino Art University (Tokio, 1991) absolvierte er seinen M. Arch. am Shibaura Institute of Technology in Tokio (1993). Er arbeitete für die Tokioter Büros Archiwerk (1994) und Sasaki Architect (1998), bevor er 2002 gemeinsam mit Satoshi Yamaguchi sein Büro **AMARTERRANCE** in Tokio gründete. Satoshi Yamaguchi wurde 1968 in der Präfektur Kanagawa geboren. Er schloss 1991 sein Studium am Shibaura Institute of Technology in Tokio ab und legte dort 1993 auch die Prüfung zum M.Arch. ab. Anschließend war er für Beam Studio in Tokio tätig (1993), gründete 1997 in Yokohama IQ Architects, bevor er Amarterrance ins Leben rief. Nach Hiroshi Marubashi leitet sich der Name Amarterrance von der japanischen Gottheit *Amaterasu-o-mi-kami* ab, der „höchsten Göttin und Begründerin des japanischen Kaiserhauses". *Amaterasu* bedeutet außerdem „die Sonne, die ohne Unterschied für alle scheint". Projekte des Büros sind u. a. eine Docomo-Geschäftsstelle (Maebashi, 2003), das Harmonic Club Hotel (Karuizawa, 2004), Abstract Forest (Yamanashi, 2007, hier vorgestellt) und das Restaurant Miyokawa (Kamakura, 2008), alle in Japan.

Hiroshi Marubashi est né dans la préfecture de Gunma en 1968. Diplômé du département d'architecture de l'Université d'art Musashino (Tokyo, 1991), il a reçu son M.Arch de l'Institut de technologie Shibaura (Tokyo, 1993). Il a travaillé chez Archiwerk (Tokyo, 1994) et Sasaki Architect (Tokyo, 1998), avant de fonder **AMARTERRANCE** avec Satoshi Yamaguchi à Tokyo in 2002. Satoshi Yamaguchi est né dans la préfecture de Kanagawa en 1968. Diplômé M.Arch de l'Institut de technologie Shibaura (Tokyo, 1991–1993), il a travaillé pour Beam Studio (Tokyo, 1993) et fondé IQ Architects (Yokohama, 1997), avant de créer Amarterrance. Hiroshi Marubashi explique que le nom de l'agence vient d'*Amaterasu Oomikami*, le « dieu le plus important et l'ancêtre de l'empire japonais. » *Amaterasu* signifie également « que le soleil brille impartialement sur tout ». Parmi les travaux de l'agence figurent une boutique Docomo (Maebashi City, 2003) ; l'Harmonic Club Hotel (Karuizawa, 2004) ; Forêt abstraite (Abstract Forest, Yamanashi, 2007, publiée ici) et le restaurant Miyokawa (Kamakura, 2008), tous au Japon.

ABSTRACT FOREST

Yamanashi Prefecture, Japan, 2007

Area: 133 m². Client: not disclosed.
Cost: not disclosed

This relatively simple house is built on a forest site, with numerous oak and larch trees, which were preserved to the greatest extent possible. A laminated lumber "wall pillar" is intended to create a "grid that replaces the felled trees." This system allows open views on all four sides of the residence. Semi-rigid joints and pin joints are used in alternation, allowing a more "open and free" plan than a traditional wooden skeleton structure. Essentially a single room, the house consists, like the forest itself, "of a variety of different areas but, simultaneously, it affirms its spatial continuity." The intention of the architects was to affirm a certain unity between the house, with its interior, and the forest. This is evident in the structure itself as well as in the views that the house affords its environment.

Das eher schlichte Haus steht auf einem Waldgrundstück mit zahlreichen Eichen und Lärchen, die weitgehend erhalten werden konnten. Eine „Pfeilerwand" aus Furnierschichtholz soll „das Bild der zuvor hier gewachsenen Bäume nachempfinden". Dank dieser Konstruktion ist ein freier Ausblick in alle vier Richtungen möglich. Durch den abwechselnden Einsatz von halbstarren Verbindungen und Bolzenverbindungen ließ sich ein weitaus „offenerer und freierer" Grundriss umsetzen als mit einer herkömmlichen Holzskelettbauweise. Das Haus, im Grunde ein einziger großer Raum, umfasst wie der Wald „verschiedene Zonen, wahrt aber dennoch eine räumliche Kontinuität". Ziel der Architekten war es, eine Einheit zwischen Haus, Innenraum und Wald herzustellen. Dies wird am Bau selbst sowie durch die Ausblicke unterstrichen, die das Haus in seine Umgebung bietet.

Cette maison, relativement simple, est édifiée dans un site forestier abondamment planté de chênes et de mélèzes qui ont été, le plus possible, préservés. Un « mur-pilier » crée une « trame qui remplace les arbres abattus ». Ce système permet de conserver des perspectives sur les quatre côtés de l'habitation. Des joints semi-rigides et des agrafes utilisés en alternance autorisent un plan « plus ouvert et plus libre » que dans une maison traditionnelle à ossature en bois. Essentiellement constituée d'une pièce unique, la maison se compose, comme la forêt, « d'une variété de zones différenciées, tout en affirmant simultanément sa continuité spatiale ». L'intention des architectes était de trouver une certaine unité entre la maison, son intérieur et la forêt, ce qui apparaît clairement dans la construction, mais aussi dans les vues cadrées de l'environnement.

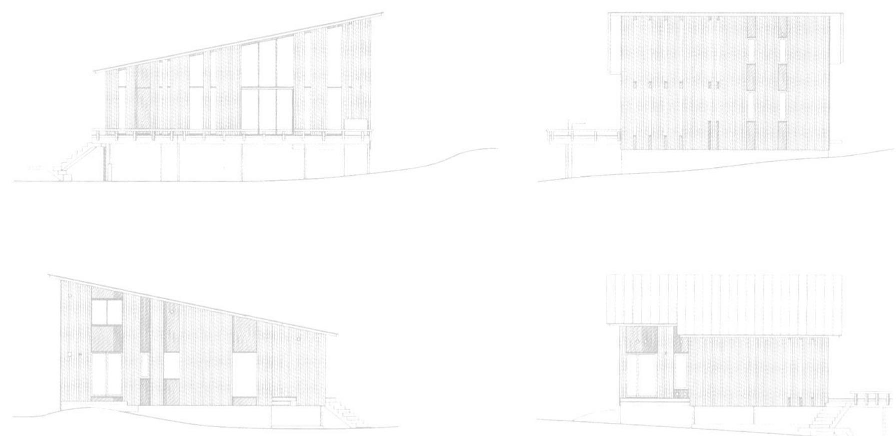

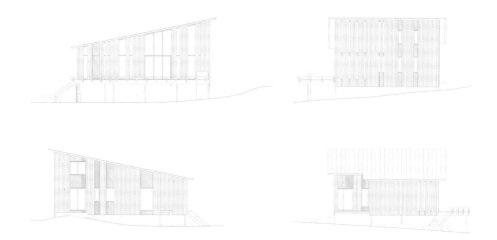

Elevation drawings (above) and a similarly oriented photo (left) show the simple, wedge-like form of the house, which is partially lifted off the ground. Below, the main living space.

Aufrisse (oben) und eine Frontalaufnahme (links) veranschaulichen die schlichte, keilartige Form des Hauses, das zum Teil über den Boden aufgeständert ist. Unten der Hauptwohnraum.

Les élévations (ci-dessus) et la photo prise selon la même orientation (à gauche) montrent la forme en coin de la maison en partie surélevée. Ci-dessous, le séjour principal.

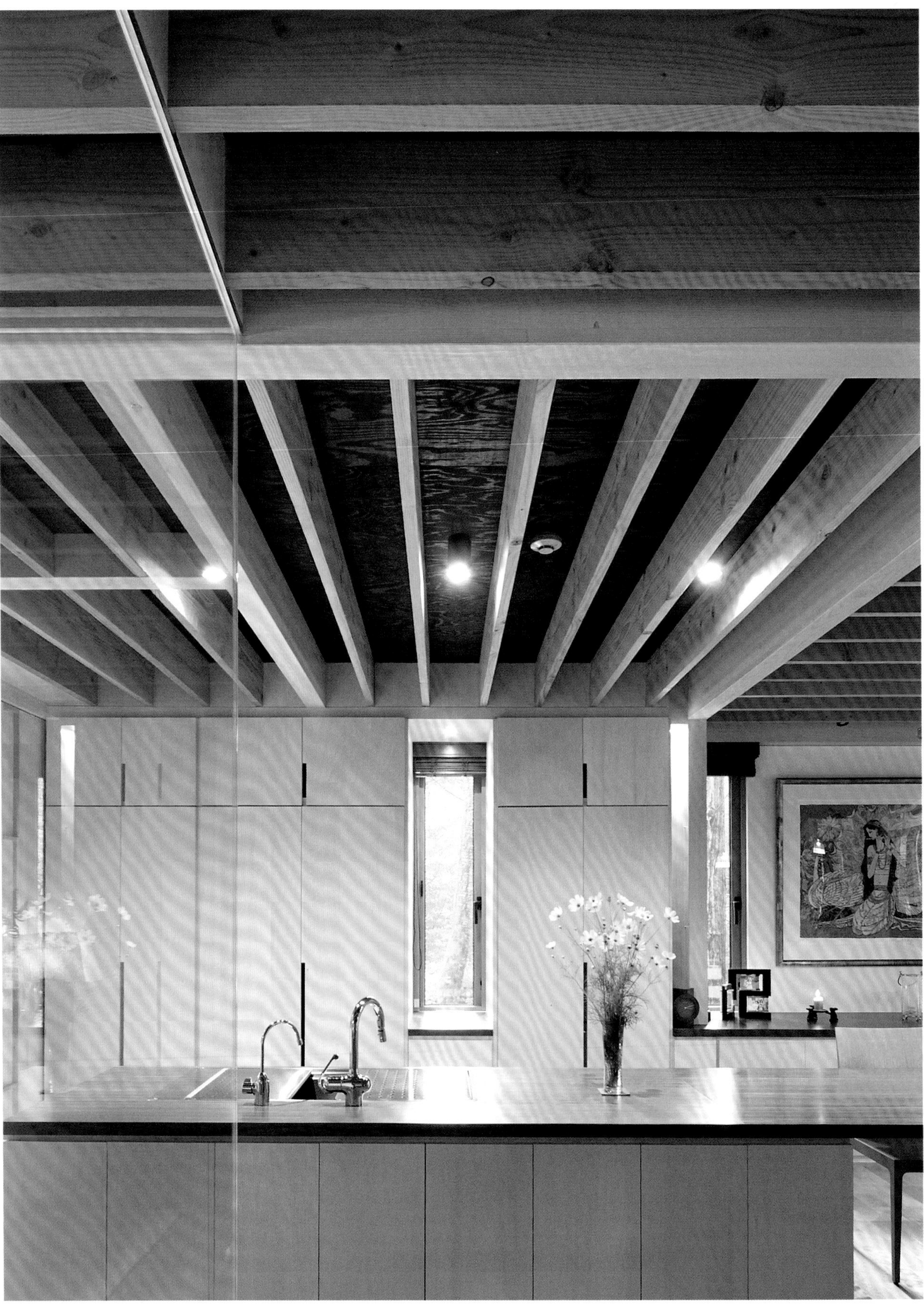

The interior of the house emphasizes the proximity of the architecture to its natural setting, including the sunken bathtub to the right.

Das Interieur des Hauses unterstreicht die Nähe der Architektur zu ihrem landschaftlichen Kontext; ebenso auch die in den Boden eingelassene Badewanne rechts im Bild.

L'intérieur de la maison fait ressortir la proximité de l'architecture et de son cadre naturel, comme par exemple à travers une baignoire creusée dans le sol (à droite).

ARKPABI

Arkpabi I Giorgio Palù & Michele Bianchi architetti
Via Trecchi 20
26100 Cremona
Italy

Tel: +39 03 72 41 38 87
Fax: +39 03 72 80 04 67
Web: www.arkpabi.it
E-mail: arkpabi@arkpabi.it

Giorgio Palù was born in Cremona, Italy, in 1964. He graduated from the Politecnico di Milano in 1990 and in 1994 he founded **ARKPABI**, in Cremona, with Michele Bianchi. Michele Bianchi was also born in Cremona in 1964 and graduated from the Politecnico di Milano in 1990. Their work includes the Dellearti Design Hotel (Cremona, 1999–2002); an Apartment Building (Cremona, 2002–04); another Apartment Complex in Milan (2004–08); and I Tulipani House (Cremona, 2006–09, published here). Their private residences include a house in Cigognolo (Cremona, 2000–03), one in Padenghe sul Garda (Brescia, 2005–08) and another in Piadena (Cremona, 2008– under construction), all in Italy. Current work also includes a mixed-use housing and shopping mall complex in Cremona.

Giorgio Palù wurde 1964 in Cremona, Italien, geboren. Nachdem er 1990 sein Studium an der Politecnico di Milano abgeschlossen hatte, gründete er 1994 mit Michele Bianchi sein Büro **ARKPABI** in Cremona. Michele Bianchi wurde ebenfalls 1964 in Cremona geboren und schloss sein Studium an der Politecnico di Milano 1990 ab. Zu ihren Projekten zählen das Dellearti Design Hotel (Cremona, 1999–2002), ein Apartmentgebäude (Cremona, 2002–04), ein weiterer Apartmentkomplex in Mailand (2004–08) sowie das Haus I Tulipani (Cremona, 2006–09, hier vorgestellt). Zu den von ihnen realisierten privaten Wohnbauten gehören ein Haus in Cigognolo (Cremona, 2000–03), ein Haus in Padenghe sul Garda (Brescia, 2005–08) sowie ein Haus in Piadena (Cremona, seit 2008 im Bau), alle in Italien. Zu ihren aktuellen Projekten zählt auch ein Wohnkomplex mit Einkaufszentrum in Cremona.

Giorgio Palù, né à Crémone (Italie) en 1964, est diplômé du Politecnico de Milan (1990), et a fondé **ARKPABI** à Crémone en 1994, avec Michele Bianchi. Michele Bianchi, également né à Crémone en 1964, est diplômé du Politecnico de Milan (1990). Parmi leurs réalisations : le Dellearti Design Hotel (Crémone, 1999–2002) ; un immeuble de logements (Crémone, 2002–04) ; un complexe de logements à Milan (2004–08) et la maison I Tulipani (Crémone, 2006–09), publiée ici. Parmi leurs maisons individuelles figurent des maisons à Cigognolo (Crémone, 2000–03) ; Padenghe sul Garda (Brescia, 2005–08) et Piadena (Crémone, 2008–en cours), le tout en Italie. Ils travaillent actuellement sur un complexe de centre commercial, de logements et de bureaux à Crémone.

LIBERI TUTTI

I TULIPANI HOUSE

Cremona, Italy, 2006–09

Area: 220 m² (plus 210 m² in the hanging garden area). Client: I Tulipani Soc. Coop. A R.L. Cost: €700 000

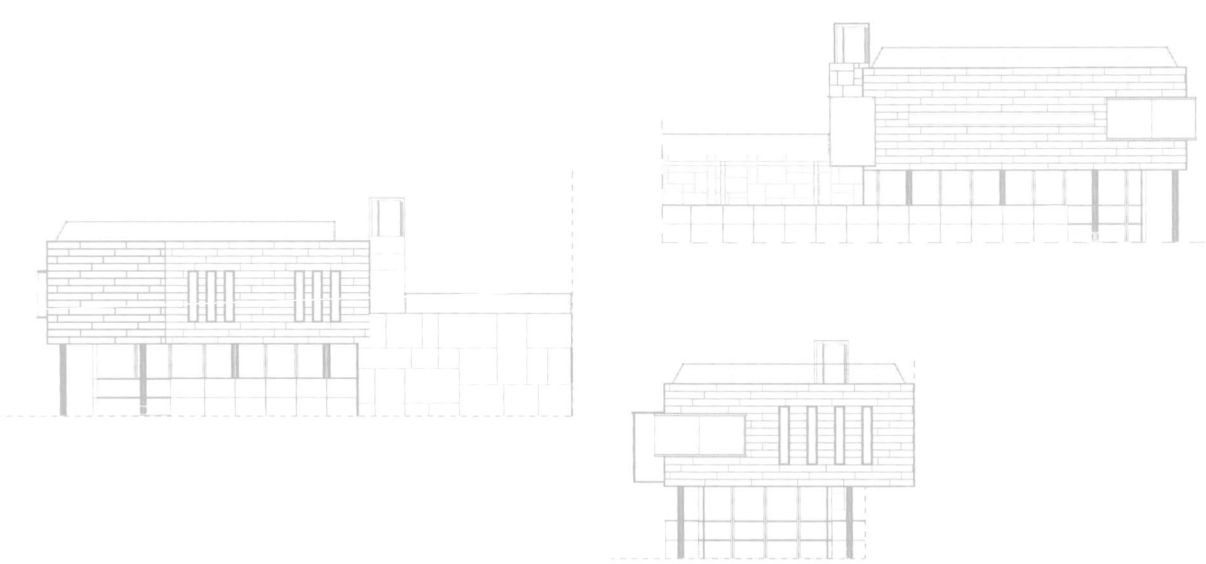

This housing scheme includes commercial space on the street level, and a suspended villa divided into two levels, forming the residence of an artist set on a preexisting building. Though the largely glazed volumes are "regular and orthogonal," they are "related in an explosive combination," according to the architects. Thin piloti supports give an impression of a dynamic relation between the volumes. Polyurethane-coated, pre-painted aluminum panels are used for cladding, with a willful contrast between black and primary red surfaces. The architects are intent on the "dematerialization" of what remains a geometric vocabulary, despite the numerous spatial and volumetric surprises integrated into the design. The lower glazed volume of the suspended villa has internal mirrored surfaces that contrast with oak floors, and walls covered in black leather in the upper area. A garden affording generous views of the city is set on the roof of the villa. A glazed stairway links the volumes.

Dieser Entwurf für einen Wohnbau umfasst Geschäftsflächen auf Straßenebene und eine über zwei Ebenen verteilte, „hängende" Villa. Das Domizil eines Künstlers wurde auf ein bestehendes Gebäude aufgesetzt. Zwar wirken die großzügig verglasten Volumina „regelmäßig und rechtwinklig", sind den Architekten zufolge jedoch „in einer explosiven Kombination angeordnet". Schlanke *pilotis* lassen den Eindruck einer dynamischen Beziehung der Volumina zueinander entstehen. Als Verkleidung wurden polyurethanbeschichtete Aluminiumpaneele verwendet, wobei die schwarzen und in der Primärfarbe Rot gehaltenen Oberflächen einen gewollten Kontrast bilden. Besonderen Wert legen die Architekten auf ihre „entmaterialisierende" Formensprache, die trotz der zahlreichen, in den Entwurf integrierten räumlichen und volumetrischen Überraschungen stets geometrisch bleibt. In den Innenräumen der unteren, verglasten Ebene der hängenden Villa wurden Spiegelflächen installiert, die mit den Eichenböden kontrastieren. Die Wände der oberen Ebene sind mit schwarzem Leder verkleidet. Auf dem Dach der Villa wurde ein Garten mit weitem Blick über die Stadt angelegt. Eine gläserne Treppe verbindet die einzelnen Volumina miteinander.

Ce petit complexe comprend des espaces commerciaux en rez-de-chaussée sur rue et la résidence d'un artiste : une villa suspendue de deux niveaux littéralement posée sur le bâtiment préexistant. Bien que les volumes, en grande partie vitrés, soient « réguliers et orthogonaux », ils se relient « dans une combinaison explosive », expliquent les architectes. De fins piloti créent un sentiment de relation dynamique entre ces volumes. Les panneaux d'aluminium peint enduits de polyuréthane qui forment le bardage créent un contraste voulu entre les surfaces noires ou couleur rouge primaire. Les architectes insistent sur la « dématérialisation » de ce vocabulaire qui reste géométrique malgré les nombreuses surprises spatiales et volumétriques que réserve le projet. Le volume vitré inférieur de la villa suspendue comprend des panneaux intérieurs en miroir qui contrastent avec les sols en chêne, tandis qu'à l'étage certains murs sont tendus de cuir noir. Un jardin bénéficiant d'amples perspectives sur la ville a été aménagé sur le toit-terrasse. Les volumes sont reliés par un escalier de verre.

The elevations (above) show the extension of the existing building, clearly showing how the architects added a residence, turning the overall structure into a mixed-use design.

Die Aufrisse (oben) zeigen die aufgestockte Erweiterung. Deutlich zu erkennen ist der von den Architekten hinzugefügte Wohntrakt, durch den das Gebäude sein gemischtes Nutzungsprofil gewinnt.

Les élévations (ci-dessus) permettent de comprendre comment la nouvelle construction a été ajoutée sur l'ancienne, et comment cette adjonction a transformé l'ensemble en petit immeuble mixte.

The design clearly makes reference to the existing building, to the extent of blurring any obvious exterior distinction between what was there before and what was added.

Formal nimmt der Entwurf so deutlich auf das bestehende Gebäude Bezug, dass Unterschiede zwischen Alt und Neu am Außenbau kaum zu erkennen sind.

La composition s'appuie sur la construction existante au point de faire disparaître toute distinction extérieure évidente entre ce qui était et ce qui a été ajouté.

Stairs (left) leading to the rooftop patio (right) and the main living space (below) show that the exterior design corresponds closely to the feeling of the interior.

Die Treppen hinauf zum Dachgarten (links) und hinunter in den Hauptwohnraum (unten) belegen, dass die Wirkung nach außen und die Atmosphäre des Innenraums eng miteinander korrespondieren.

L'escalier qui conduit au patio en toiture (à gauche) et le séjour principal (ci-dessous) montrent que le dessin des façades correspond assez fidèlement au sentiment donné par l'intérieur.

Plans of the two levels (below) and a view of the rooftop terrace reveal essentially orthogonal lines and an overall discretion seen most clearly in the inward tilting barriers at the edge of the terrace (above).

Grundrisse der zwei Wohnebenen (unten) und ein Blick auf die Dachterrasse veranschaulichen die weitgehende Orthogonalität der Linienführung und die umsichtige Gestaltung von Details, zu sehen insbesondere am nach innen geneigten Geländer der Terrasse (oben).

Les plans des deux niveaux (ci-dessous) et une vue du toit-terrasse illustrent le plan essentiellement orthogonal et la discrétion d'ensemble que l'on note dans les garde-fous inclinés vers l'intérieur au pourtour de la terrasse (ci-dessus).

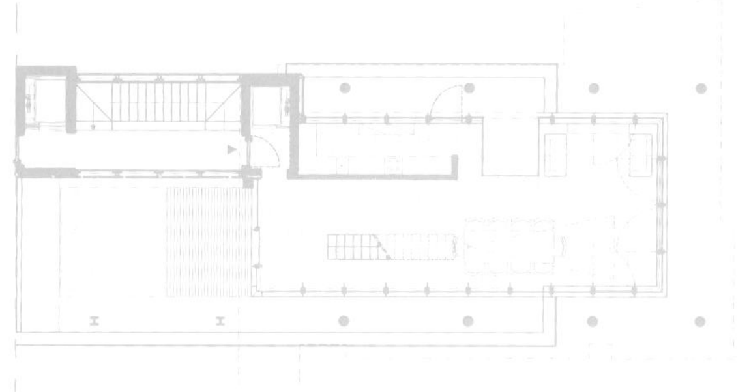

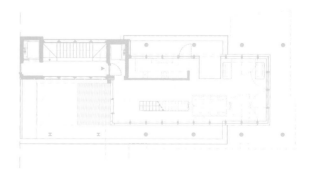

Zafra-Uceda House ►

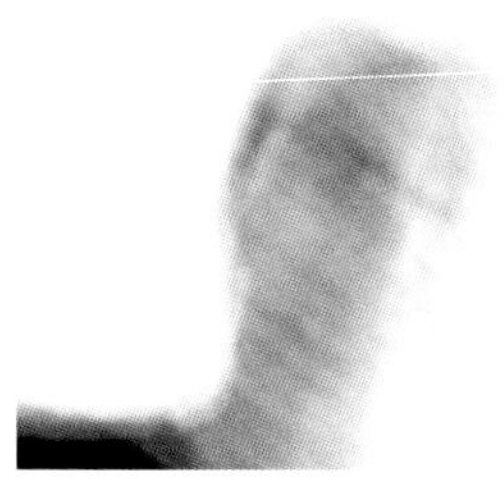

EDUARDO ARROYO – NO.MAD ARQUITECTOS

Eduardo Arroyo
NO.MAD Arquitectos, S.L.P.
C/ Pez, 27–1° Izda.
28004 Madrid
Spain

Tel: +34 91 532 70 34
Fax: +34 91 522 88 47
E-mail: nomad@nomad.as
Web: www.nomad.as

EDUARDO ARROYO was born in 1964 in Bilbao and graduated from the ETSA Madrid in 1988. He was a professor in the same school from 1996 to 2002. He has also taught in universities in Seoul, Teheran, Paris, Lausanne, Eindhoven, Graz, Ferrara, Porto, Lisbon, Oslo, Brussels, Buenos Aires, Barcelona, Alicante, Valencia, and Seville. His work includes the Euskotren Headquarters (Durango, 2003); Visitors Center and Elica Hotel (Fabriano, Italy, 2003); Kaleido Restaurant (Madrid, 2004); Musée des Beaux-Arts (Lausanne; NMBA, competition entry; 2004); Housing Tower (Durango, 2004); Housing and Sports Center (Valencia, 2004); and the Estonian National Museum (Tartu, Estonia, 2005). He has also worked on urban design at El Torico Plaza (Teruel, 2005); and the access and plaza for Etxebarria Park (Bilbao, 2005). His more recent work includes Social Housing for IVVSA (Valencia, 2006); Social Housing for EMVS (Madrid, 2006); a Single-Family House (Calas, 2006); Scenic Art Center (Zarautz, 2007); Environment Improvement Systems for EDAR (Galindo, 2007); University of Economy (Vienna, Austria, 2008); Head Office for EPSA (Seville, 2008); Zafra-Uceda House (Aranjuez, 2008–09, published here); and a Civic Center (Sestao, 2009), all in Spain unless stated otherwise.

EDUARDO ARROYO wurde 1964 in Bilbao geboren und schloss sein Studium 1988 an der ETSA Madrid ab. Von 1996 bis 2002 war er als Professor an derselben Hochschule tätig. Darüber hinaus lehrte er an Universitäten in Seoul, Teheran, Paris, Lausanne, Eindhoven, Graz, Ferrara, Porto, Lissabon, Oslo, Brüssel, Buenos Aires, Barcelona, Alicante, Valencia und Sevilla. Zu seinen Projekten zählen die Zentrale von Euskotren (Durango, 2003), das Besucherzentrum und Hotel Elica (Fabriano, Italien, 2003), das Restaurant Kaleido (Madrid, 2004), ein Wettbewerbsbeitrag für das Musée des Beaux-Arts in Lausanne (NMBA, 2004), ein Apartmenthochhaus (Durango, 2004), ein Wohn- und Sportkomplex (Valencia, 2004) sowie das Estnische Nationalmuseum (Tartu, Estland, 2005). Darüber hinaus war er an der städtebaulichen Planung der Plaza El Torico beteiligt (Teruel, 2005) sowie an der Erschließung und Platzgestaltung des Etxebarria Parks (Bilbao, 2005). Jüngste Arbeiten sind u. a. soziale Wohnbauprojekte für IVVSA (Valencia, 2006), Sozialwohnungen für EMVS (Madrid, 2006), ein Einfamilienhaus (Calas, 2006), das Centro de Artes Escenicas (Zarautz, 2007), umwelttechnische Optimierungssysteme für EDAR (Galindo, 2007), die Wirtschaftsuniversität Wien (Österreich, 2008), das Hauptkatasteramt (EPSA) in Sevilla (2008), das Haus Zafra-Uceda (Aranjuez, 2008–09, hier vorgestellt) sowie ein Bürgerzentrum in Sestao (2009), alle in Spanien, soweit nicht anders angegeben.

EDUARDO ARROYO est né en 1964 à Bilbao, et a obtenu son diplôme d'architecte de l'ETSA à Madrid en 1988. Il a enseigné dans cette même école de 1996 à 2002, ainsi que dans les universités de Séoul, Téhéran, Paris, Lausanne, Eindhoven, Graz, Ferrare, Porto, Lisbonne, Oslo, Bruxelles, Buenos Aires, Barcelone, Alicante, Valence et Séville. Parmi ses réalisations : le siège d'Euskotren (Durango, Espagne, 2003) ; le centre des visiteurs et l'Elica Hotel (Fabriano, Italie, 2003) ; le restaurant Kaleido (Madrid, 2004) ; le Musée des beaux-arts (Lausanne, Suisse, NMBA, participation au concours, 2004) ; une tour de logements (Durango, 2004) ; le Musée national de l'Estonie (Tartu, Estonie, 2005). Il est également intervenu comme urbaniste sur le projet de la place d'El Torico (Teruel, 2005) ; l'accès et la place du Parc Etxebarria (Bilbao, 2005). Ses projets actuels, pratiquement tous en Espagne, comprennent des logements sociaux pour l'IVVSA (Valence, 2007) et pour l'EMVS, Madrid (2006) ; une maison familiale (Calas, 2006) ; un Centre des arts de la scène (Zarautz, 2007) ; des systèmes pour l'amélioration de l'environnement pour l'EDAR (Galindo, 2007) ; l'Université d'économie (Vienne, Autriche, 2008) ; le siège de l'EPSA (Séville, 2008) ; la maison Zafra-Uceda (Aranjuez, 2008-09 publiée ici) ; un Centre municipal (Sestao, 2009), tous en Espagne sauf mention contraire.

ZAFRA-UCEDA HOUSE

Aranjuez, Spain, 2008–09

Area: 250 m² (320 m² with terraces).
Clients: J. C. Zafra, M. A. Uceda. Cost: €560 000

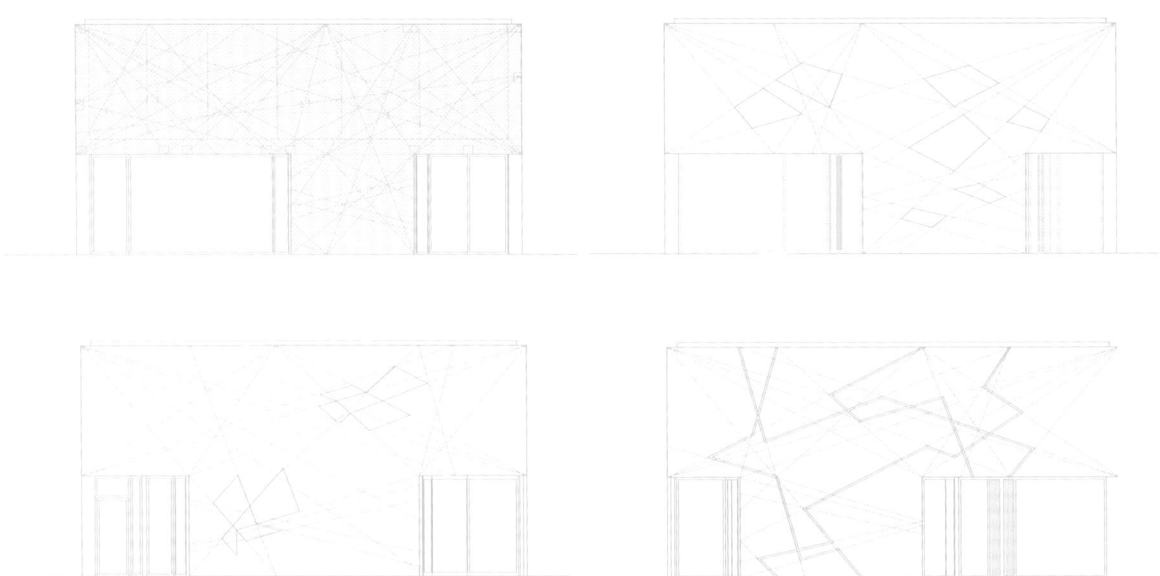

The architect calls the surroundings of this house a golf course with "a dubious-quality built environment." The volumes are determined by the "empty character" of the surroundings, responding thus to distant landscape views. A mountain view, the old city, or the river are framed intentionally through the orientation of the openings of the house. Two enclosed terraces on the upper level open to the sky and contain a cactus garden, while a southern terrace again frames distant perspectives. The house, according to the architect, is thus the result of a series of "accidents." At the request of the clients, there are no doors, but each space does have a defined function. An "iridescent polycarbonate wall changes colors with the light and runs parallel to a reflecting mirroring wall that multiplies the interior spaces." The living room is a double-height area with panoramic perforations. An expanded metal mesh façade to the south protects the dining and sleeping areas from direct sun (and golf balls), while a concrete wall on the east isolates the house from neighbors. "To the north," concludes Eduardo Arroyo, "pieces of green marble, cut out with invisible lines, send a public message reminding us that the time for luxurious buildings has probably passed."

Dem Architekten zufolge ist die Umgebung des Hauses, ein Golfplatz, geprägt von „Bebauung von fragwürdiger Qualität". Die Volumina des Hauses wurden als Reaktion auf die „Leere" der Umgebung gestaltet und bieten einen weiten Blick in die Landschaft. Durch die Ausrichtung der Fassadenöffnungen werden bewusst Ausblicke auf Berge, Altstadt oder Fluss gerahmt. Im Obergeschoss öffnen sich zwei umbaute Terrassen zum Himmel. Hier wurde auch ein Kakteengarten angelegt. Eine Südterrasse wiederum rahmt den Blick in die Ferne. Der Architekt versteht das Haus als Resultat einer Reihe von „Zufällen". Auf Wunsch der Auftraggeber gibt es keine Türen, dennoch hat jeder Raum eine klar definierte Funktion. Eine „irisierende Wand aus Polycarbonat verändert sich farblich mit dem Lichteinfall und verläuft parallel zu einer verspiegelten Wand, in der sich die Innenräume vervielfachen". Der Wohnraum hat doppelte Geschosshöhe und ist mit Panoramafenstern ausgestattet. Nach Süden hin schützt ein Streckmetallgitter die Ess- und Schlafbereiche vor direktem Sonnenlicht (und den Golfbällen). Im Osten schirmt eine Betonmauer das Haus zur Nachbarschaft hin ab. „Im nördlichen Teil des Hauses", bemerkt Eduardo Arroyo abschließend, „lassen die fast nahtlosen Zuschnitte des grünen Marmors jedem unmissverständlich bewusst werden, dass die Zeit der Luxusbauten vermutlich vorüber ist."

Les architectes qualifient le voisinage de cette maison implantée sur un terrain de golf « doté d'un environnement bâti de qualité douteuse ». Les volumes sont déterminés par le « caractère vide » du paysage et répondent ainsi aux perspectives sur le paysage lointain. Les vues sur les montagnes, la vieille ville ou la rivière ont été intentionnellement cadrées par l'orientation des ouvertures. Au niveau supérieur, deux terrasses closes, mais ouvertes sur le ciel, contiennent un jardin de cactus, tandis que la terrasse sud cadre, elle aussi, des perspectives lointaines. Selon l'architecte, cette maison serait ainsi le résultat d'une série « d'accidents ». À la demande des clients, les portes ont été éliminées, mais chaque espace possède une fonction bien définie. Un « mur en polycarbonate iridescent change de couleurs selon la lumière et court parallèlement à une paroi en miroir qui multiplie les espaces intérieurs. » Le séjour représente un volume double hauteur, percé de baies panoramiques. Au sud, la façade en treillis de métal étiré protège la zone de repas et les chambres du soleil direct (et des balles de golf), tandis qu'à l'est, un mur en béton isole des voisins. « Au nord », conclut Eduardo Arroyo, « des plaques de marbre vert, découpées selon des lignes invisibles, envoient le message que l'époque des constructions de luxe est probablement passée. »

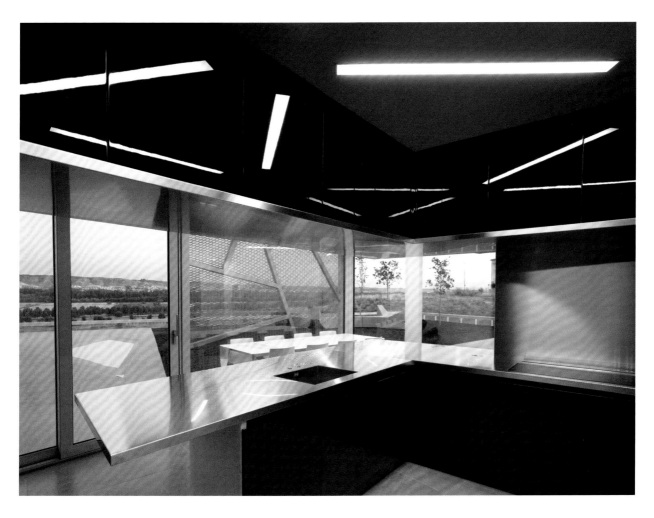

The fractured design of the house seen in the plans (below) is circumscribed within an essentially square form. This duality is visible in the interior photos here, where unexpected frames and openings are juxtaposed with relatively calm inside space.

Der zersplittert anmutende Entwurf des Hauses, zu sehen in den Grundrissen unten, wird von einer quadratischen Hülle umfangen. Dieselbe Dualität ist auch in den Innenaufnahmen zu erkennen: Dort kontrastieren überraschende Rahmungen und Öffnungen mit einem vergleichsweise ruhigen Innenraum.

Le plan fracturé de la maison (plans ci-dessous) est circonscrit dans un cadre à peu près carré. Cette dualité apparaît dans les photos de l'intérieur, où des cadrages et des ouvertures inattendues se juxtaposent dans un espace relativement apaisé.

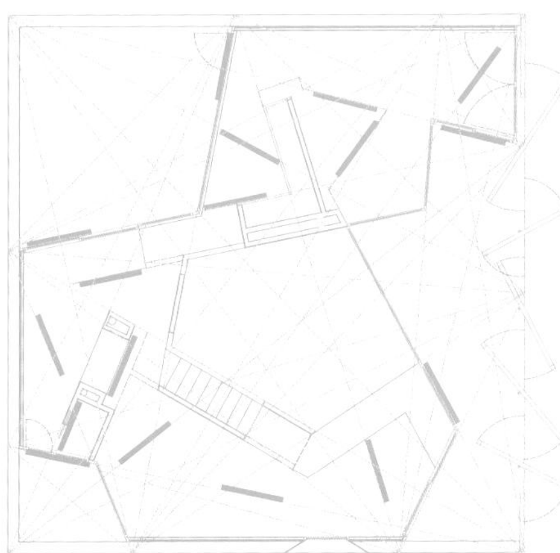

Double Chimney ►

ATELIER BOW-WOW

Atelier Bow-Wow
8–79 Suga-Cho
Shinjuku-ku
Tokyo 160–0018
Japan

Tel: +81 3 3226 5336
E-mail: info@bow-wow.jp

ATELIER BOW-WOW was established in 1992 by Yoshiharu Tsukamoto and Momoyo Kaijima. Yoshiharu Tsukamoto was born in 1965 in Tokyo and graduated from the Tokyo Institute of Technology (Doctorate in Engineering, 1987). He also studied at the École d'Architecture (Paris, Belleville, UP8, 1987–88). He has been a Visiting Associate Professor at UCLA (2007–08). Momoyo Kaijima was born in 1969 in Tokyo, and graduated from Japan Women's University (1991), the Graduate School of the Tokyo Institute of Technology (1994), and studied at the ETH (Zurich, 1996–97). Their main works in 2006 include the Mado Building, House Tower, and Nora House. In 2007, they completed the Crane House, and in 2008, the Sway House, Double Chimney (Nagano, published here), Ikushima Library and Pony Garden, and Mountain House (California, USA, also published here). Current work includes Housing on Rue Rebière (Paris, France) and the Global Citizen Communication Center (Aichi World Expo Memorial Park, Aichi, Japan).

1992 gründeten Yoshiharu Tsukamoto und Momoyo Kaijima ihr Büro **ATELIER BOW-WOW**. Yoshiharu Tsukamoto, 1965 in Tokio geboren, schloss sein Studium am Tokyo Institute of Technology mit einer Promotion im Bauingenieurwesen ab (1987). Darüber hinaus studierte er an der École d'Architecture (Paris, Belleville, UP8, 1987–88) und war außerordentlicher Gastprofessor an der UCLA (2007–08). Momoyo Kaijima wurde 1969 in Tokio geboren und absolvierte ihr Studium an der Japan Women's University (1991), der Graduiertenfakultät des Tokyo Institute of Technology (1994) sowie der ETH Zürich (1996–97). Zu ihren wichtigsten Projekten 2006 zählen das Mado Building, der House Tower und das Nora House. 2007 konnte das Crane House fertiggestellt werden, 2008 das Sway House, Double Chimney (Nagano, hier vorgestellt), eine Bibliothek mit Ponyhof in Ikushima sowie das Mountain House (Kalifornien, USA, ebenfalls hier vorgestellt). Aktuelle Projekte sind u. a. ein Wohnbauprojekt an der Rue Rebière (Paris) sowie das Global Citizen Communication Center (Aichi World Expo Memorial Park, Aichi, Japan).

L'**ATELIER BOW-WOW** a été fondé en 1992 par Yoshiharu Tsukamoto et Momoyo Kaijima. Yoshiharu Tsukamoto, né en 1965 à Tokyo, est diplômé de l'Institut de technologie de Tokyo (doctorat en ingénierie, 1987). Il a également étudié à l'École d'architecture de Belleville (UP8, Paris, 1987–88), et a été professeur associé invité à UCLA (2007–08). Momoyo Kaijima, née en 1969 à Tokyo, est diplômée de l'Université féminine du Japon (1991), de l'École supérieure de l'Institut de technologie de Tokyo (1994) et a étudié à l'ETH (Zurich, 1996–97). Parmi leurs principales réalisations : l'immeuble Mado ; la maison tour (House Tower) et la maison Nora en 2006 ; la maison « Grue » (Crane House) en 2007 et, en 2008 : la Sway House ; la maison à deux cheminées (Double Chimney House, Nagano, publiée ici) ; la bibliothèque Ikushima ; le Pony Garden et la maison de montagne (Mountain House, Californie, également publiée ici). Actuellement, ils travaillent sur un projet de logements à Paris, et le Centre de communication citoyenne globale (Aichi World Expo Memorial Park, Aichi, Japon).

DOUBLE CHIMNEY

Nagano, Japan, 2007–08

Area: 176 m². Client: not disclosed. Cost: not disclosed

The plan of this house constitutes two intersecting triangular volumes. The site is wooded and the residence appears hardly to disturb its environment, with its barnlike sloping roofs and generous ground-floor openings. The light-colored wood on the inner walls of the volumes is contrasted with black rear façades, and the more visible, equally black roof. Each volume has a chimney, hence the name of the house. There is a hint of more traditional forms in these designs, but their unexpected juxtaposition and site placement make their contemporary nature fully evident.

Der Grundriss des Hauses wurde aus zwei ineinandergreifenden dreieckigen Flächen entwickelt. Das Grundstück ist bewaldet, wobei das Haus mit seinen scheunenähnlich geneigten Dächern und großzügigen Fensterflächen im Erdgeschoss sein Umfeld kaum zu stören scheint. Das helle Holz der Innenseite der Fassaden kontrastiert mit der schwarzen Rückfassade und dem dort deutlicher sichtbaren schwarzen Dach. Wie schon der Name des Hauses ahnen lasst, verfügt jeder der beiden Baukörper über einen eigenen Kamin. Am Entwurf lassen sich weitere traditionelle Bauformen ausmachen, doch die überraschende Nebeneinanderstellung und die Aufteilung des Grundstücks machen zweifelsfrei deutlich, dass es sich hier um zeitgenössische handelt.

Le plan de cette maison se compose de deux volumes triangulaires qui s'entrecoupent. Avec ses toits qui rappellent une grange et ses généreuses ouvertures au niveau du rez-de-chaussée, elle trouble à peine son site boisé. Le bois clair des aménagements intérieurs contraste avec le noir des façades arrière et de la toiture, très visibles. Chaque volume possède sa propre cheminée, d'où le nom de la maison. On note des rappels de formes traditionnelles, mais leur juxtaposition inattendue et l'implantation dans le site n'en rendent leur nature contemporaine que plus évidente.

The architects make ample use of the Japanese concept of space that is neither clearly interior nor entirely exterior, as seen in the image above and at the top of the right page. Bottom right, the two chimneys that give the name to the house can be seen.

Die Architekten nehmen auffällig auf ein japanisches Raumverständnis Bezug, das Innen- und Außenraum nicht strikt trennt, wie oben und rechts oben zu sehen. Unten rechts die zwei Schornsteine, denen das Haus seinen Namen verdankt.

Les architectes ont largement utilisé le concept japonais d'un espace qui n'est ni vraiment intérieur ni entièrement extérieur, comme le montrent l'image ci-dessus et celle du haut de la page de droite. En bas à droite, on aperçoit les deux cheminées qui donnent son nom à la maison.

Interior spaces are quite unencumbered in these views, where light and unexpected angles combine to make space that is not easily defined.

Hier sind die Innenräume noch unverstellt; Lichteinfall und überraschende Winkel sorgen dafür, dass der Raum auf diesen Aufnahmen nicht leicht zu erschließen ist.

Les espaces intérieurs sont très dégagés. La lumière mais aussi des plans inclinés ou en biais inattendus constituent un espace qui ne se laisse pas aisément définir.

MOUNTAIN HOUSE

California, USA, 2008

Area: 115 m². Client: not disclosed. Cost: not disclosed

This small retreat in an isolated site in Nevada is quite unexpected, with its large-scale timber upper terrace. Wood is also present on the lower level, with a timber ceiling. Beds are inserted into alcoves, and there is even an exterior bathtub for those who dare use it. There is a sense of economy in this architecture, and also of symbiosis with the natural environment; the architects have surely not been directly inspired by local residences, but have brought with them their very specific sense of surprising volumes and an ability to integrate architecture into a natural setting that clearly has a relationship to Japanese thinking, despite the US site involved here.

Das kleine, einsam gelegene Wochenendhaus in Nevada überrascht mit seiner großen Dachterrasse aus Holz. Der gleiche Werkstoff ist in Form einer Holzdecke auch in der unteren Ebene präsent. Die Betten wurden in Alkoven integriert, und für die Mutigen gibt es sogar eine Badewanne unter freiem Himmel. Die Architektur wirkt zurückhaltend und scheint sich geradezu symbiotisch in die landschaftliche Umgebung zu fügen. Ganz offensichtlich wurden die Architekten hier nicht von lokalen Bauten inspiriert. Vielmehr brachten sie ihr höchst eigenes Gespür für unerwartete Baukörper und die Einbindung von Architektur in ihr natürliches Umfeld mit – ein Ansatz, der zweifellos im japanischen Denken wurzelt, trotz des amerikanischen Bauplatzes.

Cette petite retraite édifiée dans un site isolé du Nevada est assez surprenante, en particulier par sa vaste terrasse couverte en bois. Ce matériau est également présent dans les aménagements du rez-de-chaussée et dans les plafonds. Les lits sont logés dans des alcôves et l'on trouve même une baignoire extérieure pour ceux qui ont le courage de l'utiliser. On note un certain sens de l'économie dans cette architecture, mais aussi une recherche de symbiose avec l'environnement naturel. Les architectes ne se sont pas directement inspirés de l'habitat local, mais ont appliqué leur sens très particulier du volume et montré leur habileté à intégrer l'architecture dans un cadre naturel – attitude clairement en relation avec la pensée architecturale japonaise, bien que l'on soit ici aux États-Unis.

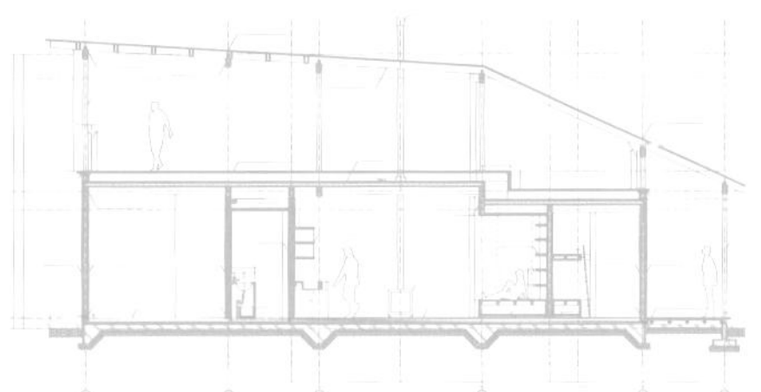

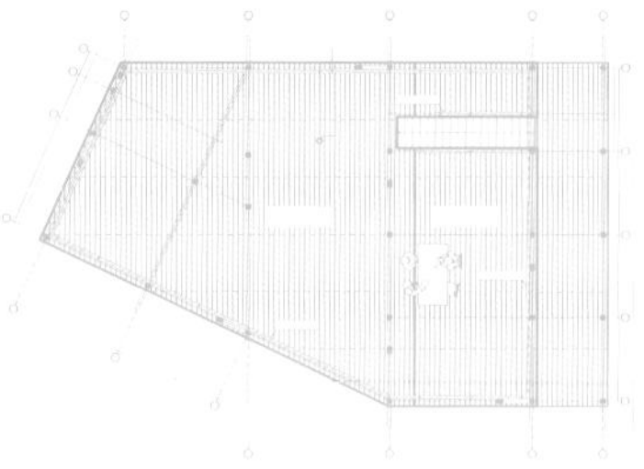

The impression of a symbiosis with nature is emphasized by the outside bathtub seen to the right. Plans, a section, and photos show how wood is used to shelter space while leaving it in good part open to the outside.

Der Eindruck einer Symbiose mit der Natur erhält durch die Badewanne unter freiem Himmel eine zusätzliche Betonung. Grundrisse, ein Schnitt und die Aufnahmen veranschaulichen, wie Holz eingesetzt wurde, um schützende Räume zu schaffen, diese aber zugleich überwiegend zum Außenraum hin zu öffnen.

L'impression de symbiose avec la nature est mise en relief par l'implantation d'une baignoire à l'extérieur (à droite). Les plans, une coupe et les photographies montrent comment une structure en bois vient abriter le vaste volume supérieur tout en le laissant en grande partie ouvert sur l'extérieur.

Wood is present throughout, even in the old-style wood burning stove (left). Simple hanging light bulbs, or such architectural details as the bed surrounded by bookshelves seen below, emphasize a feeling of rural simplicity.

Holz ist überall präsent, selbst in Gestalt des altmodischen Holzofens (links). Schlichte herabhängende Glühbirnen und architektonische Details wie das von Bücherregalen gerahmte Bett (unten) unterstreichen die schlichte Rustikalität.

Le bois est omniprésent, y compris par la présence d'un ancien poêle à bois (à gauche). De simples ampoules suspendues ou des détails architecturaux comme l'alcôve du lit entouré de rayonnages (ci-dessous) rappellent la simplicité campagnarde.

BELLEMO & CAT

Bellemo & Cat
23A Eastment Street
Northcote, Victoria 3070
Australia

Tel: +61 3 9489 5812
Fax: +61 3 9 4895 5735
E-mail: bellemocat@bigpond.com.au
Web: www.bellemocat.com

Michael Bellemo was born in 1967 in Melbourne. He received his B.Arch degree from the University of Melbourne in 1992, and registered as an architect in 1996. He has been a director of **BELLEMO & CAT** since the establishment of the firm in 1998. Cat Macleod was born in 1963 in Penang, Malaysia. She received a B.F.A. from the Victorian College of the Arts (Melbourne) in 1992. She has also been a Director of Bellemo & Cat since 1998. The work of Bellemo & Cat includes Polywrap Private Collection (Geelong, 2004), Balga (Point Lonsdale, 2007), the Australian Technical College (East Melbourne, 2007), Sidle (Carawatha Reserve, 2008), Polygreen (Northcote, Melbourne, 2007–08, published here), and the Administration Center, Saint Joseph's College (Ferntree Gully, Melbourne, 2009–10), all in Australia. Given the varied background of the partners, Bellemo & Cat undertakes large-scale artworks as well as architecture.

Michael Bellemo wurde 1967 in Melbourne geboren. Er absolvierte seinen B. Arch. 1992 an der University of Melbourne und ist seit 1996 eingetragener Architekt. Seit der Firmengründung 1998 ist er Direktor von **BELLEMO & CAT**. Cat Macleod wurde 1963 in Penang, Malaysia, geboren. 1992 schloss sie ihr Studium am Victorian College of the Arts (Melbourne) mit einem B. F. A. ab. Auch sie ist seit 1998 Direktorin von Bellemo & Cat. Zu den Projekten von Bellemo & Cat zählen die Polywrap Private Collection (Geelong, 2004), Balga (Point Lonsdale, 2007), das Australian Technical College (East Melbourne, 2007), Sidle (Carawatha Reserve, 2008), Polygreen (Northcote, Melbourne, 2007–08, hier vorgestellt) und das Verwaltungszentrum des Saint Joseph's College (Ferntree Gully, Melbourne, 2009–10), alle in Australien. Aufgrund der unterschiedlichen Ausbildung der beiden Partner realisiert Bellemo & Cat sowohl künstlerische Großprojekte als auch Architektur.

Michael Bellemo, né en 1967 à Melbourne, a un B.Arch de l'université de Melbourne (1992), et est architecte licencié depuis 1996. Il dirige **BELLEMO & CAT** depuis la fondation de l'agence en 1998. Cat Macleod, née en 1963 à Penang (Malaisie), est B.F.A. du Victorian College of the Arts (Melbourne) en 1992. Elle est également directrice de Bellemo & Cat depuis 1998. Parmi les réalisations de Bellemo & Cat, toutes en Australie : la collection privée Polywrap (Geelong, 2004) ; Balga (Point Lonsdale, 2007) ; l'Australian Technical College (East Melbourne, 2007) ; Sidle (Carawatha Reserve, 2008) ; la maison Polygreen (Northcote, Melbourne, 2007–08, publiée ici) et le Centre administratif du Saint Joseph's College (Ferntree Gully, Melbourne, 2009–10), le tout en Australie. Étant donnée l'expérience variée de leurs associés, Bellemo & Cat interviennent aussi bien en architecture que dans le domaine des créations artistiques à grande échelle.

POLYGREEN

Northcote, Melbourne, Australia, 2007–08

Area: 155 m². Clients: Michael Bellemo, Cat Macleod.
Cost: € 220 000

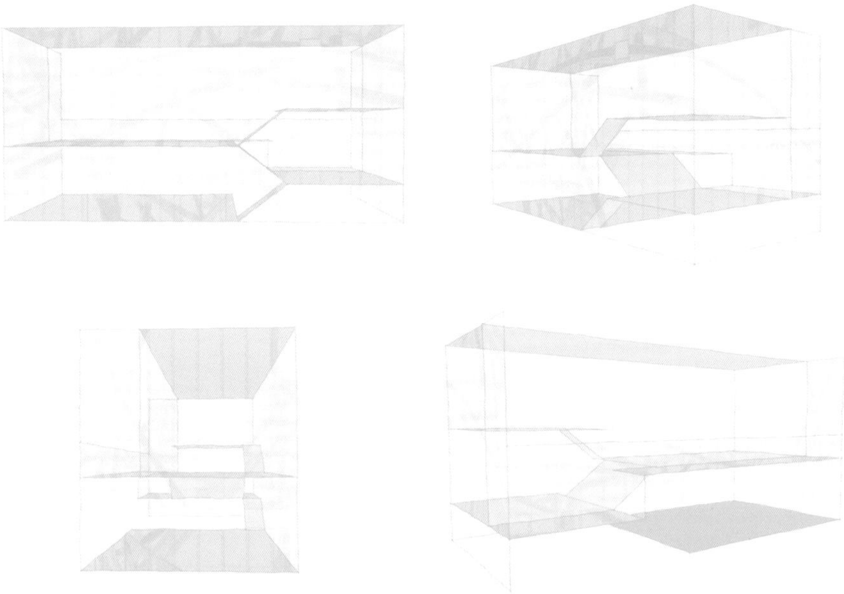

Located in a narrow service lane for old brick warehouses, sheds, and garages, this house is both a living and a working space. The architects state: "Our response to this context and our need was to create a new warehouse/container building, using the same formal language and going for maximum site coverage with a building wrapped on three sides in a translucent printed skin." They relate the pattern and printed skin to artworks that they have produced, and to their "Polywrap" project (Geelong, 2004), thus giving a sense of continuity to their work and to this new place of work and life. The office is on the ground floor facing the street. Children's bedrooms are downstairs, and the rest of the space is open "with split-level floors enabling kids' play areas." The design of this low-budget house was in part influenced by a neighbor who asked the architects for "a bit of greenery."

Das Haus, gelegen an einer schmalen Zufahrtsstraße zu alten Lagerhäusern aus Backstein, Schuppen und Garagen, ist sowohl Wohnhaus als auch Arbeitsraum. Die Architekten erläutern: „Unsere Reaktion auf den Kontext und unsere persönlichen Bedürfnisse war es, ein neues ‚Lagerhaus' zu gestalten und dabei die entsprechende Formensprache aufzugreifen. Wir entschieden uns für die maximale Bebauung des Grundstücks und umhüllten das Gebäude an drei Seiten mit einer transluzenten, bedruckten Außenhaut." Das Team stellt das Muster der bedruckten Außenhaut in einen Zusammenhang mit von ihnen realisierten Kunstwerken sowie ihrem Projekt Polywrap (Geelong, 2004). Offensichtlich zeichnet sich eine Kontinuität in ihren Projekten ab, die auch diesen neuen Lebens- und Arbeitsraum umfasst. Im Erdgeschoss des Hauses befindet sich ein Büro, das zur Straße orientiert ist. Die Kinderzimmer liegen im Untergeschoss, während die übrigen Bereiche offen gestaltet sind, mit „versetzten Geschossebenen, die die Kinder als Spielflächen nutzen können". In die Gestaltung des kostengünstigen Hauses floss auch der Wunsch eines Nachbarn ein, der die Architekten um „ein bisschen Grün" gebeten hatte.

Située dans une étroite voie de service entre d'anciens entrepôts, hangars et garages en brique, cette maison est à la fois un espace de vie et de travail. L'architecte précise : « Notre réponse à ce contexte et à nos besoins a consisté à créer un bâtiment de type entrepôt/conteneur selon le même langage formel que ceux du voisinage, et d'occuper au maximum le terrain par cette construction enveloppée sur trois côtés d'une peau translucide imprimée. » Ce principe de peau imprimée est dans la continuité des œuvres d'art qu'ils ont produites ou de leur projet « Polywrap » (Geelong, 2004). Le bureau, qui se trouve au rez-de-chaussée, donne sur la rue. Les chambres des enfants sont situées en bas, et le reste de l'espace est ouvert « avec des sols à niveaux différenciés qui dégagent des zones de jeux pour les enfants ». La conception de cette maison réalisée pour un faible budget a été en partie influencée par un voisin qui avait demandé aux architectes de créer « un peu de verdure ».

Despite its strictly rectangular form, visible both in the drawings above and in the photo to the right, the Polygreen House is most unusual, both in appearance and in the way its internal spaces flow into one another.

Trotz seiner strengen Rechtecksform, zu sehen in den Zeichnungen oben und dem Foto rechts, ist das Polygreen House höchst ungewöhnlich: sowohl in seiner Erscheinung als auch durch seine ineinanderfließenden Innenräume.

Malgré sa forme strictement rectangulaire (dessins ci-dessus et photo de droite), la maison Polygreen est extrêmement inhabituelle dans son aspect et la façon dont ses volumes internes se fondent les uns dans les autres.

23A

Below, a drawing of the exterior design of the house, partially visible in the photo of the generous living space (bottom).

Unten das Design der Außenfassade des Hauses, das ausschnittsweise auch auf der Aufnahme des großzügigen Wohnraums (unten) sichtbar ist.

Ci-dessous un dessin d'une façade de la maison, partiellement visible de l'intérieur dans la photo du vaste séjour (ci-dessous).

Inside spaces are very open, but retain a sense of privacy through elements such as the partial screen seen in both images on this page.

Die Innenräume sind sehr offen, wahren jedoch ein gewisses Maß an Privatsphäre, etwa durch den teilweise blickdichten Wandschirm, zu sehen auf beiden Abbildungen dieser Seite.

Les volumes intérieurs largement ouverts maintiennent un certain sentiment d'intimité grâce à des éléments comme l'écran partiel visible sur ces deux photographies.

BERNARDES + JACOBSEN

Bernardes + Jacobsen Arquitetura
Rua Corcovado 250
Jardim Botânico
22460–050 Rio de Janeiro, RJ
Brazil

Tel/Fax: +55 21 2512 7743
E-mail: bjrj@bja.com.br
Web: www.bja.com.br

Thiago Bernardes was born in Rio de Janeiro in 1974. The office of **BERNARDES + JACOBSEN** was created in 1980 by his father, Claudio Bernardes, and Paulo Jacobsen, pioneers of a new type of residential architecture based on an effort to combine contemporary design and Brazilian culture. Thiago Bernardes worked in his father's office from 1991 to 1996, when he left to create his own firm, working on more than 30 residential projects between that date and 2001. With the death of his father, Thiago Bernardes reintegrated the firm and began to work with Paulo Jacobsen, who was born in 1954 in Rio. He studied photography in London before graduating from the Bennett Methodist Institute in 1979. The office of Bernardes + Jacobsen currently employs approximately 50 people in Rio de Janeiro and São Paulo and they work on roughly 40 projects per year. Some of their significant projects include the Gerdau Headquarters (Santa Catarina, 2005); FW House (Guaruja, 2005); and the MPM Agency Main Office (São Paulo, 2006). Recent work includes the JH House (São Paulo, 2008); the JZ House (Camaçari, Bahia, 2006–08, published here); RW House (Búzios, Rio de Janeiro, 2009); and the FN and DB Houses (both in São Paulo, 2009), all in Brazil.

Thiago Bernardes wurde 1974 in Rio de Janeiro geboren. Schon 1980 gründete sein Vater Claudio Bernardes mit Paulo Jacobsen das Büro **BERNARDES + JACOBSEN**. Die beiden Partner waren Pioniere einer neuartigen Wohnarchitektur, die zeitgenössische Gestaltung und brasilianische Kultur miteinander vereinte. Von 1991 bis 1996 war Thiago Bernardes im Büro seines Vaters tätig und gründete anschließend sein eigenes Büro, mit dem er zwischen 1996 und 2001 über 30 Wohnbauprojekte realisierte. Nach dem Tod seines Vaters führte Thiago Bernardes die beiden Firmen zusammen und begann seine Zusammenarbeit mit Paulo Jacobsen, der 1954 in Rio geboren wurde. Jacobsen studierte Fotografie in London, bevor er sein Studium 1979 am Bennett Methodist Institute abschloss. Bernardes + Jacobsen beschäftigt derzeit rund 50 Mitarbeiter in Rio de Janeiro und São Paulo und arbeitet an etwa 40 Projekten pro Jahr. Wichtige Projekte sind u. a. die Gerdau Zentrale (Santa Catarina, 2005), das Haus FW (Guaruja, 2005) sowie die Hauptniederlassung der Agentur MPM (São Paulo, 2006). Neuere Projekte sind u. a. das Haus JH (São Paulo, 2008), die Residência JZ (Camaçari, Bahia, 2006–08, hier vorgestellt), das Haus RW (Búzios, Rio de Janeiro, 2009) sowie die Häuser FN und DB (beide in São Paulo, 2009), alle in Brasilien.

Thiago Bernardes est né à Rio de Janeiro en 1974. L'agence **BERNARDES + JACOBSEN** a été fondée en 1980 par son père, Claudio Bernardes et Paulo Jacobsen, pionniers d'un nouveau type d'architecture résidentielle qui voulait associer modernité et culture brésilienne. Thiago a travaillé dans l'agence de son père de 1991 à 1996, puis a fondé sa propre structure, intervenant sur plus de trente projets résidentiels entre cette date et 2001. Après le décès de son père, il a réintégré l'agence et commencé à collaborer avec Paulo Jacobsen, né en 1954 à Rio de Janeiro. Jacobsen a étudié la photographie à Londres, avant d'étudier au Bennett Methodist Institute, dont il sort diplômé en 1979. L'agence Bernardes + Jacobsen emploie actuellement environ cinquante personnes à Rio et São Paulo, pour une quarantaine de projets environ chaque année. Parmi leurs réalisations les plus significatives ; le siège de Gerdau (Santa Catarina, 2005) ; la maison FW (Guaruja, 2005) et le siège de l'agence MPM (São Paulo, 2006). Plus récemment, ils ont achevé la maison JH (São Paulo, 2008, publiée ici) ; la maison JZ (Bahia, 2008, également publiée ici) ; la maison RW (Búzios, Rio de Janeiro, 2009) et les maisons FN et DB (São Paulo, 2009), le tout au Brésil.

JZ HOUSE

Camaçari, Bahia, Brazil, 2006–08

Area: 1850 m². Client: not disclosed. Cost: not disclosed.
Collaboration: Ricardo C. Branco, Veridiana Ruzzante, Marina Nogaró

The architects deal with the delicate placement of the house on a sand dune by lifting it up in good part on pilotis. Its unusual form is clearly visible in the image below.

Die Architekten reagierten auf die problematische Lage des Hauses auf einer Düne, indem sie es zu einem Großteil auf pilotis *aufständerten. Die ungewöhnliche Form des Hauses ist unten im Bild deutlich zu sehen.*

Les architectes ont résolu le délicat problème de l'implantation dans une dune en soulevant une grande partie de la maison par des pilotis. La forme très particulière du projet est mise en valeur dans l'image ci-dessous.

Built on a sand dune, this house has a reinforced-concrete base, but is otherwise made entirely of wood. A volume containing bedrooms is lifted on pilotis, creating parking space below. The main part of the house is a "great room" with a view of the ocean and garden. The fact that this volume and much of the house is lifted up on the dune assures ample cross-ventilation from sea winds. This main living space directs the organization of the remaining parts of the house. An effort was made to use local materials, such as eucalyptus trellises and Bahia beige marble for the floors, and also to select tones that blend harmoniously with the sand, for example. A solarium and swimming pool on the beach side complete this undeniably spectacular house.

Das auf einer Düne gelegene Haus hat ein Fundament aus Stahlbeton, besteht ansonsten jedoch ausschließlich aus Holz. Die Schlafzimmer befinden sich im auf *pilotis* aufgeständerten Bau, unter dem auf diese Weise Pkw-Stellplätze entstanden. Hauptbereich des Hauses ist ein „großer Raum“ mit Blick auf das Meer und den Garten. Dank der Lage dieses Hausbereichs und eines Großteils des Baus auf der Düne werden die Räume ausreichend mit Wind vom Meer durchlüftet. Nach Möglichkeit wurden lokale Baumaterialien genutzt, wie bei den Gittern aus Eukalyptusholz und den cremefarbenen Böden aus Bahia-Marmor. Darüber hinaus wurde darauf geachtet, eine Palette von Farbtönen zu wählen, die mit dem Sand am Strand harmoniert. Eine Sonnenterrasse und ein Pool auf der Strandseite des Gebäudes vervollständigen das zweifellos spektakuläre Haus.

Cette maison entièrement en bois se dresse sur un socle en béton armé au sommet d'une dune de sable. Le volume des chambres est surélevé par des pilotis, libérant un espace de parking au niveau du sol. La partie principale est une « grande pièce » qui donne sur l'océan et le jardin. La surélévation de ce volume et de la plus grande partie de la construction assure une importante ventilation croisée par les vents de la mer. L'espace de séjour principal dicte l'organisation du reste de la résidence. On s'est efforcé d'utiliser des matériaux locaux, comme, par exemple, des treillis en bois d'eucalyptus, du marbre beige de Bahia pour les sols, ou des couleurs harmonisées avec celle du sable. Du côté de la plage, un solarium et une piscine complètent les installations de cette maison spectaculaire.

The house exudes a tropical atmosphere befitting its seaside location. Wood is the most prominent cladding material inside.

Passsend zur Lage am Meer vermittelt das Haus eine tropische Atmosphäre. Holz ist das dominierende Material im Innenraum.

L'atmosphère tropicale de l'intérieur de la maison est en accord avec la nature environnante. À l'intérieur, le bois est le matériau d'habillage de prédilection.

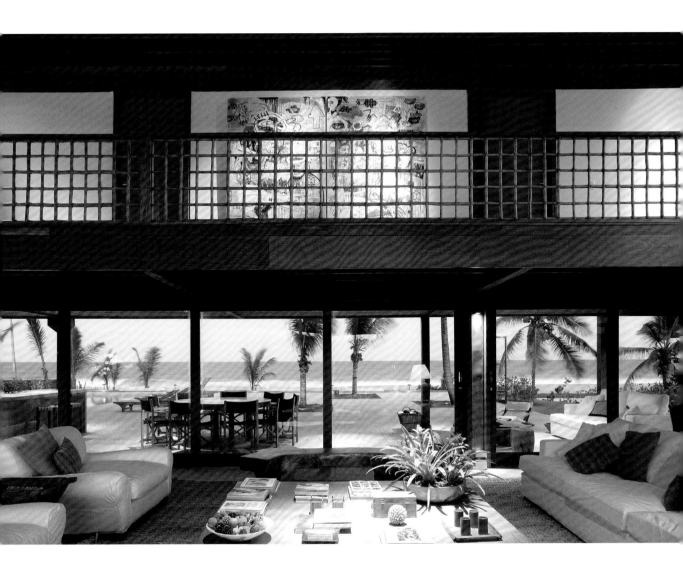

Plans and, above all, the image above show how the residence opens out toward the beach. From the living space, both the mid ground with the balcony and the background ocean view are part of a carefully designed and luxurious composition.

Die Grundrisse und vor allem die Aufnahme oben illustrieren, wie sich das Haus zum Strand hin öffnet. Vom Hauptwohnraum aus wirken der Mittelgrund mit der Empore und der Meerblick im Hintergrund wie eine sorgfältig gestaltete, luxuriöse Komposition.

Les plans, et mieux encore, l'image ci-dessus, montrent l'ouverture totale de la maison sur la plage. Vus du séjour, le balcon intérieur et la vue sur l'océan font partie d'une composition soignée, placée sous le signe du luxe.

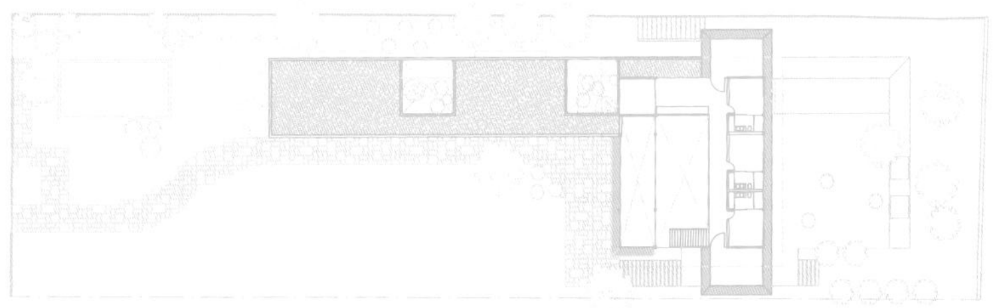

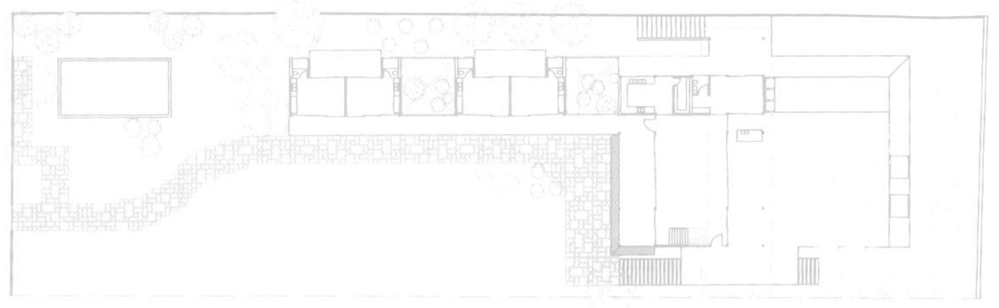

ALBERTO CAMPO BAEZA

Estudio Arquitectura Campo Baeza
C/ Almirante 9, 2 izq
28004 Madrid
Spain

Tel: +34 91 701 06 95
Fax: +34 91 521 70 61
E-mail: estudio@campobaeza.com
Web: www.campobaeza.com

Born in Valladolid in 1946, **ALBERTO CAMPO BAEZA** studied in Madrid, where he obtained his Ph.D. in 1982 (ETSAM). He has taught in Madrid, at the ETH in Zurich (1989–90), at Cornell University, and at the University of Pennsylvania (1986 and 1999), and the ETSAM, where he has served as Head Professor of Design. His work includes the Fene Town Hall (1980); S. Fermin Public School (Madrid, 1985); Public Library (Orihuela, 1992); a Public School (Cádiz, 1992); and the BIT Center in Mallorca (1998); as well as a number of private houses, such as the Belvedere, De Blas House, Sevilla de la Nueva, Madrid (2000). In 2001 he completed what he considers his most prestigious building, the Headquarters of the Caja General de Ahorros de Granada. In 2002 he finished an office building for the Consejería de Salud de la Junta de Andalucia in Almeria, and the SM Editorial building in Madrid. More recent work includes the NMAC Museum (Cádiz, 2006); Montecarmelo Public School (Madrid, 2006); Olnik Spanu House (Garrison, New York, 2005–07, published here); Falla Square Housing (Cádiz, 2007); Centro de Interpretación Salinas de Janubio (Lanzarote, 2008); San Sebastián Castle (Cádiz, 2008); and Offices for Benetton (Samara, Russia, 2009), all in Spain unless stated otherwise.

ALBERTO CAMPO BAEZA, 1946 in Valladolid geboren, studierte in Madrid, wo er 1982 promovierte (ETSAM). Er lehrte in Madrid, an der ETH Zürich (1989–90), der Cornell University, der University of Pennsylvania (1986 und 1999) und der ETSAM, wo er als Professor den Fachbereich Entwerfen leitete. Zu seinen Projekten zählen das Rathaus in Fene (1980), die Schule S. Fermin (Madrid, 1985), eine öffentliche Bibliothek (Orihuela, 1992), eine Schule (Cádiz, 1992), das BIT Center in Mallorca (1998) sowie eine Reihe privater Wohnbauten, darunter das Belvedere, das Haus De Blas, Sevilla de la Nueva, Madrid (2000). 2001 wurde das in seinen Augen bisher repräsentativste Projekt fertiggestellt: die Zentrale der Caja General de Ahorros de Granada. 2002 wurden ein Bürogebäude für die Consejería de Salud de la Junta de Andalucía in Almería fertiggestellt sowie ein Gebäude für SM Editorial in Madrid. Jüngere Projekte sind u. a. das Museum NMAC (Cádiz, 2006), die Montecarmelo-Schule (Madrid, 2006), das Olnik Spanu House (Garrison, New York, 2005–07, hier vorgestellt), ein Wohnkomplex an der Plaza de Falla (Cádiz, 2007), das Centro de Interpretación Salinas de Janubio (Lanzarote, 2008), das Kastell San Sebastián (Cádiz, 2008) sowie Büros für Benetton (Samara, Russland, 2009), alle in Spanien, soweit nicht anders angegeben.

ALBERTO CAMPO BAEZA, né à Valladolid en 1946, a fait ses études d'architecture à Madrid. Il est docteur de l'Escuela Tecnica Superior de Arquitectura (ETSAM) en 1982. Il a enseigné à l'ETSAM, à l'ETH de Zurich (1989–90) à l'université Cornell et à l'université de Pennsylvanie (1986 et 1989) où il a été professeur principal de conception. Parmi ses réalisations figurent l'hôtel de ville de Fene (1980) ; l'école S. Fermin (Madrid, 1985), une bibliothèque publique (Orihuela, 1992), une école (Cadix, 1992) et le Centre BIT de Mallorca (1998) ; ainsi qu'un certain nombre de résidences privées comme les maisons Belvedere, De Blas, et Sevilla de la Nueva à Madrid (2000). Il a achevé en 2001 ce qu'il considère être son œuvre la plus emblématique, le siège de la Caja General de Ahorros de Granada. En 2002, il a réalisé un immeuble de bureaux pour la Consejería de Salud de la Junta de Andalucía à Almería ; et l'immeuble des Éditions SM à Madrid. Plus récemment, il a construit le musée NMAC (Cádiz, 2006) ; l'école publique de Montecarmelo (Madrid, 2006) ; la maison Olnik Spanu (Garrison, New York, 2005–07, publiée ici) ; l'immeuble de logements de la place Falla (Cádiz, 2007) ; le Centro de Interpretación Salinas de Janubio (Lanzarote, 2008) ; le château de San Sebastián (Cádiz, 2008) ; et des bureaux pour Benetton (Samara, Russie, 2009), le tout en Espagne, sauf mention contraire.

OLNIK SPANU HOUSE

Garrison, New York, USA, 2005–07

Area: 900 m². Clients: Nancy Olnik, Giorgio Spanu. Cost: not disclosed.
Collaboration: Miguel Garcia Quismondo, Ignacio Aguirre

This project originally dates from 2003. Demolition of an existing structure on the site was carried out in 2004, and construction of the new house advanced from 2005 to 2007. The house was furnished in 2008. On a site that the architect calls "a place that is very close to heaven," he designed a platform and placed a long concrete box (37 meters long, 16 meters wide, 3.6 meters high). The flat roof is clad in travertine so that it can be used as a terrace, covered by a light roof held up by cylindrical steel pillars. The roof cantilevers over the sides of the house by about three meters. "This construction on the platform," says Campo Baeza, "resembles a large table with ten legs. Three areas are created within it, divided by two white boxes that do not reach the ceiling, containing the stairs and service spaces. The central space is the living area, and the dining room has a large white table. On one side, closer to the swimming pool, is the kitchen, and on the other side, in the manner of a *pensatorio*, the area around the hearth." Bedroom and bath areas are located below, in the concrete box. A gallery for a collection of Arte Povera and other Italian pieces is part of the design. The architect seeks here to create what he calls "the hut over the cave."

Die Anfänge des Projekts reichen bis 2003 zurück. 2004 wurde ein Altbau auf dem Grundstück abgerissen, der Neubau des Hauses dauerte von 2005 bis 2007. Eingerichtet wurde der Bau schließlich 2008. Für das Grundstück, das der Architekt einen Ort nennt, „der dem Himmel sehr nahe ist", entwarf er eine Plattform, auf die er einen länglichen Kasten aus Beton setzte (37 m lang, 16 m breit und 3,6 m hoch). Das Flachdach wurde mit Travertin gedeckt und lässt sich als Terrasse nutzen. Darüber schwebt eine leichte Dachkonstruktion, die auf zylindrischen Stahlstützen ruht. Vorne kragt das Dach rund 3 m über die Hauskante aus. „Die Konstruktion auf der Plattform", so Campo Baeza, „lässt an einen großen Tisch mit zehn Beinen denken. Im Innern des Hauses sind drei Bereiche definiert, gegliedert durch zwei weiße Boxen, die bis knapp unter die Decke reichen und in denen Treppen und Nebenräume untergebracht sind. Zentraler Raum ist der Wohnbereich, der Essraum wird von einem großen weißen Tisch dominiert. Die Küche liegt zum Schwimmbecken hin, während sich auf der anderen Seite – wie bei einem *pensatorio* – der Bereich um das Kaminfeuer befindet." Schlafbereiche und Badezimmer sind im darunter liegenden Baukörper aus Beton untergebracht. In den Entwurf integriert wurde eine Galerie für eine Sammlung von Arte-Povera-Werken und anderen Arbeiten italienischer Künstler. Mit diesem Haus, erklärt der Architekt, habe er eine „Hütte über einer Höhle" schaffen wollen.

Ce projet a débuté en 2003. La démolition d'une construction préexistante a été effectuée en 2004. Le chantier de construction s'est étalé de 2005 à 2007 et la maison a été meublée en 2008. Pour ce site dont l'architecte a dit « qu'il était très proche du paradis », Campo Baeza a conçu une plate-forme sur laquelle il a posé une boîte de béton (37 x 16 x 3,6 m). La partie supérieure est habillée de travertin pour servir de terrasse que vient recouvrir un toit léger soutenu par des piliers cylindriques en acier. Cette toiture se projette en porte-à-faux de 3 m environ. « Cette construction sur la plate-forme », explique l'architecte, « ressemble à une grande table à dix pieds. À l'intérieur ont été créées trois zones, divisées par deux importantes boîtes blanches qui ne touchent pas le plafond et contiennent les escaliers et les espaces de service. L'espace central est réservé au séjour et à la salle à manger que agrémentée d'une grande table blanche. D'un côté, près de la piscine, se trouve la cuisine et de l'autre, à la manière d'un pensatorio, la zone autour de la cheminée. » Les chambres et les installations sanitaires sont implantées dans la boîte en béton. Le projet comprend également une galerie pour une collection d'Arte Povera, et diverses œuvres d'art italiennes. L'architecte a cherché à créer ici ce qu'il appelle « une hutte au-dessus d'une caverne ».

As a sketch by the architect shows, the basic design of the house has an almost classical simplicity, with a transparent upper level sitting on a more closed base.

Wie eine Skizze des Architekten belegt, ist die Grundidee des Hauses von geradezu klassischer Schlichtheit. Das transparente Obergeschoss ruht auf einem vergleichsweise geschlossenen Sockel.

Comme le montre ce croquis de l'architecte, le projet est d'une simplicité quasi classique : une boîte transparente posée sur un socle assez massif.

The geometric rigor of the house, with its full-height glazing topped by an overhanging horizontal roof contrasts with the natural setting in the image below.

Die geometrische Strenge des Hauses mit der deckenhohen Verglasung und dem auskragenden Flachdach kontrastiert mit der landschaftlichen Umgebung (unten).

La rigueur géométrique de la maison aux parois vitrées toute hauteur surmontées d'un toit plat en porte-à-faux contraste avec le cadre naturel dans l'image ci-dessous.

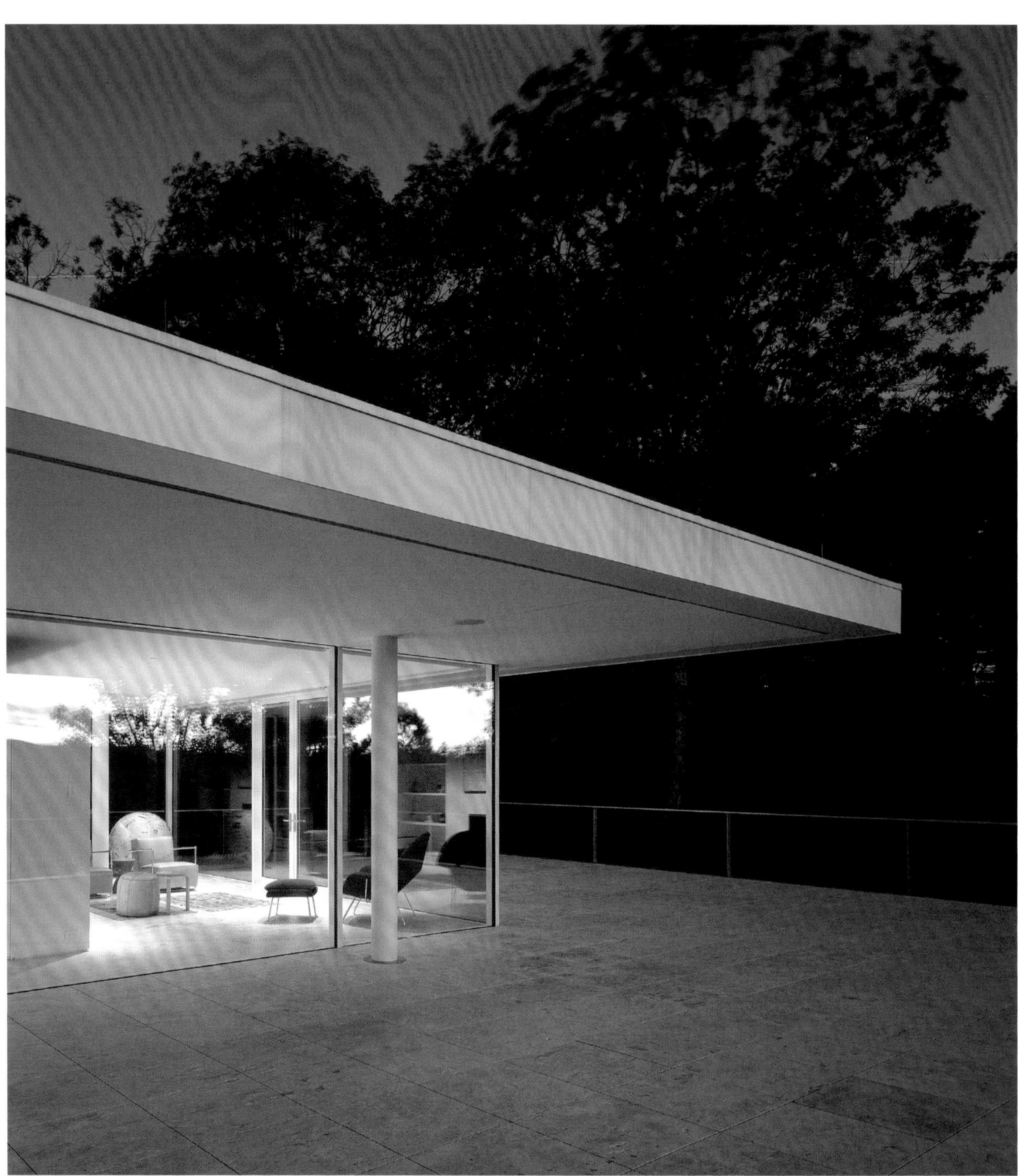

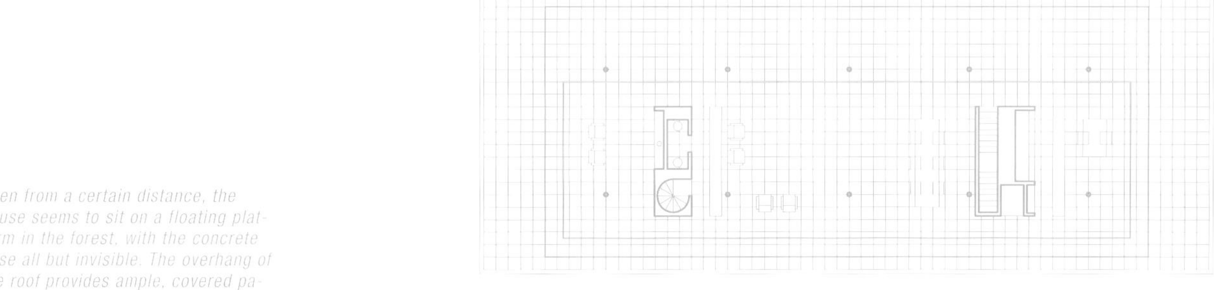

Seen from a certain distance, the house seems to sit on a floating platform in the forest, with the concrete base all but invisible. The overhang of the roof provides ample, covered patio space.

Aus der Distanz wirkt das Haus, als schwebe es auf einer Plattform mitten im Wald; das Sockelgeschoss aus Beton ist kaum auszumachen. Durch die Auskragung des Dachs wird eine großzügiger Bereich der Terrasse überdacht.

Vue d'une certaine distance, le socle de béton étant pratiquement invisible, la maison semble reposer sur une plate-forme flottante en pleine forêt. À gauche, le porte-à-faux de la toiture offre un généreux espace protégé.

The simplicity of the furnishings of the house emphasizes its Miesian purity, while floor-to-ceiling glazing almost makes it appear that the entire top level is open to the forest.

Die schlichte Möblierung des Hauses betont dessen Mies'sche Klarheit. Die deckenhohe Verglasung lässt den Eindruck entstehen, das gesamte Obergeschoss öffne sich zu seiner bewaldeten Umgebung.

La simplicité du mobilier fait ressortir la pureté très miesienne de cette maison. Le vitrage toute hauteur donne l'impression que le niveau supérieur est entièrement ouvert sur la forêt.

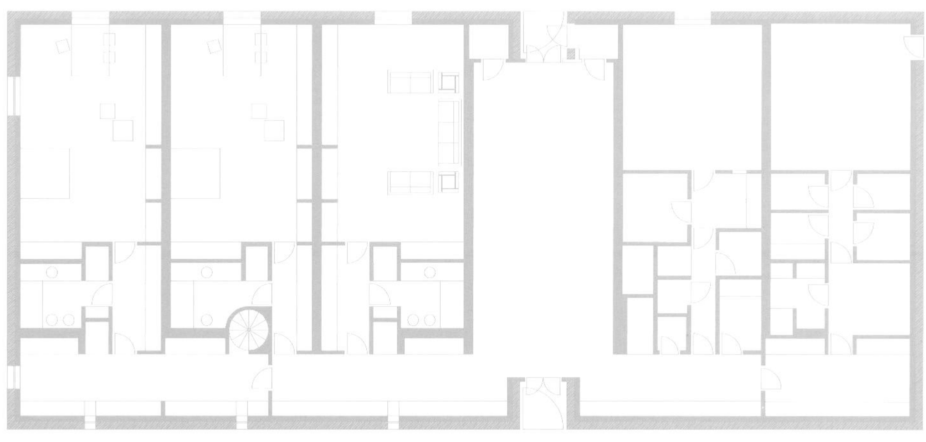

The floor plan above has all the rigor shown in the photographs of the house. In the image above, floor and ceiling frame the view, with the intermediate living space almost seeming to be entirely open, aside from the simple, central column.

Der Grundriss (oben) vermittelt dieselbe Strenge wie die Aufnahmen des Hauses. Auf dem Foto oben rahmen Boden und Decke das Panorama. Abgesehen von der schlichten Stütze in der Mitte ist der Raum vollständig offen.

Le plan au sol (ci-dessus) présente la même rigueur que le traduisent les photographies. Dans l'image ci-dessus, le sol et le plafond cadrent la vue. Entre les deux, le séjour semble presque totalement ouvert, mis à part la présence d'une colonne centrale.

CASEY BROWN

Casey Brown Architecture
Level 1, 63 William Street
East Sydney, NSW 2010
Australia

Tel: +61 2 9360 7977
Fax: +61 2 9360 2123
E-mail: cb@caseybrown.com.au
Web: www.caseybrown.com.au

Robert Brown received his degrees in architecture from the University of New South Wales (1976 and 1979) and from Columbia University Graduate School of Architecture in New York (1992–93). He worked with Fisher Lucas Architects in Sydney (1976), Julian Harrap Architects in London (1983), and the Heritage Council NSW (1984–86), before creating Dawson Brown Partnership (1986–89), Dawson Brown + Ackert Architecture (1989–92), and Dawson Brown Architecture (1993–2004). In 2004, he created the firm **CASEY BROWN** with partner Caroline Casey. The James-Robertson House (Great Mackeral Beach, Sydney, NSW, 2001–03) won a 2004 Residential Architecture Award from the Royal Australian Institute of Architects (NSW Chapter). Recent projects include the Sastrugi Ski Lodge (Thredbo, NSW, 2000); Graigee Lee House (Palm Beach, Sydney, NSW, 2001); and the Bungan Beach House (Bungan Beach, Sydney, NSW, 2003). More recently, they have completed the Permanent Camping House (Mudgee, NSW, 2007, published here); the Stanwell Park House (Stanwell Park Beach, Sydney, NSW, 2007); and Eagles Rest Winery (Hunter Valley, NSW, 2010), all in Australia.

Robert Braun machte seine Abschlüsse in Architektur an der University of New South Wales (1976 und 1979) und dem Graduiertenkolleg für Architektur an der Columbia University in New York (1992–93). Er arbeitete für Fisher Lucas Architects in Sydney (1976), Julian Harrap Architects in London (1983) und das Heritage Council NSW (1984–86), bevor er die Büros Dawson Brown Partnership (1986–89), Dawson Brown + Ackert Architecture (1989–92) und Dawson Brown Architecture (1993–2004) gründete. 2004 schließlich eröffnete er mit Caroline Casey als Partnerin das Büro **CASEY BROWN**. Das James-Robertson House (Great Mackeral Beach, Sydney, NSW, 2001–03) wurde 2004 mit dem Preis für Wohnhausarchitektur des Royal Australian Institute of Architects (Abteilung New South Wales) ausgezeichnet. Jüngere Projekte sind die Sastrugi Ski Lodge (Thredbo, NSW, 2000), das Graigee Lee House (Palm Beach, Sydney, NSW, 2001) sowie das Bungan Beach House (Bungan Beach, Sydney, NSW, 2003). In letzter Zeit konnten das Hausprojekt Permanent Camping (Mudgee, NSW, 2007, hier vorgestellt), das Stanwell Park House (Stanwell Park Beach, Sydney, NSW, 2007) und das Weingut Eagles Rest (Hunter Valley, NSW, 2010) fertiggestellt werden, alle in Australien.

Robert Braun est diplômé en architecture de l'université de Nouvelle-Galles-du-Sud (1976 et 1979) et de l'École supérieure d'architecture de l'université Columbia à New York (1992–93). Il a travaillé avec les agences Fisher Lucas Architects à Sydney (1976), Julian Harrap Architects à Londres (1983) et pour l'Heritage Council NSW (1984–86), avant de fonder le Dawson Brown Partnership (1986–89), Dawson Brown + Ackert Architecture (1989–92) et Dawson Brown Architecture (1993–2004). En 2004, il crée l'agence **CASEY BROWN** avec Caroline Casey. La maison James-Robertson (Great Mackeral Beach, Sydney, NGS, 2001–03) a remporté le prix de l'architecture résidentielle du Royal Australian Institute of Architects (section de Nouvelle-Galles-du-Sud). Parmi leurs projets récents : le chalet de ski Sastrugi (Thredbo, NGS, 2000), la maison Graigee Lee (Palm Beach, Sydney, NGS, 2001), et la maison de plage de Bungan (Bungan Beach, Sydney, NGS, 2003), la maison de camping permanent (Permanent Camping House, Mudgee, NGS, 2007, publiée ici), la maison de Stanwell Park (Stanwell Park Beach, Sydney, NGS, 2007), et le chais d'Eagles Rest (Hunter Valley, NGS, 2010), le tout en Australie.

PERMANENT CAMPING

Mudgee, NSW, Australia, 2007

Area: 18 m². Client: not disclosed. Cost: not disclosed.
Collaboration: Hernan Alvarez (Project Architect),
Jeffrey Broadfield (Builder)

This tiny house is located on a mountain site in a sheep station in central western New South Wales. The panoramic view from the house reaches hundreds of kilometers around the site. The two-story, copper-clad structure has a very small three-meter by three-meter footprint, and has sides that open to provide verandahs to the north, east, and west. The sides close entirely to protect the house from bush fires. Recycled ironbark (eucalyptus) is used inside the house, which contains a sleeping loft and kitchen with a wood-fired stove. The roof collects rainfall and a toilet is located outside. Heavy insulation protects residents from both cold wind and daytime heat. Because of the extreme isolation of its location, the house was entirely prefabricated in Sydney and transported on site.

Das winzige Haus liegt auf einem Hügel mitten auf einer Schaffarm im Herzen von New South Wales. Der Panoramablick vom Haus reicht Hunderte von Kilometer weit in das Umland. Der zweigeschossige kupferverkleidete Bau hat eine ungewöhnlich kleine Grundfläche von 3 x 4 m und lässt sich nach Norden, Osten und Westen öffnen, sodass kleine Veranden entstehen. Die Seiten lassen sich vollständig schließen, um das Haus vor Buschfeuern zu schützen. Im Innern, in dem es ein Podest mit Bett und eine Küche mit Holzofen gibt, kam recyceltes Ironbark-Holz (eine Eukalyptusart) zum Einsatz. Über das Dach wird Regenwasser gesammelt, draußen befindet sich ein separates Außen-WC. Dank starker Dämmung sind die Bewohner vor kalten Winden ebenso wie vor der tagsüber herrschenden Hitze geschützt. Aufgrund der extrem isolierten Lage des Grundstücks wurde das gesamte Haus in Syndey vorgefertigt und zum Standort transportiert.

Cette minuscule maison est située dans les montagnes de Nouvelle-Galles-du-Sud, au cœur d'alpages pour brebis. La vue panoramique que l'on a de ses ouvertures porte sur des centaines de kilomètres. La construction – deux niveaux habillés de cuivre – n'occupe qu'une emprise au sol de 3 x 3 m. Ses côtés s'ouvrent pour former des vérandas au nord, à l'est et à l'ouest. Ces côtés se referment entièrement pour protéger la maison des incendies naturels. L'intérieur, qui contient une pièce pour dormir et une cuisine à cuisinière à bois, est habillé d'écorce d'eucalyptus recyclé. La toiture collecte l'eau de pluie et les toilettes sont extérieures. Une épaisse couche d'isolant protège des vents froids et de la chaleur diurne. Du fait de son isolement extrême, l'ensemble a été entièrement préfabriqué à Sydney et transporté sur place.

With its very small area and protective cladding, the house might almost appear to be a military surveillance point. Sitting lightly on the ground, this is architecture that speaks clearly to environmental concerns.

Mit seiner besonders kleinen Grundfläche und der schützenden Verkleidung wirkt das Haus fast wie ein militärischer Wachturm. Das leicht vom Boden abgesetzte Haus ist Architektur, die deutlich von Umweltbewusstsein zeugt.

Par sa petite taille et son habillage de protection, la maison pourrait presque faire penser à une tour de guet. Reposant à peine sur le sol, elle exprime clairement dans son architecture ses préoccupations environnementales.

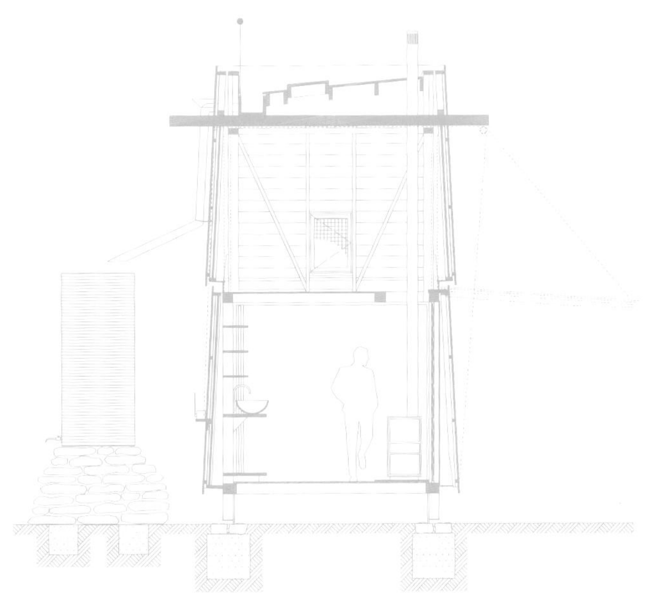

A square plan makes way for generous open space when the outer shutters of the house are raised. A wood-burning stove provides warmth in the dry surroundings.

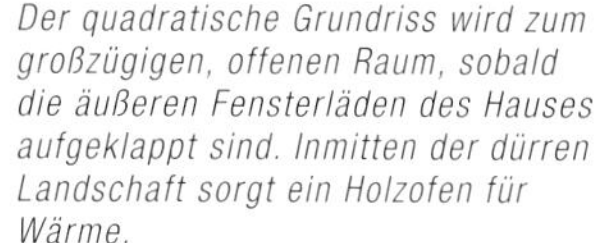

Der quadratische Grundriss wird zum großzügigen, offenen Raum, sobald die äußeren Fensterläden des Hauses aufgeklappt sind. Inmitten der dürren Landschaft sorgt ein Holzofen für Wärme.

Le plan de forme carré dégage un généreux volume ouvert quand les volets extérieurs sont relevés. Le poêle à bois apporte un peu de chaleur dans cet environnement sauvage.

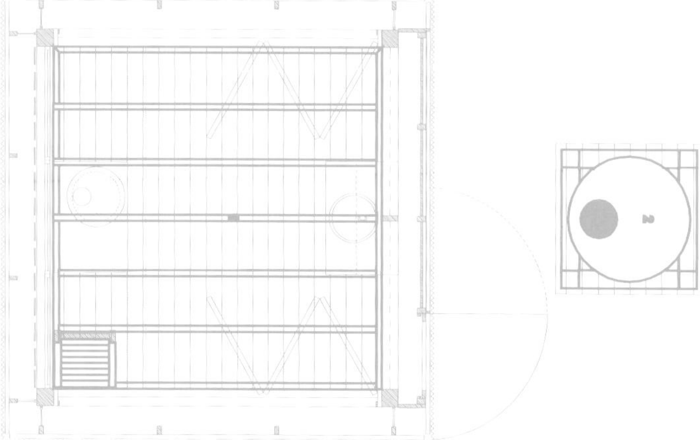

The spartan upper-level living spaces are covered in wood slats, echoing the rather blank and protected appearance of the little house in its closed mode.

Der spartanische Wohnbereich im Obergeschoss ist holzvertäfelt und greift die eher schmucklose Optik des schützenden Äußeren des kleinen Hauses im geschlossenen Zustand auf.

Les pièces de style spartiate de l'étage sont doublées d'un lattis de bois. Leur aspect refermé fait écho au style assez neutre et défensif de cette petite maison.

PADRAIC CASSIDY

Padraic Cassidy Architect
1003 Diamond Avenue #201
South Pasadena, CA 91030
USA

Tel: +1 626 441 8880
Fax: +1 626 441 8881
E-mail: info@padraiccassidy.com
Web: www.padraiccassidy.com

Born in 1966 in Nantucket, **PADRAIC CASSIDY** received his B.F.A. (1989) and B.Arch (1990) degrees from the Rhode Island School of Design (Providence, Rhode Island). He worked in the offices of Daly Genik (1991), and of Frank O. Gehry (1991–95), before creating his own office. Padraic Cassidy has been designing private homes and offices since 1988. His most recent work includes the Red House (Los Angeles, California, 2004–06, published here); Apatow Productions (Los Angeles, California, 2007); Loggia LeGros Residence (Wilson, Wyoming, 2008); Benedict House (Santa Monica, California, 2009); and the Mt. Washington House (Los Angeles, California, 2009), all in the USA.

PADRAIC CASSIDY, 1966 in Nantucket geboren, erhielt seinen B.F.A. (1989) und seinen B.Arch. (1990) an der Rhode Island School of Design (Providence Rhode Island). Er arbeitete für Daly Genik (1991) und Frank O. Gehry (1991–95), ehe er sein eigenes Büro gründete. Seit 1988 entwirft Padraic Cassidy private Wohnbauten und Büros. Zu seinen jüngsten Projekten zählen das Red House (Los Angeles, Kalifornien, 2004–06, hier vorgestellt), Apatow Productions (Los Angeles, Kalifornien, 2007), die Loggia LeGros Residence (Wilson, Wyoming, 2008), das Benedict House (Santa Monica, Kalifornien, 2009) sowie das Mt. Washington House (Los Angeles, Kalifornien, 2009), alle in den USA.

Né en 1966 à Nantucket, **PADRAIC CASSIDY** a obtenu son B.F.A. (1989) et son B.Arch (1990) de l'École de design de Rhode Island (RISD, Providence, Rhode Island). Il a travaillé chez Daly Genik (1991) et Frank O. Gehry (1991–95) avant d'ouvrir sa propre agence. Padraic Cassidy conçoit des résidences privées et des bureaux depuis 1988. Parmi ses réalisations les plus récentes : la maison rouge (Red House, Los Angeles, Californie, 2004–06, publiée ici) ; les Productions Apatow (Los Angeles, Californie, 2007) ; la résidence Loggia LeGros (Wilson, Wyoming, 2008) ; la maison Benedict (Santa Monica, Californie, 2009) ; et la maison du Mt Washington (Los Angeles, Californie, 2009), le tout aux États-Unis.

RED HOUSE

Los Angeles, California, USA, 2004–06

*Area: 310 m². Clients: Larry and Emily Karaszewski.
Cost: not disclosed*

The architect has designed a rather complex and angled volume that sits on top of the more orthogonal (red) base of the residence.

Der Architekt entwarf ein recht komplexes, verwinkeltes Volumen, das auf dem rechtwinkligen (roten) Sockelgeschoss des Hauses aufliegt.

L'architecte a dessiné un volume incliné assez complexe qui repose sur une base plus régulière (en rouge).

This house was built for Larry Karaszewski and his family. Karaszewski, together with Scott Alexander, was the screenwriter for such films as Tim Burton's *Ed Wood* (1994), *The People vs. Larry Flynt* (1996), and *Man on the Moon* (1999). Overlooking Runyon Canyon Park south of Mulholland Drive in the Hollywood hills, the Red House is set in a eucalyptus forest. Concrete siding and a metal roof are used to avoid fire hazards in a house that appears quite simple from its driveway, but more complex from below. Views of the park opposite are framed by a three-meter-high pivoting window in the master bedroom, while nearby vegetation was preserved during construction with the help of an arborist. All furniture was custom-designed and/or built in by the architect. The choice of red for the house is related to the screenwriter's memories of his Indiana childhood.

Cassidy entwarf dieses Haus für Larry Karaszewski und dessen Familie. Karaszewski hatte gemeinsam mit Scott Alexander Drehbücher für Filme wie Tim Burtons *Ed Wood* (1994), *Larry Flynt – Die nackte Wahrheit* (1996) oder *Der Mondmann* (1999) verfasst. Das Rote Haus liegt inmitten eines Eukalyptuswaldes und bietet einen Ausblick auf den Runyon Canyon Park südlich vom Mulholland Drive in den Hollywood Hills. Die Verkleidung aus Beton sowie ein Dach aus Metall bieten Schutz bei Waldbränden. Während sich das Haus von der Einfahrt aus recht einfach gibt, zeigt es sich vom Fuß des Hügels weitaus komplexer. Die Aussicht in den gegenüber gelegenen Park wird von einem 3 m hohen Schwingflügelfenster im Hauptschlafzimmer gerahmt. Mithilfe eines Baumpflegers konnten die um das Haus wachsenden Pflanzen während der Bauphase erhalten werden. Sämtliche Möbel wurden vom Architekten eigens entworfen und/oder von ihm eingebaut. Die Entscheidung, das Haus rot zu streichen, geht auf Erinnerungen des Drehbuchautors an seine Kindheit in Indiana zurück.

Cette maison a été construite pour Larry Karaszewski et sa famille. Karaszewski, avec Scott Alexander, est le scénariste de films comme *Ed Wood* (1994) de Tim Burton, ou *The People vs. Larry Flynt* (1996), et *Man on the Moon* (1999). Dominant Runyon Canyon Park au sud de Mulholland Drive dans les collines d'Hollywood, la maison rouge se dresse au milieu d'une forêt d'eucalyptus. Des parements en béton et une toiture métallique ont été mis en place pour réduire les risques dus aux incendies. La maison semble assez simple vue de son allée d'accès, mais beaucoup plus complexe du contrebas. Dans la chambre principale, les perspectives sur le parc sont cadrées par une baie pivotante de 3 m de haut. La végétation a été protégée pendant la durée du chantier. Tout le mobilier a été conçu sur mesure et/ou fabriqué par l'architecte. Le choix du rouge pour les façades est un rappel de l'enfance du propriétaire dans l'Indiana.

The house is carefully inserted into its natural environment, as can be seen in the double page at the beginning of this chapter. A swimming pool is sheltered by low trees (below). A roof plan can also be seen below.

Das Haus ist einfühlsam in seine landschaftliche Umgebung eingebunden, wie die Doppelseite zu Beginn dieses Kapitels zeigt. Ein Swimmingpool wird von niedrigen Bäumen beschattet. Unten eine Dachaufsicht.

La maison s'insère soigneusement dans son environnement naturel, comme le montre la double page précédente. La piscine est abritée par des arbustes (ci-dessous). Ci-dessous également, le plan du toit.

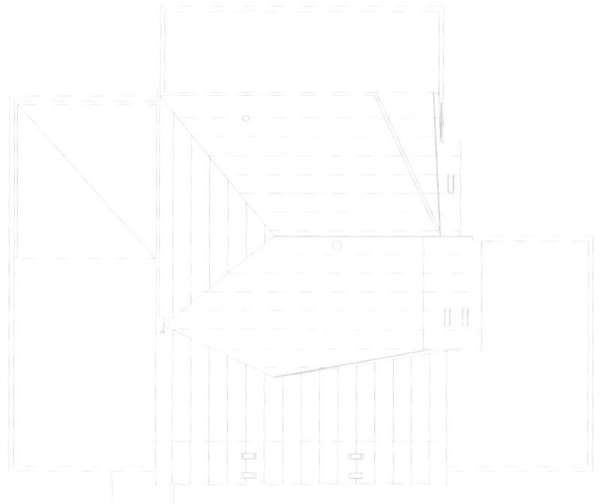

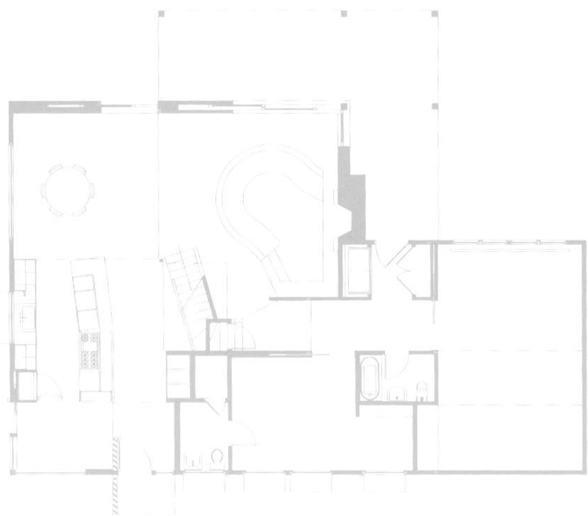

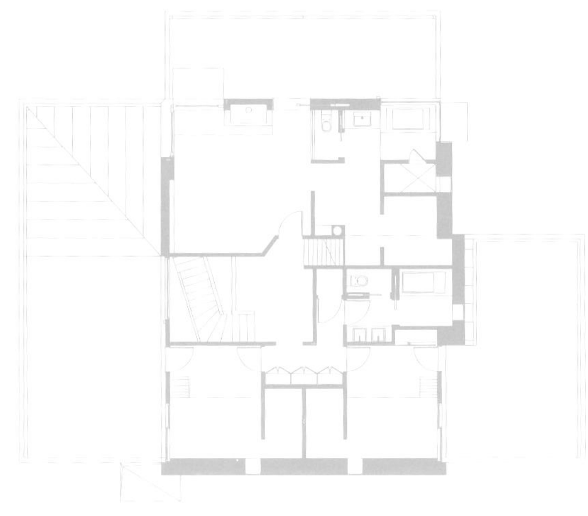

Floor plans (left) are basically orthogonal. Inside the house, green or red surfaces recall the bright red used outside, while kitchen or bedroom spaces (this page) offer generous openings to the forested environment.

Die Grundrisse (links) sind primär rechtwinklig definiert. Im Innern des Hauses greifen grüne und rote Oberflächen das leuchtende Rot der Fassade auf. Küche und Schlafzimmer (diese Seite) haben großzügige Fenster mit Blick in die waldige Umgebung.

Les plans au sol (à gauche) sont pratiquement orthogonaux. À l'intérieur, les plans vert ou rouge rappellent la couleur de la façade. La cuisine et les chambres (sur cette page) offrent d'amples perspectives sur l'environnement boisé.

CELULA ARQUITECTURA

Celula Arquitectura / Jorge Covarrubias + Benjamin Gonzalez Henze
Campos Eliseos 432
Colonia Polanco
México D.F. 11560
Mexico

Tel: +52 55 5281 7640
E-mail: info@celulaarquitectura.com
Web: www.celulaarquitectura.com

CELULA ARQUITECTURA is a "multidisciplinary practice focused on integrating architecture, landscape and art." The firm partners are Jorge Covarrubias, born in 1969 in Los Mochis, and Benjamin Gonzalez Henze, born in 1965 in Mexico City. Covarrubias graduated from the Universidad Iberoamericana in Mexico City and Gonzalez from La Salle University, also in Mexico. Their work includes the Casa SA (2005–08) and Casa Club Bosque Altozano (2006–09), both in Mexico City; and Clay House (Valle de Bravo, 2007–08, published here). They did the exhibition design for "Luis Barragan, The Quiet Revolution" (2002), and for a show of the work of the artist Fernando Ortega (2009), both in Mexico City.

CELULA ARQUITECTURA ist ein „multidisziplinäres Team, das sich darauf spezialisiert hat, Architektur, Landschaft und Kunst miteinander zu verbinden". Partner der Firma sind Jorge Covarrubias, 1969 in Los Mochis geboren, und Benjamin Gonzalez Henze, 1965 in Mexiko-Stadt geboren. Covarrubias schloss sein Studium an der Universidad Iberoamericana in Mexiko-Stadt ab, Gonzalez an der Universidad La Salle, ebenfalls in Mexiko-Stadt. Zu ihren Projekten zählen Casa SA (2005–08) sowie Casa Club Bosque Altozano (2006–09), beide in Mexiko-Stadt, sowie die Casa en el Bosque Altozano (Valle de Bravo, 2007–08, hier als Clay House vorgestellt). Sie gestalteten die Ausstellungsarchitektur für „Luis Barragan, The Quiet Revolution" (2002) und für eine Ausstellung des Künstlers Fernando Ortega (2009), beide in Mexiko-Stadt.

CELULA ARQUITECTURA est « une agence multidisciplinaire aux activités axées sur l'intégration de l'architecture, du paysage et de l'art ». Ses associés sont Jorge Covarrubias, né en 1969 à Los Mochis, et Benjamin Gonzalez Henze, né en 1965 à Mexico. Covarrubias est diplômé de l'Université ibéro-américaine de Mexico et Gonzalez de l'université La Salle, également à Mexico. Leurs réalisations comprennent la Casa SA (2005–08) ; la Casa Club Bosque Altozano (2006–09), toutes deux à Mexico ; et la maison d'argile (Clay House, Valle de Bravo, 2007–08, publiée ici). Ils ont conçu l'exposition « Luis Barragan, The Quiet Revolution » (Luis Barragan, la révolution tranquille, 2002, Mexico), et une autre autour de l'œuvre de l'artiste Fernando Ortega (2009, Mexico).

CLAY HOUSE

Valle de Bravo, Mexico, 2007–08

Area: 450 m². Client: not disclosed.
Cost: $1.4 million

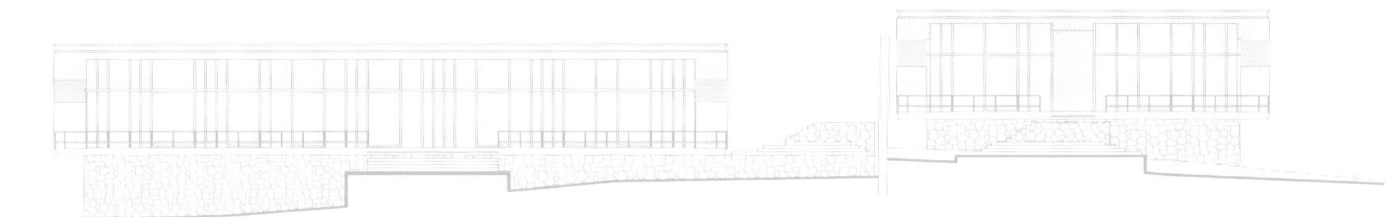

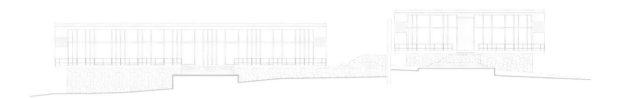

Elevations of the house (this page and bottom, right) show that the largely glazed upper portion sits on a solid base whose form is adapted to the levels of the site. Mature trees shelter the glazed upper deck.

Aufrisse des Hauses (diese Seite und rechts unten) zeigen einen weitgehend verglasten Aufsatz auf einem kompakten Sockel, der sich den verschiedenen Ebenen des Geländes anpasst. Alte Bäume beschatten den verglasten Aufsatz.

Les élévations de la maison (sur cette page et en bas à droite) montrent que le volume supérieur en grande partie vitré repose sur une base massive dont la forme est adaptée au profil du terrain. De grands arbres protègent la terrasse supérieure vitrée.

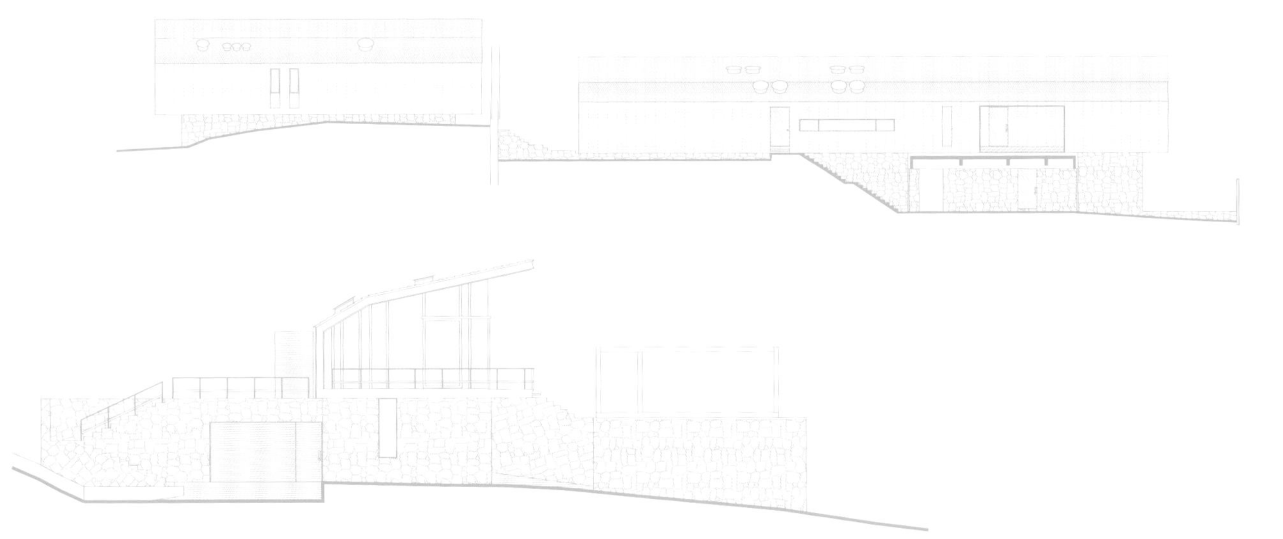

Located 150 kilometers southwest of Mexico City, this house is set on a 3500-square-meter site on a hillside. The architects state: "The house evokes the feeling of floating above the landscape, accentuating the sense of contact with nature." A structural window system seeks to overcome the "conventional distinctions between inside and outside." A large pavilion located near the pool contains living, dining, kitchen, and workspaces. Two bedrooms are located in a second, smaller pavilion. The location of the pavilions was selected to preserve existing trees on the site. A steel enclosure greets visitors, contrasting with the openness of the living spaces. A clay veneer inspired by the texture of local houses was used for cladding on the steel-frame structure.

Das Haus liegt 150 km südwestlich von Mexiko-Stadt auf einem 3500 m² großen Grundstück in einer hügeligen Landschaft. Die Architekten erklären: „Der Bau wirkt, als würde er über der Landschaft schweben und unterstreicht die Verbundenheit mit der Natur." Mithilfe eines Fenstersystems, das zugleich tragende Funktion hat, sollen die „konventionellen Grenzen zwischen innen und außen" überwunden werden. In einem großzügigen Pavillon neben dem Pool sind Wohn- und Essbereich, Küche und Arbeitsräume untergebracht. Zwei Schlafzimmer befinden sich in einem zweiten, kleineren Pavillon. Die Lage der Pavillons wurde vom Wunsch bestimmt, den Baumbestand des Grundstücks zu erhalten. Besucher betreten das Haus durch ein mit Stahl umbautes Entrée – ein Kontrast zu den offenen Wohnbereichen. Angeregt durch die Textur lokaler Bauten wurde die Stahlrahmenkonstruktion mit einer Verkleidung aus Ton versehen.

Située à 150 km au sud-ouest de Mexico, cette maison occupe un terrain de 3500 m² inscrit dans la pente d'une colline. « Elle donne la sensation de flotter au-dessus du paysage, et renforce l'impression de contact avec la nature », expliquent les architectes. Un jeu de baies structurelles efface les « distinctions habituelles entre l'intérieur et l'extérieur ». Un grand pavillon près de la piscine regroupe le séjour, la zone des repas, la cuisine et des espaces de travail. Deux chambres sont aménagées dans un second pavillon de dimensions inférieures. L'implantation de ces pavillons fut choisie dans l'objectif de préserver les arbres existants. La clôture en acier qui accueille le visiteur contraste avec l'immense ouverture des espaces de vie. Un revêtement en argile, inspiré de la texture des maisons de la région, protège cette construction à ossature d'acier.

In the broadly glazed living area, trees and blinds provide protection from the sun, while residents feel almost as though they are a part of the landscape.

Im großzügig verglasten Wohnbereich bieten Bäume und Jalousien Schutz vor der Sonne. Die Bewohner gewinnen den Eindruck, Teil der Landschaft zu sein.

Dans le séjour largement vitré, les arbres et les stores protègent du soleil mais laissent aux résidants l'impression de se trouver au milieu du paysage.

The house looks out onto a swimming pool and the more distant water. Furnishings are kept to a minimum, further emphasizing the lines of the architecture and the spectacular view.

Das Haus bietet Ausblick auf einen Pool und das Wasser in der Ferne. Die Möblierung wurde auf ein Minimum reduziert, was die Linienführung der Architektur und die spektakuläre Aussicht zusätzlich betont.

La maison donne sur une piscine et le fleuve dans le lointain. Le mobilier est réduit, ce qui laisse toute son importance à l'architecture et à la vue spectaculaire.

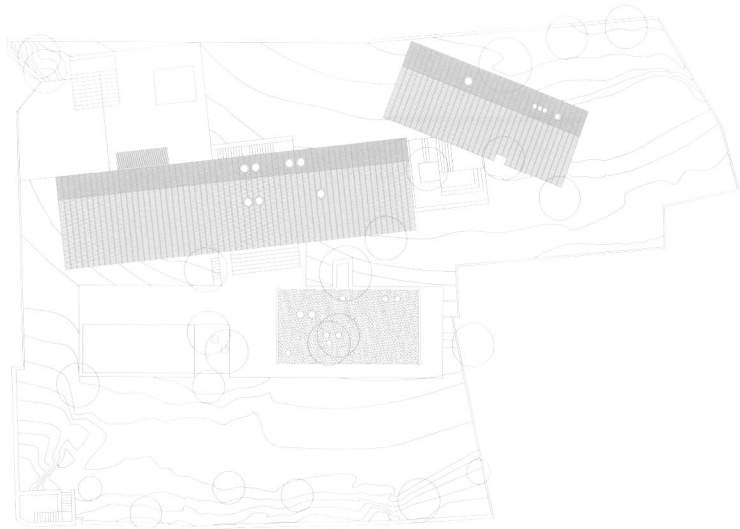

JOSÉ CRUZ OVALLE

Estudio de Arquitectura José Cruz Ovalle
Espoz 2902
Vitacura, Santiago de Chile
Chile

Tel: +56 2 206 6145
Fax: +56 2 206 0857
E-mail: cruzarquitectura@mi.cl

JOSÉ CRUZ OVALLE was born in Santiago in 1948, and began studying architecture at the Universidad Católica de Chile in 1968 and continued, beginning in 1970, at the School of Architecture of the Universitat Polytècnica de Catalunya, from which he graduated in 1973. He worked as an independent architect in Barcelona between 1974 and 1987, the year when he moved back to Chile where he associated himself with his partners Turell Ana in 1988, Juan Purcell Mena in 1995, and Hernán Cruz in 2000. His most significant works include the Pavilion of Chile at the Expo '92 (Seville, Spain); Hotel Explora Patagonia (1995); and the Campus of the Universidad Adolfo Ibáñez in Penalolen (Santiago de Chile), which was awarded First Prize for the best work of architecture at the IV Bienal Iberoamericana de Arquitectura, 2004. Juan Purcell Mena was born in Viña del Mar in 1963. He studied architecture at the Universidad Católica de Chile. He graduated as an architect in 1991. In 1995 he joined José Cruz Ovalle as a partner and later as an associated architect. The Valle Escondido House (Lo Barnechea, Santiago, Chile, 2007, published here) forms part of their work.

JOSÉ CRUZ OVALLE wurde 1948 in Santiago geboren. Sein Architekturstudium nahm er 1968 an der Universidad Católica de Chile auf und führte es 1970 an der Fakultät für Architektur der Universitat Politècnica de Catalunya fort, wo er 1973 seinen Abschluss machte. Von 1974 bis 1987 war er als freier Architekt in Barcelona tätig. 1987 zog er zurück nach Chile, wo er sich 1988 zunächst mit Turell Ana, 1995 dann mit Juan Purcell und 2000 schließlich mit Hernán Cruz zusammenschloss. Seine bedeutendsten Projekte sind u. a. der chilenische Pavillon für die Expo '92 in Sevilla (Spanien), das Hotel Explora Patagonia (1995) sowie der Campus der Universidad Adolfo Ibáñez in Peñalolén (Santiago de Chile), für den er mit dem ersten Preis für ein Architekturprojekt auf der IV. Bienal Iberoamericana de Arquitectura (2004) ausgezeichnet wurde. Juan Purcell Mena wurde 1963 in Viña del Mar geboren. Er studierte Architektur an der Universidad Católica de Chile und machte seinen Abschluss 1991. 1995 schloss er sich mit José Cruz Ovalle zusammen, zunächst als Partner und später als assoziierter Architekt. Die Casa Valle Escondido (Lo Barnechea, Santiago, Chile, 2007, hier vorgestellt) zählt zu ihren gemeinsamen Arbeiten.

JOSÉ CRUZ OVALLE, né à Santiago en 1948, a commencé ses études d'architecture à l'Université catholique du Chili en 1968, et les a poursuivies à partir de 1970 à l'École d'architecture de l'Université polytechnique de Barcelone, dont il est sorti diplômé en 1973. Il a travaillé comme architecte indépendant à Barcelone de 1974 à 1987, puis est rentré au Chili où il s'est associé avec Turell Ana en 1988, Juan Purcell Mena en 1995 et Hernán Cruz en 2000. Parmi ses réalisations les plus notables : le pavillon du Chili à l'Exposition universelle de Séville (1992) ; l'hôtel Explora Patagonie (1995) et le campus de l'université Adolfo Ibáñez de Penalolen (Santiago du Chili), qui a reçu le premier prix de la meilleure œuvre d'architecture à la IVe Biennale ibéro-américaine d'architecture, en 2004. Juan Purcell Mena, né à Viña del Mar en 1963, a étudié l'architecture à l'Université catholique du Chili dont il est diplômé en 1991. Il rejoint José Cruz Ovalle, en 1995, comme partenaire, puis architecte associé. La maison du Valle Escondido située à Lo Barnechea (Santiago, Chili, 2007, publiée ici) fait partie de leurs réalisations.

VALLE ESCONDIDO HOUSE

Lo Barnechea, Santiago, Chile, 2007

Area: 460 m². Client: Hernán Besom. Cost: not disclosed.
Collaboration: Juan Purcell (Partner)

Located in the foothills of the Andes near Santiago, the house provides an intentional counterpoint to a group of large native trees growing on the site. An access courtyard opens into the house, where stairs and bridges announce the spatial complexity of the design, which is inscribed in a sloped site. José Cruz Ovalle writes: "The lowest floor levels expand out in to the exterior space to create the courtyards. The highest levels protrude from the building in order to cast shadows into the courtyards which, together with the quivering variations in light and shadow of the tree foliage, give the house its unique vitality, something which the architecture achieves when the house is inhabited in relation to nature."

Das in den Ausläufern der Anden unweit von Santiago gelegene Haus bildet einen bewussten Kontrapunkt zu einer Gruppe großer einheimischer Bäume auf dem Grundstück. Zugang bietet ein Hof, zu dem hin das Haus sich öffnet. Treppen und Brücken sind ein Hinweis auf die räumliche Komplexität des Baus, der in ein Hanggrundstück eingebettet ist. José Cruz Ovalle schreibt: „Die unteren Ebenen greifen in den Außenraum aus und definieren die Höfe. Die oberen Ebenen kragen aus dem Bau aus und schaffen so Schattenzonen in den Höfen. Im Zusammenspiel mit dem flirrenden Licht und den Schattenwürfen des Laubes gewinnt das Haus jene unverwechselbare Vitalität, die Architektur erreicht, wenn ein Haus in eine lebendige Beziehung zur Natur gesetzt wird."

Implantée dans les collines du pied des Andes près de Santiago du Chili, cette résidence se présente en contrepoint volontaire d'un important bosquet. Une cour donne accès à cette construction, dont les escaliers et passerelles annoncent la complexité spatiale de ce projet inscrit dans une forte pente. José Cruz Ovalle explique : « Les niveaux inférieurs s'ouvrent sur l'extérieur pour créer des cours. Les niveaux supérieurs se projettent pour générer des ombres dans ces cours, ce qui, en dehors des variations permanentes de l'ombre et de la lumière provoquées par la présence des arbres, confère au lieu une vitalité exceptionnelle. La maison est habitée par sa relation avec la nature. »

As the drawings on the left page and below show clearly, the house is integrated into a natural drop in the site, giving it a real connection to the earth, also expressed in the interiors, where more than one level is visible in each of the images above.

Wie die Zeichnungen links und unten deutlich zeigen, wurde das Haus in das abschüssige Terrain eingebettet. So entsteht eine echte Beziehung zum Baugrund, die sich auch im Innenraum spiegelt, von dem auf den Fotos oben mehrere Ebenen zu sehen sind.

Comme ces dessins (page de gauche et ci-contre) le montrent, la maison est insérée dans un creux naturel du terrain. Ce lien concret avec la terre s'exprime également à l'intérieur où l'on perçoit partout les différences de niveaux (images ci-dessus).

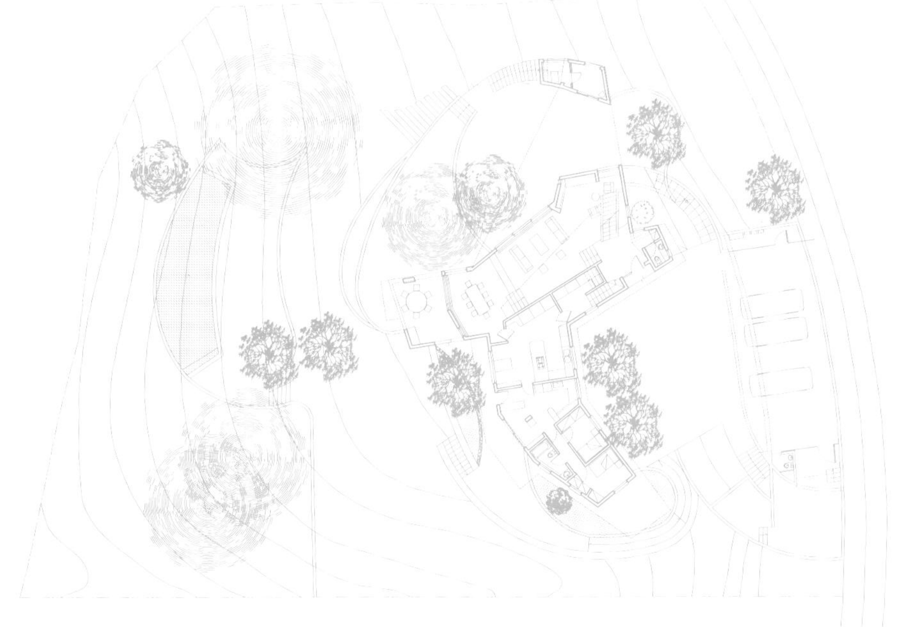

dRMM

dRMM
de Rijke Marsh Morgan Architects
1 Centaur Street
London SE1 7EG
UK

Tel: +44 20 78 03 07 77
Fax: +44 20 78 03 06 66
E-mail: mail@drmm.co.uk
Web: www.drmm.co.uk

Alex de Rijke is the Director of **dRMM**. He attended the Royal College of Art (London, M.Arch, 1984–86), Polytechnic South West, School of Architecture (Plymouth, Dip Arch RIBA Part II, 1987–89), and South Bank University (London, Professional Practice course RIBA Part III, 1992–93). He worked as an assistant in the offices of Rick Mather Architects (London, 1986), and Tchaik Chassay Architects (London, 1990–91), before forming dRMM Architects with Sadie Morgan and Philip Marsh in 1995. The practice now employs 30 people. Their recent work includes No. One Centaur Street (private housing, London, 2002–03); Wansey Street Housing (private and social housing, London, 2005–06); buildings for Kingsdale School (remodeling and new buildings, London, 2000–07); Clapham Manor Primary School (contemporary extension to Victorian school, London, 2006–09); Sliding House (Suffolk, 2006–09, published here); and the Stratford City North/Athlete's Village (private and social housing, London, 2008–), all in the UK.

Alex de Rijke ist Direktor von **DRMM**. Er studierte am Royal College of Art (London, M.Arch., 1984–86), an der Architekturfakultät der Polytechnic South West (Plymouth, Dip. Arch. RIBA Part II, 1987–89) sowie der South Bank University (London, Professional Practice Course RIBA Part III, 1992–93). Er war als Assistent bei Rick Mather Architects (London, 1986) und Tchaik Chassay Architects (London, 1990–91) tätig, bevor er 1995 dRMM Architects mit Sadie Morgan und Philip Marsh gründete. Inzwischen beschäftigt das Büro 30 Mitarbeiter. Jüngere Projekte sind No. One Centaur Street (privates Wohnhaus, London, 2002–03), Wansey Street Housing (privater und sozialer Wohnungsbau, London, 2005–06), Umbau und Neubauten für die Kingsdale School (London, 2000–07), die Clapham Manor Primary School (Anbau an ein viktorianisches Schulgebäude, London, 2006–09), Sliding House (Suffolk, 2006–09, hier vorgestellt) sowie Stratford City North/Athlete's Village (privater und sozialer Wohnungsbau, London, seit 2008), alle in Großbritannien.

Alex de Rijke qui dirige **DRMM** a étudié au Royal College of Art (Londres, M.Arch, 1984–86), à l'École d'architecture de Polytechnic South West (Plymouth, Dip Arch RIBA Part II, 1987–89) et à South Bank University (Londres, Professional Practice course RIBA Part III, 1992–93). Il a travaillé en qualité d'assistant à Londres dans les agences Rick Mather Architects (1986) et Tchaik Chassay Architects (1990–91), avant de fonder dRMM Architects avec Sadie Morgan et Philip Marsh en 1995, qui emploie aujourd'hui trente personnes. Parmi leurs réalisations récentes : N°1 Centaur Street (résidence privée, Londres, 2002–03) ; des logements sociaux et en copropriété (Wansey Street Housing, Londres, 2005–06) ; des restaurations et des bâtiments nouveaux pour l'École Kingsdale (Londres, 2000–07) ; l'extension de la Clapham Manor Primary School, une école victorienne (Londres (2006–09) ; la maison coulissante (Sliding House, Suffolk, 2006–09, publiée ici) ; et des logements sociaux et en copropriété à Stratford City North/Athlete's Village (Londres, 2008), le tout en Grande-Bretagne.

SLIDING HOUSE

Suffolk, UK, 2006–09

*Area: 256 m² (388 m² including porches, garages).
Clients: Mr. and Mrs. Ralph Marketa. Cost: not disclosed*

The greenhouse-like form of the house can be covered by its wood-clad exterior that slides on rails.

Die an ein Gewächshaus erinnernde Grundform des Hauses mit einer holzverblendeten Außenhülle, die auf Schienen bewegt werden kann.

La partie de la maison en forme de serre peut être recouverte de son double en bois, qui coulisse sur des rails.

The drawing below shows the potential for movement or expansion of the house, seen below in its closed mode.

Die Zeichnung illustriert die Bewegungs- und Erweiterungsmöglichkeiten des Hauses, das auf dem Foto unten in geschlossenem Zustand zu sehen ist.

Ce schéma montre le potentiel de mouvement ou d'expansion de la maison vue ci-dessous en mode « fermé ».

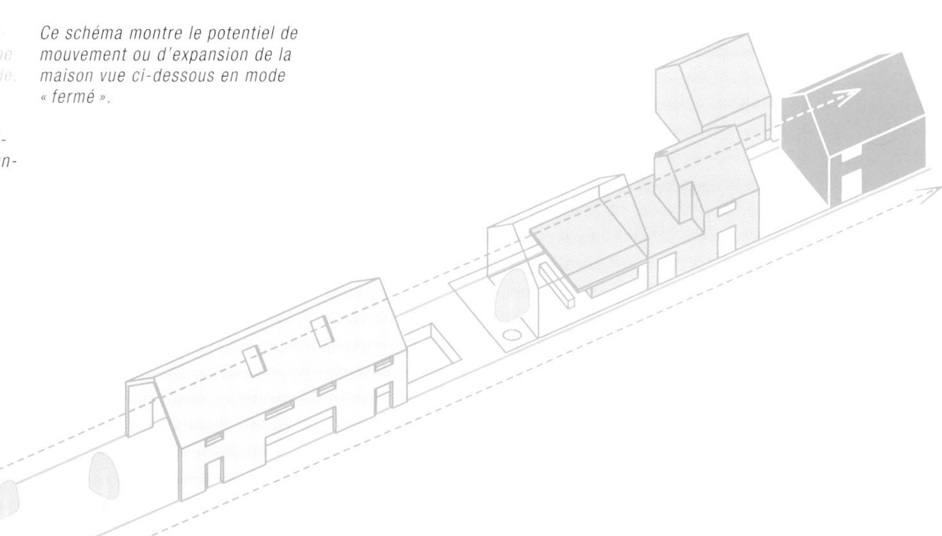

Located on a rural site in Suffolk, East Anglia, this project is designed to local rural development standards and with a respect for vernacular farm buildings. One unusual aspect of the project was that it was actually built by the client. The resulting 28-meter-long building includes a house, garage, and annex. The buildings are finished in red rubber membrane and glass, or red and black stained larch. The architect states: "The annex and garage are constructed with a modular timber cassette system with Scandinavian laminated section windows and doors. The surprise is that these separated forms can be transformed by the fourth and largest element in the group, the 20-ton mobile roof and wall enclosure that traverses the site." This mobile roof, set on concealed railway tracks, "passes over the annex, house and glasshouse" creating new enclosures. Hidden electric motors drive this surprising transformation of the structure, which may potentially be extended also to cover a planned swimming pool. A house that can be modified in form and area is certainly innovative.

Das auf dem Land in Suffolk, East Anglia, gelegene Haus wurde den ländlichen Bauvorgaben gemäß und mit Respekt vor der typischen Architektur bäuerlicher Nutzbauten entworfen. Ungewöhnlich war bei diesem Projekt, dass es tatsächlich vom Auftraggeber selbst gebaut wurde. Das 28 m lange Gebäude umfasst Wohnhaus, Garage und Anbau. Die Außenhaut besteht aus einer roten Kunststoffmembran und Glas bzw. aus rot oder schwarz gebeiztem Lärchenholz. „Anbau und Garage", so erklären die Architekten, „wurden aus einem Holzkassetten-Modulsystem gefertigt und haben skandinavische Fenster und Türen mit Verbundholzrahmen. Die Überraschung besteht darin, dass sich diese separaten Formen mithilfe des vierten und größten Elements – einer 20 t schweren, beweglichen Dach-Wandeinheit, die sich quer über das ganze Grundstück verschieben lässt – transformiert werden können." Dieses bewegliche Element ruht auf versenkten Eisenbahnschienen und „gleitet über Anbau, Haus und Glashaus", wodurch sich neue Raumkonstellationen ergeben. Verdeckt installierte Elektromotoren ermöglichen die erstaunliche Verwandlung des Baus, der sich erweitern lässt, um einen für die Zukunft geplanten Pool zu überdachen. Ein Haus, das sich in Form und Fläche modifizieren lässt, ist zweifelsohne innovativ zu nennen.

Située dans une région agricole du Suffolk, en East Anglia, cette maison a été conçue selon les standards ruraux locaux, dans le respect des formes des bâtiments vernaculaires. L'une de ses spécificités est aussi d'avoir été construite par le client lui-même. L'ensemble de 28 m de long réunit une maison, un garage et une annexe habillés d'une membrane de caoutchouc rouge, de verre ou de mélèze teinté en rouge ou noir. L'architecte explique que « [...] l'annexe et le garage sont construits selon un système de caissons (« cassettes ») de bois modulaire ; les portes et fenêtres sont fabriquées en usine en Scandinavie. La surprise vient de ce que ces blocs individualisés sont métamorphosés par l'apparition d'un quatrième élément – le plus grand – qui est un immense capotage mobile de vingt tonnes ». Ce toit et ces murs mobiles qui coulissent sur des rails dissimulés « passent au-dessus de l'annexe, de la maison et de la serre », modifiant l'enveloppe apparente. Des moteurs électriques cachés animent cette transformation surprenante qui pourrait aller potentiellement jusqu'à recouvrir la piscine prévue. Une maison qui peut modifier sa forme et sa surface, voilà certainement une idée neuve.

The glass-enclosed volume glows from within at night, while the apparently more conventional, wood-clad volume resembles a normal house.

Der gläserne Baukörper leuchtet nachts von innen, während das vermeintlich konventionellere, holzverblendete Volumen wie ein konventionelles Haus wirkt.

La lumière irradie du volume vitré pendant la nuit. Le volume habillé de bois fait davantage penser à une résidence classique.

An interior view of the glass-covered volume, where both walls and the roof are fully glazed, allowing residents to be visually in contact with the natural setting.

Eine Innenansicht des gläsernen Volumens. Wände und Dach sind vollständig verglast, was den Bewohnern Sichtkontakt zur landschaftlichen Umgebung ermöglicht.

Vue intérieure du volume aux murs et à la toiture entièrement vitrés qui permettent un rapport visuel intégral avec le cadre naturel.

Los Canteros Mountain Refuge

dRN ARCHITECTS

dRN Architects
Isidora Goyenechea 3200
Santiago
Chile

Tel: +56 2 231 4114
E-mail: contacto@drn.cl
Web: www.drn.cl

dRN ARCHITECTS was established in 2005 by Nicolás del Río and Max Núñez in Santiago. Born in Santiago in 1975, Nicolás del Río studied at the Universidad Católica de Chile, obtaining his degree in 2001. He also studied at the Politecnico di Milano (Italy, 1998–99). Since 2005 he has taught a first-year Design Studio at the Universidad Andrés Bello (Santiago). Born in Santiago in 1976, Max Núñez received his M.Arch degree from the Universidad Católica de Chile in 2004. He also studied prior to that at the Politecnico di Milano (1998–99). Since 2005 he has taught a second-year Design Studio at the Universidad Andrés Bello, in Santiago. Their work includes the Skibox (Portillo, 2006); Mountain Refuge Chalet C6 (Portillo, 2006); Mountain Refuge Chalet C7 (Portillo, 2008); Cerro Tacna Beach House (Maintencillo, 2008, published here); Los Canteros Mountain Refuge (Farellones, 2008, also published here); Beach House (Cachagua, 2009); Beach House (La Baronia, 2009); and Chiloe Island House (Punta Chilen, 2009), all in Chile.

dRN ARCHITECTS wurde 2005 von Nicolás del Río und Max Núñez in Santiago gegründet. Nicolás del Río, 1975 in Santiago geboren, studierte an der Universidad Católica de Chile, wo er 2001 seinen Abschluss machte. Ein Studienaufenthalt führte ihn außerdem an das Politecnico di Milano (1998–99). Seit 2005 leitet er ein Entwurfsseminar für Studenten des ersten Studienjahrs an der Universidad Andrés Bello in Santiago. Max Núñez, 1976 in Santiago geboren, absolvierte seinen M.Arch. 2004 an der Universidad Católica de Chile. Auch er hatte zuvor am Politecnico di Milano studiert (1998–99). Seit 2005 leitet er ein Entwurfsseminar für Studenten des zweiten Studienjahrs an der Universidad Andrés Bello in Santiago. Zu ihren Projekten zählen Skibox (Portillo, 2006), Refugio Chalet C6 (Portillo, 2006), Refugio Chalet C7 (Portillo, 2008), Strandhaus am Cerro Tacna (2008, hier vorgestellt), Refugio Los Canteros (Farellones, 2008, ebenfalls hier vorgestellt), zwei weitere Strandhäuser (Cachagua und La Baronia, 2009) sowie ein Haus auf der Insel Chiloe (Punta Chilen, 2009), alle in Chile.

L'agence **dRN ARCHITECTS** a été fondée en 2005 par Nicolás del Río et Max Núñez à Santiago du Chili. Né à Santiago en 1975, Nicolás del Río a étudié à l'université catholique du Chili, dont il est diplômé en 2001, et au Politecnico de Milan (1998–99). Depuis 2005, il enseigne en première année de conception à l'université Andrés Bello à Santiago. Né à Santiago en 1976, Max Núñez a passé son diplôme d'architecture à l'Université catholique du Chili en 2004, et avait précédemment étudié au Politecnico de Milan (1998–99). Depuis 2005, il enseigne une seconde année de design à l'université Andrés Bello de Santiago. Parmi leurs réalisations : la Skibox (Portillo, 2006) ; le refuge de montagne C6 (Portillo, 2006) ; le refuge de montagne C7 (Portillo, 2008) ; une maison de plage (Cerro Tacna, 2008, publiée ici) ; le refuge de montagne de Los Canteros (Farellones, 2008, également publié ici) ; deux maisons de plage (Cachagua et La Baronia, 2009) ; et une maison sur l'île de Chiloe (Punta Chilen, 2009), le tout au Chili.

LOS CANTEROS MOUNTAIN REFUGE

Farellones, Chile, 2008

Area: 140 m². Client: Moral family. Cost: $150 000.
Collaboration: Oltmann Ahlers

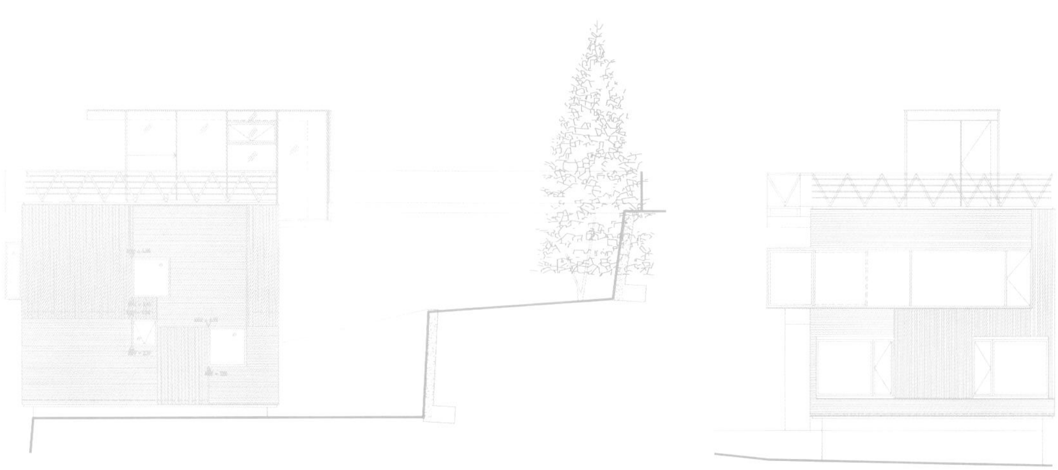

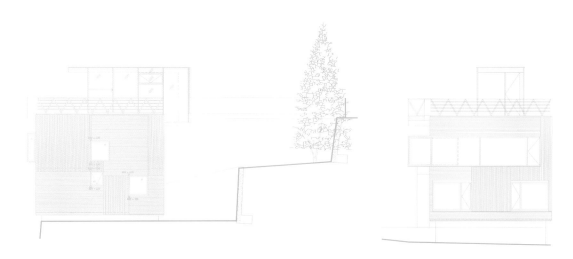

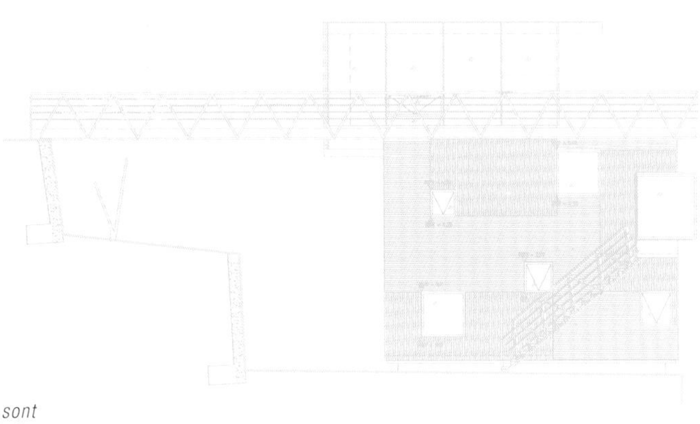

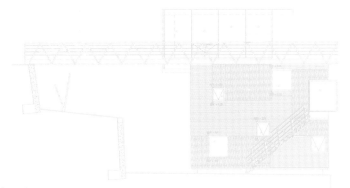

Glass-enclosed volumes sit above and on the front of the otherwise rather closed house. A rooftop terrace (seen on the left page) offers a spectacular view of the surrounding mountains.

Verglaste Volumina sitzen auf und an dem ansonsten eher geschlossenen Baukörper. Eine Dachterrasse (linke Seite) bietet eine spektakuläre Aussicht auf die umliegenden Berge.

De volumes entièrement vitrés sont fixés au-dessus et en façade de la maison, par ailleurs assez fermée. Le toit-terrasse (page de gauche) offre une vue spectaculaire sur les montagnes environnantes.

Existing containment walls on the site of this house defined its area. Set at an altitude of 2000 meters in the Andes, the house is designed with "a monolithic volume of stone that partially fills the void left by the existing containment walls." The glazing is kept to a minimum for reasons of heat loss in winter, and in order to frame specific views. A light, steel walkway links the road to the upper level of the structure. A prefabricated steel-frame structure was used to take advantage of the short building season in the region (about six months). An interior plywood cladding was covered with double thermal insulation, topped with waterproof membrane material and an outside cladding of black slate. Though this cladding does recall earlier stone structures of the region, it does not play a structural role. The refuge has three levels—a first floor with four small bedrooms, a second level with spaces for eating, playing, sitting, and cooking, and the top-floor access area with extra space for storing mountain gear.

Vorhandene Stützmauern auf dem Grundstück des Hauses gaben den Bauplatz vor. Das Haus, auf 2000 m Höhe in den Anden gelegen, wurde als „monolithischer Steinkörper" entworfen, der „den Raum zwischen den Stützmauern zum Teil ausfüllt". Um Wärmeverlusten im Winter zu begegnen und einen Rahmen für besondere Ausblicke zu schaffen, wurden die verglasten Fensteröffnungen auf ein Minimum reduziert. Eine leichte Stahlbrücke bindet das Haus im oberen Geschoss an die Straße an. Um mit der kurzen, sechsmonatigen Bauperiode in der Region auskommen zu können, wurde mit einer vorgefertigten Stahlrahmenkonstruktion gearbeitet. Die Verkleidung der Innenräume aus Schichtholz wurde mit doppelter Wärmedämmung versehen, auf die eine wasserdichte Membran aufgebracht ist. Außen wurde der Bau mit schwarzem Schiefer verkleidet. Obwohl die Verblendung des Hauses Assoziationen an ältere Steinbauten der Region weckt, hat sie keinerlei tragende Funktion. Das Feriendomizil verfügt über drei Ebenen: ein Erdgeschoss mit vier kleinen Schlafzimmern, eine zweite Ebene mit Ess-, Spiel-, Wohn- und Kochbereich sowie die oberste Ebene mit dem Eingang und einem separaten Raum für Sportausrüstungen.

L'emprise au sol de la maison est définie par des murs de soutènement. Situé à une altitude de 2000 m dans les Andes, ce refuge est « un volume monolithique en pierre qui comble partiellement le vide délimité par les murs de soutènement ». Les ouvertures vitrées sont réduites au minimum pour éviter les pertes de chaleur en hiver, mais cadrent néanmoins des vues choisies. Une passerelle légère en acier relie la route au niveau supérieur. L'ossature en acier préfabriquée a dû tenir compte de la courte saison de construction dans la région (six mois environ). Le parement intérieur en contreplaqué vient s'appliquer sur une double couche d'isolation thermique recouverte d'une membrane étanche et d'un bardage extérieur en ardoise noire. Si celui-ci rappelle d'anciennes constructions en pierre de la région, il ne joue pas de rôle structurel. Le refuge s'étage sur trois niveaux : le premier contient quatre petites chambres, le second le séjour, le coin repas, jeux et cuisine, et le niveau supérieur une pièce pour entreposer le matériel d'alpinisme.

At night, the glazed areas of the house are prominent while the main, lower volume remains more enigmatic and dark.

Nachts fallen die verglasten Bereiche des Hauses besonders auf, während der untere Teil des Baukörpers rätselhaft und dunkel bleibt.

La nuit, les parties vitrées de la maison ressortent particulièrement, mais le volume inférieur conserve une présence plus sombre et énigmatique.

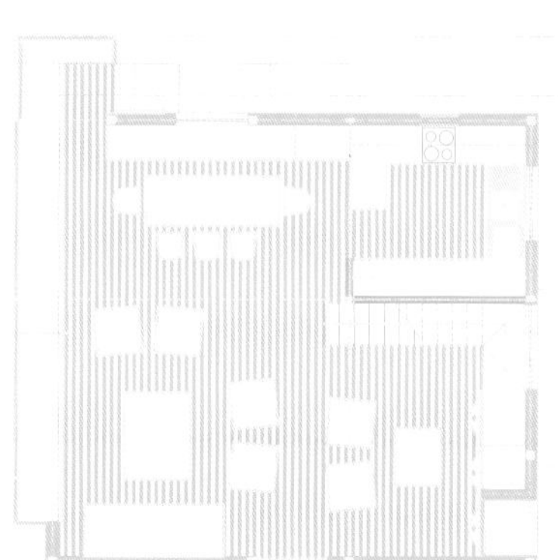

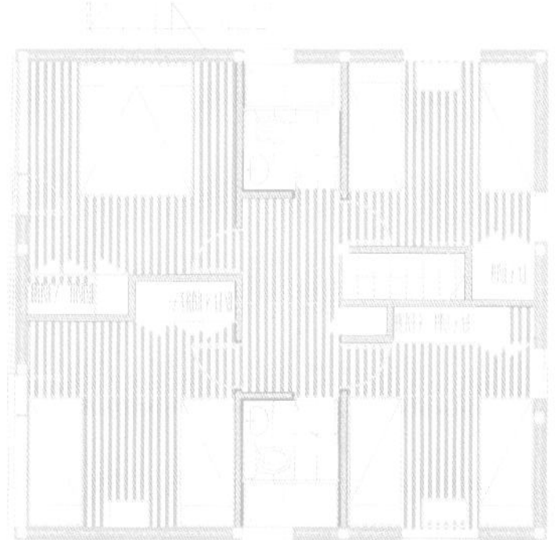

Plans show the essentially square form of the house, with the fully glazed front of the living area looking out onto the mountains (above).

Grundrisse zeigen die quadratische Grundform des Hauses. Die voll verglaste Front des Wohnbereichs bietet einen Ausblick auf die Berge (oben).

Les plans montrent la forme essentiellement carrée de la maison. Dans le séjour, une immense baie s'ouvre sur les montagnes (ci-dessus).

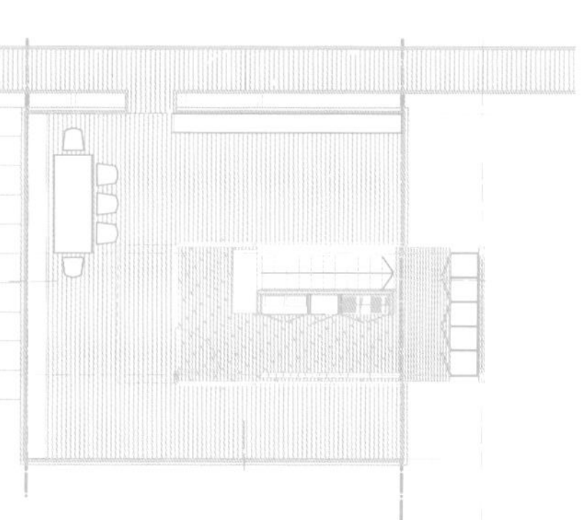

CERRO TACNA BEACH HOUSE

Maintencillo, Chile, 2008

Area: 122 m². Client: Patricio Miñano. Cost: $90 000.
Collaboration: Olivier Tayeb

The wooden house is set high off the ground to avoid problems in periods of storm or flooding. The two elevations on the right page reveal its light, hovering design.

Das Holzhaus wurde hoch über den Boden aufgeständert, um vor Schäden durch Sturm und Flut zu schützen. Die beiden Aufrisse auf der rechten Seite belegen den leichten, fast schwebenden Eindruck des Entwurfs.

La maison construite en bois est fortement surélevée par rapport au sol pour limiter les risques en cas de tempête ou d'inondations. Les deux élévations de la page de droite illustrent clairement sa légèreté et son principe de suspension.

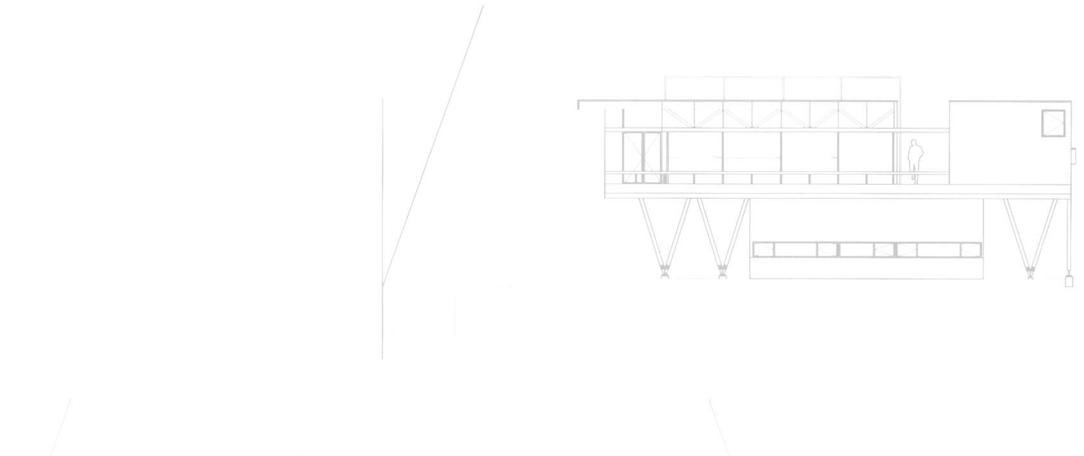

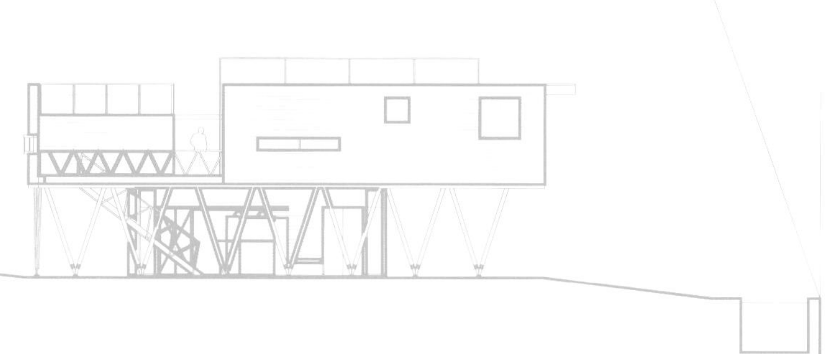

The house is located on Tacna Hill, south of Maitencillo, a well-known Chilean beach resort. Built as an elevated platform, 3.8 meters above ground level, the house contains two independent volumes with living space and bedrooms and a third one below, for guest rooms. Part of the platform is left free by these three freely placed elements, facilitating the movement between interior and exterior. The living room has four 2.3 x 2.3 meter sliding windows, accentuating the interpenetration of exterior and interior. The actual locations of the volumes are related to views from the house. The house is built of impregnated pine, like many neighboring residences. The entire design and construction process took just ten months.

Das Haus liegt am Cerro Tacna, südlich von Maitencillo, einem bekannten chilenischen Badeort. Es ist 3,8 m hoch auf einer Plattform aufgeständert und besteht aus zwei separaten Baukörpern mit Wohnbereich und Schlafzimmern sowie einem dritten, darunter gelegenen, in dem sich Gästezimmer befinden. Dank der freien Platzierung der drei Volumina bleibt ein Teil der Plattform unbebaut, was den Bewohnern die Bewegung zwischen Innen- und Außenraum erleichtert. Der Wohnbereich ist mit 2,3 x 2,3 m großen Schiebefenstern ausgestattet, wodurch die Durchdringung von Innen- und Außenraum zusätzlich betont wird. Die Positionierung der Volumina wurde so gewählt, dass sich verschiedene Ausblicke bieten. Wie viele seiner Nachbarbauten wurde das Haus aus imprägniertem Kiefernholz gebaut. Die gesamte Entwurfs- und Bauphase nahm nicht mehr als zehn Monate in Anspruch.

La maison est située sur la colline de Tacna au sud de Maitencillo, plage chilienne très connue. Construite sur une plate-forme surélevée de 3,8 mètres par rapport au sol, elle contient deux volumes indépendants (séjour et chambres) et un troisième pour les chambres d'amis. Une partie de la plate-forme reste libre, ce qui facilite les passages entre l'extérieur et l'intérieur. Les baies coulissantes de 2,3 x 2,3 m du séjour accentuent l'impression d'interpénétration entre le dedans et le dehors. Les volumes ont été disposés en fonction des vues. Comme beaucoup de résidences voisines, la maison est en pin imprégné. Sa conception et sa construction n'ont pris que dix mois.

A broad, wooden deck allows residents to sit high above the beach, looking out to the water.

Die breite Holzterrasse bietet Platz, um hoch über dem Strand zu sitzen und auf das Meer zu blicken.

Une large terrasse à sol en bois offre une position d'observation dominante vers l'océan.

The interior has simple, modern lines, echoed in the deck view seen to the right.

Schlichte, moderne Linien prägen das Interieur und finden sich auch auf der Terrasse (rechts) wieder.

L'intérieur de style simple et moderne se retrouve sous un autre angle dans une vue de la terrasse (à droite).

House for a Sculptor

THOMAS FABRINSKY

Thomas Fabrinsky
Hirschstr. 89
76137 Karlsruhe
Germany

Tel: +49 721 46 47 09–0
Fax: +49 721 46 47 09–29
E-mail: info@fabrinsky.com
Web: www.fabrinsky.com

THOMAS FABRINSKY was born in Ludwigshafen am Rhein in 1964. He trained as an architectural draftsman (1981–84) before studying architecture at the University of Applied Sciences, Karlsruhe (1986–93). He worked in the offices of Rainer Maul (Karlsruhe, 1991–93), and Baesler, Schmidt und Partner (Berlin, 1993–96), before creating his own office in Karlsruhe in 1996. He has taught at the University of Applied Sciences, Faculty of Architecture, Karlsruhe since 2006. His recent work includes a House for a Sculptor (Kleinmachnow, 2007, published here); four Row Houses (Hockenheim, 2007); a new, Semi-Detached House (Oberhausen, 2007); another Semi-Detached House in Malsch (2008); and a House in Rheinstetten (Karlsruhe, 2008), all in Germany.

THOMAS FABRINSKY wurde 1964 in Ludwigshafen am Rhein geboren. Nach einer Ausbildung als Bauzeichner (1981–84) studierte er Architektur an der Fachhochschule Karlsruhe (1986–93). Er arbeitete für die Architekturbüros Rainer Maul (Karlsruhe, 1991–93) und Baesler, Schmidt und Partner (Berlin, 1993–96), bevor er 1996 sein eigenes Büro in Karlsruhe gründete. Seit 2006 ist er Lehrbeauftragter an der Hochschule Karlsruhe, Fakultät für Architektur. Zu seinen jüngeren Projekten zählt ein Einfamilienhaus mit Bildhaueratelier (Kleinmachnow, 2007, hier vorgestellt), vier Reihenhäuser (Hockenheim, 2007), ein Doppelhaus in Oberhausen (2007), ein weiteres Doppelhaus in Malsch (2008) sowie ein Wohnhaus in Rheinstetten (Karlsruhe, 2008), alle in Deutschland.

THOMAS FABRINSKY, né à Ludwigshafen am Rhein en 1964, a suivi une formation de dessinateur en architecture (1981–84), avant d'étudier l'architecture à l'Université des sciences appliquées de Karlsruhe (1986–93). Il a travaillé dans les agences du Rainer Maul (Karlsruhe, 1991–93), et Baesler, Schmidt und Partner, à Berlin (1993–96), avant de créer sa propre agence à Karlsruhe en 1996. Il enseigne à la faculté d'architecture de l'Université des sciences appliquées de Karlsruhe depuis 2006. Parmi ses réalisations récentes ; une maison avec atelier pour un sculpteur (Kleinmachnow, 2007, publiée ici) ; deux maisons en alignement (Hockenheim, 2007) ; deux maisons semi-indépendantes (Oberhausen, 2007 et Malsch, 2008) ; et une maison à Rheinstetten (Karlsruhe, 2008), le tout en Allemagne.

HOUSE FOR A SCULPTOR

Kleinmachnow, Germany, 2007

Area: 226 m². Clients: Aletta and Andreas Theurer. Cost: not disclosed.
Collaboration: Christiane Neumüllers, Michael Totz

Kleinmachnow is a well-known residential area located at the southern edge of Berlin. The 900-square-meter site for this house is surrounded by older, large homes. The program called for a house for four people and a double-height studio for the artist. Existing trees on the site had to be preserved, which dictated the long, thin form of the house (22.5 x 5.75 meters). Works of art are displayed in a courtyard adjacent to the studio facilities, which include a complete kitchen and bathroom. A first floor living area includes the kitchen, and dining and living areas. Broad glazing and a terrace offer views of the pines that surround the house. The house is equipped with a geothermal heat pump, reducing heating costs considerably. The house has a titanium zinc roof, timber sliding windows, cast plaster on the basement floor, slate on the ground floor, and a parquet on the top level. The house received a 2007 Reiners Foundation Award and a 2008 Prize from the BDA (German Association of Architects) of the Brandenburg region.

Kleinmachnow ist eine begehrte Wohngegend am südlichen Stadtrand von Berlin. Das 900 m² große Grundstück ist von älteren, großzügigen Wohnbauten umgeben. Das Programm sah ein Haus für vier Personen sowie ein Künstleratelier mit doppelter Geschosshöhe vor. Um den alten Baumbestand auf dem Grundstück erhalten zu können, bot sich eine schmale, gestreckte Form für das Haus (22,5 x 5,75 m) an. Angrenzend an das Atelier, zu dem eine komplett eingerichtete Küche und ein Bad gehören, liegt ein Hof, in dem Kunstwerke zu sehen sind. Die Wohnflächen im Erdgeschoss umfassen Küche, Ess- und Wohnbereich. Großzügige Verglasung und eine Terrasse erlauben Ausblicke auf die Kiefern, die das Haus umstehen. Das Gebäude ist mit einer Erdwärmepumpe ausgestattet, was die Heizkosten erheblich senkt. Das Haus verfügt über ein Titanzinkdach und Holzschiebefenster, einen Gussestrich im Untergeschoss, Schieferböden im Erdgeschoss und Parkett in der oberen Etage. 2007 wurde der Bau mit dem Preis der Reiners-Stiftung und 2008 mit dem BDA-Preis „Gute Bauten im Land Brandenburg" ausgezeichnet.

Kleinmachnow est un quartier résidentiel connu, à la limite sud de Berlin. Le terrain de 900 m² occupé par cette maison est entouré de grandes demeures anciennes. Le programme portait sur une résidence pour quatre personnes et un atelier à double hauteur de plafond pour l'artiste. Les arbres existants devaient être préservés, ce qui explique le choix du plan en longueur (22,5 x 5,75 m). Des œuvres d'art sont présentées dans une cour adjacente au studio qui comprend aussi une cuisine et une salle de bains. Le séjour en rez-de-chaussée inclut la cuisine et un coin pour les repas. De grandes baies vitrées et une terrasse offrent des vues sur les pins environnants. Une pompe à chaleur géothermique participe au chauffage de l'ensemble. La toiture est équipée d'une toiture en zinc au titane, de baies coulissantes en bois, d'un sol en ardoise au rez-de-chaussée, et de parquets à l'étage. L'ensemble a reçu un prix de la Fondation Reiners en 2007 et un prix de l'Association des architectes allemands (BDA) de la région du Brandebourg en 2008.

The form of the house follows the gently sloping site, as is evident in the elevations seen above.

Der Baukörper folgt dem sanft abfallenden Grundstück, wie die Aufrisse oben zeigen.

La forme de la maison suit la pente douce du terrain, comme le montrent les élévations ci-dessus.

The basic shed-like form of the house takes on an almost industrial appearance as seen from the side (right). Above, the outdoor terrace opening onto a carefully groomed lawn.

Von der Seite wirkt das formal reduzierte, scheunenartige Haus fast industriell (rechts). Oben die Terrasse, die sich zu einer gepflegten Rasenfläche hin öffnet.

Vue de côté, la forme basique de la maison revêt un aspect quasi industriel (à droite). Ci-dessus, la terrasse ouvre sur un gazon soigneusement entretenu.

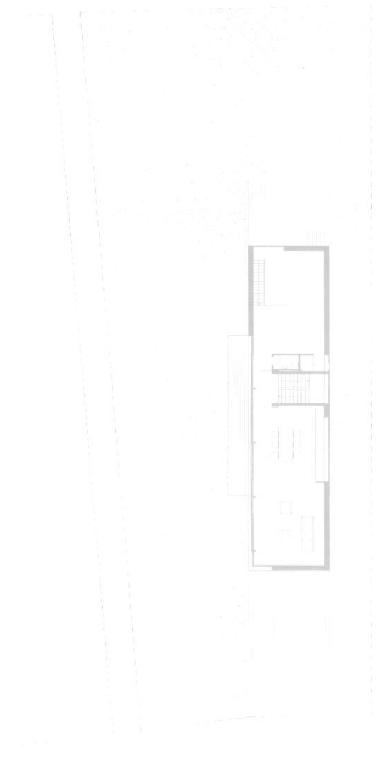

The overall form of the house is rectangular, as is readily visible in the site plan (above). The atelier has double ceiling height, while living spaces are generously glazed, offering ample views onto the green setting of the house.

Die Grundform des Hauses ist ein Rechteck, wie der Lageplan oben deutlich zeigt. Die Atelierräume haben doppelte Geschosshöhe; die Wohnräume sind großzügig verglast und erlauben unverstellte Ausblicke in die grüne Umgebung des Hauses.

Le plan d'ensemble de la maison est rectangulaire (en haut à droite). L'atelier occupe un volume double hauteur tandis que les espaces de vie généreusement vitrés offrent des vues panoramiques sur le cadre de verdure de la maison.

FEARON HAY

Fearon Hay Architects Ltd.
PO Box 90311
Victoria Street West
Auckland 1142
New Zealand

Tel: +64 9 309 0128
Fax: +64 9 309 0827
E-mail: contact@fearonhay.com
Web: www.fearonhay.com

Jeffrey Fearon was born in 1972 in Auckland. He received his B.Arch degree from the University of Queensland (1990–95). Tim Hay was born in 1973, also in Auckland, and received a B.Arch degree from Auckland University (1993–97). They established **FEARON HAY ARCHITECTS** in 1998. As they describe their own practice and its largely residential work: "Fearon Hay projects include commissions in diverse environments—coastal, urban, rural, lakeside, and alpine. Works are located in both North and South Islands of New Zealand." Their projects include Coromandel Beach House (Coromandel Peninsula, 2000); Kellands Commercial Office Building (Auckland, 2001); Darling Point Apartment (Sydney, 2002); Parnell House (Auckland, 2002); Shark Alley Retreat (Great Barrier Island, 2002–03); Lake Wakatipu House (Queenstown, 2003); Sergeant to Dunn House (Auckland, 2005); Clooney Restaurant (Auckland, 2006); Northland Beach House (Rawhiti, 2007); Yates-Allison House (Tutukaka Coast, 2007); Sandhills Road House (Great Barrier Island, 2007); Sandy Bay Farm House (Sandy Bay, Tutukaka Coast, 2007–08, published here); Closeburg Station Guest House (Queenstown, 2008); Tribeca Loft (Manhattan, New York, USA, 2008); and Wintergarden @ The Northern Club (Auckland, 2008), all in New Zealand unless stated otherwise.

Jeffrey Fearon wurde 1972 in Auckland geboren. Er schloss sein Studium an der University of Queensland (1990–95) mit einem B. Arch. ab. Tim Hay wurde 1973 ebenfalls in Auckland geboren und absolvierte seinen B. Arch. an der Universität seiner Heimatstadt (1993–97). 1998 gründeten die beiden ihr Büro **FEARON HAY ARCHITECTS**. Sie beschreiben ihre Firma und deren überwiegendes Engagement im Wohnbau wie folgt: „Zu den Projekten von Fearon Hay zählen Aufträge in den verschiedensten Kontexten – an der Küste, in der Stadt, auf dem Land, an Seen und in den Bergen. Die Projekte liegen auf der Nord- und Südinsel Neuseelands." Zu ihren Arbeiten zählen Coromandel Beach House (Coromandel-Halbinsel, 2000), Kellands Commercial Office Building (Auckland, 2001), Darling Point Apartment (Sydney, 2002), Parnell House (Auckland, 2002), Shark Alley Retreat (Great Barrier Island, 2002–03), Lake Wakatipu House (Queenstown, 2003), Umbau des Sargent House (1973) zum Dunn House (Auckland, 2005), Clooney Restaurant (Auckland, 2006), Northland Beach House (Rawhiti, 2007), Yates-Allison House (Tutukaka Coast, 2007), Sandhills Road House (Great Barrier Island, 2007), Sandy Bay Farm House (Sandy Bay, Tutukaka Coast, 2007–08, hier vorgestellt), Gästehaus Closeburg Station (Queenstown, 2008), ein Loft in Tribeca (New York, New York, 2008) sowie Wintergarden @ The Northern Club (Auckland, 2008), alle in Neuseeland, sofern nicht anders vermerkt.

Jeffrey Fearon, né en 1972 à Auckland, reçu son B.Arch de l'université du Queensland (1990–95). Tim Hay, né en 1973, également à Auckland, a un diplôme B.Arch de l'université d'Auckland (1993–97). Ils ont fondé l'agence **FEARON HAY ARCHITECTS** en 1998, et présentent ainsi leur agence et leurs interventions qui portent essentiellement sur le secteur résidentiel : « Les projets de Fearon Hay répondent à des commandes reçues pour divers types d'environnement – côtier, urbain, rural, lacustre et de montagne. Les réalisations sont situées aussi bien dans l'île Nord que dans l'île Sud de la Nouvelle-Zélande. » Parmi leurs réalisations : la maison de plage de Coromandel (Coromandel Peninsula, 2000) ; l'immeuble de bureaux Kellands (Auckland, 2001) ; la maison Parnell (Auckland, 2002) ; un appartement à Darling Point (Sydney, 2002) ; un chalet à Shark Alley (Great Barrier Island, 2002–03) ; la maison du lac Wakatipu (Queenstown, 2003) ; la maison Sergeant to Dunn (Auckland, 2005) ; le restaurant Clooney (Auckland, 2006) ; la maison de Northland Beach (Rawhiti, 2007) ; la maison Yates-Allison (Tutukaka Coast, 2007) ; la maison de Sandhills Road (Great Barrier Island, 2007) ; la ferme de Sandy Bay (Sandy Bay, Tutukaka Coast, 2007–08, publiée ici) ; la maison d'hôtes de Closeburg Station (Queenstown, 2008) ; le Wintergarden @ The Northern Club (Auckland, 2008) ; et, aux États-Unis, un loft à Tribeca (New York, 2008), le tout en Nouvelle-Zélande, sauf mention contraire.

SANDY BAY FARM HOUSE

Sandy Bay, Tutukaka Coast, New Zealand, 2007–08

Area: 220 m². Client: not disclosed.
Cost: not disclosed.

Like other houses designed by Fearon Hay, the Sandy Bay Farm House has a spectacular natural setting, on the Tutukaka Coast of New Zealand's Northland region. The site overlooks the Pacific Ocean in the direction of the Poor Knights Archipelago. This is a holiday residence located on a high ridge in the midst of a cattle farm. The architects state: "The building twists to follow the contour with the living space elevated on a concrete plinth to provide a glazed screen to the sheltered courtyard behind." The single-story structure with full height glazing in the living areas facing the view adapts a modest profile that makes it fit into the landscape as much as a modern house can. Indeed, the house is almost more about the site and the view than it is about the architecture, but it does provide a remarkable setting for a vacation residence.

Wie andere Bauten von Fearon Hay steht das Sandy Bay Farm House in spektakulärer landschaftlicher Umgebung an der Küste von Tutukaka, in der neuseeländischen Region Northland. Das Grundstück bietet einen Ausblick auf den Pazifik in Richtung der Poor Knights Islands. Auf einem hohen Bergrücken, mitten auf einer Rinderfarm, liegt das Feriendomizil. „Das Haus", erläutern die Architekten, „folgt der Kontur des Geländes mit einem Knick, der Wohnbereich ruht erhöht auf einem Betonsockel und dient zugleich als verglaster Windschutz für den dahintergelegenen geschützten Innenhof." Der eingeschossige Bau mit seinem voll verglasten, zum Panorama hin ausgerichteten Wohnraum gibt sich bescheiden und fügt sich soweit in die Landschaft, wie es für ein modernes Bauwerk nur möglich ist. Tatsächlich geht es bei diesem Haus fast stärker um die Lage und die Aussicht als um die Architektur – es ist ein bemerkenswerter Standort für ein Ferienhaus.

Comme d'autres maisons conçues par Fearon Hay, la ferme de Sandy Bay bénéficie d'un cadre naturel spectaculaire sur la côte de Tutukaka, dans la région nord de la Nouvelle-Zélande. Ce site qui domine l'océan Pacifique regarde vers l'archipel de Poor Knights Islands. C'est une résidence de vacances située sur une crête au milieu du domaine d'une ferme d'élevage de bétail. « La construction s'articule pour suivre le contour du terrain ; le séjour surélevé sur un socle de béton s'ouvre par un écran de verre sur une cour abritée à l'arrière », précise l'architecte. D'un seul niveau, cette maison aux immenses baies du séjour s'ouvrant sur le panorama, adopte néanmoins un profil discret qui l'intègre dans le paysage autant qu'une construction moderne puisse le faire. Il s'agit en effet davantage d'une réflexion sur le site et la vue que sur l'architecture elle-même, mais qui offre véritablement un cadre remarquable pour une maison de vacances.

Drawings (right) show the long, low profile of the house, and its gentle projection over the hilltop setting.

Zeichnungen (rechts) zeigen das gestreckte, niedrige Profil des Hauses und dessen verhaltene Auskragung über das hügelige Terrain.

Les dessins de droite montrent la silhouette allongée et surbaissée de la maison et son léger porte-à-faux par rapport au sommet de la colline.

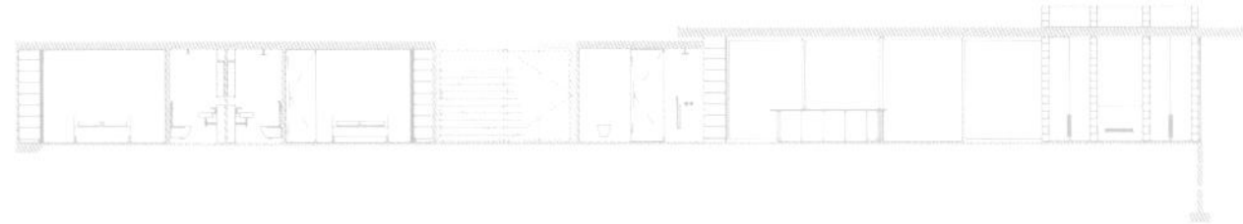

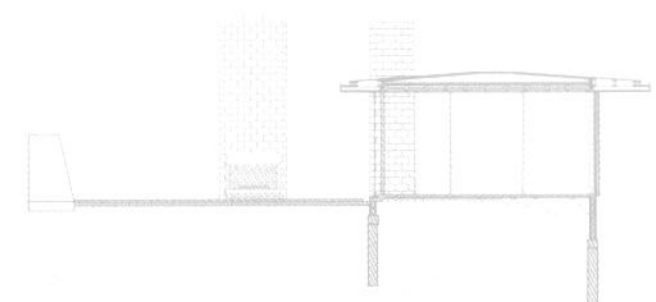

Given its protected natural setting, the house is designed to intrude as little as possible on the site, giving its residents a spectacular setting with views in all directions.

Aufgrund seiner Lage in einem Naturschutzgebiet wurde das Haus so geplant, dass es so wenig wie Möglich in das Gelände eingreift. Die Bewohner profitieren von der spektakulären Lage mit Ausblicken in alle Richtungen.

La maison a été conçue pour limiter au maximum les atteintes au site protégé. Ses résidants bénéficient de vues spectaculaires dans toutes les directions.

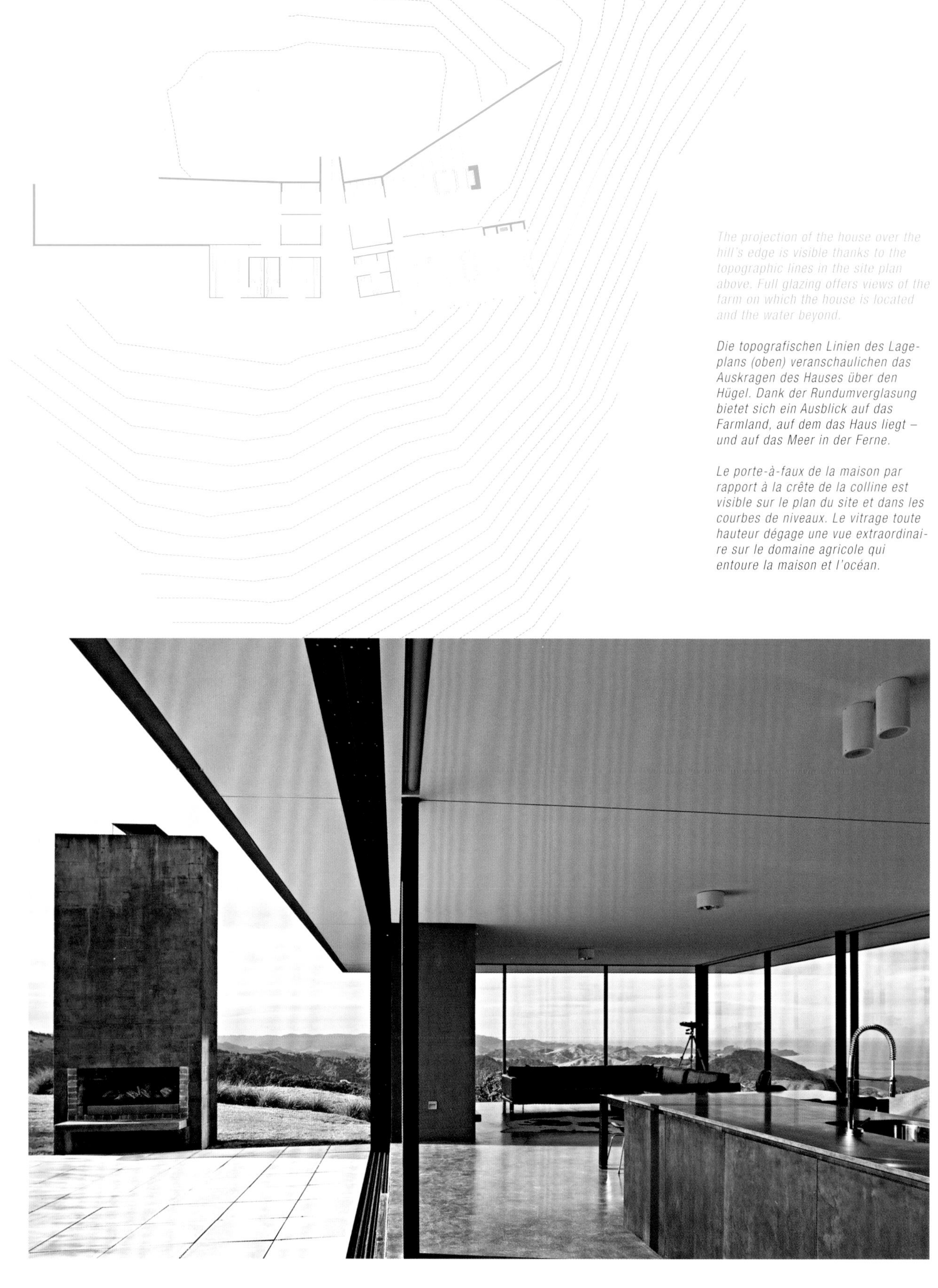

The projection of the house over the hill's edge is visible thanks to the topographic lines in the site plan above. Full glazing offers views of the farm on which the house is located and the water beyond.

Die topografischen Linien des Lageplans (oben) veranschaulichen das Auskragen des Hauses über den Hügel. Dank der Rundumverglasung bietet sich ein Ausblick auf das Farmland, auf dem das Haus liegt – und auf das Meer in der Ferne.

Le porte-à-faux de la maison par rapport à la crête de la colline est visible sur le plan du site et dans les courbes de niveaux. Le vitrage toute hauteur dégage une vue extraordinaire sur le domaine agricole qui entoure la maison et l'océan.

The relatively light window frames give the impression that the living space is practically floating between the ceiling and the floor, making the view part of the architecture.

Durch die vergleichsweise schmalen Fensterrahmen entsteht der Eindruck, als schwebe der Wohnraum zwischen Decke und Boden, sodass die Aussicht zum integralen Bestandteil der Architektur wird.

La menuiserie métallique relativement légère donne presque l'impression que le séjour flotte entre plafond et plancher, faisant de la vue une partie intégrante de l'architecture.

CARLOS FERRATER

Carlos Ferrater Partnership (OAB)
C/ Balmes 145 bajos
08008 Barcelona
Spain

Tel: +34 93 238 51 36
Fax: +34 93 416 13 06
E-mail: carlos@ferrater.com
Web: www.ferrater.com

CARLOS FERRATER LAMBARRI was born in Barcelona in 1944 and received his diploma from the Architecture School of Barcelona (ETSAB, 1971) and his doctorate from the same institution in 1987. He created his current office, OAB, with Xavier Martí, Lucía Ferrater, and Borja Ferrater in 2006. He contributed to the exhibition design of the very popular M. C. Escher show (Madrid, 2006–07); and has built House for a Photographer 2 (Ebro Delta, Tarragona, 2006, published here); Empordà Golf Club (Gualta, Girona, 2005–07); 16 houses in Teià (near Barcelona, 2008); and the Granada Science Park (Granada, 2008, with Jiménez Brasa Architects). He is the lead designer of a house in New Delhi (India, 2007–); and is working on the Acogida Pavilion (Sierra de Atapuerca, Burgos, 2007–), all in Spain unless stated otherwise.

CARLOS FERRATER LAMBARRI wurde 1944 in Barcelona geboren und machte 1971 sein Diplom an der Escuela Técnica Superior de Arquitectura de Barcelona (ETSAB), wo er 1987 auch promovierte. 2006 gründete er sein aktuelles Büro, OAB, mit Xavier Martí, Lucía Ferrater und Borja Ferrater. Beteiligt war er u. a. an der architektonischen Gestaltung der außerordentlich populären M. C. Escher-Ausstellung in Madrid (2006–07). Darüber hinaus baute er das Haus für einen Fotografen 2 (Ebrodelta, Tarragona, 2006, hier vorgestellt), den Empordà Golf Club (Gualta, Girona, 2005–07), 16 Häuser in Teià (bei Barcelona, 2008) sowie den Wissenschaftspark Granada (Granada, 2008, mit Jiménez Brasa Arquitectos). Er entwarf ein Haus in Neu-Delhi (Indien, im Bau seit 2007) und arbeitet derzeit am Acogida-Pavillon (Sierra de Atapuerca, Burgos, im Bau seit 2007), alle in Spanien, sofern nicht anders angegeben.

CARLOS FERRATER LAMBARRI, né à Barcelone en 1944, a obtenu son diplôm de l'École technique supérieure d'architecture de Barcelone (ETSAB) en 1971, et a été promu docteur par la même institution en 1987. Il a fondé son agence actuelle, OAB, avec Xavier Martí, Lucía Ferrater et Borja Ferrater en 2006. Il a participé à la conception d'une exposition très populaire sur M. C. Escher (Madrid, 2006–07) ; et a construit la maison pour un photographe 2 (Delta de l'Èbre, Tarragone, 2006, publiée ici) ; le golf club d'Empordà (Gualta, Girona, 2005–07) ; seize maisons à Teià (près de Barcelone, 2008) ; le Parc des sciences de Grenade (Grenade, 2008, avec Jiménez Brasa Architects) ; une maison à New Delhi (Inde, 2007 – en cours) et le pavillon de réception d'Acogida (Sierra de Atapuerca, Burgos, 2007 – en cours).

HOUSE FOR A PHOTOGRAPHER 2

Ebro Delta, Tarragona, Spain, 2006

Area: 120 m². Client: José Manuel Ferrater. Cost: €360 600.
Collaboration: Carlos Escura

The crisp, white lines of the house alternate with glazed or screened openings. To the right, the extremely long and narrow site runs to the beach, with the house placed at its inner extremity.

Die klaren, weißen Linien des Hauses bilden ein Wechselspiel mit den verglasten oder gitterartigen Fassadenöffnungen. Oben rechts das extrem lange, schmale Grundstück, das bis zum Strand reicht und an dessen äußerstem Ende das Haus liegt.

Les parties pleines et tendues de la maison d'un blanc immaculé alternent avec des ouvertures entièrement vitrées ou filtrées par des écrans. Ci-dessus, à droite, le terrain extrêmement long et étroit, qui s'étend jusqu'à la plage. La maison est implantée à l'extrémité opposée.

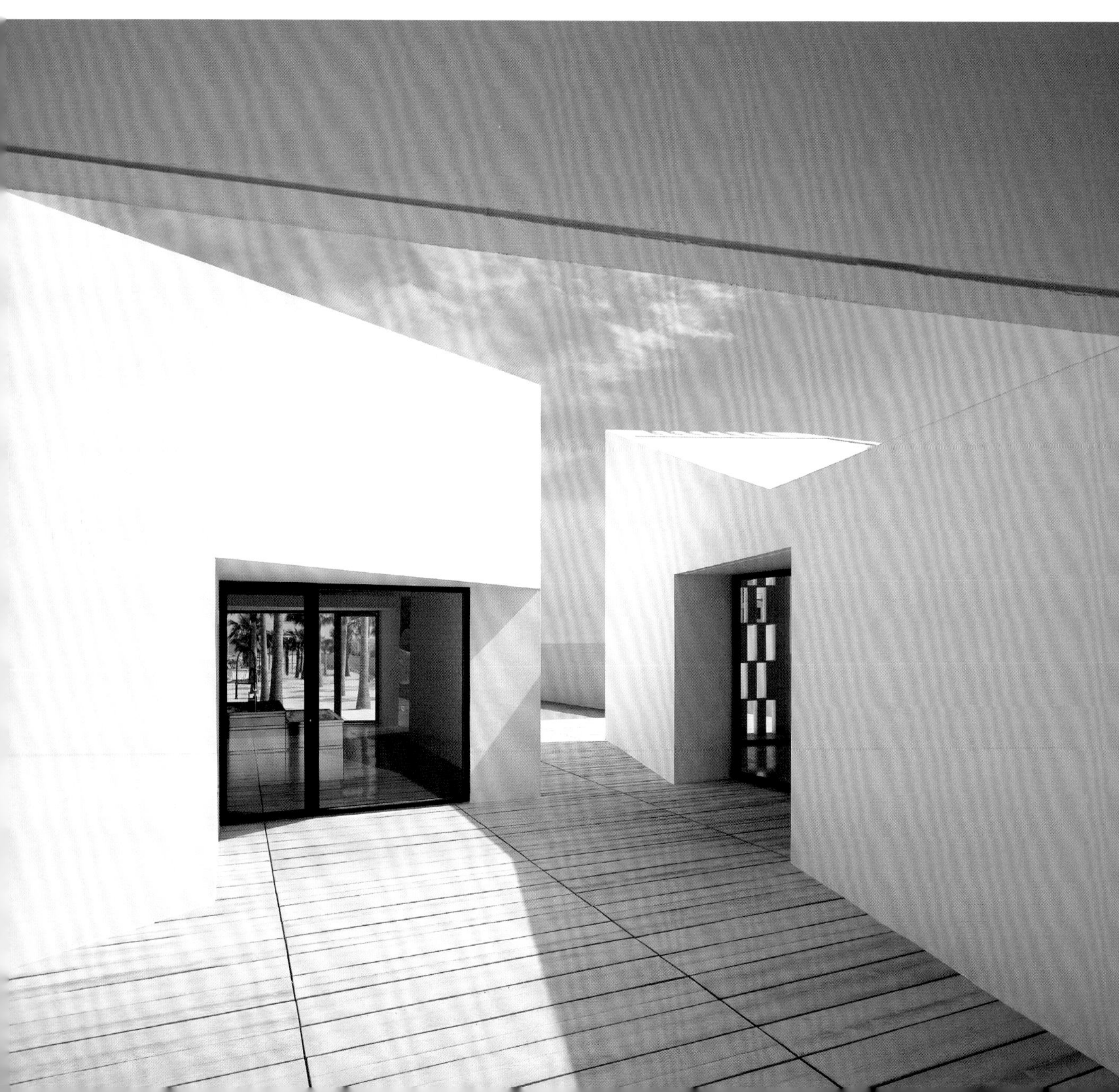

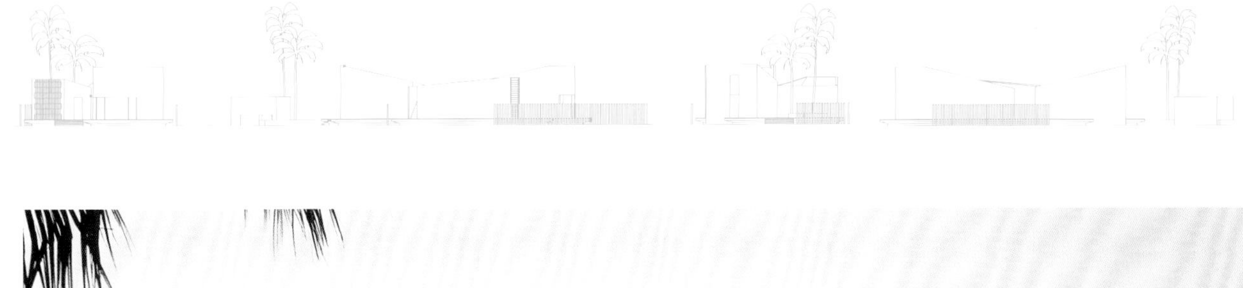

The 250-meter-long, 18-meter-wide site for this house is located at right angles to the sea. The house is perched just above the natural flood level, at the upper end of the sloping site. Sixty palm trees lead from the beach up to the house. The architect cites a Cubist work by Picasso, from the Musée Picasso in Paris, as a source of inspiration. The main space in the house is a central void, with irregular pavilions disposed around it on a main deck level. The actual Cubist inspiration of the design may be more apparent in plan than in elevation, but the net result is a spectacular house that stands on its own above the sea, defining its space in a taut, white composition.

Das 250 m lange und 18 m breite Grundstück liegt im rechten Winkel zum Strand. Das Haus, am oberen Ende des sanft abfallenden Geländes gelegen, befindet sich knapp oberhalb der natürlichen Hochwassermarke. 60 Palmen führen vom Strand hinauf zum Gebäude. Inspirieren ließ sich der Architekt von einem kubistischen Werk Picassos aus dem Musée Picasso in Paris. Zentraler Bereich des Hauses ist eine offene Terrasse, um die mehrere, unregelmäßig geformte Pavillons gruppiert sind. Obwohl sich die kubistische Inspiration des Entwurfs womöglich deutlicher am Grundriss als am Aufriss zeigt, ist das Ergebnis ein spektakuläres Haus, das sich mit seiner straffen, weißen Komposition zu behaupten weiß.

Le terrain de 250 m de long par 18 m de large vient perpendiculairement à la mer. La maison se trouve à l'extrémité supérieure de la pente, juste au-dessus du niveau d'une éventuelle montée des eaux. L'ancien jardin entre la mer et la maison est planté de soixante palmiers. L'architecte cite une œuvre cubiste de Picasso conservée au musée Picasso de Paris parmi ses sources d'inspiration. L'espace principal est un vide central autour duquel s'organisent des pavillons de forme irrégulière disposés sur une plate-forme. L'inspiration cubiste est plus apparente en plan qu'en élévation, mais n'en produit pas moins une résidence spectaculaire qui domine la mer et définit son espace propre dans une composition tendue immaculée.

Left, a bedroom with high book-shelves and a narrow, equally high opening that recalls the form of the site of the house.

Links ein Schlafzimmer mit hohen Bücherregalen und einer schmalen, ebenso hohen Fensteröffnung, die formal an den Zuschnitt des Grundstücks erinnert.

À gauche, une chambre équipée de bibliothèques hautes et dont l'étroite baie vitrée toute hauteur rappelle la forme du terrain.

Screens of various sorts filter the light and provide an element of privacy for an interior working space (above) or an outdoor terrace (left).

Sicht- und Blendschutzvorrichtungen unterschiedlichster Art filtern das Licht und schaffen Privatsphäre in einem Arbeitszimmer (oben) oder auf einer Terrasse (links).

Différents types d'écrans filtrent la lumière ou assurent un peu plus d'intimité, par exemple dans cet espace de travail (ci-dessus) ou cette terrasse (à gauche).

FLOAT

Float Architectural Research and Design
Erin Moore
Architecture Department
University of Oregon
210 Lawrence Hall
1206 University of Oregon
Eugene, OR 97403–1206
USA

Tel: +1 520 400 2900
E-mail: erin@floatarch.com
Web: www.floatarch.com

Erin Moore graduated from Smith College, Northampton, Massachusetts (1996) and received her M.Arch degree from the University of California-Berkeley (2003). She worked with Van Der Ryn Architects (Sausalito, California, 2002–03), Ibarra Rosano Design Architects (Tucson, 2003–05), and Line and Space Architects in Tucson (2005–06), before founding **FLOAT** Architectural Research and Design, where she has been the Principal since 2006. She is an Assistant Professor in the Architecture Department of the University of Oregon since 2008. Her work includes Floodspace, research and design (ongoing, in collaboration with Simi Hoque Ph.D., Massachusetts Institute of Technology); Rainette Verte, a studio in Bordeaux (France; design in development); the Watershed (Willamette Valley, Oregon, 2006–07, published here); and CEK Cabin (Tenakee Springs, Alaska, remodel, 2008).

Erin Moore graduierte am Smith College, Northampton, Massachusetts (1996) und erhielt ihren M.Arch. an der University of California-Berkeley (2003). Sie arbeitete für Van Der Ryn Architects (Sausalito, Kalifornien, 2002–03), Ibarra Rosano Design Architects (Tucson, 2003–05) und Line and Space Architects in Tucson (2005–06), bevor sie das Büro **FLOAT** Architectural Research and Design gründete, dessen Chefin sie seit 2006 ist. Seit 2008 ist sie Dozentin an der Fakultät für Architektur der Universität Oregon. Zu ihren Projekten zählen Floodspace, Forschung und Gestaltung (eine Kooperation mit Simi Hoque Ph.D., Massachusetts Institute of Technology), Rainette Verte, ein Studio in Bordeaux (Frankreich, Entwurf in der Entwicklung), Watershed (Willamette Valley, Oregon, 2006–07, hier vorgestellt) sowie CEK Cabin (Tenakee Springs, Alaska, Umbau, 2008).

Erin Moore, diplômée de Smith College, Northampton, Massachusetts, en1996, a obtenu son M.Arch de l'université de Californie-Berkeley en 2003. Elle a travaillé avec Van Der Ryn Architects à Sausalito, Californie, de 2002 à 2003, Ibarra Rosano Design Architects à Tucson de 2003 à 2005, et Line and Space Architects à Tucson de 2005 à 2006, avant de fonder **FLOAT** Architectural Research and Design, qu'elle dirige depuis 2006. Elle est professeur assistante au département d'architecture de l'université de l'Oregon depuis 2008. Parmi ses réalisations : Floodspace, recherche et projet (en cours, en collaboration avec Simi Hoque Ph.D., Massachusetts Institute of Technology) ; Rainette Verte, un studio à Bordeaux (France – en cours) ; le Watershed (Willamette Valley, Oregon, 2006–07, publié ici) ; et la CEK Cabin (Tenakee Springs, Alaska, rénovation, 2008).

WATERSHED

Willamette Valley, Oregon, USA, 2006–07

Area: 6.5 m². Client: not disclosed. Cost: not disclosed

This writing studio for a philosophy professor and nature writer (the mother of Erin Moore) is a project intended to "engage architecture with ecology." The first request of the client was to be able to hear rain falling on the roof of the structure. Located in the watershed of the Marys River, the structure is designed to make visitors aware of local plant and animal life—for example with small tunnels beneath the Watershed that encourage reptiles and amphibians to come into view. A water collection basin serves as a front step, but also attracts birds and deer. Built without road access, without electricity on site, and without significant excavation, the structure is both removable and recyclable. The Watershed was built with poured-on-site concrete foundation piers, topped by a steel frame. Cedar planks are bolted to the frame and can be individually removed and replaced.

Bei dieser Schreibwerkstatt für eine Philosophieprofessorin und Naturschriftstellerin (Erin Moores Mutter) geht es um „die Verbindung von Architektur und Ökologie". Erste Vorgabe der Auftraggeberin war der Wunsch, den Regen auf das Hausdach fallen hören zu können. Das Häuschen liegt an der Wasserscheide des Marys River und soll Besuchern die Pflanzen- und Tierwelt der Gegend vor Augen führen – etwa durch kleine Tunnel unter dem Watershed, die Reptilien und Amphibien anlocken. Ein Wasserbecken dient als Eingangsstufe und zieht zugleich Vögel und Wild an. Der Bau hat keinen Zufahrtsweg, keine Stromanschlüsse und wurde ohne substanziellen Erdaushub realisiert, ist demontierbar und recycelbar. Gebaut wurde die Hütte mit vor Ort gegossenen Gründungspfeilern aus Beton, auf die ein Stahlrahmen gesetzt wurde. Zedernholzbohlen wurden auf den Rahmen geschraubt. Sie lassen sich einzeln entfernen und austauschen.

Ce petit studio pour une femme professeur de philosophie et écrivain sur le thème de la nature (mère d'Erin Moore) est un projet qui veut « intégrer l'architecture à l'écologie ». La première demande de la cliente était d'entendre la pluie tomber sur le toit. Située dans le bassin hydrographique de la Marys River, la construction prend en compte les plantes et la vie animale. Par exemple, de petits tunnels ont été prévus sous la maison pour les reptiles et les amphibiens. Le bassin de collecte des eaux sert de seuil, mais attire aussi les oiseaux et les daims qui viennent y boire. Construit sans voie d'accès ni branchement à l'électricité et sans que le sol ait été creusé significativement, cette maisonnette est à la fois déplaçable et recyclable. Son ossature en acier s'appuie sur des pieux en béton coulé sur place. Les planches de cèdre vissées sur l'ossature peuvent être facilement démontées et remplacées.

The Watershed can be seen as a minimal form of shelter in a natural environment. Aside from its four, small, concrete foundation piers, the house actually sits above the earth.

Das Watershed-Projekt lässt sich als ein aufs Minimum reduzierter Schutzraum in der Landschaft verstehen. Abgesehen von den vier kleinen Gründungspfeilern aus Beton schwebt das Haus über dem Boden.

Le Watershed peut s'interpréter comme une forme d'abri minimal isolé dans son environnement naturel. En dehors de ses quatre petits pieux de fondation en béton, la maison est littéralement posée sur le sol.

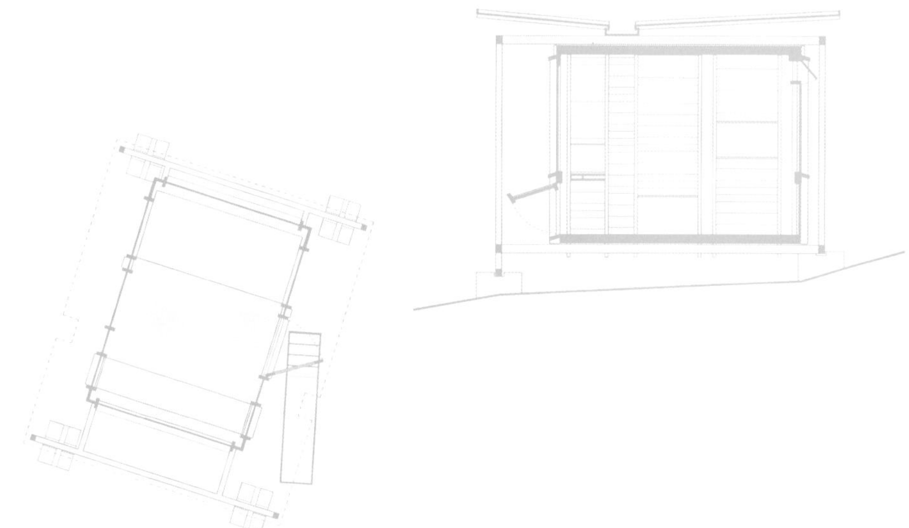

An observation point as much as a residence, the Watershed provides for generous views of the terrain, and the careful collection of rainwater (right).

Egal, ob man Watershed als Haus oder als eine Beobachtungsstation begreift, – es bietet rundum einen Ausblick in das Gelände. Auch Regenwasser wird hier gesammelt (rechts).

Point d'observation aussi bien qu'habitation, le Watershed offre des vues généreuses sur la campagne et récupère avec soin l'eau de pluie (à droite).

Crooked House

FOVEA

FOVEA
Comte Sandoz Architectes SARL
Faubourg de la Gare 5a
2000 Neuchâtel
Switzerland

Tel: +41 32 724 68 67
Fax: +41 32 724 68 69
E-mail: contact@fovea-web.ch
Web: www.fovea-web.ch

FOVEA, created in 2005 by François Comte and Pierre Sandoz, works in the areas of art, and architectural or environmental research. François Comte was born in 1972 in Switzerland and educated at the HES-SO in Fribourg (1997). Pierre Sandoz was also born in 1972 in Switzerland and graduated from the EPFL (Lausanne) in 1998. Each of the architects worked on large-scale projects in other offices before teaming up—Pierre Sandoz on the Neuchâtel elements of Expo '02 and the Stade de Suisse football stadium (Bern, 2000, for Luscher Architectes); and François Comte on the Pourtales Hospital (Neuchâtel, 2000, for NHP Architectes). Their recent work includes the Crooked House (Montet, Vaud, 2007, published here); a house (Bevaix, Neuchâtel, 2008); and the construction of seven row houses (Cudrefin, Vaud, 2009), all in Switzerland.

FOVEA, ein 2005 von François Comte und Pierre Sandoz gegründetes Büro, ist in den Bereichen Kunst, Architektur und Umweltforschung tätig. François Comte, 1972 in der Schweiz geboren, studierte an der HES-SO in Fribourg (1997). Auch Pierre Sandoz wurde 1972 in der Schweiz geboren und schloss sein Studium 1998 an der EPFL (Lausanne) ab. Beide Architekten arbeiteten in verschiedenen Büros an Großprojekten, bevor sie sich zusammenschlossen – Pierre Sandoz an den Bauten für die Expo '02 in Neuchâtel sowie am Fußballstadion Stade de Suisse (Bern, 2000, für Luscher Architectes), François Comte am Pourtalès-Krankenhaus (Neuchâtel, 2000, für NHP Architectes). Ihre jüngeren Projekte sind u. a. das Schiefe Haus (Montet, Vaud, 2007, hier vorgestellt), ein Wohnhaus in Bevaix (Neuchâtel, 2008) und der Bau von sieben Reihenhäusern in Cudrefin (Vaud, 2009), alle in der Schweiz.

Fondée en 2005 par François Comte et Pierre Sandoz, l'agence **FOVEA** intervient dans les domaines de l'art et des recherches architecturale et environnementale. François Comte, né en 1972 en Suisse, a étudié à l'HES-SO à Fribourg en 1997. Pierre Sandoz, également né en 1972 en Suisse, est sorti diplômé de l'EPFL-Lausanne en 1998. Chacun a travaillé sur d'importants projets avec d'autres agences avant de s'associer : Pierre Sandoz sur certains pavillons pour Expo '02 à Neufchâtel et le Stade de Suisse (stade de football, Berne, 2000, pour Luscher Architectes), et François Comte sur le projet de l'hôpital Pourtalès (Neuchâtel, 2000, pour NHP Architectes). Ils ont récemment réalisé la maison biscornue (Crooked House, Montet, canton de Vaud, 2007, publiée ici) ; une maison à Bevaix (Neuchâtel, 2008) ; et sept maisons en alignement (Cudrefin, canton de Vaud, 2009), tous en Suisse.

CROOKED HOUSE

Montet, Vaud, Switzerland, 2007

Area: 226 m². Client: not disclosed.
Cost: €400 000

The architects first visited the 970-square-meter site for this house at the end of January 2006. Construction started in January 2007 and was completed six months later. The house has a wooden frame on a reinforced-concrete base—and is clad in painted pine planks. It uses an air-water heat pump to save energy. Although the residence was the first to be built in its rural setting, it is seen as a prototype for other future houses in the vicinity. The most surprising architectural feature of the design is the 40° inclination of the front façade, looking down on the garden and affording a good deal of privacy despite the size of the windows. The prefabricated wooden-frame elements were installed in just two days, while finishes and cladding were added on site. The form of the house is intended to recall that of typical tobacco barns.

Die Architekten besuchten das 970 m² große Grundstück für das Haus erstmals im Januar 2006. Die Bauarbeiten konnten im Januar 2007 aufgenommen und sechs Monate später abgeschlossen werden. Das Haus ist eine Holzrahmenkonstruktion auf einem Stahlbetonfundament und wurde mit farbig gestrichenem Kiefernholz verkleidet. Dank einer Luft-Wasser-Wärmepumpe kann Energie gespart werden. Obwohl das Haus als Einzelbau in seiner ländlichen Umgebung realisiert wurde, soll es als Prototyp für weitere potenzielle Bauvorhaben in der Nähe dienen. Das überraschendste architektonische Merkmal des Hauses ist die 40°-Neigung der Frontfassade zum Garten hin, durch die trotz der Größe der Fenster ein hohes Maß an Privatsphäre gewährleistet ist. Die vorgefertigten Holzrahmenelemente wurden in nur zwei Tagen montiert. Ausbau und Verkleidung wurden vor Ort realisiert. Formal soll das Haus an traditionelle Tabakscheunen erinnern.

Les architectes ont découvert ce terrain de 970 m² fin janvier 2006. Le chantier, qui a débuté en janvier 2007, a été achevé en six mois. La maison à ossature de bois sur socle en béton armé est habillée d'un bardage peint en pin. Une pompe à chaleur air-eau contribue aux économies d'énergie. Première construction dans ce cadre rural, elle est un prototype pour de futurs développements dans le voisinage. Sa caractéristique architecturale la plus surprenante est évidemment l'inclinaison à 45° de la façade sur jardin qui permet de préserver l'intimité, malgré les dimensions de la baie. Les éléments préfabriqués de l'ossature ont été montés en deux jours seulement et le bardage posé sur place. La forme générale rappelle celle des granges à tabac de la région.

In its rural setting, the house takes on the appearance of a barn, aside, surely, from its outwardly tilted upper façade.

Inmitten der ländlichen Umgebung wirkt das Haus fast wie eine Scheune – abgesehen natürlich von dem nach vorn gekippten oberen Teil der Fassade.

Dans son cadre rural, la maison évoque la forme d'une grange, mise à part l'inclinaison de la partie supérieure de sa façade.

Minimal landscaping around the house echoes the simple concrete patio (above). Drawings show the unusual roof angles, and in particular the façade that seems to bow over the outdoor terrace.

Die minimale Landschaftsgestaltung am Haus passt zur schlichten Terrasse aus Beton (oben). Zeichnungen zeigen den ungewöhnlichen Winkel des Dachs und insbesondere der Fassade, die sich über die Terrasse zu neigen scheint.

Le style minimaliste de l'aménagement paysager autour de la maison se manifeste aussi dans la terrasse en béton brut (ci-dessus). Les dessins montrent le profil étrange de la toiture et en particulier celui de la façade inclinée sur la terrasse.

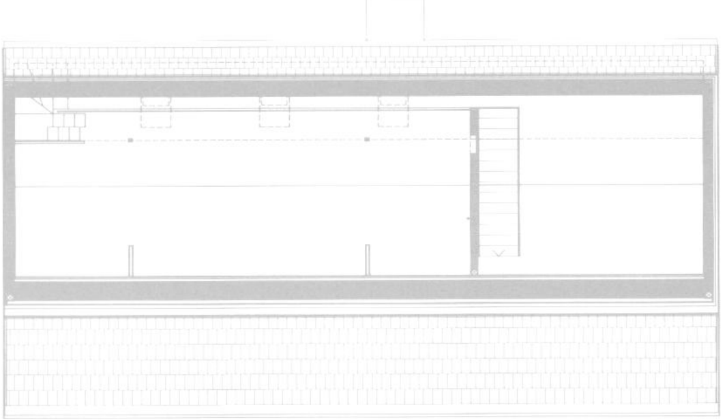

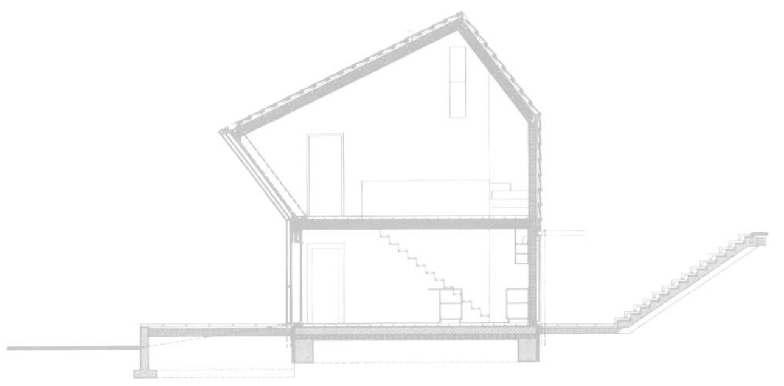

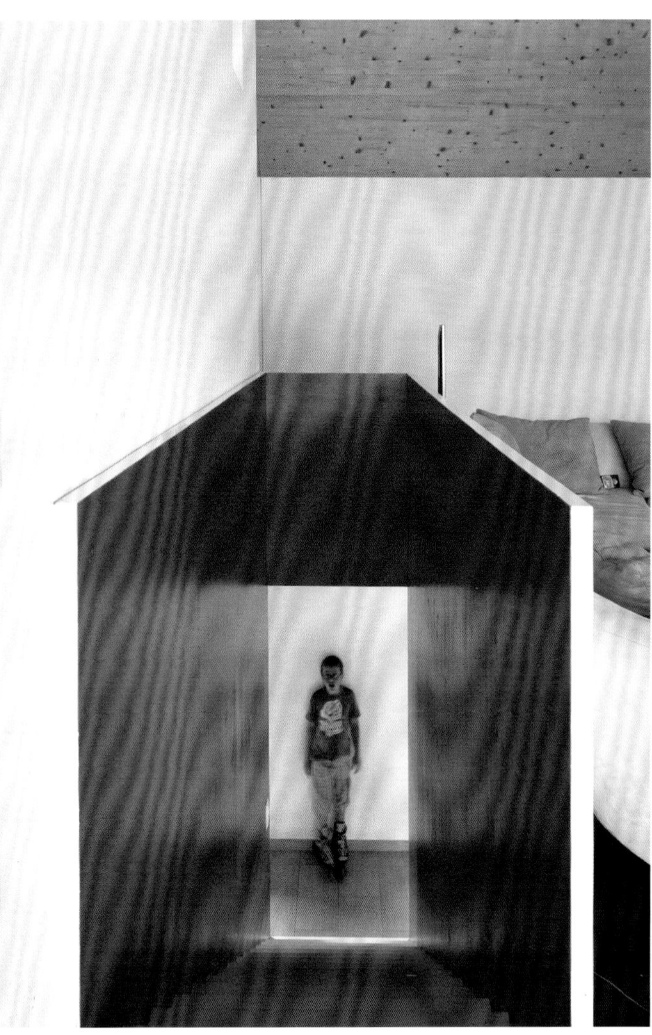

The basic form of the house is strictly rectangular, as the plans show (below). Despite this regularity, the architects succeed in creating unusual interior spaces with windows in unexpected locations, for example.

Die Grundform des Hauses ist konsequent rechteckig, wie die Grundrisse unten belegen. Trotz dieser Regelmäßigkeit gelingt es den Architekten, ungewöhnliche Innenräume zu gestalten, etwa durch überraschende Platzierung der Fensteröffnungen.

Le plan de la maison est strictement rectangulaire (ci-dessous). Malgré cette régularité formelle, les architectes ont réussi à créer des espaces intérieurs intéressants, par exemple à travers l'implantation recherchée de certaines ouvertures.

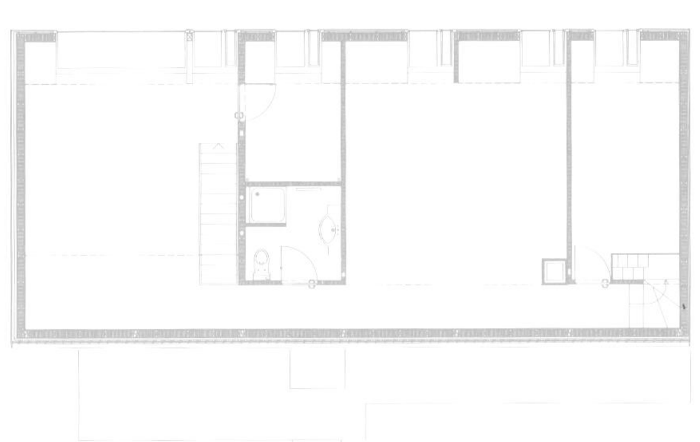

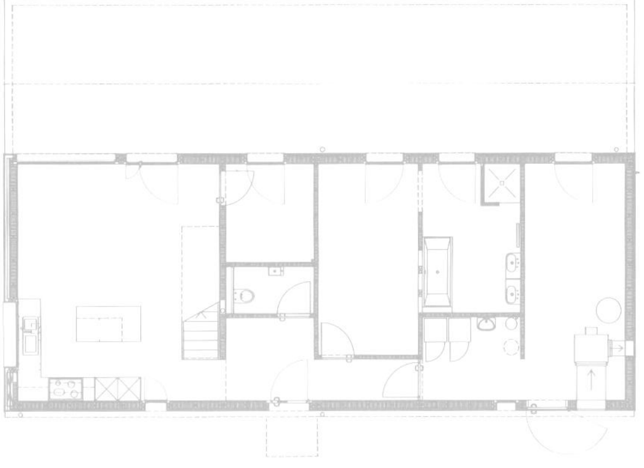

SOU FUJIMOTO

Sou Fujimoto Architects
10–3 Ichikawa-Seihon Building 6F
Higashi-Enoki-Cho Shinjuku
Tokyo 162–0807
Japan

Tel: +81 3 3513 5401
Fax: +81 3 3513 5402
E-mail: sosuke@tka.att.ne.jp
Web: www.sou-fujimoto.com

SUO FUJIMOTO was born in 1971. He received a B.Arch degree from the University of Tokyo, Faculty of Engineering, Department of Architecture (1990–94). He established his own firm, Sou Fujimoto Architects, in 2000. He is considered to be one of the most interesting rising Japanese architects, and his forms usually evade easy classification. He has been a lecturer at the Tokyo University of Science (2001–), Tokyo University (2004), and Kyoto University (2007–). His work includes Industrial Training Facilities for the Mentally Handicapped (Hokkaido, 2003); the Environment Art Forum for Annaka (Gunma, 2003–06); Treatment Center for Mentally Disturbed Children (Hokkaido, 2006); a Tokyo apartment (Tokyo, 2006–07); House O (Chiba, 2007); N House (Oita Prefecture, 2007–08, published here); Final Wooden House (Kumamura, Kumamoto, 2007–08, also published here); and Namba and Hayashi (both in Tokyo, 2008), all in Japan.

SOU FUJIMOTO wurde 1971 geboren. Sein Architekturstudium an der Fakultät für Bauingenieurwesen der Universität Tokio schloss er mit einem B.Arch. ab (1990–94). Sein eigenes Büro, Sou Fujimoto Architects, gründete er 2000. Er gilt als einer der interessantesten jungen Architekten Japans, seine Formensprache entzieht sich einfachen Zuordnungen. Als Dozent lehrte er an der Tokioter Universität der Wissenschaften (seit 2001) sowie den Universitäten von Tokio (2004) und Kioto (seit 2007). Zu seinen Projekten zählen Ausbildungsstätten für geistig Behinderte (Hokkaido, 2003), das Umweltkunstforum in Annaka (Gunma, 2003–06), ein Behandlungszentrum für psychisch kranke Kinder (Hokkaido, 2006), ein Apartment in Tokio (Tokio, 2006–07), Haus O (Chiba, 2007), Haus N (Präfektur Oita, 2007–08, hier vorgestellt), das Final Wooden House in Kumamoto (Kumamoto, 2007–08, ebenfalls hier vorgestellt) sowie Namba und Hayashi (beide in Tokio, 2008), alle in Japan.

SOU FUJIMOTO, né en 1971, a obtenu son B.Arch à l'université de Tokyo, Faculté d'ingénierie, département d'architecture (1990–94). Il crée sa propre agence, Sou Fujimoto Architects, en 2000. On le considère comme l'un des jeunes architectes japonais les plus intéressants apparus récemment. Son vocabulaire formel échappe à toute classification aisée. Il a été assistant à l'université de Kyoto (2007 – en cours), à l'université de Tokyo (2004) et à l'Université des sciences de Tokyo (2001–en cours). Parmi ses réalisations : des installations de formation pour handicapés mentaux (Hokkaido, 2003) ; l'Environment Art Forum pour Annaka (Gunma, 2003–06) ; un Centre de traitement pour les enfants souffrant de troubles mentaux (Hokkaido, 2006) ; un appartement à Tokyo (Tokyo, 2006–07) ; la maison O (Chiba, 2007) ; la maison N (Préfecture d'Oïta, 2007–08, publiée ici ; la maison de bois définitive (Kumamura, Kumamoto (2007–08, également publiée ici) ; et Namba and Hayashi (tous deux à Tokyo, 2008), tous au Japon.

N HOUSE

Oita Prefecture, Japan, 2007–08

Area: 85 m². Client: not disclosed. Cost: ¥34.965 million.
Collaboration: Yumiko Nogiri

The architect describes this house as being made up of "three shells of progressive size nested inside one another." The outer shell covers 150 square meters of the 236-square-meter site, while only the final, inner shell holds the actual interior areas. Sou Fujimoto states: "I have always had doubts about streets and houses being separated by a single wall, and wondered if a gradation of this rich domain accompanied by various senses of distance between streets and houses might be a possibility, such as: a place inside the house that is fairly near the street; a place that is a bit further from the street; and a place as far removed from the street as possible, in secure privacy." The final result is that there is no longer a distinct barrier between the house and the street—a sensation that Fujimoto compares to "living in the clouds." Despite its multiple layers, separating residents from the city, the architect speaks of "an undulation of primordial space where humans dwell" when referring to the urban condition. "This," he says, "is a presentation of an ultimate house in which everything from the origins of the world to a specific house is conceived together under a single method."

Der Architekt beschreibt das Haus als „drei Hüllen von zunehmender Größe, die ineinander verschachtelt sind". Die äußere Schale umfängt 150 m² des 236 m² großen Grundstücks; die eigentlichen Innenräume sind in der kleinsten, innersten Bauhülle untergebracht. Sou Fujimoto erklärt: „Es schien mir schon immer zweifelhaft, Straßen und Häuser durch eine einzige Mauer zu trennen, und so fragte ich mich, ob es nicht denkbar sei, eine Abstufung dieser komplexen Zone vorzunehmen, die ein Gefühl für die unterschiedlich großen Entfernungen zwischen Häusern und Straßen vermitteln würde: ein Ort im Haus beispielsweise, der sich recht nah an der Straße befindet, dahinter ein weiterer Ort mit etwas größerem Abstand zur Straße und zuletzt einer, der so weit wie möglich von der Straße entfernt ist und einen abgeschlossenen privaten Bereich bildet." Resultat eines solchen Prozesses ist, dass sich keine klaren Grenzen zwischen Haus und Straße ausmachen lassen – ein Eindruck, den Fujimoto damit vergleicht, „in den Wolken zu wohnen". Trotz der verschiedenen Schichten, die die Bewohner des Hauses von der Stadt trennen, nennt der Architekt die urbane Lebensform „einen wellenförmig ausgeprägten Ur-Raum, in dem Menschen leben". „Dieses Bauwerk", so der Architekt, „ist das Sinnbild des ultimativen Hauses, in dem alles – von den Anfängen der Welt bis hin zum spezifisch ausgeprägten Haus – in einer einzigen Methode zusammengeführt ist."

L'architecte décrit sa maison comme « trois coques de plus en plus grandes l'une dans l'autre ». La coque extérieure occupe 150 m² du terrain de 246 m², mais seule la coque interne, la plus petite, contient les espaces de vie. « J'ai toujours eu des interrogations sur les maisons séparées de la rue par un simple mur », explique Fujimoto, « et je me suis demandé s'il n'était pas intéressant d'étudier une certaine gradation dans ce domaine encore inexploré, en considérant les différentes perceptions de la distance entre la rue et la maison, par exemple : un lieu assez proche de la rue, un autre un peu plus éloigné, un autre enfin le plus loin possible pour assurer l'intimité ». Au final, il n'existe plus de barrière distincte entre la maison et la rue – sensation que Fujimoto compare à « vivre dans les nuages… » Malgré ces strates multiples qui isolent les résidants de la ville, l'architecte parle d'une « vibration de l'espace originel dans lequel vivent les humains… C'est la représentation de la maison ultime dans laquelle tout, des origines du monde à une maison spécifique, est conçu ensemble, avec une même méthode ».

In a typical Japanese residential neighborhood, the N House stands out because of its sharply defined white forms, but also because of its completely unexpected openings.

Inmitten eines typischen japanischen Wohngebiets fällt das Haus N durch seine scharf definierten weißen Formen, aber auch wegen seiner höchst überraschenden Fassadenöffnungen auf.

Insérée dans un quartier résidentiel japonais de style typique, la maison N se singularise par des formes très définies, sa blancheur étincelante et ses surprenantes ouvertures.

As these views from opposite angles demonstrate, the N House is open in almost every direction, providing light and an abundance of "intermediate" space that is not readily defined as being either interior or exterior.

Wie die Blicke aus gegenläufigen Perspektiven belegen, ist das Haus N in fast allen Richtungen offen, wodurch es sehr hell ist und eine Vielzahl von „Zwischenräumen" bietet, die sich nur bedingt als Innen- oder Außenraum definieren lassen.

Comme le montrent ces vues prises d'angles opposés, la maison N s'ouvre dans pratiquement toutes les directions, ce qui apporte beaucoup de lumière et crée une multiplicité d'espace « intermédiaires » que l'on ne peut définir comme intérieurs ou extérieurs.

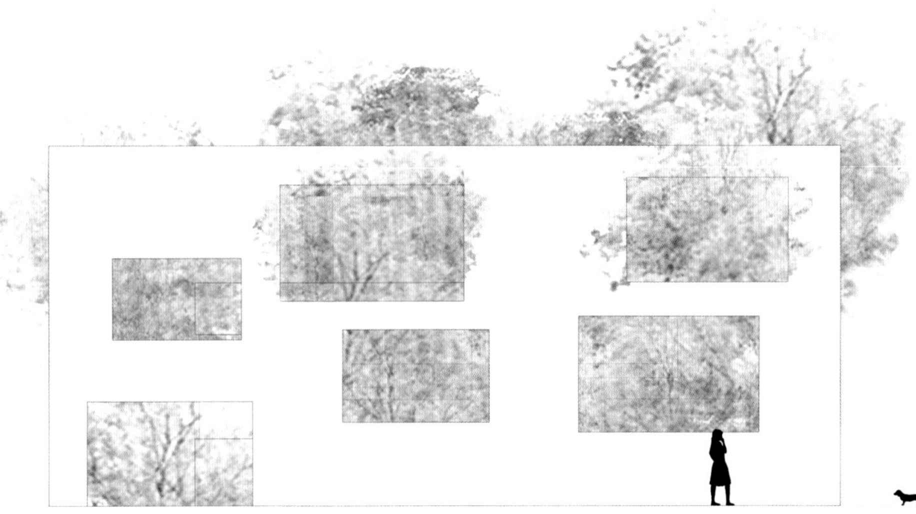

FINAL WOODEN HOUSE

Kumamura, Kumamoto, Japan, 2007–08

*Area: 22 m². Client: Kumamura Forestry Association. Cost: ¥4.246 million.
Collaboration: Hiroshi Kato*

The Final Wooden House has a sharply delineated cubic form, but the openings in its wooden façades are clearly irregular. Right, the natural wooden setting of the structure.

Grundform des Final Wooden House ist ein scharf umrissener Kubus, während die Öffnungen in der Fassade aus Holz deutlich unregelmäßig ausfallen. Rechts im Bild die waldige Umgebung des Hauses.

La maison de bois définitive est de forme cubique, mais ses ouvertures forment une composition de nature irrégulière. À droite, le cadre naturel boisé de la maison.

As usual, it is the architect himself who most clearly expresses the nature of the project. He engaged in a "mindless" stacking of 350-millimeter square pieces of lumber on a tiny, 15-square-meter site. "I envisioned the creation of new spatiality that preserves primitive conditions of a harmonious entity before various functions and roles differentiated," he says. There are no separations, no floors, no real walls or ceilings in this house, allowing visitors to "distribute themselves three-dimensionally in space." Floors become walls or chairs, as he says, causing visitors to rethink the entire idea of a building. "Rather than just a new architecture," Fujimoto concludes, "this is a new origin, a new existence."

Wie üblich ist es der Architekt selbst, der das Wesen seines Projekts am klarsten vermittelt. In diesem Fall entschied er sich, Bauholz mit einem quadratischen Querschnitt von 350 mm x 350 mm auf einem winzigen, 15 m² großen Grundstück „ohne Sinn und Verstand" übereinanderzuschichten. „Ich hatte die Vision von einem neuartigen Raumerlebnis, das die Urbeschaffenheit einer harmonischen Ganzheit ahnen lässt – bevor man begann, verschiedene Funktionen und Typen zu unterscheiden." Es gibt keine räumliche Gliederung, keine Geschosse, keine echten Wände oder Decken in diesem Haus, was Besuchern erlaubt, „sich dreidimensional im Raum zu verteilen". Böden werden zu Wänden oder Stühlen und regen die Besucher laut Fujimoto an, die Idee, was ein Haus sei, neu zu überdenken. „Es ist mehr als bloß ein neues Stück Architektur," fasst Fujimoto zusammen, „es ist ein neuer Anfang, eine neue Daseinsweise."

Comme souvent, c'est l'architecte lui-même qui exprime le mieux la nature de son projet. Il a entrepris d'empiler « de façon gratuite » des grumes de bois de section carrée de 35 cm de côté sur un petit espace de 15 m². « J'ai envisagé de créer une nouvelle spatialité qui préserve les conditions primitives d'une entité harmonieuse avant que n'interviennent certaines fonctions et rôles différenciés », explique-t-il. Il n'y a ni séparations, ni sols, ni vrais murs, ni plafonds dans cette maison pour permettre aux visiteurs de « se distribuer eux-mêmes en trois dimensions dans cet espace ». Comme il l'explique, les sols deviennent des murs ou des sièges entraînant chacun à repenser l'idée même de maison. « Plutôt que d'être simplement une nouvelle architecture », conclut Fujimoto, « c'est une nouvelle origine, une nouvelle existence. »

The unusual stacking method employed by the architect generates spaces that, in a sense, challenge residents (or rather users) to find a place to sit or to make the architecture theirs.

Die ungewöhnliche Stapelmethode, mit der der Architekt hier arbeitet, lässt einen Raum entstehen, der seine Bewohner (oder vielmehr Besucher) herausfordert, einen Sitzplatz zu finden und sich die Architektur zu eigen zu machen.

Le principe d'empilement pratiqué par l'architecte génère des volumes qui incitent les résidants (ou plutôt les usagers) à trouver d'eux-mêmes leur place et à s'approprier l'espace architectural.

Elevation drawings show how the façades echo the cutout forms of the interior volumes, where openings provide views of the outside where "normal" structures surely would not.

Die Aufrisse zeigen, wie die Fassaden mit den Aussparungen des Innenraums korrespondieren. Die Öffnungen bieten Ausblicke in den Außenraum, wie es „normale" Bauten sicher nicht tun würden.

Les élévations montrent comment la façade est déterminée par la découpe des volumes intérieurs. Les ouvertures offrent des vues sur l'extérieur à des endroits que des constructions « normales » ne permettraient pas.

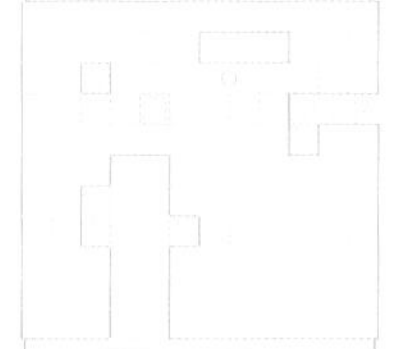

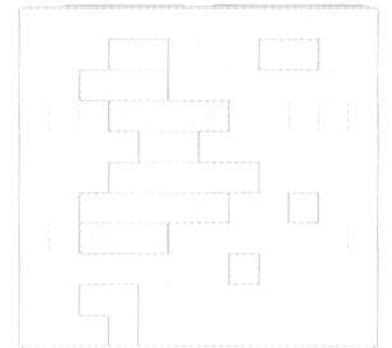

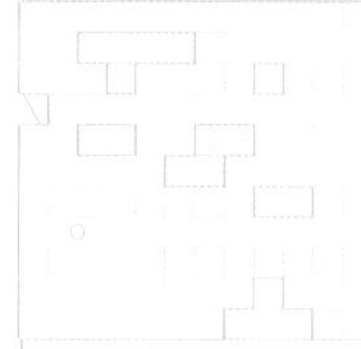

ALEXANDER GORLIN

Alexander Gorlin Architects
137 Varick Street
New York, NY 10013
USA

Tel: +1 212 229 1199
Fax: +1 212 206 3590
E-mail: agorlin@gorlinarchitects.com
Web: www.gorlinarchitects.com

ALEXANDER GORLIN received his Bachelor's degree from the Cooper Union School of Architecture (1978), his M.Arch from Yale (1980), and then worked in the offices of I. M. Pei and Partners (1981–82) and Kohn Pederson Fox (1984–85), before creating his own firm in 1986. He has been an Adjunct Professor at Yale (1982–90) and a Visiting Professor of Architecture at the Cooper Union (1999, 2000). He has designed housing in Santa Fe, Chicago, Nova Scotia, and Miami; synagogues in New York and Tulsa, Oklahoma; a boathouse at Yale (1998); the Gravesend Community Center in Brooklyn (2002); and participated in the competitions for the Berlin Spreebogen district (1993) and Madrid's Prado (1995). He has done residential work for such prestigious clients as Alexander Liberman, Grace Mirabella, and S. I. Newhouse. His World Trade Center Memorial proposal was exhibited at the 2002 Venice Biennale and he completed the apartment of Daniel Libeskind in New York (2004). Recent and current work includes the Aqua Apartment Tower in Miami; the Liberty Harbor townhouses in Jersey City (New Jersey); the Nir/Braufman's Southampton Beach House (Southampton, New York, 2005–08, published here); Nehemiah Spring Creek Affordable Housing (Brooklyn, New York, ongoing); and Common Ground Supportive Housing, a 200-unit facility for the formerly homeless, designed to achieve LEED Gold rating (Bronx, New York, 2010), all in the USA.

ALEXANDER GORLIN schloss sein Studium an der Cooper Union School of Architecture mit einem Bachelor ab (1978), erhielt seinen M.Arch. in Yale (1980) und arbeitete anschließend für I. M. Pei and Partners (1981–82) sowie für Kohn Pederson Fox (1984–85). 1986 gründete er sein eigenes Büro. Er war Lehrbeauftragter in Yale (1982–90) und Gastprofessor für Architektur an der Cooper Union (1999, 2000). Er entwarf Wohnbauten in Santa Fe, Chicago, Nova Scotia und Miami, Synagogen in New York und Tulsa, Oklahoma, ein Bootshaus in Yale (1998) und das Gravesend Community Center in Brooklyn (2002). Darüber hinaus beteiligte er sich an Wettbewerben für den Spreebogen in Berlin (1993) sowie den Prado in Madrid (1995). Er baute Häuser für so renommierte Auftraggeber wie Alexander Liberman, Grace Mirabella und S. I. Newhouse. Sein Entwurf für das World Trade Center Memorial wurde 2002 auf der Biennale von Venedig präsentiert, 2004 stellte er ein New Yorker Apartment für Daniel Libeskind fertig. Zu seinen jüngeren und aktuellen Projekten zählen der Aqua Apartment Tower in Miami, die Liberty Harbor Townhouses in Jersey City (New Jersey), ein Strandhaus für Nir/Braufman (Southampton, New York, 2005–08, hier vorgestellt), die kostengünstigen Wohnbauten in Nehemiah Spring Creek (Brooklyn, New York, in Arbeit) sowie das Projekt Common Ground Supportive Housing mit 200 Wohneinheiten für ehemalige Obdachlose, ausgezeichnet mit einer LEED-Goldmedaille für umweltschonendes Bauen (Bronx, New York, 2010), alle in den USA.

ALEXANDER GORLIN a reçu son B.Arch. de l'École d'architecture de la Cooper Union (1978), son M.Arch de l'université Yale (1980), puis a travaillé dans les agences d'I. M. Pei and Partners (1981–82) et Kohn Pederson Fox (1984–85), avant de fonder sa propre agence en 1986. Il a été professeur adjoint à Yale (1982–90) et professeur invité d'architecture à la Cooper Union (1999, 2000). Il a conçu des logements à Santa Fe, Chicago, Nova Scotia et Miami ; des synagogues à New York et Tulsa (Oklahoma) ; un hangar à bateaux à Yale (1998) ; le Gravesend Community Center à Brooklyn (2002) ; et participé aux concours pour le quartier du Spreebogen à Berlin (1993) et le musée du Prado à Madrid (1995). Il a construit des maisons pour des clients prestigieux, tels qu'Alexander Liberman, Grace Mirabella et S. I. Newhouse. Sa proposition de mémorial pour le World Trade Center a été exposée à la Biennale de Venise en 2002 ; et il aménagé l'appartement de Daniel Libeskind à New York (2004). Plus récemment, il a réalisé l'Aqua Apartment Tower à Miami ; les maisons de ville de Liberty Harbor à Jersey City (New Jersey) ; la maison de plage Nir/Braufman (Southampton, New York, 2005–08, publiée ici) ; des logements sociaux à Nehemiah Spring Creek (Brooklyn, New York, en cours) ; et le Common Ground Supportive Housing, un ensemble de deux cents logements pour les sans-abri répondant aux critères LEED Gold (Bronx, New York, 2010), le tout aux États-Unis.

SOUTHAMPTON BEACH HOUSE

Southampton, New York, USA, 2005–08

Area: 1022 m². Client: not disclosed.
Cost: not disclosed

At over 1000 square meters, this is by no means a modest house. The architect differentiates the façades, providing a continuous band of openings on the beach side (right).

Mit über 1000 m^2 ist dies zweifellos kein bescheidenes Haus. Der Architekt differenziert die Fassadenflächen und definiert ein durchgängiges Fensterband zur Strandseite (rechts).

Mesurant plus de 1000 m^2, cette résidence n'est certainement pas modeste. L'architecte a différencié les façades et créé un bandeau continu d'ouvertures du côté de la plage (à droite).

This ample summerhouse is located on a narrow piece of land situated between ocean and bay. African teak and pale limestone are prevalent cladding elements for the residence, which was designed for a family of four. There are three master bedrooms, three guest suites, staff quarters, and 557 square meters of living and entertainment space. The second-floor volume is cantilevered near the entrance to the house, creating a sheltered patio. A two-story staircase rises through an atrium to the main level of the house, where a central fireplace partitions the generous space into sitting and dining areas. The living space opens to a terraced patio and pool. The architect states: "Above, a great winglike canopy extends from the building, shading the house. In marked contrast to the substantial mass of the limestone building, this finely tapered form floats above the patio. Clad in a soft gray metal, it seems almost to disappear against a pale sky." A wood boardwalk leads from the pool to a private beach.

Das großzügige Sommerhaus liegt auf einer schmalen Landzunge zwischen dem offenen Meer und der Bucht. Verblendmaterialien für das Anwesen, das für eine vierköpfige Familie entworfen wurde, sind in erster Linie afrikanisches Teakholz und heller Sandstein. Es gibt drei Hauptschlafzimmer, drei Gästesuiten, Unterkünfte für Angestellte und 557 m^2 Wohn- und Freizeitfläche. Unweit des Eingangs kragt der Baukörper im ersten Obergeschoss aus, wodurch ein schattiger Terrassenplatz entsteht. Eine zweigeschossige Treppe führt vom Atrium in die Hauptebene des Hauses hinauf, wo ein zentraler Kamin den großzügigen Raum in Wohn- und Essbereich gliedert. Der Wohnbereich öffnet sich zur Terrasse mit Pool. „Ein großes Vordach", erläutert der Architekt, „ragt wie ein Flügel über den Bau hinaus und spendet Schatten. Die spitz zulaufende Form ist ein ausgeprägter Kontrast zur eindrucksvollen Masse des Sandsteinbaus und scheint über der Terrasse zu schweben. Verblendet mit mattgrauem Metall verschwindet das Dach beinahe gegen den blassen Himmel." Ein Holzsteg führt vom Pool hinunter zum privaten Strand.

Cette vaste résidence d'été aux murs en calcaire de couleur claire et teck africain se dresse sur une bande de terrain étroite entre l'océan et une baie. Elle a été conçue pour une famille de quatre personnes. On y trouve trois chambres principales, trois suites pour invités, des chambres pour domestiques et 557 m^2 de séjour et de réception. Le volume de l'étage en porte-à-faux de la maison crée un patio protégé de l'entrée. Un escalier s'élève de l'atrium vers le niveau principal, où une cheminée centrale divise le volume entre séjour et salle à manger. Le séjour ouvre sur un patio en terrasse et une piscine. « Un avant-toit important en forme d'aile se projette de la maison qu'il protège. Cette forme légèrement effilée semble flotter au-dessus du patio en contraste marqué avec la masse substantielle de la construction en pierre calcaire. Habillé de métal gris lisse, il semble presque disparaître sur le fond du ciel pâle », explique l'architecte. Une allée en planches de bois relie la piscine à une plage privée.

A pool and outdoor terrace allow residents to take in broad views of the ocean. A narrow wooden walkway (below) leads to the beach itself.

Pool und Terrasse bieten den Bewohnern einen weiten Blick auf das Meer. Ein schmaler Holzweg (unten) führt zum Strand hinunter.

Une piscine et une terrasse permettent de bénéficier d'une vue panoramique sur l'océan. Une étroite passerelle en bois (ci-dessous) donne accès à la plage.

A view of the living room shows how the architect has carefully orchestrated views up the steps, to the left, or out the front window, to the right. Below, a site plan showing the house and its walkway to the beach.

Ein Blick in den Wohnraum belegt, wie sorgsam der Architekt die Blickbeziehungen orchestriert, sei es nach links die Treppe hinauf oder nach rechts aus dem Hauptfenster hinaus. Unten ein Lageplan mit dem Haus und dem Steg zum Strand.

Une vue du séjour montre la façon dont l'architecte a soigneusement orchestré les vues vers l'escalier à gauche, ou la baie panoramique à droite. Ci-dessous, le plan du terrain montrant la maison et la passerelle qui conduit à la plage.

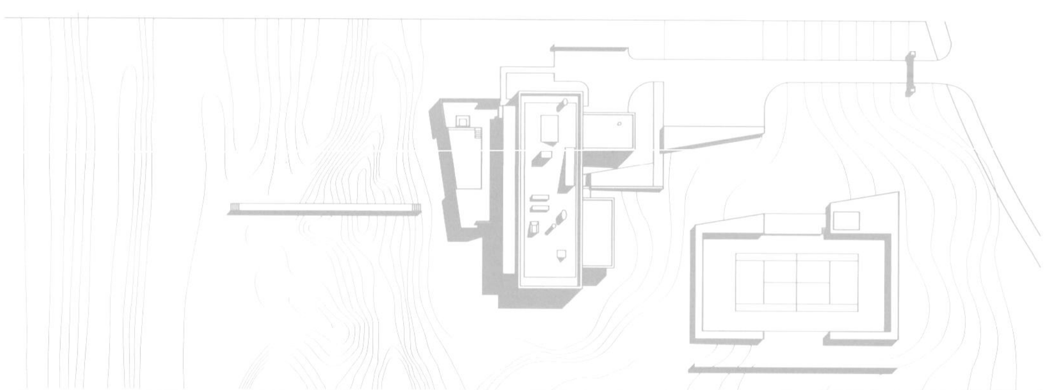

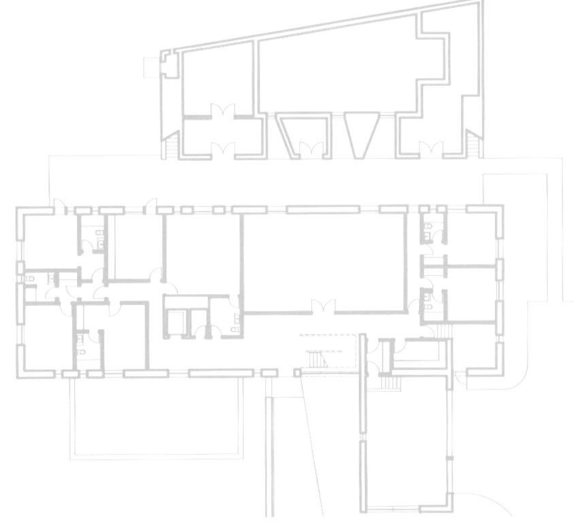

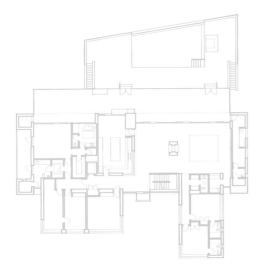

Floor plans (above), and kitchen and dining room views, with the ever-present views toward the broad beach.

Grundrisse (oben) sowie Innenansichten der Küche und des Essbereichs mit dem allgegenwärtigen Blick zum Strand.

Plans au sol (ci-dessus) et vues de la cuisine et de la salle à manger donnant sur l'océan omniprésent.

Todos Santos House

JORGE GRACIA GARCIA

Gracia Studio
6151 Progressive Avenue, Suite 200
San Diego, CA 92154
USA

Tel: +1 619 795 7864
E-mail: jorge@graciastudio.com
Web: www.graciastudio.com

JORGE GRACIA GARCIA was born in 1973 in Tijuana, Mexico, and graduated from the Universidad Iberoamericana Noroeste (Tijuana, Mexico, 1991–97). He worked in the Sebastian Mariscal Studio (2003–04), before creating his own firm in 2004. His recent projects are Casa GA (Tijuana, Mexico, 2004); Todos Santos House (Todos Santos, Baja California Sur, Mexico, 2006, published here); Casa Becerril (Tijuana, Mexico, 2006); a Design Center in Brickell (Miami, Florida, 2006/09–); a Hotel and Winery in Mexico's wine country Valle de Guadalupe (under construction); and a Culinary School (Tijuana, Mexico, under construction).

JORGE GRACIA GARCIA wurde 1973 in Tijuana, Mexiko, geboren und schloss sein Studium an der Universidad Iberoamericana Noroeste (Tijuana, Mexiko, 1991–97) ab. Er war für Sebastian Mariscal Studio (2003–04) tätig, bevor er 2004 sein eigenes Büro gründete. Zu seinen jüngeren Projekten zählen Casa GA (Tijuana, Mexiko, 2004), ein Haus in Todos Santos (Baja California Sur, Mexiko, 2006, hier vorgestellt), Casa Becerril (Tijuana, Mexiko, 2006), ein Design Center in Brickell (Miami, Florida, seit 2006/09), ein Hotel und Weingut in Mexikos Weinbauregion Valle de Guadalupe (im Bau) sowie eine Kochschule (Tijuana, Mexiko, im Bau).

JORGE GRACIA GARCIA, né en 1973 à Tijuana au Mexique, est diplômé de l'Université ibéro-américaine Noroeste (Tijuana, Mexique, 1991–97). Il a travaillé pour le Sebastian Mariscal Studio (2003–04), avant de créer sa propre agence en 2004. Parmi ses projets récents : la Casa GA (Tijuana, Mexique, 2004) ; la Maison Todos Santos (Todos Santos, Basse-Californie-du-Sud, Mexique, 2006, publié ici) ; la Casa Becerril (Tijuana, Mexique, 2006) ; un centre de design à Brickell (Miami, Floride, depuis 2006/09) ; un hôtel et un chais dans la région viticole mexicaine Valle de Guadalupe (en construction) ; et une école de cuisine (Tijuana, Mexique, en construction).

TODOS SANTOS HOUSE

Todos Santos, Baja California Sur, Mexico, 2006

Area: 320 m². Client: Arnaud Gregori.
Cost: not disclosed

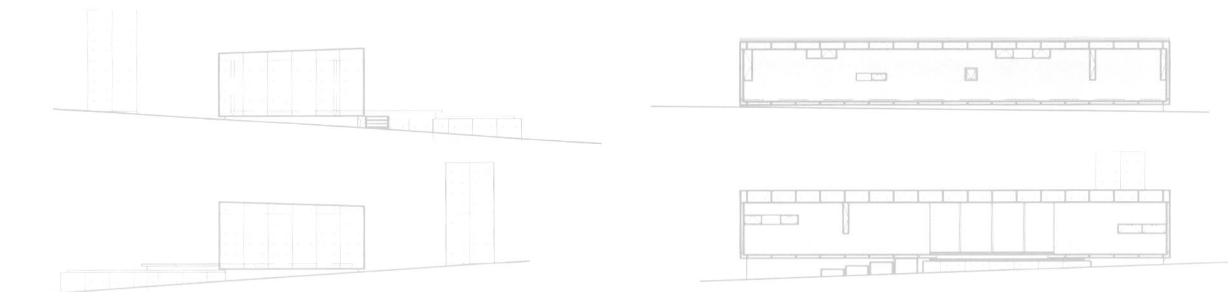

One hour south of La Paz Baja California Sur, this is the town where the Hotel California of the Eagles 1976 song stands. The location required that all materials and labor be local, this in a town with just two hardware stores. Two comparable houses, each with an ocean view, were required. An "indoor-outdoor" area at the heart of the structure was also part of the scheme. Sand-colored exposed concrete walls and typical *talavera* tiles were the main construction materials. Three bedrooms and two bathrooms compliment the main area of the house reserved for dining and living space opening to the pool and terrace. The architect states: "The most important thing for us was to create a place where people can enjoy the company of friends and family, and at the same time enjoy nature and get to the basics of life."

Eine Stunde südlich von La Paz Baja California Sur liegt der Ort Todos Santos, in dem das Hotel aus dem Eagles-Song „Hotel California" von 1976 steht. Aufgrund der Lage des Hauses mussten sämtliche Materialien lokal verfügbar sein und von örtlichen Firmen verbaut werden, schließlich gibt es in diesem Städtchen nur zwei Eisenwarenhandlungen. Gewünscht waren zwei ähnliche Baukörper, beide mit Blick aufs Meer. Teil des Konzepts war ein zentraler „Innen-/Außenbereich". Hauptmaterialien sind sandfarbene Mauern aus Sichtbeton und regionaltypische Fliesen, die *talavera*. Drei Schlafzimmer und zwei Bäder ergänzen den zentralen Wohn- und Essbereich des Hauses, der sich zu Terrasse und Pool hin öffnet. „Am wichtigsten für uns war es," erklärt der Architekt, „einen Ort zu schaffen, an dem man Zeit mit Freunden und Familie verbringen und zugleich die Natur genießen, zu den wesentlichen Dingen des Lebens zurückfinden kann."

La maison se trouve à une heure au sud de La Paz, dans l'État de Basse-Californie-du-Sud, la ville du fameux Hotel California de la chanson des Eagles (1976). Éloigné de tout, le lieu choisi faisait que tous les matériaux et la main d'œuvre devaient être locaux, même si l'approvisionnement sur place était difficile. Le programme comprenait deux maisons avec vue sur l'océan, chacune possédant un espace dedans/dehors intégré. Les principaux matériaux de construction sont le béton apparent pour les murs de couleur sable et les tuiles locales typiques, les *talaveras*. En dehors du volume principal consacré au séjour et à la zone des repas et ouvrant sur la piscine et la terrasse, trois chambres et deux salles de bains ont été aménagées. « La chose la plus importante pour nous était de créer un lieu où recevoir agréablement la famille et les amis, et, en même temps, de profiter simplement de la nature et des plaisirs essentiels de la vie », précise l'architecte.

Long and low, the house fits into its arid natural setting as though it is meant to be there. A pool and exterior terrace retain the same minimal appearance, at the edge of the desert.

Das langgestreckte, niedrige Haus fügt sich in die trockene Landschaft ein, als müsse es hier stehen. Auch Pool und Terrasse sind ein ähnlich minimalistischer Eingriff in diesen Ausläufer der Wüste.

Allongée et surbaissée, la maison s'intègre dans son cadre naturel comme si elle n'aurait pu être ailleurs. La piscine et la terrasse en limite du désert sont traitées dans le même esprit minimaliste.

GRAFT

Graft Gesellschaft von Architekten GmbH
Heidestr. 50
10557 Berlin
Germany

Tel: +49 30 24 04 79 85
Fax: +49 30 24 04 79 87
E-mail: berlin@graftlab.com
Web: www.graftlab.com

GRAFT was created in Los Angeles in 1998 "as a label for architecture, art, music, and the pursuit of happiness." Lars Krückeberg, Wolfram Putz, Thomas Willemeit, Gregor Hoheisel, and Alejandra Lillo are the partners of Graft, which today employs about 20 architects and artists in the United States, Europe, and Asia. Graft has offices in Los Angeles, Berlin, and Beijing. Lars Krückeberg was educated at the Technische Universität Braunschweig, Germany, as an engineer (1989–96), and at SCI-Arc in Los Angeles (1997–98). Wolfram Putz attended the Technische Universität Braunschweig (1988–95), the University of Utah, Salt Lake City (1992–93), and SCI-Arc in Los Angeles (1996–98). Thomas Willemeit was also educated in Braunschweig, and at the Bauhaus Dessau (1991–92), before working in the office of Daniel Libeskind (1998–2001). Taking advantage of their German background combined with US training, they have built a studio and house for the actor Brad Pitt in Los Angeles (2000–03); designed a private dental clinic; and Hotel Q! in Berlin. They have designed restaurants in the Mirage and Bellagio Casinos in Las Vegas and worked on several luxury resort hotels in the Caribbean, including locations in the Turcs and Caicos and in the Dominican Republic. Working with Brad Pitt and William McDonough + Partners, Graft helped organize the Pink Project and Make it Right initiative in New Orleans and are one of the group of architects designing the houses (two houses published here).

GRAFT entstand 1998 in Los Angeles als „ein Label für Architektur, Kunst, Musik und das Streben nach Glück". Lars Krückeberg, Wolfram Putz, Thomas Willemeit, Gregor Hoheisel und Alejandra Lillo sind Partner bei Graft, das heute in den Vereinigten Staaten, Europa und Asien etwa 20 Architekten und Künstler beschäftigt und Büros in Los Angeles, Berlin und Peking unterhält. Lars Krückeberg studierte an der Technischen Universität Braunschweig Bauingenieurwesen (1989–96) und am SCI-Arc in Los Angeles (1997–98). Wolfram Putz studierte von 1988 bis 1995 an der TU Braunschweig, 1992 bis 1993 an der University of Utah in Salt Lake City und von 1996 bis 1998 schließlich an der SCI-Arc in Los Angeles. Thomas Willemeit wurde ebenfalls in Braunschweig ausgebildet, anschließend am Bauhaus Dessau (1991–92), ehe er im Büro von Daniel Libeskind arbeitete (1998–2001). Die Architekten profitieren von ihrem deutschen Hintergrund und ihrer Ausbildung in den USA. Sie bauten in Los Angeles ein Studio und Haus für den Schauspieler Brad Pitt (2000–03) und entwarfen eine private Zahnklinik sowie das Hotel Q! in Berlin. Sie gestalteten Restaurants in den Kasinos Mirage und Bellagio in Las Vegas und arbeiteten an mehreren Luxusresorts in der Karibik, darunter an Standorten auf den Turks- und Caicosinseln und in der Dominikanischen Republik. Gemeinsam mit Brad Pitt und William McDonough + Partners war Graft bei der Organisation des Pink Project und der Make-it-Right-Initiative in New Orleans beteiligt und ist Teil eines Architektenteams, das dort Häuser entworfen hat (von denen zwei hier vorgestellt werden).

L'agence **GRAFT** a été fondée à Los Angeles, en 1998, « comme label d'architecture, d'art, de musique, et de recherche du bonheur ». Lars Krückeberg, Wolfram Putz, Thomas Willemeit, Gregor Hoheisel et Alejandra Lillo sont les associés de Graft qui emploie aujourd'hui une vingtaine d'architectes et d'artistes aux États-Unis, en Europe et en Asie. L'agence possède des bureaux à Los Angeles, Berlin et Pékin. Lars Krückeberg a fait ses études d'ingénieur à l'université technique de Braunschweig (Allemagne, 1989–96) et à SCI-Arc à Los Angeles (1997–98). Wolfram Putz a également étudié à l'université technique de Braunschweig (1988–95), à l'université de l'Utah à Salt Lake City (1992–93) et à SCI-Arc à Los Angeles (1996–98). Thomas Willemeit a également fait ses études à Braunschweig et au Bauhaus Dessau (1991–92), avant de travailler chez Daniel Libeskind (1998–2001). Ils proposent ainsi une formation à la fois allemande et américaine. Ils ont construit un atelier et une maison pour l'acteur Brad Pitt à Los Angeles (2000–03) ; conçu une clinique dentaire privée ; l'hôtel Q à Berlin. Ils ont conçu les restaurants des casinos Mirage et Bellagio à Las Vegas et travaillé sur plusieurs projets d'hôtels de vacances de luxe dans la Caraïbe (Turks et Caicos, République dominicaine). En collaboration avec Brad Pitt et William McDonough + Partners, Graft a travaillé à l'organisation du Pink Project et du programme Make it Right à la Nouvelle-Orléans, et fait partie des architectes chargés d'y construire des maisons (dont les deux publiées ici).

MAKE IT RIGHT

New Orleans, Louisiana, USA, 2007–

Area: 167 m² (MIR Camelback House); 111 m² (MIR Shotgun House). Client: Make it Right Foundation. Cost: not disclosed. Curators: Brad Pitt / Graft

The Lower Ninth Ward, long known for its high proportion of resident ownership, was left devastated and homeless in the wake of Hurricane Katrina in August 2005. The Pink Project, the inaugural event for Brad Pitt's **MAKE IT RIGHT** initiative, was intended to focus attention on the Lower Ninth Ward. The organizers called Pink "the virtual city of hope," erecting pink tents where it is hoped 150 homes will be built again. Graft and William McDonough + Partners collaborated with Brad Pitt, Reed Kroloff, and the Lower Ninth Ward Community Coalition to develop a scheme that would eventually call on a total of 13 local, national, and international architects to design low-cost houses for the area. By April 2009, six houses had been erected. Two of these, shown here, were designed by Graft, and received LEED Platinum certification. The Camelback concept involves the local tradition of adding a partial second story to a house, while the Shotgun House is characterized by "an expressive, almost exaggerated, gable roof and generous front porch." Both of the houses are prefabricated modular units, assembled off site.

Das Stadtviertel Lower Ninth Ward in New Orleans, lange bekannt für seinen hohen Anteil an Eigenheimbesitzern, lag nach dem Hurrikan Katrina 2005 in Trümmern, viele Anwohner waren obdachlos. Das sogenannte Pink Project, der Startschuss für Brad Pitts Initiative **MAKE IT RIGHT**, sollte die öffentliche Aufmerksamkeit auf Lower Ninth Ward lenken. Die Organisatoren erklärten das Pink Project zur „virtuellen Stadt der Hoffnung" und errichteten pinkfarbene Zelte auf einem Gelände, auf dem in Zukunft wieder 150 Eigenheime entstehen sollen. Graft und William McDonough + Partners erarbeiteten gemeinsam mit Brad Pitt, Reed Kroloff und der Anwohnerinitiative des Lower Ninth Ward ein Konzept, das 13 ortsansässige, nationale und internationale Architekten zusammenführt, um kostengünstige Häuser für die Gegend zu entwerfen. Im April 2009 waren bereits sechs Häuser realisiert. Zwei dieser Bauten, hier vorgestellt, wurden von Graft entworfen und erhielten eine LEED-Platinzertifizierung. Der Haustyp Camelback greift eine ortstypische Bauweise auf – Häuser mit einem kleineren Obergeschoss –, während sich der Typ Shotgun durch ein „expressives, fast überzeichnetes Giebeldach und eine Veranda an der Vorderseite" auszeichnet. Beide Haustypen werden mit Fertigbaumodulen außerhalb der Baustelle montiert.

Le Lower Ninth Ward, un quartier de la Nouvelle-Orléans longtemps connu pour sa forte proportion de propriétaires résidants, a été dévasté par l'ouragan Katrina en août 2005 qui a fait de nombreux sans-abri. Le « Pink Project », manifestation inaugurale du programme **MAKE IT RIGHT** lancé par l'acteur Brad Pitt, avait pour but d'attirer l'attention sur cette zone ravagée. Ses organisateurs ont parlé de « cité virtuelle de l'espoir » et érigé des tentes roses là où ils prévoyaient de reconstruire cent cinquante maisons. Graft et William McDonough + Partners ont collaboré avec Brad Pitt, Reed Kroloff et la Lower Ninth Ward Community Coalition pour mettre au point un plan d'action faisant appel à treize agences d'architecture locales, nationales ou internationales pour concevoir des maisons économiques. En avril 2009, six maisons avaient été édifiées. Deux d'entre elles, montrées ici, conçues par Graft, ont reçu la certification LEED Platinum. Le concept de la maison Camelback fait appel à la tradition locale d'ajout d'un étage partiel, tandis que la maison Shotgun se caractérise par « une façade à pignon expressive, presque exagérée, et un généreux porche à l'avant ». Ces deux maisons ont été construites à l'aide d'éléments modulaires préfabriqués assemblés sur le site.

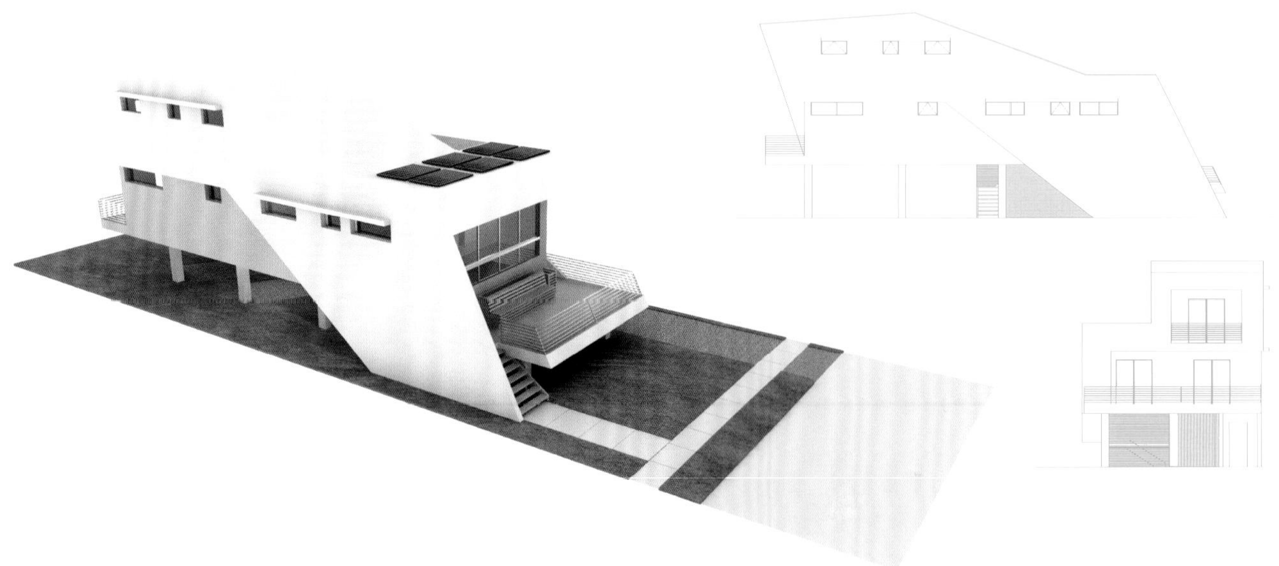

Lifting the house off the ground in good part, the architects create a sheltered parking area, but also protect the house from future flooding.

Indem die Architekten das Haus größtenteils aufständerten, schufen sie Raum für einen überdachten Carport und schützen den Bau zugleich vor potenziellen Überschwemmungen.

En soulevant une grande partie de la maison sur des pilotis, les architectes ont créé un parking abrité et protègent la maison du danger d'éventuelles inondations.

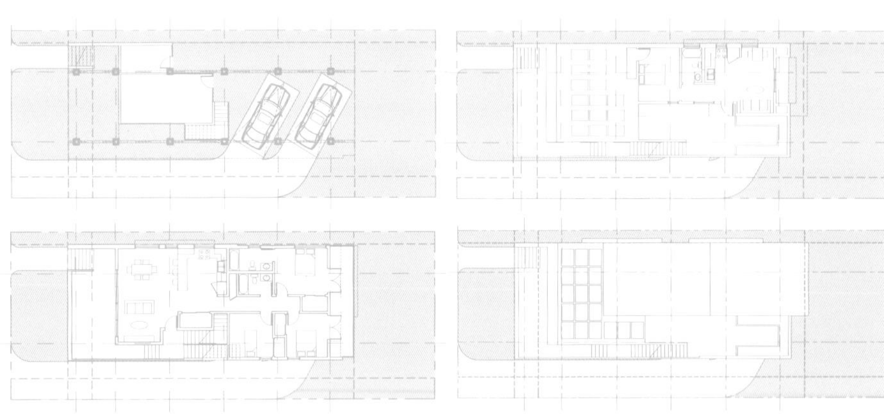

The basic modesty of row houses is retained in these designs, but, again, the structures are lifted, at least partially, above the ground. Interior spaces are modern and generous.

Die Entwürfe wahren die prinzipielle Bescheidenheit solcher Reihenhäuser. Auch hier sind die Bauten, zumindest teilweise, aufgeständert. Die Innenräume sind großzügig und modern.

La modestie des anciennes maisons alignées a été conservée dans ces projets. Les constructions sont partiellement suspendues. Les volumes intérieurs sont modernes et généreux.

HANGAR DESIGN GROUP

Hangar House
Via Terraglio 89/b
31021 Mogliano Veneto
Treviso
Italy

Tel: +39 041 593 60 00
Fax: +39 041 593 60 06
E-mail: hdg@hangar.it
Web: www.hangar.it

HANGAR DESIGN GROUP is a multidisciplinary firm founded in 1980 by Alberto Bovo (born in Padua, Italy, in 1954) and Sandro Manente (born in Venice, Italy, in 1957). Both graduated from the Università IUAV di Venezia, respectively in 1980 and 1982. Hangar has offices in Milan, New York, Barcelona, and Shanghai. Notable projects developed by the firm include the renovation of La Rinascente headquarters in Milan (2002); the signage system for Lotto Headquarters in Treviso (2002); several design products, including technical lighting systems (2003); the corporate image of the Peggy Guggenheim Collection in Venice (2004); the renovation of the Pratt Institute in New York (USA, 2005); the Environmental Graphics for San Siro Stadium in Milan for Pivato Group (2006); an office table (2006); the interior design for Manhattan apartments and townhouses (USA, 2005–07); the signage system for Wujiang Road in Shanghai (China, 2007); the packaging of the Ferrarelle "Platinum Edition" official water bottle of the Salone Internazionale del Mobile (Milan, 2008); a multi-brand store design for Zucchi in Milan (2008); urban furniture (2008); the brand image for luxury apartments in Rome (2009); and outdoor furniture (2009), all in Italy unless stated otherwise. The Joshua Tree Mobile Home project published here received a mention in the ADI contest for the 2011 Golden Compass.

Die multidisziplinäre **HANGAR DESIGN GROUP** wurde 1980 von Alberto Bovo (geboren 1954 in Padua) und Sandro Manente (geboren 1957 in Venedig) gegründet. Beide schlossen ihr Architekturstudium an der Università IUAV di Venezia ab, Bovo 1980, Manente 1982. Hangar unterhält Büros in Mailand, New York, Barcelona und Shanghai. Namhafte Projekte des Büros sind u. a. die Sanierung der Zentrale von La Rinascente in Mailand (2002), das Leitsystem der Lotto-Zentrale in Treviso (2002), diverse Designprodukte, darunter auch technische Beleuchtungssysteme (2003), das Erscheinungsbild der Peggy-Guggenheim-Sammlung in Venedig (2004), die Sanierung des Pratt Institute in New York (USA, 2005), das Gesamtdesignkonzept für das San-Siro-Stadion in Mailand für die Pivato-Gruppe (2006), ein Bürotisch (2006), die Innenarchitektur für Apartments und Townhouses in Manhattan (USA, 2005–07), das Leitsystem für die Wujiang-Straße in Shanghai (China, 2007), das Verpackungsdesign für die Ferrarelle „Platinum Edition", die offizielle Wasserflasche des Salone Internazionale del Mobile (Mailand, 2008), die Ladengestaltung eines Multi-Brand-Stores für Zucchi in Mailand (2008), Stadtmöbel (2008), die Markenentwicklung für Luxusapartments in Rom (2009) sowie Gartenmöbel (2009), alle in Italien, soweit nicht anders vermerkt. Das hier vorgestellte Joshua Tree Mobile Home fand im ADI-Wettbewerb für den Golden Compass 2011 lobende Erwähnung.

HANGAR DESIGN GROUP est une agence pluridisciplinaire fondée en 1980 par Alberto Bovo, né à Padoue, Italie, en 1954, et Sandro Manente, né à Venise en 1957. Tous deux sont diplômés de l'Université IUAV de Venise, respectivement en 1980 et 1982. Hangar possède des bureaux à Milan, New York, Barcelone et Shanghaï. Parmi leurs principales réalisations : la rénovation du siège de La Rinascente (Milan, 2002) ; la signalétique du siège du lotto (Trévise, 2002) ; le design de plusieurs produits, dont des systèmes d'éclairage (2003) ; l'image institutionnelle de la Collection Peggy Guggenheim (Venise, 2004) ; la rénovation du Pratt Institute à New York (2005) ; le décor graphique du stade San Siro pour le groupe Pivato (Milan, 2006) ; une table de bureau (2006) ; la décoration intérieure d'appartements et de maisons à Manhattan (New York, 2005–07) ; la signalétique de Wujiang Road (Shanghaï, 2007) ; le conditionnement de la bouteille d'eau officielle Ferrarelle « Platinum Edition » pour le Salon international du meuble (Milan, 2008) ; un magasin multimarques pour Zucchi (Milan, 2008) ; du mobilier urbain (2008) ; l'image de marque d'un programme d'appartements de luxe (Rome, 2009) ; et du mobilier d'extérieur (2009), le tout en Italie, sauf mention contraire. Le projet d'habitat mobile Joshua Tree publié ici a reçu une mention de l'ADI (Associazione per il Designo Industriale) au Compas d'Or 2011.

JOSHUA TREE MOBILE HOME

Italy, 2008

Area: 32 m². Client: Agora Prefab.
Cost: not disclosed

The idea of this house was to challenge some of the presuppositions concerning mobile homes. Despite its very restricted size, the Joshua Tree has "living areas (kitchen and living room), space for rest and well-being (bedrooms and baths) or relaxation (verandas), giving forms and functions to suit different moods." Factory assembled, the house might best be used in an Alpine setting, with its sloped roof that includes windows, and its mountain cabin appearance. But all is not as it seems in this instance, because rather than wood cladding, steel, zinc, and titanium plates are used in the place of traditional wood shingles. With an external height of 3.5 meters, the house is 8.5 meters long and 4 meters wide. It includes one bedroom with a double bed, one with two single beds, two bathrooms, one shower, and a kitchen/living area.

Die Idee zur Schaffung dieses Hauses war, bestehende Vorurteile gegenüber Mobilhäusern infrage zu stellen. Trotz der sehr begrenzten Größe verfügt das Joshua Tree Mobile Home über „Wohnbereiche (Küche und Wohnzimmer), Räume für Ruhe und Wellness (Schlafzimmer und Bäder) oder Entspannung (Veranden), sodass Formen und Funktionen den verschiedensten Stimmungen gerecht werden". Das werksmontierte Haus hat ein Satteldach mit Fenstern und erinnert optisch an eine Berghütte, weshalb es sich besonders gut in alpinen Gegenden einsetzen lässt. Doch hier ist nicht alles wie es scheint: Denn anstelle einer Holzverkleidung dienen Stahl-, Zink- und Titanplatten als Ersatz für traditionelle Holzschindeln. Bei einer Außenhöhe von 3,5 m ist das Haus 8,5 m lang und 4 m breit. Es umfasst ein Schlafzimmer mit Doppelbett, ein Schlafzimmer mit einem Etagenbett, zwei Bäder, eine Dusche und einen Küchen- und Wohnbereich.

L'idée de cette maison part de la remise en cause d'un certain nombre de présupposés liés à l'habitat mobile. Malgré ses dimensions réduites, elle possède « une aire de vie (séjour et cuisine), un espace pour le repos et le bien-être (chambres et bains), un pour la relaxation (vérandas), permettant des dispositifs et des fonctions adaptées à différents modes de vie ». Montée en atelier, elle convient à un cadre alpestre par son toit en pente à fenêtres intégrées et son aspect de chalet. Mais tout n'est pas tel qu'on pourrait le penser puisque le bardage de bois traditionnel a été remplacé par des plaques d'acier, de zinc et de titane. L'ensemble mesure 3,5 m de haut, 8,5 m de long et 4 m de large pour une chambre à lit double, une à deux lits simples, deux cabinets de toilette, une douche et un séjour cuisine.

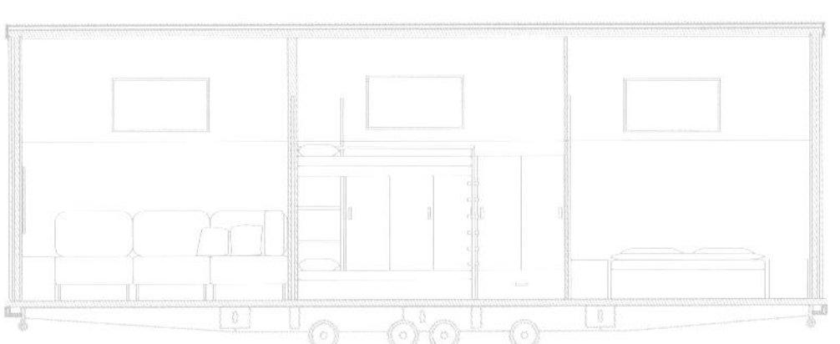

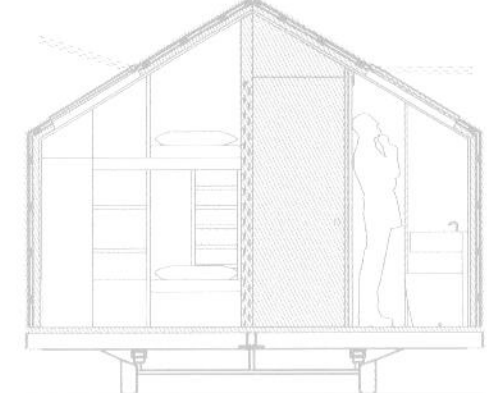

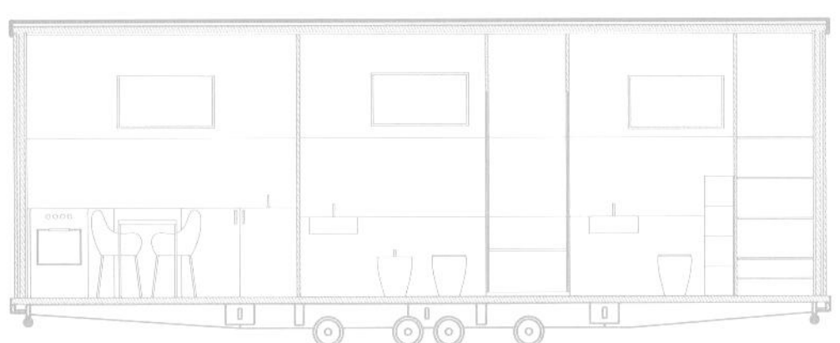

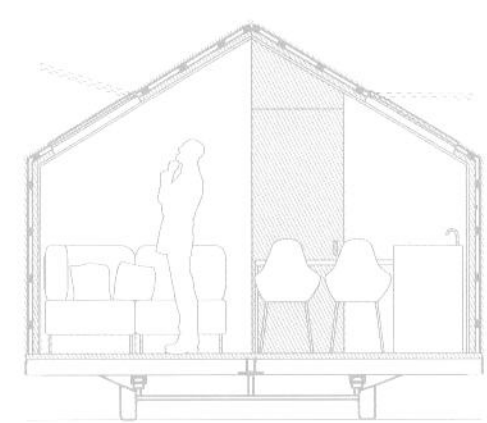

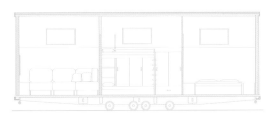

The extremely simple house might appear to be set up on pillars, but as the drawings (above) show, four sets of wheels are incorporated into the base, making this a truly mobile home.

Das höchst einfache Haus wirkt, als ruhe es auf Pfählen. Doch die Zeichnungen oben verraten, dass vier Radpaare in den Sockel integriert wurden, wodurch das Heim tatsächlich zum Mobilheim wird.

Extrêmement simple d'aspect, la maison semble montée sur pilotis, mais comme le montrent les dessins ci-dessus, elle repose en fait sur des roues qui en font un vrai mobile home.

Interiors look less like a typical mobile home than a modestly sized prefabricated house of another type.

Das Interieur erinnert weniger an ein typisches Mobilheim als vielmehr an ein bescheiden dimensioniertes Fertighaus anderer Machart.

L'intérieur fait moins penser à un mobile home qu'à une maison préfabriquée de taille modeste.

Right, a drawing showing a community of mobile homes. The integration of beds or kitchen space into the minimal floor area shows a careful attention to detail.

Rechts der Entwurf einer Mobilheimsiedlung. Der Einbau der Betten und Kücheneinheiten auf engstem Raum zeugt von hoher Aufmerksamkeit für Details.

À droite, illustration mettant en scène une petite communauté composée de mobile homes. L'implantation des lits comme les aménagements de la cuisine dans cet espace réduit témoignent de l'attention portée aux détails.

HHF

HHF architects
Allschwiler Str. 71A / 4055 Basel
Switzerland

Tel: +41 61 756 70 10 / Fax: +41 61 756 70 11
E-mail: info@hhf.ch / Web: www.hhf.ch

HHF architects was founded in 2003 by Tilo Herlach, Simon Hartmann, and Simon Frommenwiler. Tilo Herlach was born in 1972 in Zurich. He studied architecture at the ETH Zurich and at the EPFL in Lausanne (1992–98). He subsequently worked with d-company in Bern (2001–03), and with Rolf Furrer Architekten (Basel, 2003). Simon Hartmann was born in 1974 in Bern, and studied architecture at the EPFL, TU Berlin, and the ETH Zurich (1994–2003). From 1997 to 2003, he worked with Nicola di Battista in Rome, A.B.D.R., Garofalo & Miura, Steuerwald + Scheiwiller Architekten, Basel, and Rolf Furrer Architekten, in Basel. Hartmann has been a teaching assistant at the ETH Studio Basel, working with Jacques Herzog, Pierre de Meuron, Roger Diener, and Marcel Meili since 2002, and head of teaching there since 2005. Simon Frommenwiler was born in London in 1972. He attended the ETH in Zurich (1994–2000), and worked subsequently with Bearth & Deplazes, Chur, ARchos Architecture, Basel, and Skidmore, Owings & Merrill in New York. Simon Frommenwiler has been a teaching assistant working with Harry Gugger at the EPFL in Lausanne since 2005. HHF have recently worked on the Jinhua Sculpture Park Baby Dragon (Jinhua, China, 2006); "Ono" Bar-Café-Lounge (Basel, Switzerland, 2006); SonVida Housing (Bottmingen, Switzerland, 2003–07); Artfarm, showroom and storage for art (Clinton, New York, USA, 2006–07); Tsai Residence (Ancram, New York, USA, 2006–08, published here); Cafeteria Kirschgarten High School (Basel, Switzerland, 2006–08); Dune House (Ordos, Inner Mongolia, China, 2008–09, also published here); and Fashion Center Labels 2 (Berlin, Germany, 2007–10).

HHF wurde 2003 von Tilo Herlach, Simon Hartmann und Simon Frommenwiler gegründet. Tilo Herlach, 1972 in Zürich geboren, studierte Architektur an der ETH Zürich und der EPFL in Lausanne (1992–98). Anschließend arbeitete er für d-company in Bern (2001–03) und Rolf Furrer Architekten (Basel, 2003). Simon Hartmann wurde 1974 in Bern geboren und studierte Architektur an der EPFL, der TU Berlin und der ETH Zürich (1994–2003). Von 1997 bis 2003 arbeitete er für Nicola di Battista in Rom, A.B.D.R., Garofalo & Miura, Steuerwald + Scheiwiller Architekten, Basel, und Rolf Furrer Architekten in Basel. Ab 2002 war Hartmann Lehrassistent am ETH Studio Basel, wo er mit Jacques Herzog, Pierre de Meuron, Roger Diener und Marcel Meili zusammenarbeitete, seit 2005 leitet er dort die Lehre. Simon Frommenwiler wurde 1972 in London geboren. Nach seinem Studium an der ETH Zürich (1994–2000) war er für Bearth & Deplazes, Chur, ARchos Architecture, Basel, und Skidmore, Owings & Merrill in New York tätig. Simon Frommenwiler ist seit 2005 Lehrassistent bei Harry Gugger an der EPFL in Lausanne. In letzter Zeit arbeitete HHF am „Baby Dragon" im Skulpturenpark Jinhua (Jinhua, China, 2006), der Bar-Café-Lounge „Ono" (Basel, Schweiz, 2006), dem Wohnbauprojekt SonVida (Bottmingen, Schweiz, 2003–07), der Artfarm, einem Ausstellungsraum und Lager für Kunst (Clinton, New York, USA, 2006–07), der Tsai Residence (Ancram, New York, USA, 2006–08, hier vorgestellt), der Kirschgarten Schulcafeteria (Basel, Schweiz, 2006–08), dem Dune House (Ordos, Innere Mongolei, China, 2008–09, ebenfalls hier vorgestellt) sowie dem Modezentrum Labels 2 (Berlin, Deutschland, 2007–10).

L'agence **HHF** architects a été fondée en 2003 par Tilo Herlach, Simon Hartmann et Simon Frommenwiler. Tilo Herlach, né en 1972 à Zurich, a étudié l'architecture à l'ETH à Zurich et à l'EPFL à Lausanne (1992–98). Il a ensuite travaillé pour d-company à Berne (2001–03) et Rolf Furrer Architekten (Bâle, 2003). Simon Hartmann, né en 1974 à Berne, a étudié l'architecture à l'EPFL, à la TU Berlin et à l'ETH à Zurich (1994–2003). De 1997 à 2003, il a travaillé pour Nicola di Battista à Rome, A.B.D.R., Garofalo & Miura, Steuerwald + Scheiwiller Architekten (Bâle), et Rolf Furrer Architekten, à Bâle. Hartmann a été enseignant assistant à l'ETH à Bâle et a travaillé avec Jacques Herzog, Pierre de Meuron, Roger Diener et Marcel Meili depuis 2002, avant de devenir directeur de l'enseignement en 2005. Simon Frommenwiler, né à Londres en 1972, a étudié à l'ETH à Zurich (1994–2000), puis travaillé pour Bearth & Deplazes (Chur), ARchos Architecture (Bâle) et Skidmore, Owings & Merrill à New York. Simon Frommenwiler a été enseignant assistant, travaillant avec Harry Gugger à l'EPFL à Lausanne depuis 2005. HHF est récemment intervenu sur le projet du Jinhua Sculpture Park, Baby Dragon (Jinhua, Chine, 2006) ; le « Ono » Bar-Café-Lounge (Bâle, Suisse, 2006) ; les logements SonVida (Bottmingen, Suisse, 2003–07) ; le showroom et entrepôt d'art Artfarm (Clinton, New York, USA, 2006–07) ; la résidence Tsai (Ancram, New York, 2006–08, publiée ici) ; la Cafeteria du collège du Kirschgarten (Bâle, 2006–08) ; la maison sur la dune (Ordos, Mongolie intérieure, Chine, 2008–09, publiée ici) ; et le Centre de mode Labels 2 (Berlin, Allemagne, 2007–10).

TSAI RESIDENCE

Ancram, New York, USA, 2006–08

Area: 375 m². Clients: Christopher Tsai, André Stockamp.
Cost: not disclosed. Collaboration: Ai Wei Wei

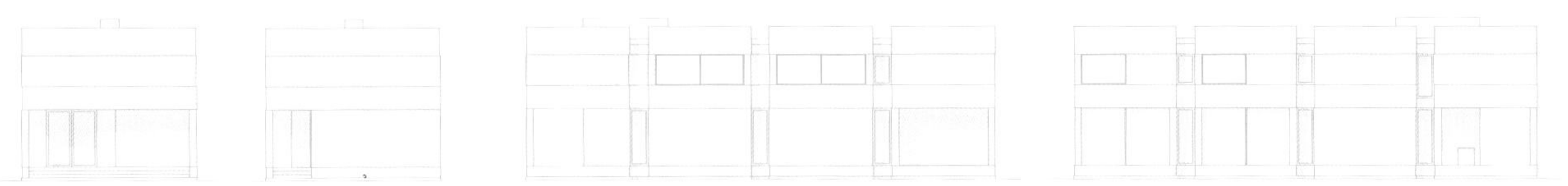

This country house was designed for two young art collectors. They asked the architects for a "simple, abstract looking piece, sitting almost without scale on the site." Four equally sized, connected, rectangular wooden volumes were covered with metal panels on the exterior and gypsum panels on the interior walls. Natural light penetrates through the openings of the outer shell of the house, which is as much a private art gallery as a country house. Views of the surrounding countryside are present, but do not dominate the architecture. The project, like others that HHF has worked on, was designed in collaboration with the noted Chinese artist Ai Wei Wei.

Dieses Landhaus wurde für zwei junge Kunstsammler entworfen. Sie baten die Architekten um einen „schlichten, abstrakt wirkenden Entwurf, der fast maßstabslos auf dem Grundstück steht." Vier gleich große, miteinander verbundene, rechteckige Baukörper mit einem Tragwerk aus Holz wurden außen mit Metallpaneelen und innen mit Gipswandplatten verkleidet. Durch Öffnungen in der Außenhaut fällt Tageslicht in das Haus, das ebenso private Kunstgalerie wie Landhaus ist. Ausblicke in die landschaftliche Umgebung sind gegeben, dominieren die Architektur jedoch nicht. Dieses Haus entstand, wie zahlreiche andere Projekte von HHF, in Zusammenarbeit mit dem namhaften chinesischen Künstler Ai Wei Wei.

Cette maison de campagne a été conçue pour deux jeunes collectionneurs d'art qui avaient demandé aux architectes « une œuvre simple, d'allure abstraite, posée sur le terrain, presque sans échelle ». Quatre volumes rectangulaires en bois de même taille ont été habillés à l'extérieur de panneaux métalliques et de plâtre à l'intérieur. L'éclairage naturel est fourni par les grandes ouvertures pratiquées dans la coque extérieure. L'ensemble est autant une galerie d'art privée qu'une résidence de campagne. Les vues sur le paysage environnant sont très présentes, mais ne dominent pas l'architecture. Ce projet, comme d'autres d'HHF, a été conçu en collaboration avec le célèbre artiste chinois Ai Wei Wei.

A site map (above) shows the generous size of the plot, with the strictly rectangular house located near the top, center.

Ein Lageplan (oben) zeigt das großzügige Grundstück. Das streng geradlinige Haus liegt mittig an dessen oberem Ende.

Le plan du site (ci-dessus) montre les généreuses dimensions de la parcelle. La maison strictement rectangulaire est située en haut, au centre.

The boxlike design allows for a variety of different openings and an overall division into four elements.

Der kastenförmige Baukörper hat unterschiedliche Fassadenöffnungen und ist in vier Teile untergliedert.

La conception de type « boîte » permet une grande variété d'ouvertures et une division de l'ensemble en quatre éléments.

Interior views give an idea of the variety of materials employed and the generous ceiling height provided (left).

Die Innenansichten vermitteln einen Eindruck von der Vielzahl unterschiedlicher Materialien, die hier zum Einsatz kommen, sowie von der großzügigen Deckenhöhe (links).

Ces vues intérieures donnent une idée de la diversité des matériaux employés et de la grande hauteur sous plafond dans certaines pièces (à gauche).

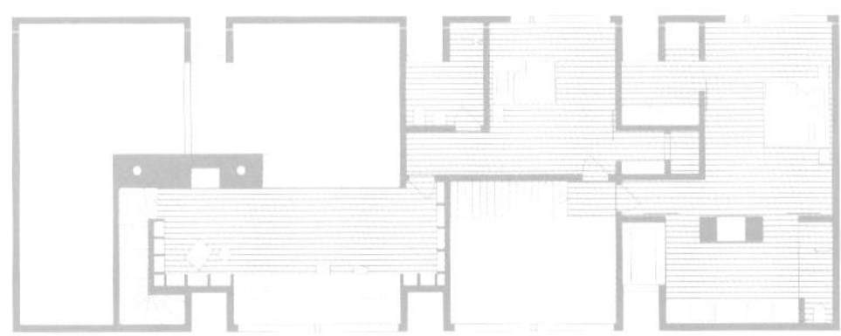

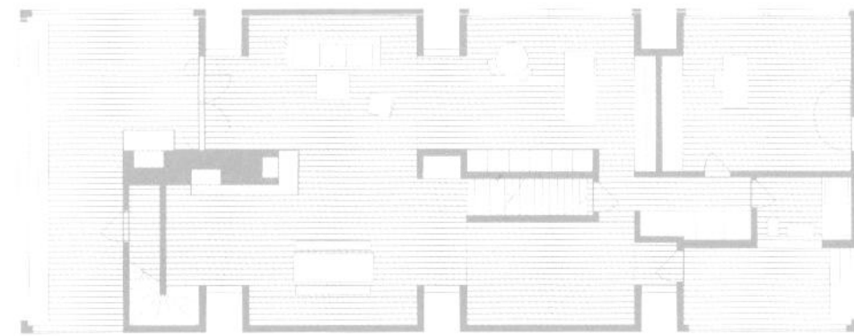

The drawings (above) show that the house is not actually divided but rather notched to create the four basic, rectangular blocks that constitute the overall larger rectangular plan.

Die Zeichnungen oben belegen, dass das Haus nicht gänzlich unterteilt, sondern nur eingeschnitten wurde, um die vier rechteckigen Grundelemente zu definieren, aus denen sich der rechteckige Gesamtgrundriss zusammensetzt.

Les plans ci-dessus montrent que la maison n'est pas réellement divisée mais plutôt indentée, pour créer quatre blocs qui, réunis, constituent un plan rectangulaire.

DUNE HOUSE

Ordos, Inner Mongolia, China, 2008–09

Area: 1000 m². Client: Ordos Jiang Yuan Water Engineering Co., Ltd.
Cost: not disclosed

Part of a series of houses designed by noted architects as a preliminary exercise in the ambitious development of a further 100 residences in this area, characterized by dunes and valleys, the Dune House "is inspired by these natural processes that shape the earth." A main space created with "soft geometries" on the lower floor is intended for all "public" activities—a dining area, fire place, and pool, as well as a living and reading space are included. All the service functions are hidden beneath the "artificial dune" imagined by the architects. The upper level is made up of "nine loose fitting boxes" that contain private spaces, including a gallery.

Das Dune House ist Teil eines ambitionierten Großprojekts, bei dem weitere 100 Wohnbauten in der von Dünen und Tälern geprägten Landschaft entstehen sollen. Namhafte Architekten haben Entwürfe für dieses Projekt geliefert. Inspiriert wurde das Dune House von „den natürlichen Prozessen, die die Erde formen". Ein in „weichen Geometrien" entworfener Hauptraum im Erdgeschoss ist den „öffentlichen" Aktivitäten gewidmet – hier wird es einen Essbereich, Kamin und Pool sowie einen Wohn- und Lesebereich geben. Sämtliche Versorgungsräume liegen eingebettet in die von den Architekten erdachte „künstlichen Düne". Das Obergeschoss besteht aus „neun lose ineinandergreifenden Boxen", in denen sich die privaten Räume befinden, darunter auch ein Raum für Kunst.

Faisant partie d'une série de maisons conçues par des architectes de renom pour la première phase d'un projet de construction d'une centaine de résidences dans une zone de dunes et de vallées, la maison de la dune « s'inspire des processus naturels qui ont donné forme à la terre ». L'espace principal du rez-de-chaussée, à base de « géométries douces », est destiné aux activités « publiques » (zone des repas, cheminée et piscine, séjour, pièce de lecture). Toutes les fonctions de service sont dissimulées derrière la « dune artificielle » imaginée par les architectes. L'étage se compose de « neuf boîtes librement ajustées » qui contiennent les espaces privatifs, dont une galerie.

The Dune House is one of a handful of Ordos-related projects to have advanced. Its four-part structure brings to mind the previous HHF house in this volume, albeit in a deliberately rougher form.

Das Dune House ist eines von einer Handvoll Bauten für das Ordos Project, die Fortschritte verzeichnen können. Die vierteilige Struktur des Baus erinnert an das andere Haus von HHF in diesem Band, wenn auch das vorliegende Projekt eine gewollt gröbere Optik hat.

La maison sur la dune fait partie des quelques projets déjà réalisés à Ordos. Sa structure en quatre parties rappelle la maison précédente d'HHF, mais avec un aspect volontairement plus brut.

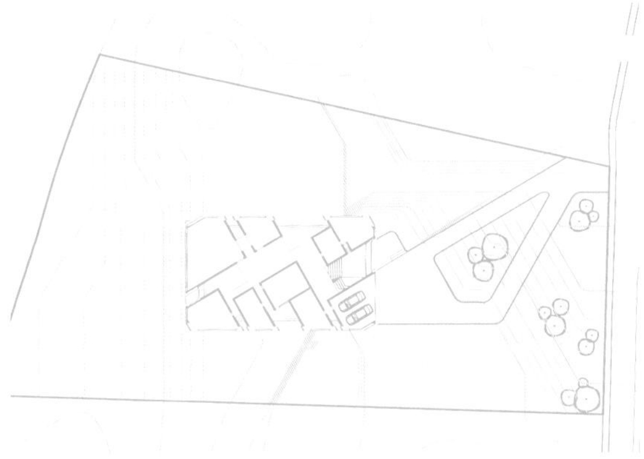

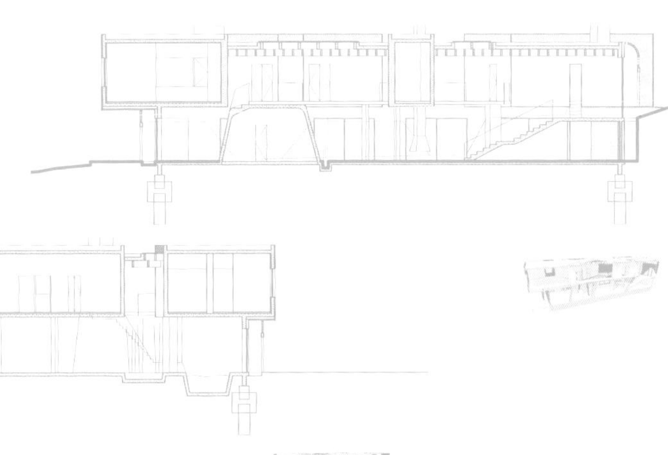

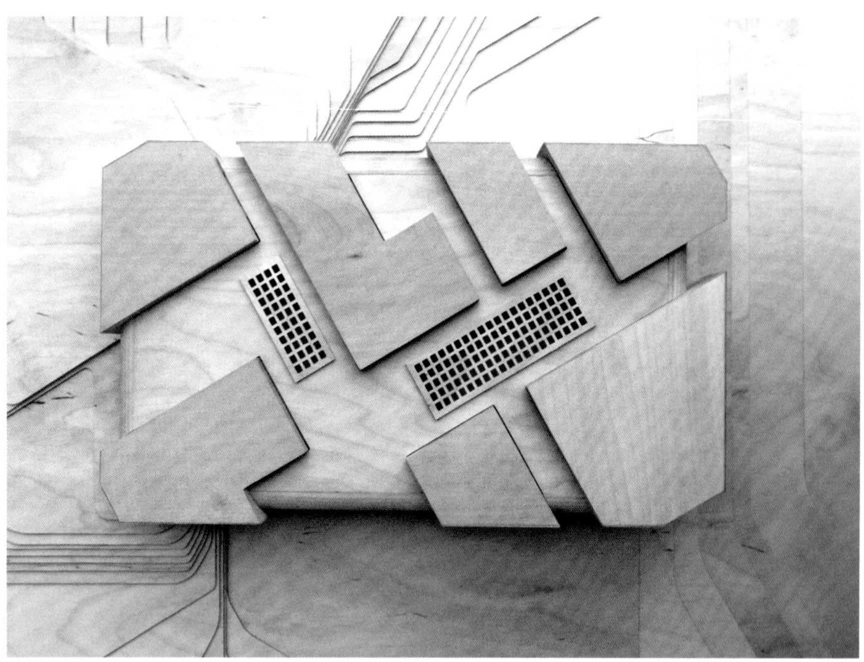

In these images of the unfinished house and its roof design (above) and plans (right bottom), strong forms in concrete create unusual spaces with desert views. Right page, top, a computer rendering of the completed house.

Die ausdrucksstarken Formen aus Beton – zu sehen auf diesen Bildern vom Rohbau, vom Dach (oben) und auf den Grundrissen (rechts unten) – definieren ungewöhnliche Räume mit Blick auf die Wüste. Auf der rechten Seite oben ein Rendering des Innenraumes.

Sur ces images de la maison encore en chantier et de sa toiture (ci-dessus) comme dans ses plans (page de droite), on perçoit la puissance formelle des volumes en béton aux baies largement ouvertes sur le désert. Page de droite, image de synthèse de la maison achevée.

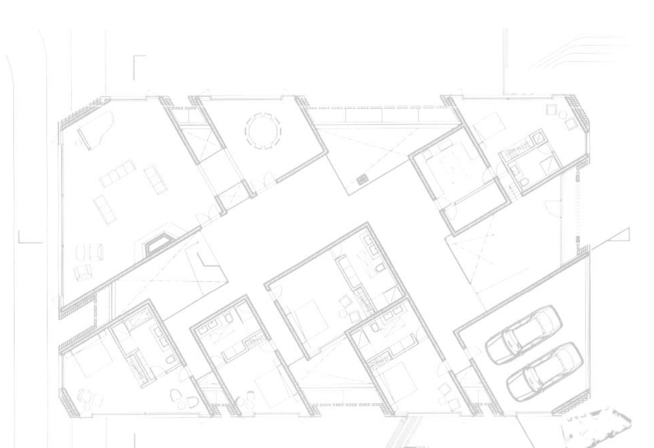

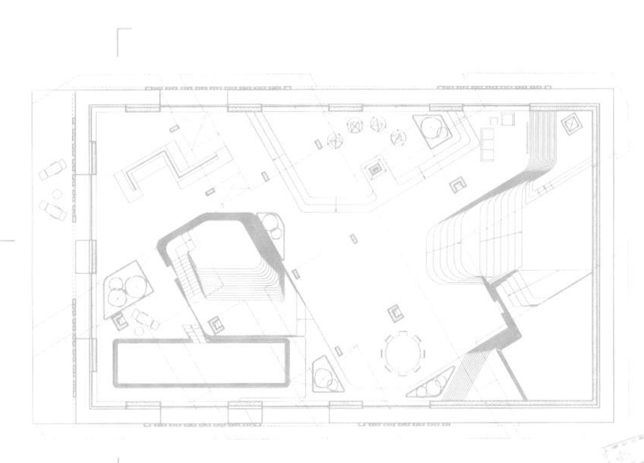

JUN IGARASHI

Jun Igarashi Associates
81 Miyamae
Saroma, Tocoro-gun
Hokkaido 093–0501
Japan

Tel: +81 1587 2 3524
Fax: +81 1587 2 3561
E-mail: jtim4550@coral.ocn.ne.jp
Web: http://jun-igarashi.web.infoseek.co.jp

JUN IGARASHI was born in Hokkaido, Japan, in 1970. He was educated at the Hokkaido Central Kougakuin Technical College (1990), and set up his own practice, Jun Igarashi Architects Inc., in 1997. He is an Instructor at the Hokkaido Institute of Technology, Nagoya Institute of Technology, and Tohoku University, and in 2006 he won an AR Award for Emerging Architecture (UK). His recent work includes Rectangle of Light (Hokkaido, 2007); House of Trough (Hokkaido, 2008); Agricultural Barn (Hokkaido, 2008); Layered House (Hokkaido, 2008); House O (Hokkaido, 2008–09, published here); Shounan House (Tokyo, 2009); and Gate Tower (Hokkaido, 2009), all in Japan.

JUN IGARASHI wurde 1970 in Hokkaido, Japan, geboren. Seine Ausbildung absolvierte er am Hokkaido Central Kougakuin Technical College (1990). 1997 gründete er sein eigenes Büro, Jun Igarashi Architects Inc. Er lehrt am Hokkaido Institute of Technology, am Nagoya Institute of Technology sowie der Tohoku University und wurde 2006 mit dem AR Award for Emerging Architecture (Großbritannien) ausgezeichnet. Zu seinen jüngeren Projekten zählen Rectangle of Light (Hokkaido, 2007), House of Trough (Hokkaido, 2008), Agricultural Barn (Hokkaido, 2008), Layered House (Hokkaido, 2008), Haus O (Hokkaido, 2008–09, hier vorgestellt), Haus Shounan (Tokio, 2009) sowie Gate Tower (Hokkaido, 2009), alle in Japan.

JUN IGARASHI, né dans l'île d'Hokkaido (Japon) en 1970 a fait ses études au Collège technique central de Kougakuin à Hokkaido (1990), avant de créer son agence, Jun Igarashi Architects Inc., en 1997. Il est enseignant à l'Institut de technologie d'Hokkaido, à l'Institut de technologie de Nagoya et à l'université Tohoku. En 2006, il a remporté un prix AR de l'architecture émergeante (G.-B.). Récemment, il a réalisé : le Rectangle de lumière (Rectangle of light, Hokkaido, 2007) ; la maison en creux (House of Trough, Hokkaido, 2008) ; une grange (Agricultural Barn, Hokkaido, 2008) ; la Maison stratifiée (Layered House, Hokkaido, 2008) ; la maison O (Hokkaido, 2008–09, publiée ici) ; la maison Shounan (Tokyo, 2009) ; et une tour d'entrée (Gate Tower, Hokkaido, 2009), tous au Japon.

HOUSE O

Hokkaido, Japan, 2008–09

Area: 112 m^2. Client: not disclosed. Cost: not disclosed

This house for a young couple is located in a small town in Eastern Hokkaido. The site for the house in this wooded region measures 2000 square meters, an unusually large size for Japan, but this area is not densely populated. It is set near a lumbermill and a hospital. The house includes an entry foyer, entry storage space, family room, kitchen, guest room, bedroom, side room, washroom closet, washroom, and bath. The architect originally considered a square plan, but found that form inefficient, preferring to cut up the various functions and to place them in more favorable locations. Each volume, radiating out from the high central space, has a lower ceiling height. Though the house does appear to be symmetrical from certain angles, a small change in the point of view means that it has an entirely different appearance. Windows are oriented to provide some protection from summer heat and extreme winter cold. The architect compares these orientations to "some cacti that thrive in the desert. A section of a cactus shows that they have folds in their surface to create shade, to keep the plant cool. Comfortable architecture is created when drawing from such a simple form in nature," says Jun Igarashi, concluding: "This is a starting point for a new type of architecture."

Dieses Haus für ein junges Paar liegt in einer Kleinstadt im Osten der Insel Hokkaido. Das 2000 m^2 große Grundstück in der waldigen Region ist ungewöhnlich groß für Japan – allerdings ist diese Gegend nicht sehr dicht besiedelt. Das in der Nähe eines Sägewerks und eines Krankenhauses gelegene Haus verfügt über Diele, Abstellraum neben dem Eingang, Wohnzimmer, Küche, Gästezimmer, Schlafzimmer, Nebenzimmer, Gästetoilette, Toilette und Bad. Ursprünglich hatte der Architekt einen quadratischen Grundriss in Betracht gezogen, fand diese Form jedoch letztendlich nicht effizient und entschied sich, die verschiedenen Funktionen voneinander zu trennen und günstiger anzuordnen. Die einzelnen Baukörper haben – ausgehend vom höchsten Raum in der Mitte – zunehmend niedrigere Deckenhöhen. Obwohl das Haus aus bestimmten Perspektiven symmetrisch scheint, genügt ein kleiner Blickpunktwechsel, um es vollkommen anders wirken zu lassen. Die Fenster wurden so ausgerichtet, dass im Sommer Schutz vor Hitze und im Winter Schutz vor der extremen Kälte gewährleistet ist. Der Architekt vergleicht diese Ausrichtung mit „bestimmten Kakteenarten, die in der Wüste gedeihen. Ein Schnitt durch einen Kaktus zeigt, dass die Oberfläche Einbuchtungen hat, wodurch Schattenzonen entstehen, die die Pflanze kühlen. Inspiriert von so einfachen Formen der Natur kann wohnliche Architektur entstehen", betont Jun Igarashi und fasst zusammen: „Dies ist der Ausgangspunkt für eine neue Form von Architektur."

Cette maison, construite pour un jeune couple, se trouve dans une petite ville d'une région boisée de l'est d'Hokkaido, non loin d'une usine et d'un hôpital. Le terrain choisi mesure 2000 m^2 – surface inhabituellement importante pour le Japon –, mais l'endroit n'est guère peuplé. La maison comprend un vestibule, un volume de rangement près de l'entrée, une salle commune familiale, une cuisine, une chambre d'amis, une chambre, une chambre d'enfant, une salle d'eau, et une salle de bains. L'architecte avait réfléchi au départ à un plan carré, mais l'avait jugé inefficace, et a préféré isoler les différentes fonctions pour les disposer de manière plus pratique. Chaque volume, qui rayonne de l'espace central, présente une hauteur de plafond plus réduite que celui-ci. Même si la maison semble symétrique sous certains angles, un léger changement de point de vue en modifie entièrement l'aspect. Les fenêtres sont orientées pour protéger de la chaleur de l'été et du froid extrême de l'hiver. L'architecte compare ces orientations à « des cactus qui fleurissent dans le désert. Une coupe de cactus montre qu'ils ont des plis à leur surface pour créer de l'ombre, et se garder au frais. Une architecture confortable peut s'inspirer des formes simples de la nature », explique Jun Igarashi, « c'est le point de départ d'un nouveau type d'architecture ».

The enigmatic, black forms of the house constitute an assembly of elements with different ceiling heights, as can be seen in the section drawing above.

Die rätselhaften schwarzen Formen des Hauses bilden ein Arrangement aus baulichen Elementen unterschiedlicher Höhe, wie auch der Schnitt oben zeigt.

L'assemblage des formes sombres et énigmatiques de cette maison crée des volumes de hauteurs de plafonds différentes, comme le montre la coupe ci-dessus.

A plan of the house shows its unusual configuration, with different possible uses for many spaces.

Der Grundriss des Hauses veranschaulicht die ungewöhnliche Konfiguration, die differenzierte Nutzungen für viele Räume zulässt.

Le plan de la maison présente une composition très inhabituelle qui offre différentes possibilités d'utilisation des volumes.

The angles of the house create views and openings that are unexpected, although the compartmentalized design certainly allows for privacy where required.

Durch die verwinkelte Struktur des Hauses ergeben sich überraschende Sichtachsen und Öffnungen; durch die Gliederung des Baukörpers wird dennoch, wo notwendig, Privatsphäre geschaffen.

Le plan non orthogonal génère des perspectives et des ouvertures inattendues, mais sa compartimentation permet de protéger les espaces d'intimité nécessaires.

YOSUKE INOUE

Yosuke Inoue Architect & Associates
201, 4–16–7 Ekoda
Nakano-ku
Tokyo 165–0022
Japan

Tel: +81 3 5913 3525
Fax: +81 3 5913 3526
E-mail: usun@gol.com
Web: www.yosukeinoue.com

YOSUKE INOUE was born in Tokyo in 1966. He graduated from the Department of Architecture of Kyoto University in 1991. He worked in the office of Sakakura Associates from 1991 to 2000, when he established his own office, Yosuke Inoue Architect & Associates, in Tokyo. His work includes House in Fuji (Fuji, Shizuoka, 2002); House in Nakanobu (Shinagawa, Tokyo, 2004); House in Setagaya-Sakura (Setagaya, Tokyo, 2004); House in Azamino (Yokohama, Kanagawa, 2005); Villa in Hayama (Hayama, Kanagawa, 2006); House in Ichikawa (Ichikawa, Chiba, 2006); House in Den-en-chofu (Ohta, Tokyo, 2007); House in Tsujido (Fujisawa, Kanagawa, 2008); and House in Yotsuya (Shinjuku, Tokyo, 2008, published here), all in Japan.

YOSUKE INOUE wurde 1966 in Tokio geboren. Sein Architekturstudium schloss er 1991 an der Universität Kioto ab. Von 1991 bis 2000 arbeitete er für Sakakura Associates, im selben Jahr gründete er sein eigenes Büro, Yosuke Inoue Architect & Associates, in Tokio. Zu seinen Projekten zählen ein Haus in Fuji (Fuji, Shizuoka, 2002), ein Haus in Nakanobu (Shinagawa, Tokio, 2004), ein Haus in Setagaya-Sakura (Setagaya, Tokio, 2004), ein Haus in Azamino (Yokohama, Kanagawa, 2005), eine Villa in Hayama (Hayama, Kanagawa, 2006), ein Haus in Ichikawa (Ichikawa, Chiba, 2006), ein Haus in Den-en-chofu (Ohta, Tokio, 2007), ein Haus in Tsujido (Fujisawa, Kanagawa, 2008) sowie ein Haus in Yotsuya (Shinjuku, Tokio, 2008, hier vorgestellt), alle in Japan.

YOSUKE INOUE, né à Tokyo en 1966, est diplômé du Département d'architecture de l'université de Kyoto (1991). Il a travaillé dans l'agence Sakakura Associates de 1991 à 2000 avant de fonder sa propre structure, Yosuke Inoue Architect & Associates, à Tokyo. Parmi ses réalisations figurent de nombreuses maisons : à Fuji (Fuji, Shizuoka, 2002) ; Nakanobu (Shinagawa, Tokyo, 2004) ; Setagaya-Sakura (Setagaya, Tokyo, 2004) ; Azamino (Yokohama, Kanagawa, 2005) ; Hayama (Hayama, Kanagawa, 2006) ; Ichikawa (Ichikawa, Chiba, 2006) ; Den-en-chofu (Ohta, Tokyo, 2007) ; Tsujido (Fujisawa, Kanagawa, 2008) ; et à Yotsuya (Shinjuku, Tokyo, 2008, publiée ici), le tout au Japon.

HOUSE IN YOTSUYA

Shinjuku, Tokyo, 2008

Area: 62 m². Client: not disclosed. Cost: not disclosed.
Collaboration: Masashi Miyamoto

This house for a mother and daughter is located in the dense Yotsuya residential area close to Shinjuku in Tokyo. As is often the case in Tokyo, the site area here is very limited (33 m²). The four-story, reinforced-concrete structure has a 3.7 x 9 meter footprint, covering the full site that faces a narrow street, and has apartment buildings on each either side. The entrance and bathroom are on the ground floor, living room and kitchen on the second floor, and bedrooms on the third and fourth floors. The architect states: "The main feature of this house is a three-story space with a top light in the form of a slit on the diagonal roof that introduces natural light."

Dieses Haus für eine Mutter und ihre Tochter liegt im dicht bebauten Tokioter Wohnviertel Yotsuya, in der Nähe von Shinjuku. Wie so oft in Tokio ist das Grundstück sehr knapp bemessen (33 m²). Der viergeschossige Stahlbetonbau hat eine Grundfläche von 3,7 x 9 m und nutzt damit das gesamte Grundstück aus, das an einer schmalen Straße liegt und an beiden Seiten von Mehrfamilienhäusern flankiert wird. Eingang und Badezimmer liegen im Erdgeschoss, Wohnzimmer und Küche im ersten, Schlafzimmer im zweiten und dritten Obergeschoss. Der Architekt erklärt: „Hauptmerkmal des Hauses ist ein sich über drei Geschosse erstreckender Raum mit Oberlichtern in Form von Schlitzöffnungen in der geneigten Dachfläche, durch die Tageslicht einfällt."

Cette maison, construite pour une mère et sa fille, est située dans le quartier résidentiel très dense de Yotsuya près de Shinjuku à Tokyo. Comme c'est souvent le cas dans la capitale, la surface au sol de 33 m² est très réduite. La construction en béton armé de quatre niveaux n'occupe une emprise au sol que de 3,7 x 9 m, et recouvre la totalité du terrain enserré entre deux immeubles d'appartements, et donnant sur une rue étroite. L'entrée et la salle de bains se trouvent au rez-de-chaussée, le séjour et la cuisine au premier étage, les chambres aux troisième et quatrième étages. Selon l'architecte : « La principale caractéristique de cette maison réside dans son volume sur trois niveaux, avec un éclairage zénithal fourni par des verrières en forme de fentes pratiquées dans la toiture à une seule pente. »

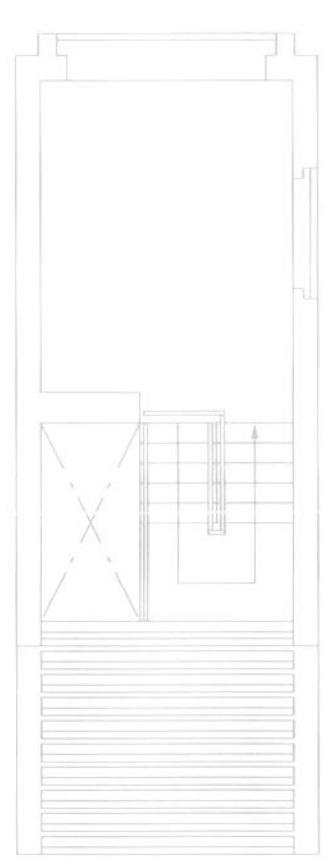

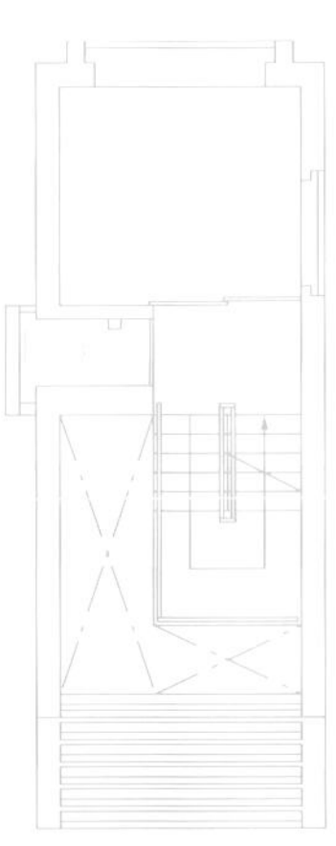

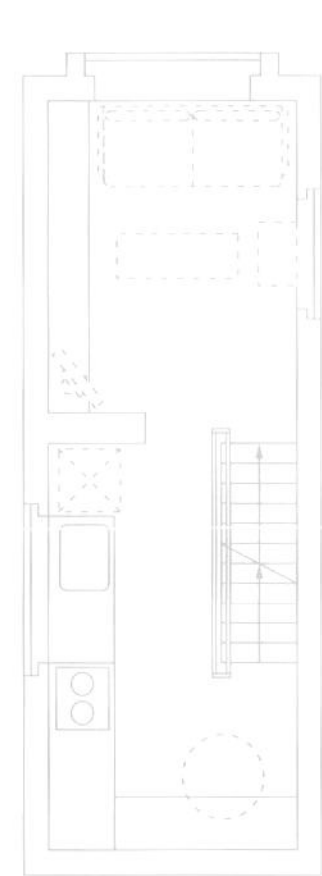

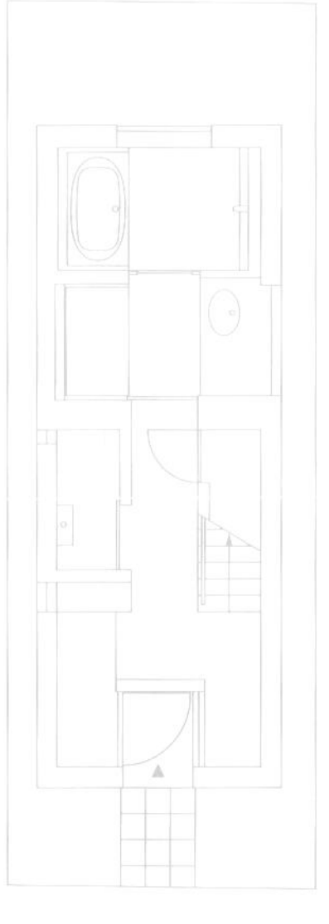

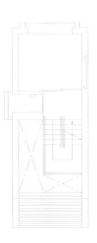

Though the long, narrow house has a rather cold appearance from the outside, its design allows for ample natural light, while the use of wood floors, for example, warms the appearance of the interior.

Obwohl das lange, schmale Haus von außen eher kühl wirkt, ermöglicht der Entwurf den großzügigen Einfall von Tageslicht; Holzfußböden sorgen für Wärme in den Innenräumen.

Bien que cette maison longue et étroite puisse sembler assez froide vue de l'extérieur, elle bénéficie d'un généreux éclairage naturel et de parquets en bois qui, parmi d'autres détails, réchauffent l'ambiance intérieure.

PRODUCED BY TOYO ITO

Toyo Ito
Toyo Ito & Associates, Architects
1–19–4 Shibuya
Shibuya-ku
Tokyo 150–0002
Japan

Tel: +81 3 3409 5822
Fax: +81 3 3409 5969
Web: www.toyo-ito.co.jp

Sou Fujimoto
Sou Fujimoto Architects
10–3 Ichikawa-Seihon Building 6F
Higashi-Enoki-Cho Shinjuku
Tokyo 162–0807
Japan

Tel: +81 3 3513 5401
Fax: +81 3 3513 5402
E-mail: sosuke@tka.att.ne.jp
Web: www.sou-fujimoto.com

Professor Terunobu Fujimori
Institute of Industrial Science
University of Tokyo
4–6–1 Komaba
Meguro-ku
Tokyo 153–8505
Japan

Tel: +81 3 5452 6370
Fax: +81 3 5452 6371
E-mail: tanpopo@iis.u-tokyo.ac.jp

Taira Nishizawa
Taira Nishizawa Architects
2–15–15–4F Takanawa
Minato-ku
Tokyo 108–0074
Japan

Tel/Fax: +81 3 3441 4806
E-mail: taira@nszw.com
Web: www.nszw.com

Born in 1941 in Seoul, Korea, **TOYO ITO** graduated from the University of Tokyo in 1965 and worked in the office of Kiyonori Kikutake until 1969. He created his own office, Urban Robot (URBOT), in Tokyo in 1971, assuming the name of Toyo Ito Architect & Associates in 1979. He was awarded the RIBA Gold Medal in 2006. His completed work includes the Silver Hut Residence (Tokyo, 1984); Tower of the Winds (Yokohama, Kanagawa, 1986); Yatsushiro Municipal Museum (Yatsushiro, Kumamoto, 1989–91); and the Elderly People's Home (1992–94) and Fire Station (1992–95), both located in the same city on the island of Kyushu. Other projects include his Odate Jukai Dome Park (Odate, 1995–97); Nagaoka Lyric Hall (Nagaoka, Niigata, 1995–97); and Ota-ku Resort Complex (Tobu-cho, Chiisagata-gun, Nagano, 1996–98), all in Japan. One of his most successful and widely published projects, the Sendai Mediatheque, was completed in 2001. He designed a temporary pavilion for the Serpentine Gallery in London (2002), and was given the Golden Lion for Lifetime Achievement at the 8th International Venice Architecture Biennale the same year. More recently, he has completed the TOD'S Omotesando Building (Shibuya-ku, Tokyo, 2002–04); Meiso no Mori Municipal Funeral Hall (Kakamigahara, Gifu, 2005–06); Hospital Cognacq-Jay (Paris, France, 2006); and the Main Stadium for the World Games 2009 (Kaohsiung, Taiwan, 2009). Toyo Ito was the producer of the Sumika Project published here.

TOYO ITO wurde 1941 in Seoul, Korea, geboren und schloss sein Studium 1965 an der Universität Tokio ab. Bis 1969 arbeitete er im Büro von Kiyonori Kikutake. Sein eigenes Büro Urban Robot (URBOT) gründete er 1971 in Tokio, seit 1979 firmiert er unter dem Namen Toyo Ito Architect & Associates. 2006 erhielt er die RIBA-Goldmedaille. Zu seinen realisierten Bauten zählen Silver Hut (Tokio, 1982–84), Tower of the Winds (Yokohama, Kanagawa, 1986), das Stadtmuseum Yatsushiro (Yatsushiro, Kumamoto, 1988–91) sowie ein Altenheim (1992–94) und eine Feuerwache (1992–95), beide in derselben Stadt auf der Insel Kyushu. Weitere Projekte sind der Odate Jukai Dome Park (Odate, 1995–97), die Nagaoka Lyric Hall (Nagaoka, Niigata, 1995–97) und das Ota-ku Resort (Tobu-cho, Chiisagata-gun, Nagano, 1996–98), alle in Japan. Eines seiner bekanntesten und meistpublizierten Projekte, die Mediathek in Sendai, wurde 2001 fertiggestellt. Er entwarf einen temporären Pavillon für die Serpentine Gallery in London (2002) und wurde im selben Jahr auf der VIII. Architekturbiennale in Venedig mit dem Goldenen Löwen für sein Lebenswerk ausgezeichnet. In jüngster Zeit realisierte er das Omotesando Building für TOD'S (Shibuya-ku, Tokio, 2002–04), die Städtische Bestattungshalle Meiso no Mori (Kakamigahara, Gifu, 2005–06), das Krankenhaus Cognacq-Jay (Paris, 2006) sowie die Sportarena für die World Games 2009 (Kaohsiung, Taiwan, 2009). Toyo Ito steht als Organisator hinter dem hier vorgestellten Sumika-Projekt.

Né en 1941 à Séoul (Corée), **TOYO ITO**, diplômé de l'université de Tokyo en 1965, a commencé par travailler chez Kiyonori Kikutake jusqu'en 1969. Il a fondé sa propre agence, Urban Robot (URBOT), à Tokyo en 1971, qui a pris le nom de Toyo Ito Architect & Associates en 1979. Il a reçu la médaille d'or du RIBA en 2006. Parmi ses œuvres réalisées : la résidence de la Hutte argentée (Silver Hut Residence, Tokyo, 1984) ; la tour des Vents (Tower of the Winds, Yokohama, Kanagawa, 1986) ; le musée municipal de Yatsushiro (Yatsushiro, Kumamoto, 1989–91) ; un foyer pour personnes âgées (1992–94) ; et un centre de secours (1992–95), tous deux dans la même ville sur l'île de Kyushu ; le Parc du dôme de Jukai (Odate, 1995–97) ; la salle de concerts lyriques de Nagaoka (Nagaoka, Niigata, 1995–97) ; et le complexe touristique d'Ota-ku (Tobu-cho, Chiisagata-gun, Nagano, 1996–98), tous au Japon. L'un de ses projets le plus réussi et le plus publié, la médiathèque de Sendaï, a été achevé en 2001. Il a conçu un pavillon temporaire pour la Serpentine Gallery à Londres (2002), et a reçu le Lion d'or pour sa carrière à la VIIIe Biennale internationale d'architecture à Venise la même année. Plus récemment, il a construit l'immeuble Tod's à Omotesando (Shibuya-ku, Tokyo, 2002–04) ; le funérarium municipal de Meiso no Mori (Kakamigahara, Gifu, 2005–06) ; l'hôpital Cognacq-Jay (Paris, 2006) ; et le stade principal des Jeux mondiaux 2009 (Kaohsiung, Taïwan, 2009). Toyo Ito est le responsable du projet Sumika publié ici.

SUMIKA PAVILION

Utsunomiya, Tochigi Prefecture, Japan, 2008

Area: 81 m^2. Client: Tokyo Gas Co. Ltd. Cost: not disclosed. Collaboration: Structural Design Office OAK (Structural Engineers), Kankyo Engineering Inc. (Mechanical Engineers), Toyota Woodyou Home Co. (Builders)

Toyo Ito was responsible for the organization of the exceptional Sumika Project, which brought together four of the most significant Japanese contemporary architects under the auspices of Tokyo Gas and is located in an industrial site in a residential area that includes a large gas tank. The idea was to create experimental houses that would be both "primitive" and contemporary at once. Ito's **SUMIKA PAVILION**, the central facility—a gathering place that has served as an information point for the complex—was built with structural, laminated lumber. The geometric system of the pavilion is based on four columns that spread and fold to become the four walls. The networked wooden structure is covered by a seamless fiber-reinforced plastic (FRP) waterproof surface and glass. Ito says: "This whole structure symbolizes the primitive living space, *sumika*, with simple facilities, creating the image of trees growing and branching overhead."

Toyo Ito war für die Organisation des ungewöhnlichen Sumika-Projekts verantwortlich, das vier der renommiertesten zeitgenössischen Architekten Japans unter der Schirmherrschaft des Energiekonzerns Tokyo Gas zusammenführte. Realisiert wurde das Projekt auf einem Industriegelände mit einem Gasometer inmitten eines Wohnviertels. Grundgedanke war die Entwicklung experimenteller Wohnbauten, die „primitiv" und zugleich zeitgenössisch sein sollten. Itos **PAVILLON SUMIKA**, das Hauptgebäude, ist ein Versammlungsort, der auch als Informationszentrale für den Komplex dient und ein Tragwerk aus Schichtholz hat. Die geometrische Struktur des Pavillons basiert auf vier Stützen, die sich falten und verzweigen und zu den vier Wänden entwickeln. Die netzartige Holzkonstruktion ist mit einer nahtlosen, wasserdichten Oberfläche aus Faserkunststoffverbund (FKV) und Glas überzogen. Ito erklärt: „Die Konstruktion steht als Symbol für den primitiven Wohnraum, *sumika*, mit einfachen technischen Einrichtungen und simuliert den Eindruck von wachsenden und sich verzweigenden Bäumen."

Toyo Ito est le responsable de ce projet exceptionnel qui a réuni quatre des plus intéressants architectes japonais contemporains, sous l'égide de la société Tokyo Gas, dans un site industriel sur lequel se dresse un énorme réservoir de gaz au milieu d'un quartier résidentiel. L'idée était de créer des maisons expérimentales qui soient à la fois « primitives » et contemporaines. Le **PAVILLON SUMIKA** d'Ito lui-même, à la fois point de rencontre et centre d'information pour le complexe, est en lamellé de bois structurel. Son système constructif repose sur quatre colonnes qui se divisent et se déploient pour former les quatre murs. La structure en bois en réseau est tendue d'une membrane en plastique renforcé de fibre (PRV) sans soudure, étanche et percée de panneaux de verre. Pour Ito : « Cette construction tout entière symbolise l'espace de vie primitif ou *sumika*, équipé d'installations simples, inspiré d'une image d'arbres étendant leurs branches par-dessus les têtes. »

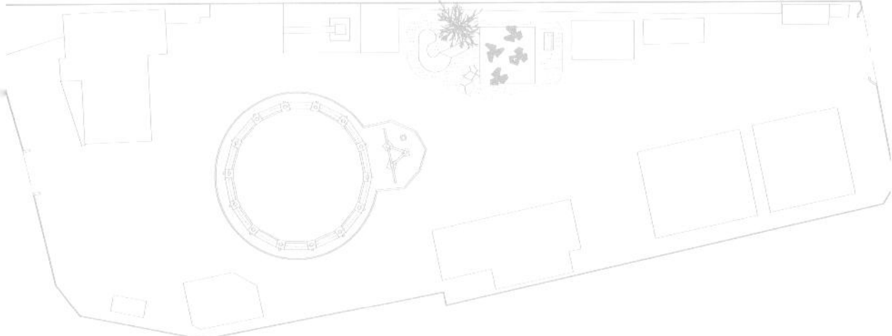

The Sumika Pavilion is both light and open, as befits a gathering place and information point for this group of houses by different architects.

Der Pavillon Sumika wirkt leicht und offen – ideal für einen Informations- und Treffpunkt in dieser von verschiedenen Architekten gestalteten Gruppe von Bauten.

Le pavillon Sumika est à la fois léger et ouvert, comme il convient pour un lieu de réunion et d'information sur ce projet d'un ensemble de maisons réalisées par différents architectes.

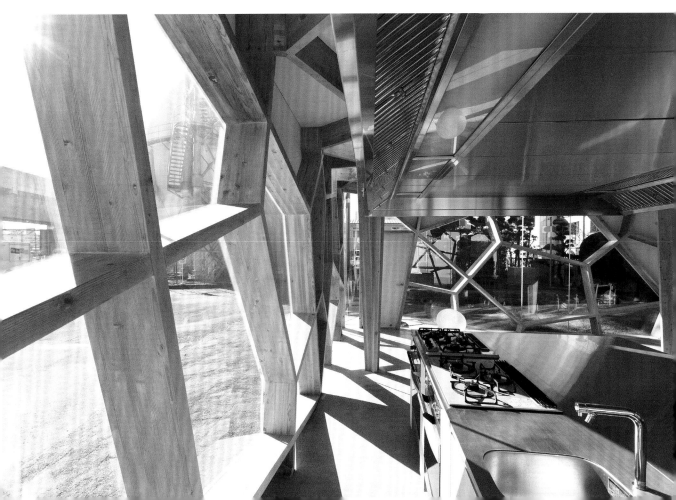

HOUSE BEFORE HOUSE

Utsunomiya, Tochigi Prefecture, Japan, 2008

Area: 61 m². Client: Tokyo Gas Co. Ltd. Cost: not disclosed.
Collaboration: Yasushi Yamanoi

SOU FUJIMOTO's House Before House is a steel-frame structure. "I envisioned creating a place that is suggestive of the primitive future, analogous to being simultaneously new and from the prehistoric age, engendered with unforeseen newness yet subsuming something akin to the unequivocal and archetypical form of a house," declares Fujimoto. He maintains that a house must be almost "indistinguishable" from the city in which it is located.

SOU FUJIMOTOs House Before House ist eine Stahlrahmenkonstruktion. „Meine Vorstellung ging dahin, einen Raum wie aus einer primitiven Zukunft zu erschaffen – der gleichzeitig neu ist und auf eine ferne Vorzeit verweist, einen Raum, in dem trotz seiner völligen Neuartigkeit die eindeutige Form des archetypischen Hauses aufscheint", erklärt Fujimoto.

La maison avant la maison, de **SOU FUJIMOTO** comporte une ossature d'acier. « J'ai eu envie de créer un lieu qui suggère un futur primitif, dans l'idée d'être à la fois nouveau et de surgir d'un âge préhistorique, d'être engendré par un esprit de nouveauté inattendu, mais qui concentre en soi quelque chose de comparable à la forme archétypique évidente d'une maison », a déclaré l'architecte. Il soutient qu'une maison doit être presque « indistinguable » de la ville dans laquelle elle se situe.

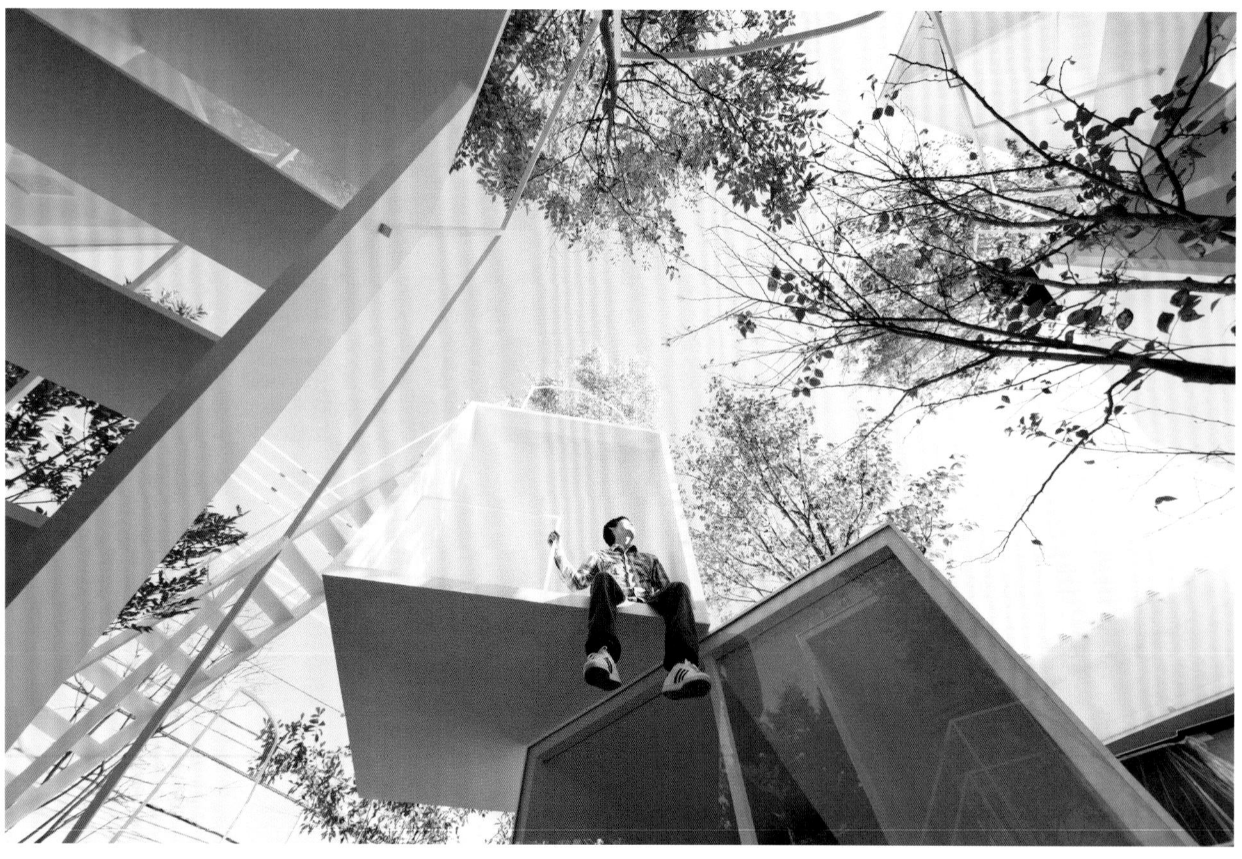

Images of Sou Fujimoto's houses often feature residents sitting or walking in unexpected places, emphasizing the radical nature of his concept of architecture. Plans and elevations show the complexity of this design (right).

Aufnahmen von Sou Fujimotos Häusern zeigen häufig die Bewohner – sitzend oder laufend an überraschenden Orten –, was den radikalen Ansatz seiner Architektur unterstreicht. Grund- und Aufrisse zeigen die Komplexität des Entwurfs (rechts).

Les images des maisons de Sou Fujimoto mettent souvent en scène leurs habitants debout, assis ou dans des endroits inattendus. C'est une manière de mettre en évidence la nature radicale de ses concepts architecturaux. Les plans et les élévations montrent la complexité du projet (à droite).

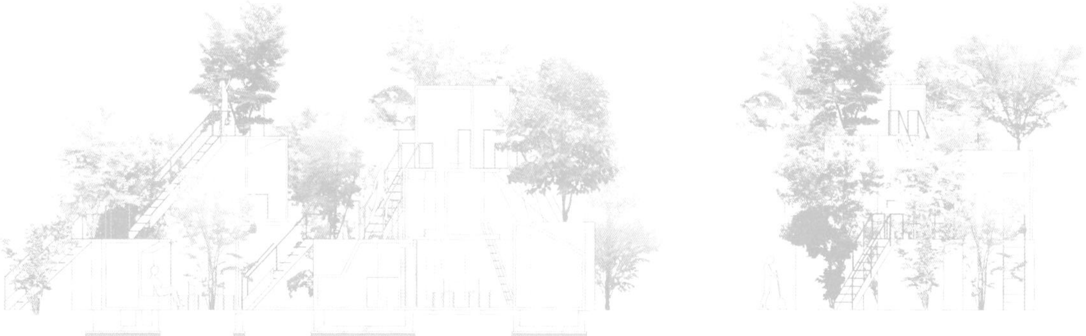

COAL HOUSE

Utsunomiya, Tochigi Prefecture, Japan, 2008

Area: 61 m². Client: Tokyo Gas Co. Ltd. Cost: not disclosed.
Collaboration: Kiyotaka Hayami

TERUNOBU FUJIMORI is known for his unusual residences and tea houses that seem at once to spring from Japanese tradition and to make gentle fun of it. In this instance, he declares that he wanted to make a "cavelike" house, inspired by the very origins of human habitation. The wood fire of an old house is here replaced by a gas fire. A red pine column brought from the mountains, and chestnut flooring, also from the mountains, mark the interior, where hand-plastered walls and ceilings also differ from most modern houses. The exterior of the "Coal House" is "scorched a full centimeter deep. I call this *yakisugi*—charred cedar—charcoal as a construction material," says Fujimori.

TERUNOBU FUJIMORI ist bekannt für seine ungewöhnlichen Wohnbauten und Teehäuser, die unmittelbar aus der japanischen Tradition zu erwachsen und zugleich humorvoll mit ihr zu spielen scheinen. In diesem Fall wollte der Architekt ein „höhlenartiges" Haus schaffen, inspiriert von den ersten Anfängen menschlicher Behausung. Das alte Holzfeuer wird hier durch den Gaskamin ersetzt. Eine Stütze aus Japanischer Rotkiefer sowie Dielen aus Kastanie, beide aus den Bergregionen Japans, prägen das Interieur. Handverputzte Wände und Decken sind ein weiterer Kontrast zu den meisten modernen Häusern. Von außen ist das „Kohlenhaus" „einen ganzen Zentimeter tief feuerversengt. Ich nenne das *yakisugi* – rußgeschwärztes Zedernholz –, Kohle als Baumaterial", erklärt Fujimori.

TERUNOBU FUJIMORI est célèbre pour ses curieuses résidences et maisons de thé qui semblent venir à la fois directement de la tradition japonaise et s'en moquer gentiment. Il a expliqué avoir voulu faire ici une maison « comme une caverne », inspirée des formes originelles de l'habitat humain. Le feu de bois des maisons anciennes est remplacé par un insert à gaz. Une colonne en pin rouge coupé dans les montagnes voisines et un sol en noyer de même origine personnalisent l'intérieur aux murs et plafonds plâtrés à la main, ce qui représente une singularité par rapport à la plupart des maisons modernes. L'extérieur de « la "maison de charbon" est calciné sur un centimètre. Pour moi, ce *yakisugi* – cèdre carbonisé – est un charbon qui devient un matériau de construction », explique Fujimori.

Fujimori's use of charred cedar for the cladding of the house is typical of old Japanese architecture, but his design is modern and unexpected.

Fujimoris Verwendung von rußgeschwärztem Zedernholz für die Verschalung des Hauses ist typisch für die traditionelle japanische Architektur, dennoch ist sein Entwurf modern und überraschend.

L'utilisation de cèdre carbonisé en habillage extérieur est typique de l'architecture japonaise ancienne, mais la conception de ce projet n'en est pas moins contemporaine et surprenante.

The open interior is intended to bring a cave to mind, but its open, bright space and the use of wood might bring a modern forest hut to mind.

Der Innenraum soll an eine Höhle erinnern. Dabei lassen der offene, helle Raum und der Einsatz von Holz eher an eine moderne Waldhütte denken.

L'intérieur ouvert veut évoquer une caverne mais son volume ample et lumineux, ainsi que l'utilisation du bois, font aussi penser à une cabane de forêt moderne.

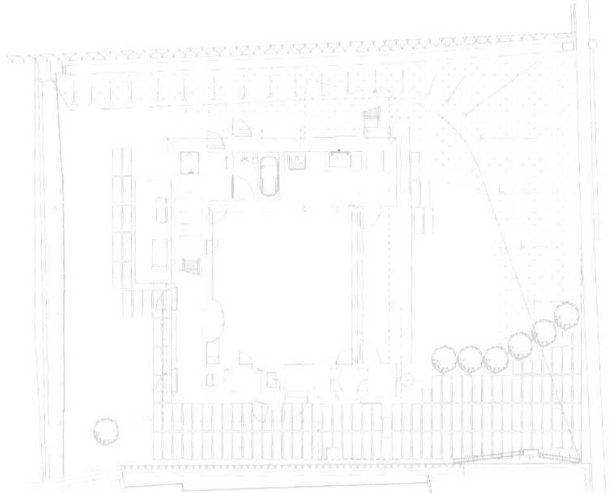

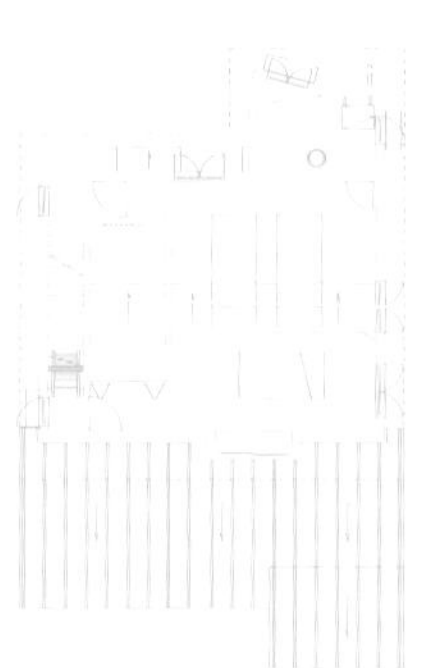

U-TSUNO-MIYA HOUSE

Utsunomiya, Tochigi Prefecture, Japan, 2008

Area: 72 m². Client: Tokyo Gas Co. Ltd.
Cost: not disclosed

The contribution of **TAIRA NISHIZAWA** (the brother of SANAA's Ryue Nishizawa) to the Sumika Project was to imagine "life in the light" by making a one-story house covered with a translucent roof slab that floats 3.5 meters above the ground and that lets the natural light penetrate into the house from above. Transparent and translucent roof areas ensure that light falls onto the bed at 8 am and in the kitchen at noon, at least part of the year. The idea of the architect is that a house should allow for natural diurnal rhythms to be reestablished. Natural ventilation is encouraged by the roof slab that has 22 louvers designed to allow wind to enter the residence.

Der Beitrag von **TAIRA NISHIZAWA**, dem Bruder des SANAA-Architekten Ryue Nishizawa, wurde vom Gedanken „Wohnen im Licht" inspiriert. Hierzu entwarf er einen Bungalow mit einer in 3,5 m Höhe scheinbar über dem Boden schwebenden, transluzenten Dachplatte, die Tageslicht von oben in das Haus fallen lässt. Transparente und transluzente Zonen im Dach erlauben, dass morgens um 8 Uhr Licht ins Schlafzimmer fällt und mittags in die Küche hinein – zumindest einen Teil des Jahres über. Es war die Vorstellung des Architekten, dass ein Haus das Erleben des natürlichen Tagesrhythmus ermöglichen sollte. 22 Lüftungsöffnungen in der Dachplatte sorgen für eine natürliche Belüftung.

La contribution de **TAIRA NISHIZAWA** (frère dc Rye Nishizawa de SANAA) à ce projet a consisté à imaginer « une vie dans la lumière », en réalisant une maison couverte d'une toiture transparente qui flotte à 3,5 m au-dessus du sol et laisse pénétrer la lumière naturelle dans chacune de ses pièces. Des zones transparentes ou translucides sont disposées de telle façon que le soleil tombe sur le lit à huit heures du matin et dans la cuisine à midi, du moins une partie de l'année. L'idée est ici qu'une maison devrait permettre de rétablir les cycles naturels diurnes. La ventilation naturelle est facilitée par vingt-deux volets placés en toiture, qui permettent de réguler l'entrée de l'air dans la maison.

The roof slab of the house appears to be quite dense, but its weightiness is lessened by its white color and, above all, by the amount of light it allows into the house.

Die Dachplatte des Hauses wirkt zunächst recht massiv, doch wird ihre Schwere durch die Farbwahl Weiß und vor allem die Menge an Licht, die sie in das Haus einfallen lässt, gemildert.

La dalle de toiture semple assez dense, mais sa pesanteur apparente est atténuée par sa couleur blanche, et surtout par le volume d'éclairage naturel qu'elle laisse pénétrer dans la maison.

MICHAEL JANTZEN

Michael Jantzen
1031 Highlands Plaza Drive West
Suite 519W
St. Louis, MO 63110
USA

Tel: +1 310 989 1897
E-mail: info@michaeljantzen.com
Web: www.michaeljantzen.com

Born in 1948, **MICHAEL JANTZEN** received a B.F.A. degree from Southern Illinois University (Edwardsville, Illinois, 1971). He received an M.F.A. degree with a major in Multimedia from Washington University (Saint Louis, Missouri, 1973). Jantzen was then hired by Washington University's School of Fine Arts and by the School of Architecture to teach studio courses as a Visiting Professor. In 1975, one of his first solar houses was featured in numerous national and international magazines. Over the next ten years, he continued to design and build energy-efficient structures with an emphasis on modular high-tech housing systems. In 1997, he was awarded a grant from Art Center College of Design Digital Media Department to develop ideas for an interface between media and architecture. In 1998, Jantzen created a conceptual house called the Malibu Video Beach House, and Elements, an interactive digital media theme park. From 1999 to 2001, he designed and built the M House, "a modular, re-locatable, environmentally responsive, alternative housing system." Since then, Jantzen has worked with various companies as a consultant to develop experimental design projects. Recent work includes Desert Winds Eco-Spa (2008), a concept design for a wellness spa that generates all of its energy from the wind and sun; Sun Rays Pavilion (2009), a concept design for a large solar-powered pavilion; and Homestead House (2009, published here).

MICHAEL JANTZEN wurde 1948 geboren und erhielt seinen B.F.A. 1971 an der Southern Illinois University (Edwardsville, Illinois). Seinen M.F.A. machte er 1973 mit dem Hauptfach Multimedia an der Washington University (Saint Louis, Missouri, 1973). Im Anschluss erhielt Jantzen einen Lehrauftrag an den Fakultäten für bildende Kunst und Architektur der Washington University und leitete dort Studiokurse als Gastprofessor. 1975 wurde eines seiner ersten Solarhäuser in zahlreichen nationalen und internationalen Zeitschriften publiziert. Im Lauf der folgenden zehn Jahre entwarf und errichtete er weitere energieeffiziente Bauten, wobei er sich auf hochtechnisierte Modulhäuser spezialisierte. 1997 erhielt er ein Forschungsstipendium der Abteilung für digitale Medien des Art Center College of Design, um Ideen für eine Schnittstelle zwischen Medien und Architektur zu entwickeln. 1998 entwarf Jantzen ein Konzepthaus, das Malibu Video Beach House, und Elements, einen interaktiven, digitalen Medienfreizeitpark. Zwischen 1999 und 2001 entwarf und baute er das M House, „ein modulares, umzugsfähiges, umweltsensibles, alternatives Wohnbausystem". Seither arbeitet Jantzen für verschiedene Firmen als Berater und entwickelt experimentelle Designprojekte. Jüngere Projekte sind u. a. das Desert Winds Eco-Spa (2008), ein Konzeptentwurf für ein Wellnesszentrum, das seinen gesamten Strombedarf aus Wind- und Solarenergie bezieht, Sun Rays Pavilion (2009), ein Konzept für einen großen, mit Solarenergie betriebenen Pavillon, sowie das Homestead House (2009, hier vorgestellt).

Né en 1948, **MICHAEL JANTZEN** a obtenu son B.F.A. de la Southern Illinois University (Edwardsville, Illinois, 1971), et son M.F.A. spécialisé en multimédias de l'université Washington (Saint Louis, Missouri, 1973). L'École des beaux-arts et l'École d'architecture de l'université Washington lui ont ensuite offert de devenir professeur d'atelier invité. En 1975, l'une de ses premières maisons solaires a été publiée dans de nombreux magazines nationaux et internationaux. Au cours des dix années suivantes, il a conçu et réalisé des constructions écologiques autour de systèmes modulaires de haute technologie. En 1997, il a obtenu une bourse du département de conception de médias numériques de l'Art Center pour développer ses idées sur une interface entre médias et architecture. En 1998, il a créé une maison conceptuelle appelée la Malibu Video Beach House, et Elements, un parc à thème sur les médias numériques interactifs. De 1999 à 2001, il a conçu et construit la maison M, « système d'habitation modulaire, transportable, écologique ». Depuis, il a travaillé comme consultant sur de nombreux projets expérimentaux. Parmi ses réalisations récentes : le Desert Winds Eco-Spa (2008), le concept d'un spa qui génère l'énergie dont il a besoin à partir des vents et du soleil ; Sun Rays, un grand pavillon à énergie solaire (2009) et la maison ferme (Homestead House, 2009, publiée ici).

HOMESTEAD HOUSE

2009

For this project, Michael Jantzen looked into "readily available agricultural building components in the creation of alternative housing systems." The house makes use of commercially available steel, and a "prefabricated, modular, high-strength, low-cost, arch building system normally used for agricultural purposes." Using simple tools, the recyclable steel sheets can be bolted together, which can also be dismounted easily. The system allows modules to be assembled in various ways. A lighter interior structure is imagined that can be filled with pulped newspaper for insulation. Photovoltaic cells, a small wind turbine, passive solar heating, and rainwater collection are all envisaged for energy independence.

Für dieses Projekt griff Michael Jantzen auf „leicht erhältliche Baukomponenten zurück, mit denen sich alternative Wohnbauprojekte realisieren lassen". Das Haus nutzt handelsübliche Stahlprofile sowie ein „vorgefertigtes, modulares, sehr belastbares und kostengünstiges Bogensystem, das üblicherweise in der Landwirtschaft Verwendung findet". Mithilfe einfacher Werkzeuge lassen sich die recyclingfähigen Stahlblechen verschrauben und ebenso einfach wieder demontieren. Das System erlaubt es, die Module auf verschiedene Weise zusammenzusetzen. Für den Innenausbau ist eine leichtere Konstruktion vorgesehen, die mit zerfasertem Zeitungspapier gedämmt werden kann. Fotovoltaikzellen, ein kleiner Windgenerator, eine Solarheizung und Regenwassernutzung sollen für energetische Unabhängigkeit sorgen.

Pour réaliser ce projet, Michael Jantzen a recherché « des éléments de constructions agricoles facilement disponibles pour créer un système d'habitat alternatif ». La maison est donc en acier et fait appel à « un système constructif en arcs préfabriqués, modulaires à haute résistance et de coût peu élevé, souvent utilisé dans les exploitations agricoles ». Les tôles d'acier recyclées sont vissées à l'aide d'outils simples et peuvent donc se démonter aisément. Le système permet d'assembler les modules de diverses façons. Une structure intérieure plus légère est isolée thermiquement de l'extérieur par de la pulpe de papier. Des cellules photovoltaïques, une petite éolienne, un chauffage solaire passif et la collecte des eaux de pluie devraient assurer une certaine indépendance énergétique.

JOHNSTON MARKLEE

Johnston Marklee
1545 Pontius Avenue
Los Angeles, CA 90025
USA

Tel: +1 310 442 4886
Fax: +1 310 442 4896
E-mail: office@johnstonmarklee.com
Web: www.johnstonmarklee.com

Diego Arraigada Arquitecto
Alvear 1569
Rosario
Argentina

Tel/Fax: +54 341 448 8393
E-mail: estudio@diegoarraigada.com
Web: www.diegoarraigada.com

SHARON JOHNSTON got her B.A. in History and Art History from Stanford University and her architectural degree from the Harvard Design School (GSD). **MARK LEE** is a graduate of the University of Southern California, where he received a B.A. in Architecture. He got his M.Arch at the GSD. Johnston Marklee was founded by Sharon Johnston and Mark Lee in 1998. Recently, Johnston Marklee designed the Kaikai Kiki Merchandise Room for the ©Murakami traveling exhibition at the Museum of Contemporary Art (MOCA), Los Angeles, California. Johnston Marklee curated the Portugal Arte '09 outdoor sculpture exhibition in Lisbon, and is designing an exhibition for the DEPART Foundation, to be featured at "New York Minute, Macro Future," Rome, Italy, and the Istituto Italiano di Cultura, Los Angeles, California, in 2010. The View House (Rosario, Argentina, 2006–09, published here) is the result of collaboration with **DIEGO ARRAIGADA**. Arraigada graduated in 1999 from the School of Architecture, Planning and Design at the National University of Rosario, Argentina. In 2003, he received an M.Arch degree from the University of California at Los Angeles (UCLA). In 2004, he established Diego Arraigada Arquitecto in Rosario. He teaches at the UAI School of Architecture in Rosario and at the Di Tella University School of Architecture and Urban Studies in Buenos Aires. Current works include a low-rise housing project in Rosario, and a coastal park in Patagonia, both in Argentina.

SHARON JOHNSTON erhielt ihren B.A. in Geschichte und Kunstgeschichte an der Universität Stanford und schloss ihr Architekturstudium an der Harvard Design School (GSD) ab. **MARK LEE** schloss sein Studium an der University of Southern California mit einem B. A. in Architektur ab. Seinen M. Arch. machte er an der GSD. 1998 gründeten Sharon Johnston und Mark Lee ihr Büro Johnston Marklee. In letzter Zeit entwarfen Johnston Marklee den Kaikai-Kiki-Shop für die ©Murakami-Wanderausstellung am Museum of Contemporary Art (MOCA) in Los Angeles. Außerdem kuratierten Johnston Marklee in Lissabon die Skulpturenausstellung im öffentlichen Raum für die Portugal Arte '09 und entwerfen eine Ausstellungsarchitektur für die DEPART Foundation, die 2010 im Rahmen von „New York Minute, Macro Future" in Rom sowie am Istituto Italiano di Cultura in Los Angeles zu sehen sein wird. Das hier vorgestellte View House (Rosario, Argentina, 2006–09) entstand in Zusammenarbeit mit **DIEGO ARRAIGADA**. Arraigada schloss 1999 sein Studium an der Fakultät für Architektur, Planung und Entwurf an der Universidad Nacional de Rosario in Argentinien ab. 2003 erwarb er seinen M. Arch. an der University of California in Los Angeles (UCLA) und gründete 2004 sein Büro Diego Arraigada Arquitecto in Rosario. Er lehrt an der Fakultät für Architektur der UAI Rosario sowie an der Fakultät für Architektur und Urbanistik der Universidad Torcuato Di Tella in Buenos Aires. Gegenwärtig arbeitet er an einer Wohnanlage mit niedriger Bebauung in Rosario sowie einem Küstenpark in Patagonien, beide in Argentinien.

SHARON JOHNSTON a obtenus son B.A. en histoire et histoire de l'art de l'université Stanford et est diplômée en architecture de l'Harvard Design School (GSD). **MARK LEE** est diplômé de l'université de Californie du Sud (USC, B.Arch) et a obtenu son M.Arch de la GSD. Ils ont fondé l'agence Johnston Marklee en 1998. Récemment, ils ont conçu la boutique Kaikai Kiki de l'exposition itinérante « ©Murakami » du Musée d'art contemporain de Los Angeles (MOCA). Johnston Marklee a été commissaire de l'exposition de sculpture de plein air « Portugal Arte '09 » à Lisbonne, et travaille actuellement sur le projet d'une exposition pour la Fondation DEPART, qui sera présentée à la manifestation « New York Minute, Macro Future », à Rome, et à l'Institut culturel italien de Los Angeles en 2010. La maison avec vue (View House, Rosario, Argentine, 2006–09, publiée ici) résulte d'une collaboration avec **DIEGO ARRAIGADA**. Arraigada est diplômé de l'École d'architecture, d'urbanisme et de design de l'Université nationale de Rosario (1999). En 2003 il a passé son M.Arch à l'UCLA et a fondé l'agence Diego Arraigada Arquitecto à Rosario en 2004. Il enseigne à l'École d'architecture de Rosario et à l'École d'architecture et d'études urbaines de l'université Di Tella à Buenos Aires. Parmi ses travaux récents figurent un projet de logements en alignement à Rosario, et un parc côtier en Patagonie.

VIEW HOUSE

Rosario, Argentina, 2006–09

Area: 269 m². Client: Lucas Ma (President, Markee LLC). Cost: not disclosed

The site of this house is considered "ecologically fragile." The architects sought to optimize "small dwelling spaces by maximizing the experience of the dramatic surrounding views and prioritizing environmental performance." This is achieved in part through a compact footprint. Views of the site are arranged through the openings that punctuate the house and its spiral internal disposition. The unusual curving concrete surfaces are in part determined by the structural logic of the house. Dependence on mechanical systems was minimized through the use of natural airflow and alternative energy systems. The loads of the house are borne in part by a "pentagonal steel ring embedded in walls and floor plates."

Der Standort des Hauses gilt als „ökologisch sensibel". Den Architekten ging es um eine Optimierung von „kleinen Wohnflächen, indem die dramatische Aussicht in einem Höchstmaß genutzt und umweltgerechtes Bauen an erste Stelle gesetzt wurde". Dies wird zum Teil durch eine kompakte Grundfläche erreicht. Ausblicke auf das Grundstück ergeben sich durch die Öffnungen, die in die Fassade eingeschnitten sind, sowie durch die spiralförmige Gliederung des Hausinneren. Die ungewöhnlichen, geschwungenen Betonoberflächen resultieren u. a. aus der baulichen Logik des Hauses. Die Abhängigkeit von Technik konnte durch die Nutzung natürlicher Lüftungsströme und alternativer Energiesysteme minimiert werden. Das Gewicht des Hauses wird zum Teil durch einen „fünfeckigen, in Wände und die Bodenplatte eingelassenen Stahlring" getragen.

Le site de cette maison est jugé « écologiquement fragile ». Les architectes ont cherché à tirer le maximum de profit « de petits espaces d'habitation, en optimisant l'expérience des vues spectaculaires sur le paysage et en donnant la priorité à la performance environnementale ». Ceci a été réalisé, en partie grâce à une emprise au sol réduite. Les vues sur le paysage sont réparties au fil des ouvertures de la maison dont le plan intérieur est en spirale. Les plans en béton curieusement incurvés sont en partie déterminés par la logique structurelle de la composition. Le recours aux systèmes mécaniques a été réduit au minimum grâce à la ventilation naturelle et à des systèmes à base d'énergies alternatives. Les charges sont en parties reportées sur « un anneau pentagonal en acier intégré aux murs et aux planchers ».

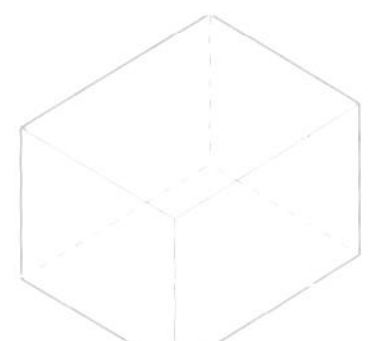
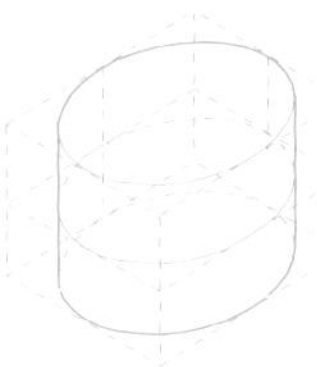
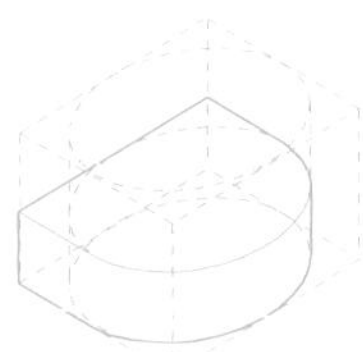
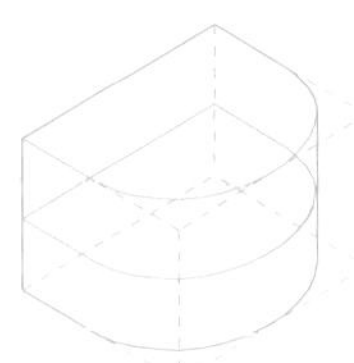
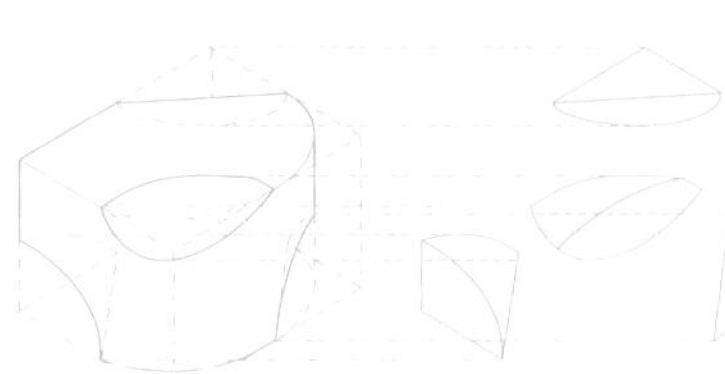

The progressive axonometric drawings (above) show how the forms of the house evolved from a cube to a cylinder, and the slicing of those basic geometric volumes.

Die Abfolge axonometrischer Zeichnungen (oben) illustriert, wie sich die Form des Hauses aus einem Kubus, dann einem Zylinder und schließlich dem Beschnitt dieser beiden geometrischen Grundformen entwickelte.

Les dessins axonométriques ci-dessus montrent comment les formes de la maison ont évolué à partir d'un cube et d'un cylindre découpés.

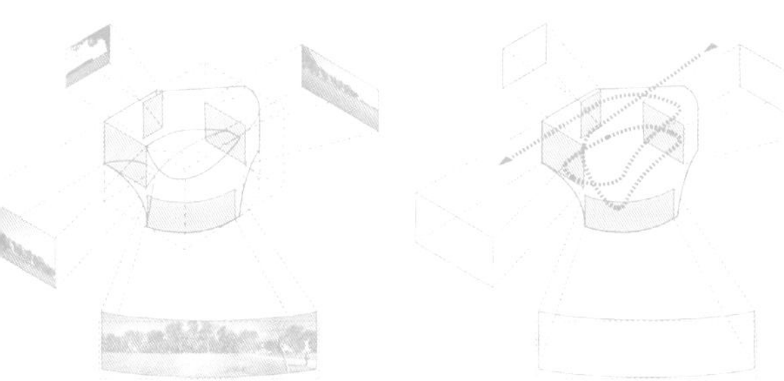

The drawing (above) and images of the house make clear the intention of the architects to provide the view(s) implied in the name of the residence.

Die Zeichnung (oben) und die Aufnahmen des Hauses verdeutlichen, wie die Architekten die Aussicht(en) ermöglichten, denen das Haus seinen Namen verdankt.

Le dessin ci-dessus et les images de la maison montrent que l'architecte a voulu privilégier les vues, comme l'implique d'ailleurs le nom de cette résidence.

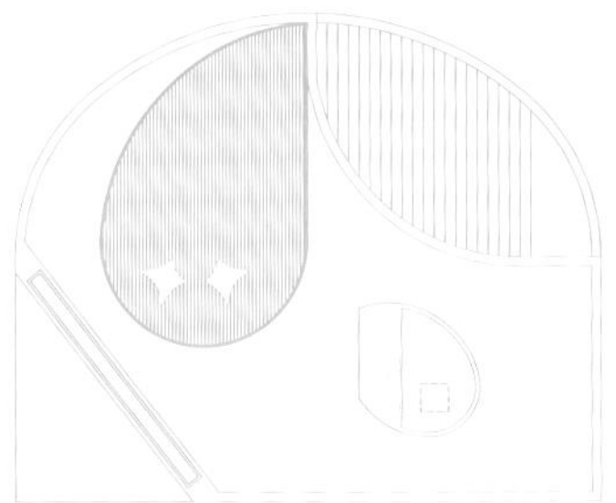

Despite its broad curves and somewhat unexpected angles, interior images demonstrate that the house provides for comfortable living space.

Die Innenansichten belegen, dass das Haus trotz seiner ausgreifenden Rundungen und zum Teil überraschenden Winkel komfortablen Wohnraum bietet.

Malgré des courbes amples et des plans inclinés assez inattendus, les images de l'intérieur montrent des espaces de vie particulièrement confortables.

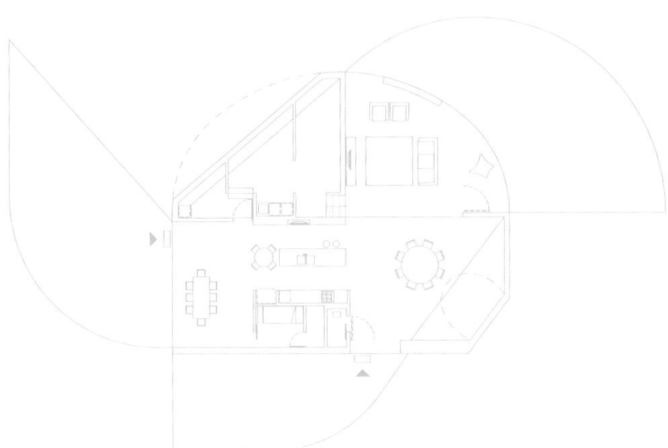

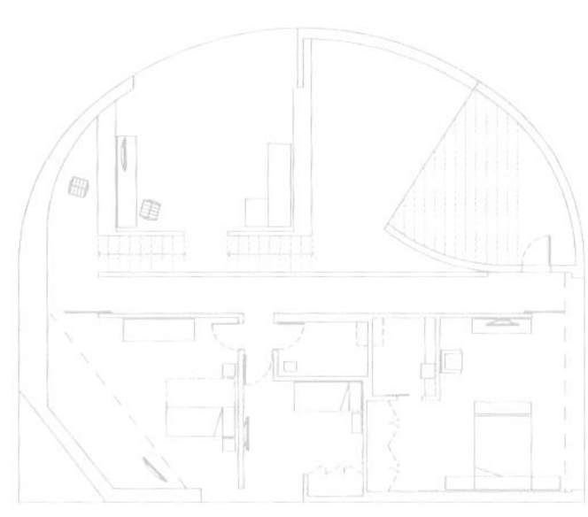

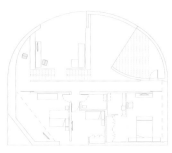

RICK JOY

Rick Joy Architects
400 South Rubio Avenue
Tucson, AZ 85701
USA

Tel: +1 520 624 1442
Fax: +1 520 791 0699
E-mail: studio@rickjoy.com
Web: www.rickjoy.com

RICK JOY's first working experience was not as an architect, but as a musician and a carpenter in Maine. He obtained his B.Arch degree from the University of Arizona in 1990 and spent three years in the office of Will Bruder, working on the design team for the Phoenix Central Library. He then set up his own practice in Tucson in 1993. "Bold, modern architecture that is rooted in the context and culture of its place," says Rick Joy, "and that is developed in combination with the basics of proper solar orientation and site protection, and the responsible use of sensible materials and fine craftsmanship will have the quality to withstand the tests of time." Rick Joy Architects currently has several residential commissions in Napa, Utah, Chile, Vermont, New Mexico, Marfa and Dallas in Texas, and Arizona, including a house for Eleanor and Francis Ford Coppola; the Hacienda de Taos in New Mexico; and the Woodstock Farm Estate in Vermont. Other recent commissions include the campus of the Holy Cross Institute and Chapel at Saint Edwards University in Austin (Texas); an eco-resort hotel and villas in Southern Utah; a town and resort on Bahia Balandra (Baja California Sur, Mexico); a town and resort in Zion (Utah); re-master planning and downtown extension in York Beach (Maine); Ventana Canyon House (Tucson, Arizona, 2004–08, published here); and a ten-story sportsmen's housing block for the 2011 Pan-American Games in Guadalajara (Mexico).

RICK JOY sammelte seine ersten Berufserfahrungen nicht als Architekt, sondern als Musiker und Schreiner in Maine. 1990 erwarb er seinen B. Arch. an der Universität von Arizona und arbeitete drei Jahre bei Will Bruder im Entwurfsteam für die Phoenix Central Library. 1993 gründete er sein eigenes Büro in Tucson. „Kühne, moderne Architektur, die in ihrem Umfeld und dessen Kultur verwurzelt ist“, erklärt Rick Joy, „bei der eine optimale Sonnenausrichtung und der Umweltschutz berücksichtigt werden und die verantwortlich mit sinnvollen Materialien und hochwertigem Handwerk umgeht, ist von einer Qualität, die die Zeit überdauert.“ Derzeit arbeitet Rick Joy Architects an mehreren Aufträgen für Wohnbauten in Napa, Utah, Chile, Vermont, New Mexico, Marfa und Dallas in Texas sowie in Arizona. Hierzu zählen u. a. ein Haus für Eleanor und Francis Ford Coppola, die Hacienda de Taos in New Mexico sowie die Woodstock Farm in Vermont. Weitere Aufträge sind der Campus des Holy Cross Institute und die Kapelle der Saint Edwards University in Austin (Texas), ein ökologisches Hotel mit Ferienhausanlage in Süd-Utah, eine Stadt und Ferienanlage auf Bahia Balandra (Baja California Sur, Mexiko), eine Stadt und Ferienanlage in Zion (Utah), ein Masterplan und der Ausbau des Stadtzentrums in York Beach (Maine), das Ventana Canyon House (Tucson, Arizona, 2004–08, hier vorgestellt), sowie eine zehngeschossige Wohnanlage für Sportler für die Panamerikanischen Spiele 2011 in Guadalajara (Mexiko).

Les premières expériences professionnelles de **RICK JOY** ne sont pas celles d'un architecte, mais d'un musicien et d'un menuisier dans le Maine. Il a obtenu son B.Arch de l'université de l'Arizona en 1990 et passé trois années dans l'agence de Will Bruder, travaillant dans l'équipe de conception de la bibliothèque centrale de Phoenix. Il a ensuite monté sa propre agence à Tucson en 1993. « Une architecture audacieuse et moderne, enracinée dans le contexte et la culture du lieu », explique-t-il, « et qui se développe en combinaison avec les principes de base de l'orientation solaire et de la protection du site, une utilisation responsable de matériaux intelligents et une réalisation soignée qui possède la qualité de résister à l'épreuve du temps. » Rick Joy Architects travaille actuellement sur plusieurs projets résidentiels à Napa, dans l'Utah, au Chili, dans le Vermont, au Nouveau-Mexique, à Marfa et Dallas au Texas et en Arizona, dont une résidence pour Eleanor et Francis Ford Coppola ; la Hacienda de Taos au Nouveau-Mexique ; et le Woodstock Farm Estate dans le Vermont. Parmi d'autres commandes figurent le campus de l'Institut Holy Cross et de sa chapelle à Saint-Edwards University à Austin (Texas) ; un éco-hôtel de vacances et des villas dans le sud de l'Utah ; une ville et une station balnéaire à Bahia Balandra (Basse-Californie-du-Sud, Mexique) ; une ville et une station touristique à Zion (Utah) ; le plan directeur et l'extension du centre de York Beach (Maine) ; la maison du canyon de Ventana (Canyon House, Ventana, Tucson, Arizona, 2004–08, publié ici) ; et un immeuble de dix étages de logements pour les sportifs des Jeux panaméricains 2011 à Guadalajara (Mexique).

VENTANA CANYON HOUSE

Tucson, Arizona, USA, 2004–08

Area: 778 m². Client: Tom Barton.
Cost: not disclosed

This house includes a 297-square-meter ground floor, a 315-square-meter upper level, and a 166-square-meter covered patio. It was designed with a post-tensioned concrete slab cantilevered over load-bearing cast-in-place concrete walls, with structural steel frame above. This is a five-bedroom family vacation house in the Catalina Mountains overlooking Tucson Valley. The swimming pool and terrace are carved from the cliff face. The house is entered from beneath the cantilevered kitchen. The family bedrooms are on the ground level. The main living area is the upper floor, with a dining room, living room, kitchen, and guesthouse, and a large horizontal window offering views of the valley. The Ventana Canyon House is clad essentially in heavy-gage steel plate, with cantilevered "brows" that block out the sun's rays and the view of gazing neighbors.

Das Haus umfasst ein 297 m² großes Erdgeschoss, ein 315 m² großes Obergeschoss sowie einen 166 m² großen überdachten Innenhof. Der Entwurf basiert auf einer auskragenden Spannbetonplatte über tragenden Wänden aus Ortbeton und einer Stahlrahmenkonstruktion darüber. Das Ferienhaus für eine Familie hat fünf Schlafzimmer und liegt in den Catalina Mountains mit Blick auf das Tucson Valley. Swimmingpool und Terrasse wurden aus dem Felshang geschlagen. Der Eingang liegt unterhalb der auskragenden Küche, die Schlafzimmer der Familie befinden sich im Erdgeschoss. Der Hauptwohnbereich mit Ess- und Wohnzimmer, Küche und einer Gästewohnung befindet sich im Obergeschoss; ein großes Panoramafenster bietet einen Blick auf das Tal. Das Ventana Canyon House ist weitgehend mit schweren Stahlplatten verkleidet; auskragende „Brauen" schützen vor Sonnenlicht und den Blicken der Nachbarn.

Cette maison familiale dans les Catalina Mountains domine la vallée de Tucson. Elle se compose d'un rez-de-chaussée de 297 m², un étage de 341,5 m² et d'un patio couvert de 166 m². Sa structure fait appel à une dalle de béton post-tensionné reposant en porte-à-faux sur des murs porteurs en béton coulé en place, sur lesquels s'appuie également une ossature en acier. Maison familiale de cinq chambres, sa piscine et sa terrasse ont été creusées dans la falaise. On pénètre dans l'habitation sous la cuisine en porte-à-faux. Les cinq chambres de la famille sont au niveau inférieur. Les espaces de vie, dont le séjour, la salle à manger, la cuisine et une section pour invités, se trouvent à l'étage, où une immense baie horizontale offre des vues sur la vallée. La maison est essentiellement habillée de lourdes plaques d'acier à « sourcils » qui protègent du soleil et des regards des voisins.

Above, the steel cladding of parts of the house, and left, the swimming pool. Below: A section drawing of the house shows its strong structural elements and slightly inclined roof.

Oben die Stahlverblendung an Teilen des Hauses, links der Pool. Auf dem Querschnitt des Hauses unten sind die kräftigen tragenden und das leicht geneigte Dach deutlich sichtbar.

Ci-dessus l'habillage en acier de certaines parties de la maison et, à gauche, la piscine. La coupe ci-dessous montre la vigueur de la composition structurelle et de la toiture légèrement inclinée.

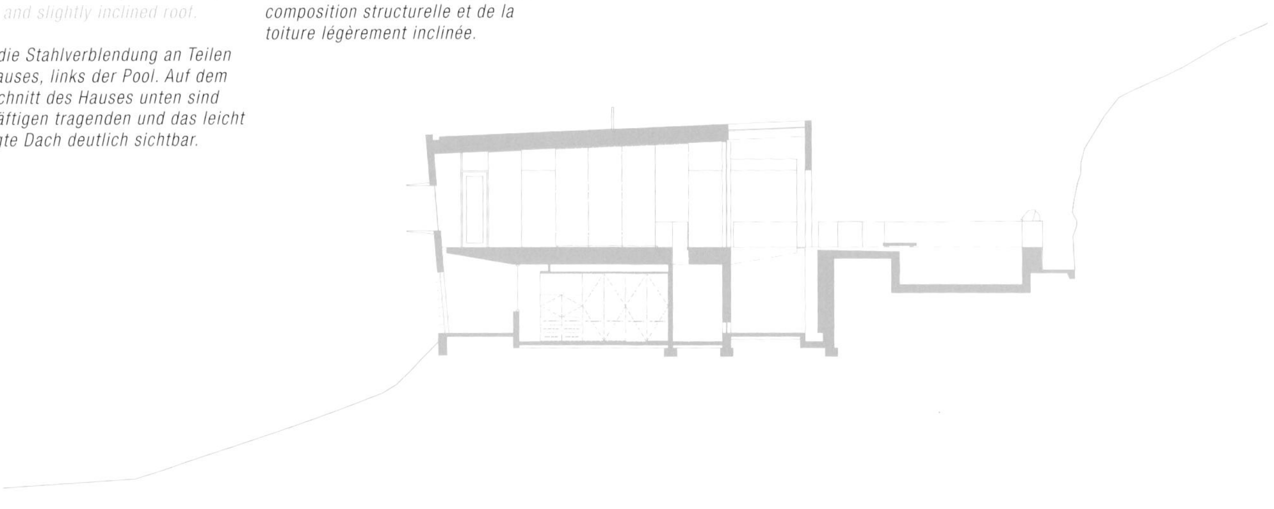

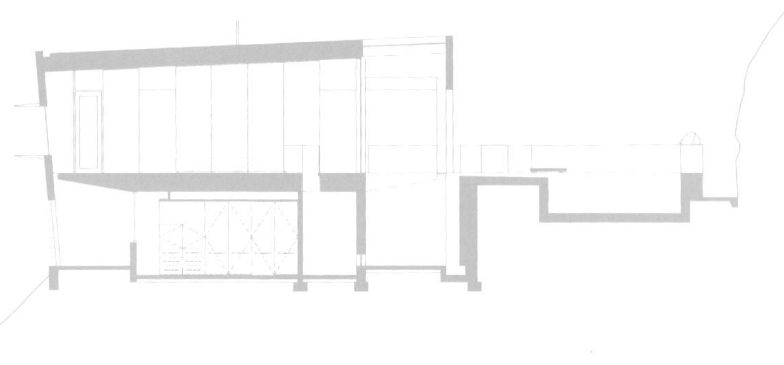

Elevations shows the substantial size of the main level of the house as opposed to its base. Below, the living and dining area.

Aufrisse zeigen die großzügig bemessene Fläche des Hauptgeschosses gegenüber dem Sockelgeschoss. Unten der Wohn- und Essbereich.

Les élévations montrent l'importance des dimensions de l'étage principal par rapport à la base. Ci-dessous, le séjour salle à manger.

Above, fully glazed walls open to the outdoor terraces. Below, plans of the main and lower levels.

Voll verglaste Fronten öffnen sich zur Terrasse (oben). Unten Grundrisse von Haupt- und unterem Geschoss.

Ci-dessus, des parois entièrement vitrées ouvrent sur des terrasses. Ci-dessous, plans du niveau principal et du niveau inférieur.

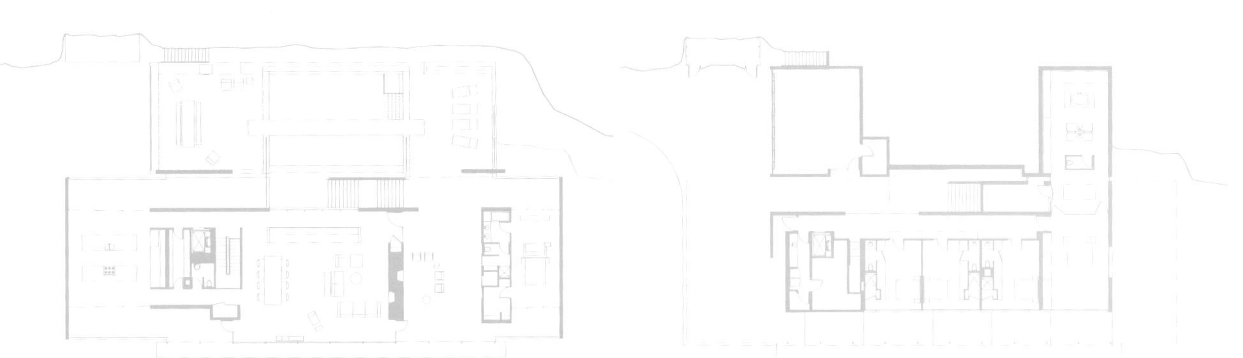

STEPHEN KANNER

Kanner Architects
1558 10th Street
Santa Monica, CA 90401
USA

Tel: +1 310 451 5400
Fax: +1 310 451 5440
E-mail: info@kannerarch.com
Web: www.kannerarch.com

STEPHEN KANNER received his M.Arch degree in 1980 from the University of California at Berkeley. He has been practicing architecture since 1980 and has been a licensed architect in the State of California since 1982. Prior to joining Kanner Architects in 1983, he worked for the Cambridge Seven in Boston on the Baltimore Aquarium and the Basketball Hall of Fame projects and subsequently for Skidmore, Owings & Merrill in Los Angeles, where he was one of the project designers on the Texaco Tower in Universal City and the Hughes Headquarters in Marina Del Rey. Kanner, a third-generation Los Angeles architect, worked closely with his father, Charles Kanner (former president of the LA Chapter of the AIA), for 18 years, and they produced more than 150 projects together. He is currently president of Kanner Architects, which celebrated its 60th anniversary in 2006. Kanner Architects has worked on numerous projects that encompass commercial and institutional projects, retail, multi-family and single-family homes. Stephen Kanner has been a guest lecturer and critic at several universities. Recent work includes Malibu 5 (Malibu, California, 2004–06, published here); 26th Street Low-Income Housing (Santa Monica, 2007); The Hollywood (Los Angeles, 2008); Nashville House (Nashville, Tennessee, 2009); and the Superior at Venice Apartments (Los Angeles, California, under construction 2009), all in the USA.

STEPHEN KANNER erhielt seinen M. Arch. 1980 an der University of California in Berkeley. Er arbeitet seit 1980 als Architekt und ist seit 1982 als solcher in Kalifornien zugelassen. Vor seinem Eintritt bei Kanner Architects 1983 arbeitete er zunächst für Cambridge Seven in Boston am Baltimore Aquarium und an der Basketball Hall of Fame und schließlich für Skidmore, Owings & Merrill in Los Angeles. Dort war er einer der Projektarchitekten für den Texaco Tower in Universal City und die Hauptverwaltung von Hughes in Marina Del Rey. Kanner stammt aus einer Architektenfamilie in Los Angeles und führt die Tradition in der dritten Generation weiter. 18 Jahre lang arbeitete er eng mit seinem Vater Charles Kanner (ehemals Präsident der AIA, Bezirk Los Angeles) zusammen. Gemeinsam realisierten sie über 150 Projekte. Gegenwärtig ist er Präsident von Kanner Architects; 2006 feierte das Büro sein 60-jähriges Bestehen. Kanner Architects betreut zahlreiche Projekte für Firmen und Institutionen, von Läden bis zu Mehr- und Einfamilienhäusern. Stephen Kanner war Gastdozent und Architekturkritiker an verschiedenen Universitäten. Jüngere Projekte sind u. a. Malibu 5 (Malibu, Kalifornien, 2004–06, hier vorgestellt), Sozialwohnungen an der 26th Street (Santa Monica, 2007), The Hollywood (Los Angeles, 2008), Nashville House (Nashville, Tennessee, 2009) sowie die Superior at Venice Apartments (Los Angeles, 2009 in Bau), alle in den USA.

STEPHEN KANNER est diplômé (M.Arch) de l'université de Californie à Berkeley (1980). Il pratique l'architecture depuis cette date, et est architecte licencié de l'État de Californie depuis 1982. Avant de rejoindre l'agence de son père, Kanner Architects, en 1983, il travaillé pour les Cambridge Seven à Boston sur les projets de l'Aquarium de Baltimore et le Basketball Hall of Fame, puis pour Skidmore, Owings & Merrill à Los Angeles, sur le projet de la tour Texaco à Universal City et le siège social de Hughes à Marina Del Rey. Kanner, représentant la troisième génération d'une famille d'architectes de Los Angeles, a travaillé en étroite collaboration avec son père, Charles Kanner (ancien président de la section locale de l'AIA), pendant dix-huit ans. Ils ont réalisé ensemble plus de cent cinquante projets. Il est actuellement président de Kanner Architects, qui a célébré son 60e anniversaire en 2006. L'agence travaille sur de multiples projets : commerciaux, institutionnels, résidentiels. Stephen Kanner a été conférencier et critique invité dans plusieurs universités. Parmi ses réalisations récentes : la maison Malibu 5 (Malibu, Californie, 2004–06, publiée ici) ; des logements économiques 26th Street (Santa Monica, 2007) ; The Hollywood (Los Angeles, 2008) ; maison Nashville (Nashville, Tennessee, 2009) ; et l'immeuble Supérieur at Venice Apartments (Los Angeles, Californie, en construction, 2009), tous aux États-Unis.

MALIBU 5

Malibu, California, USA, 2004–06

Area: 307 m². Clients: Georgia Goldfarb, Walter Zelman.
Cost: not disclosed

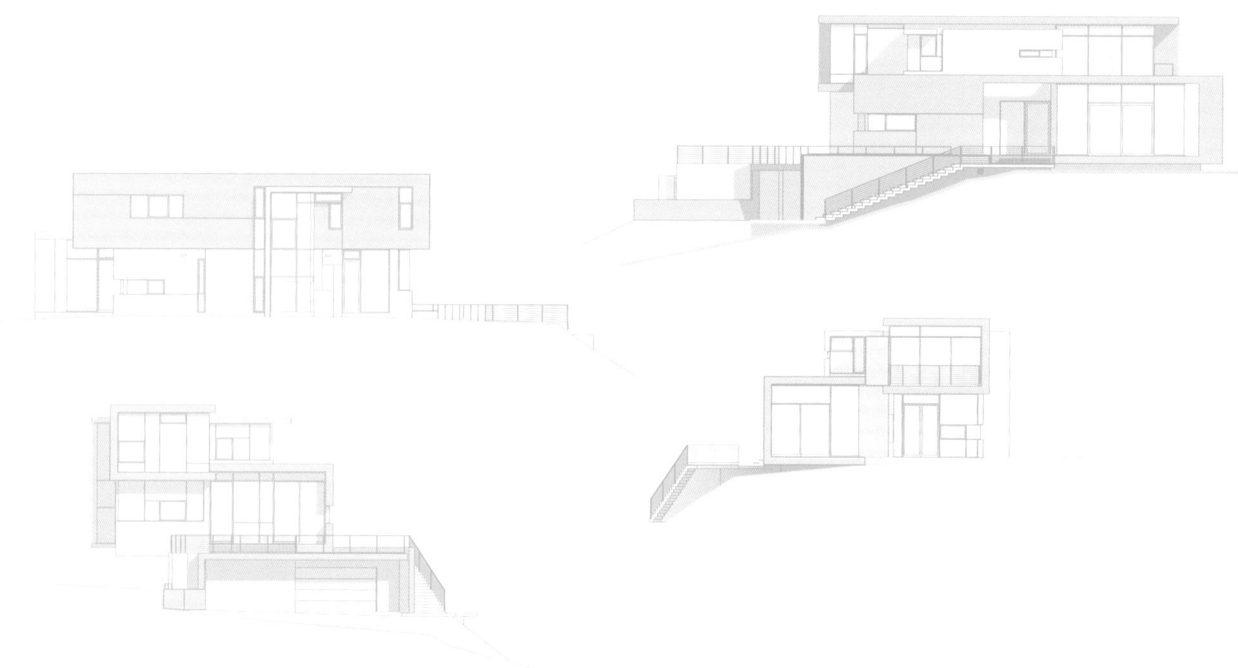

Set into a Malibu hillside, this residence is unusual in that the owners are now effectively contributing energy to the local power grid during daylight hours. It makes use of photovoltaic panels and solar thermal panels for hot water. Concrete floors at ground level absorb heat in the day and release it at night. The house is made up of "two, C-shaped, rectangular bars—one two stories, one a single story over the garage," according to Steven Kanner, and has three bedrooms and as many bathrooms. A courtyard and openings on both sides of the building allow ocean breezes to cool the house that faces the Pacific, through cross-ventilation. Double-paned low-E glass provides further thermal insulation. Balcony overhangs reduce solar gain. Artificial lighting, when necessary, is controlled by motion sensors. Local, drought-resistant plants are used in the garden, which is irrigated with recycled water. Finally, the architects state: "The inexpensive scratched-plaster exterior is painted an earthy terracotta color to provide a natural texture that smoothes the house's introduction to its environment." The color is inspired by the hue the architect found on a government building in the West African capital city of Accra.

Ungewöhnlich an dem in einen Hügel in Malibu gebauten Anwesen ist die Tatsache, dass die Eigentümer tagsüber Energie in das örtliche Stromnetz einspeisen. Das Haus nutzt Photovoltaikzellen und solarthermischen Paneele zur Warmwassererzeugung. Im Erdgeschoss absorbieren Betonböden tagsüber Wärme, die sie nachts wieder abgeben. Das Haus besteht, so Steven Kanner, aus „zwei in der Fassade C-förmigen, rechteckigen Riegeln – einer zwei-, der andere über der Garage eingeschossig". Es verfügt über drei Schlafzimmer und ebenso viele Bäder. Dank eines Innenhofs und Öffnungen auf beiden Seiten des Gebäudes weht die Meeresbrise durch das Haus mit Blick auf den Pazifik und kühlt es so durch Querlüftung. Für zusätzliche Wärmedämmung sorgt eine Isolierverglasung mit einer reflektierenden Beschichtung. Die auskragenden Balkone verhindern, dass sich das Gebäude zu stark aufheizt. Die Beleuchtung wird durch Bewegungsmelder gesteuert. Im Garten wurden regionaltypische, trockenheitsresistente Pflanzen gepflanzt, die mit Grauwasser bewässert werden. Zusammenfassend erklären die Architekten: „Der kostengünstige Grobputz der Fassade wurde in einem erdigen Terrakottaton gestrichen. Das gibt dem Haus eine natürliche Anmutung, und es fügt sich besser in seine Umgebung ein." Inspiriert zu dieser Farbwahl wurde der Architekt von einem Farbton, den er an einem Regierungsgebäude in der ghanaischen Hauptstadt Accra gesehen hatte.

Implantée pratiquement au sommet d'une colline de Malibu et dominant le Pacifique, cette résidence a pour originalité de participer à sa production d'électricité pendant le jour. Elle possède des panneaux photovoltaïques et des panneaux thermiques solaires pour fournir l'eau chaude. Les sols en béton absorbent la chaleur pendant le jour, et la restituent pendant la nuit. La maison se compose de « deux barres rectangulaires en forme de C, une de deux niveaux, une d'un seul niveau au-dessus d'un garage », explique Stephen Kanner. Elle possède trois chambres et autant de salle de bains. Une cour et des ouvertures donnant sur les deux côtés de la maison permettent une ventilation croisée assurée par la brise de l'océan. Les doubles vitrages basse énergie renforcent l'isolation thermique. Les porte-à-faux des balcons limitent le gain solaire. L'éclairage artificiel, si nécessaire, est piloté par des capteurs de mouvements. Le jardin planté de végétaux locaux résistant à la sécheresse est irrigué par de l'eau recyclée. « La façade en plâtre gratté, technique peu coûteuse, est peinte de couleur terre cuite pour produire un effet de texture naturelle qui adoucit l'irruption d'une telle maison dans son environnement. » Cette couleur est inspirée de teintes trouvées par l'architecte sur un bâtiment public d'Accra au Ghana.

The wrapping, red forms of the house assure that its appearance is different from every angle, as seen in the elevations (left page) and in two photos.

Die umeinander gefalteten, roten Fassadenflächen des Hauses sorgen dafür, dass der Bau aus jedem Blickwinkel anders wirkt, wie an den Aufrissen (linke Seite) und den zwei Aufnahmen zu sehen ist.

La structure rouge qui enveloppe la maison lui donne un aspect qui semble toujours différent, quel que soit l'angle de vision, comme le montrent les élévations (page de gauche) et ces deux vues.

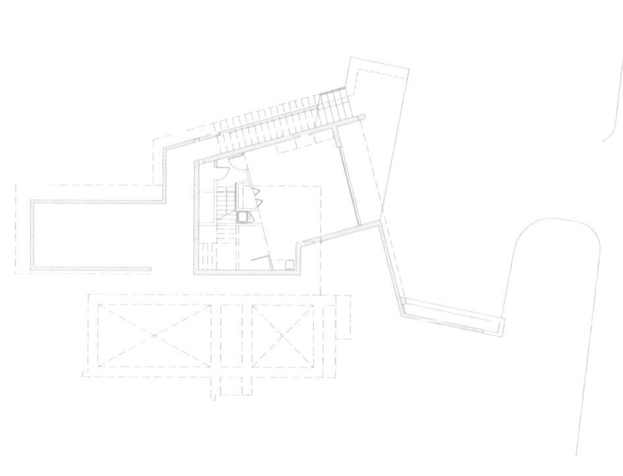

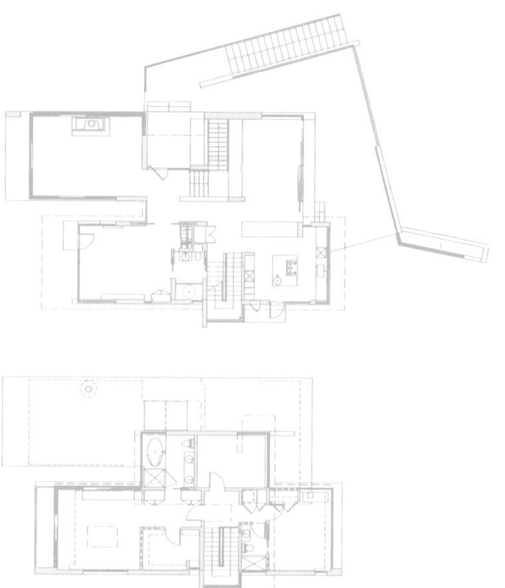

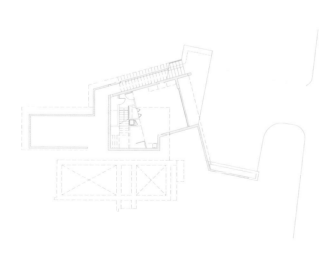

The fully glazed living room visible from inside (left page) and from the exterior (right) defines the ample, bright interior of the house.

Der voll verglaste Wohnraum auf einer Innenansicht (linke Seite) und von außen (rechts) ist beispielhaft für das großzügige, helle Interieur des Hauses.

Le séjour entièrement vitré vu de dedans (page de gauche) et de dehors (en haut à droite) est l'illustration même de cet intérieur lumineux de proportions généreuses.

Simple, mostly rectilinear alignments and a palette of neutral colors contrast with the red exterior of the house.

Die schlichte, weitgehend rechtwinklige Linienführung und die eher neutralen Farben kontrastieren mit der roten Fassade.

Les alignements simples et rationnels, ainsi que la palette chromatique neutre, contrastent avec une certaine exubérance de style, dont la couleur rouge des façades.

TAIJI KAWANO

Taiji Kawano Architects
2–13–11 Takasago
Katsushika
Tokyo 125–0054
Japan

Tel: +81 3 5668 4415
Fax: +81 3 5668 4415
E-mail: info@tk-arc.jp
Web: www.tk-arc.jp

TAIJI KAWANO was born in 1964 in Fukuoka. He received his Bachelor of Engineering Degree from Kyushu University in 1988. He worked from 1990 to 2000 in the Kohyama Atelier and established his own firm, Taiji Kawano Architects, in 2001. He has been a lecturer at the University of Tokyo since 2002. His work includes the I.S.S. Space Museum Project (Inabe, Mie, 2001, in collaboration with Yoshito Tomioka); CoCo Project (Kokonoe, Oita, 2002); J Panel Furniture (2003); Town House in Sendagi, renovation (Bunkyo, Tokyo, 2005); Town House in Takasago (Katsushika, Tokyo, 2006); Yayoi Auditorium Annex, the University of Tokyo (Bunkyo, Tokyo, 2008); House at Niiza (Niiza, Saitama, 2008); Ocha House, Ochanomizu University (Bunkyo, Tokyo, 2008–09, in collaboration with Nobuhisa Motooka, published here). His current work includes a New Dormitory for Ochanomizu University (Bunkyo, Tokyo, 2011, in collaboration with Nobuhisa Motooka). Nobuhisa Motooka was born in 1968 in Hyogo and received his Ph.D. in Architecture from the University of Tokyo in 1996. He founded his own firm in 2000.

TAIJI KAWANO wurde 1964 in Fukuoka geboren. Sein Studium an der Universität Kyushu schloss er 1988 mit einem Bachelor in Ingenieurwissenschaften ab. Von 1990 bis 2000 arbeitete er im Kohyama Atelier und gründete 2001 sein eigenes Büro, Taiji Kawano Architects. Seit 2002 ist er Dozent an der Universität Tokio. Zu seinen Projekten zählen das I.S.S. Space Museum Project (Inabe, Mie, in Zusammenarbeit mit Yoshito Tomioka, 2001), das CoCo Project (Kokonoe, Oita, 2002), die Möbelserie „J Panel" (2003), die Sanierung eines Stadthauses in Sendagi (Bunkyo, Tokio, 2005), ein Stadthaus in Takasago (Katsushika, Tokio, 2006), der Anbau an das Yayoi-Auditorium, Universität Tokio (Bunkyo, Tokio, 2008), ein Haus in Niiza (Niiza, Saitama, 2008) sowie das Haus Ocha an der Ochanomizu-Universität (Bunkyo, Tokio, 2008–09, in Zusammenarbeit mit Nobuhisa Motooka, hier vorgestellt). Aktuelle Projekte sind u. a. ein neues Wohnheim für die Ochanomizu-Universität (Bunkyo, Tokio, 2011, in Zusammenarbeit mit Nobuhisa Motooka). Nobuhisa Motooka wurde 1968 in Hyogo geboren und promovierte 1996 an der Universität Tokio in Architektur. 2000 gründete er sein eigenes Büro.

TAIJI KAWANO, né en 1964 à Fukuoka, est diplômé d'ingénierie de l'université de Kyushu (1988). Il a travaillé de 1990 à 2000 pour l'agence Kohyama Atelier et fondé la sienne, Taiji Kawano Architects, en 2001. Il est assistant à l'université de Tokyo depuis 2002. Parmi ses réalisations : le projet de musée de l'espace I.S.S. (Inabe, Mie, 2001, en collaboration avec Yoshito Tomioka) ; le projet CoCo (Kokonoe, Oita, 2002) ; une collection de meubles J Panel (2003) ; la rénovation d'une maison de ville à Sendagi (Bunkyo, Tokyo, 2005) ; une maison de ville à Takasago (Katsushika, Tokyo, 2006) ; l'annexe de l'auditorium de Yayoi à l'université de Tokyo (Bunkyo, Tokyo, 2008) ; une maison à Niiza (Niiza, Saitama, 2008) ; la maison Ocha, université d'Ochanomizu (Bunkyo, Tokyo, 2008–09, en collaboration avec Nobuhisa Motooka, publiée ici). Actuellement, il travaille sur le projet d'un nouveau dortoir pour l'université d'Ochanomizu (Bunkyo, Tokyo, 2011, en collaboration avec Nobuhisa Motooka). Nobuhisa Motooka, né en 1968 à Hyogo, a obtenu son Ph.D. en architecture de l'université de Tokyo (1996). Il a fondé son agence en 2000.

OCHA HOUSE

Ochanomizu University, Bunkyo, Tokyo, 2008–09

Area: 83 m². Client: Ochanomizu University. Cost: not disclosed.
Collaboration: Nobuhisa Motooka (Associate Professor, Ochanomizu University), Tomoya Nabeno, Masahiro Inayama (Structural Engineering)

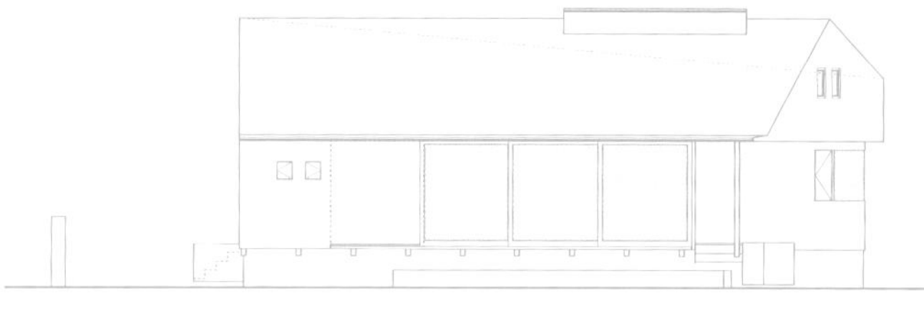

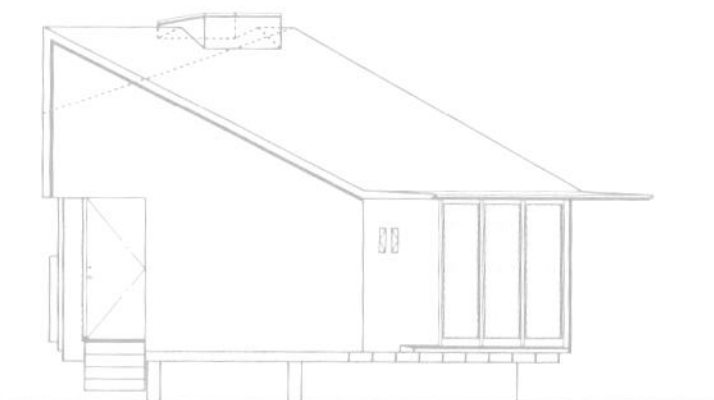

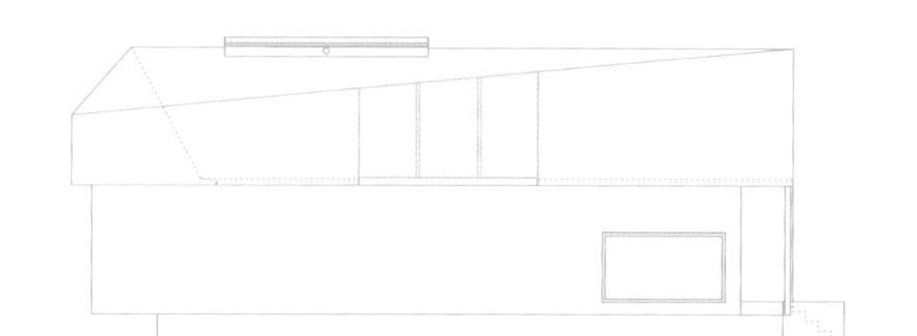

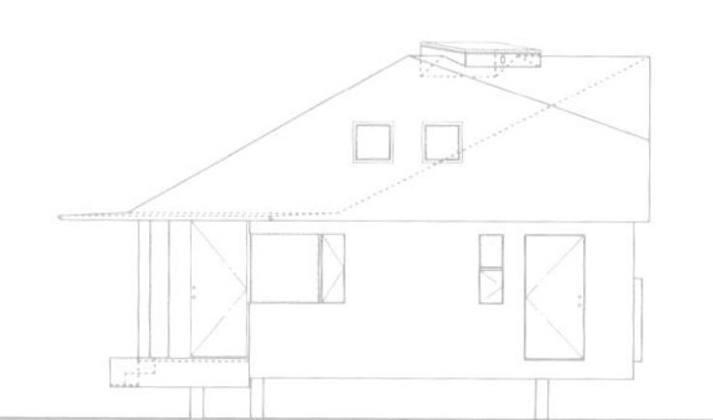

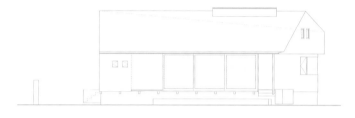

The simple lines of the house, with its elevated platform and single-slant roof, can be seen clearly in the drawings above.

Die schlichten Linien des Hauses mit seiner aufgeständerten Plattform und dem Pultdach ist auf den Zeichnungen oben deutlich zu erkennen.

Les dessins ci-dessus illustrent la composition en lignes simples de la maison, sa suspension au-dessus du sol et son toit à pente unique.

The architect describes this structure as "an experimental house for ubiquitous computing." The idea was to create a concept house so that computer devices can be utilized and custom-made according to the lifestyle of inhabitants. The adaptability of partitions, the electrical wiring, or even pipes were thus significant factors in the design. New construction techniques were employed for lightweight housing on this small urban site near the heart of Tokyo. Cedar panels with three layers glued and screwed together without any metal fittings were employed in the house, which rises to a maximum height of 5.9 meters on its 260-square-meter site. A straightforward concept and simple lines are the most obvious characteristics of this design. Ceilings and walls are lit with LEDs placed in the gutter around the outside frame. The architect compares his technique to that of Jean Pouvé's use of standardized parts for housing.

Der Architekt nennt das Gebäude ein „experimentelles Haus, in dem der Computer allgegenwärtig ist". Die Idee war es, ein Konzepthaus zu entwerfen, in dem Computertechnik eingesetzt und für den Lebensstil der Bewohner maßgeschneidert werden kann. Dementsprechend war die Anpassungsfähigkeit der Trennwände, der elektrischen Leitungen und sogar der Rohrleitungen ein entscheidender Faktor im Entwurf. So kamen auf diesem kleinen Grundstück unweit des Stadtzentrums von Tokio neue Konstruktionstechniken für Leichtbauhäuser zum Einsatz. Gearbeitet wurde mit dreilagig verleimten Zedernholzplatten, die ohne Beschläge miteinander verschraubt wurden. Das Haus auf seinem 260 m² großen Grundstück ist an seiner höchsten Stelle 5,9 m hoch. Besonders auffällig an diesem Entwurf sind die schlichte Konzeption und Linienführung. Decken und Wände werden mit LEDs beleuchtet, die in den Dachüberstand eingelassen sind. Der Architekt vergleicht seine Vorgehensweise mit Jean Prouvés Einsatz von standardisierten Fertigteilen für den Wohnbau.

L'architecte décrit cette réalisation comme « une maison expérimentale livrée à l'omniprésence de l'informatique ». L'idée était ici de créer une maison concept dans laquelle les ordinateurs puissent être utilisés et personnalisés en fonction du style de vie de ses occupants. L'adaptabilité des cloisonnements, le câblage électrique et même la tuyauterie constituaient donc des facteurs importants du projet. De nouvelles techniques de construction ont été employées pour édifier cette habitation légère sur une petite parcelle de 260 m², non loin du centre de Tokyo. Des panneaux de cèdre triple épaisseur, collés et vissés sans autre articulation métallique, ont été utilisés pour réaliser ce volume qui s'élève jusqu'à 5,9 m. Le projet se caractérise par des lignes et une conception d'une simplicité évidente. Les plafonds et les murs sont éclairés par des DELs disposées dans une gouttière périphérique. L'architecte compare sa démarche à celle de Jean Prouvé qui utilisait lui aussi des éléments préfabriqués pour construire ses maisons.

The Ocha House, inspired to some extent by the work of Jean Prouvé, has the appearance of a temporary structure, and it certainly sits lightly on its narrow site.

Das Ocha House, zum Teil vom Werk Jean Prouvés beeinflusst, wirkt fast wie ein temporärer Bau und liegt leicht auf seinem schmalen Grundstück.

La maison Ocha, inspirée dans une certaine mesure de l'œuvre de Jean Prouvé, présente l'aspect d'une structure temporaire et s'insère avec légèreté et délicatesse dans une parcelle très étroite.

The house is angular, both in plan and in the interior images seen on this double page. The LED lighting along the beams is complemented by a lot of natural light. The kitchen island (left) seems to be a natural component of the overall design.

Das Haus weist viele Schrägen auf, zu sehen am Grundriss und den Innenansichten auf dieser Doppelseite. Die entlang der Dachsparren verlaufenden LED-Leuchten werden von großzügig einfallendem Tageslicht unterstützt. Die Kücheninsel (links) fügt sich selbstverständlich in den Gesamtentwurf.

La maison respecte une géométrie anguleuse stricte comme le montrent ce plan et ces images de l'intérieur. L'éclairage à base de DEL installés le long des poutres complète la lumière naturelle. La cuisine en îlot (à gauche) semble faire naturellement partie du plan d'ensemble.

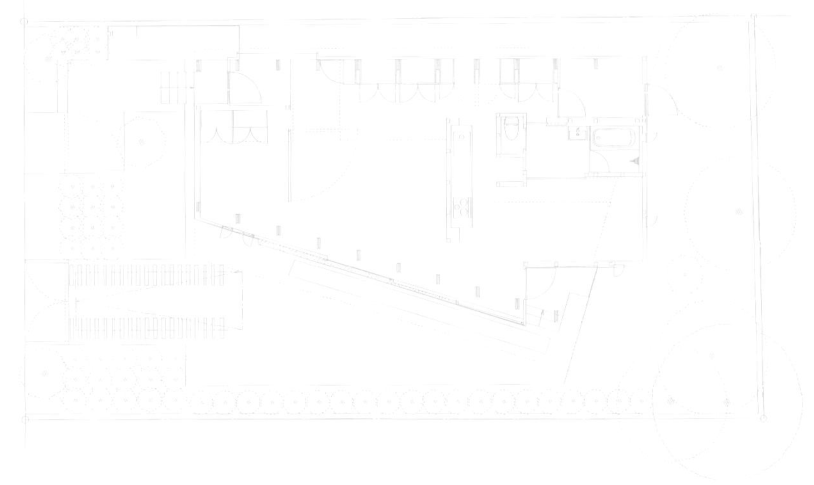

KWK PROMES

KWK PROMES
Robert Konieczny
ul. Rymera 3/5
40–048 Katowice
Poland

Tel/Fax: +48 32 206 91 26
E-mail: biuro@kwkpromes.pl
Web: www.kwkpromes.pl

Robert Konieczny was born in 1969 in Katowice, Poland. He graduated from the New Jersey Institute of Technology (Newark, New Jersey, 1996) and obtained an M.Arch degree from the Silesian University of Technology (Gliwice, Poland). Robert Konieczny established **KWK PROMES** in 1999 with Marlena Wolnik, who then left the firm in 2005. Recent work includes Aatrial House (Lower Silesia, 2003–06); Safe House (Okrzeszyn, 2005–08, published here); OUTrial House (Ksiazenice, 2005–08, also published here); and Standard House (near Pszczyna, 2009). Work now being realized includes a House near Poznan; House near Wrocław; the Ribbon House (Plock); Hidden House (Lower Silesia); and a Hotel on Czorsztyn Lake (Kluczkowce), all in Poland.

Robert Konieczny wurde 1969 in Katowice in Polen, geboren. Sein Studium schloss er am New Jersey Institute of Technology ab (Newark, New Jersey, 1996) und machte seinen M.Arch. an der Politechnika Slaska (Gliwice, Polen). 1999 gründete Robert Konieczny sein Büro **KWK PROMES** mit Marlena Wolnik, die die Firma 2005 wieder verließ. Zu seinen jüngeren Projekten zählen das Haus Aatrial (Niederschlesien, 2003–06), das Safe House (Okrzeszyn, 2005–08, hier vorgestellt), das Haus OUTrial (Ksiazenice, 2005–08, ebenfalls hier vorgestellt) sowie das Standardhaus (bei Pszczyna, 2009). Derzeit realisiert werden u. a. ein Haus bei Posen, ein Haus bei Breslau, das Ribbon House (Plock), das Hidden House (Niederschlesien) sowie ein Hotel am See von Czorsztyn (Kluczkowce), alle in Polen.

Robert Konieczny, né en 1969 à Katowice en Pologne, est diplômé de l'Institut de technologie du New Jersey (Newark, New Jersey, 1996), et a obtenu son M.Arch de l'Université de technologie de Silésie (Gliwice, Pologne). Il a fondé **KWK PROMES** en 1999 en association avec Marlena Wolnik, qui a quitté l'agence en 2005. Parmi ses réalisations récentes, toutes en Pologne : la maison Aatrial (Basse-Silésie, 2003–06) ; la maison sécurisée (Safe House, Okrzeszyn, 2005–08, publiée ici) ; la maison OUTrial (Ksiazenice, 2005–08, publiée ici) ; et la maison standard (près de Pszczyna, 2009). Il travaille actuellement à des projets de maisons individuelles près de Poznan ; une maison près de Wrocław ; la maison ruban (Ribbon House, Plock) ; la maison cachée (Hidden House, Basse-Silésie) ; et un hôtel sur le lac de Czorsztyn (Kluczkowce),le tout en Pologne.

SAFE HOUSE

Okrzeszyn, Poland, 2005–08

Area: 566 m². Client: not disclosed. Cost: not disclosed.
Collaboration: Marcin Jojko

This house was built on a 2500-square-meter site located in a small town near Warsaw. Safety was an important element for the client, hence the name of the house, and many aspects of its design. A gate leads visitors to the main entrance of the residence, a point through which they must pass to enter the house itself or the garden. Forty-centimeter-thick moving walls and drawbridge-like elements are part of the design. A 14 x 6 meter rolling gate opens toward the garden and can be used as a movie screen by the client, who is a young director. An alarm system completes the safety features. The architect states: "Almost all of the mechanisms are based on standard systems, often industrial, which reduces the costs. Everything can be remotely controlled, and in case of loss of power supply, an electrical accumulator is on stand-by. Manual control is possible as well."

Gebaut wurde dieses Haus auf einem 2500 m² großen Grundstück in einer Kleinstadt bei Warschau. Ein wesentliches Anliegen des Bauherrn war die Sicherheit, was zahlreiche Aspekte des Entwurfs beeinflusste – daher auch der Name des Hauses. Durch ein Tor gelangen Besucher zum Haupteingang des Anwesens. Diesen Punkt muss zwingend passieren, wer in das Haus oder den Garten gelangen will. Zum Entwurf gehören 40 cm starke bewegliche Wände sowie zugbrückenartige Bauteile. Ein 14 x 16 m großes Rolltor lässt sich zum Garten hin öffnen und dient dem Bauherrn, einem jungen Regisseur, zugleich als Kinoleinwand. Abgerundet werden die Sicherheitsvorkehrungen durch eine Alarmanlage. Der Architekt erklärt: „Fast alle technischen Einrichtungen sind Standardsysteme, häufig aus der Industrie, was die Kosten reduziert. Alles lässt sich per Fernbedienung steuern. Im Fall eines Stromausfalls steht ein Notstromaggregat bereit. Auch eine manuelle Bedienung der Technik ist möglich."

Cette maison a été édifiée sur un terrain de 2500 m² dans une petite ville proche de Varsovie. La sécurité comptait beaucoup pour ce client, d'où le nom de la maison et certains aspects de sa conception. Les visiteurs accèdent à l'entrée principale après avoir franchi un sas d'entrée, passage obligé pour aller à la maison ou dans le jardin. Des parois mobiles de 45 cm d'épaisseur et des éléments de type pont-levis caractérisent ce projet. Un volet roulant de 14 x 6 m s'ouvre sur le jardin et peut servir à l'occasion d'écran de projection pour le propriétaire, jeune metteur en scène. Un système d'alarme complète ces dispositifs de sécurité. Pour l'architecte : « Presque tous les mécanismes reposent sur des systèmes standard, souvent industriels, pour en réduire les coûts. Tout est contrôlable à distance et, en cas de panne de courant, un accumulateur électrique prend le relais. Un contrôle manuel est également prévu. »

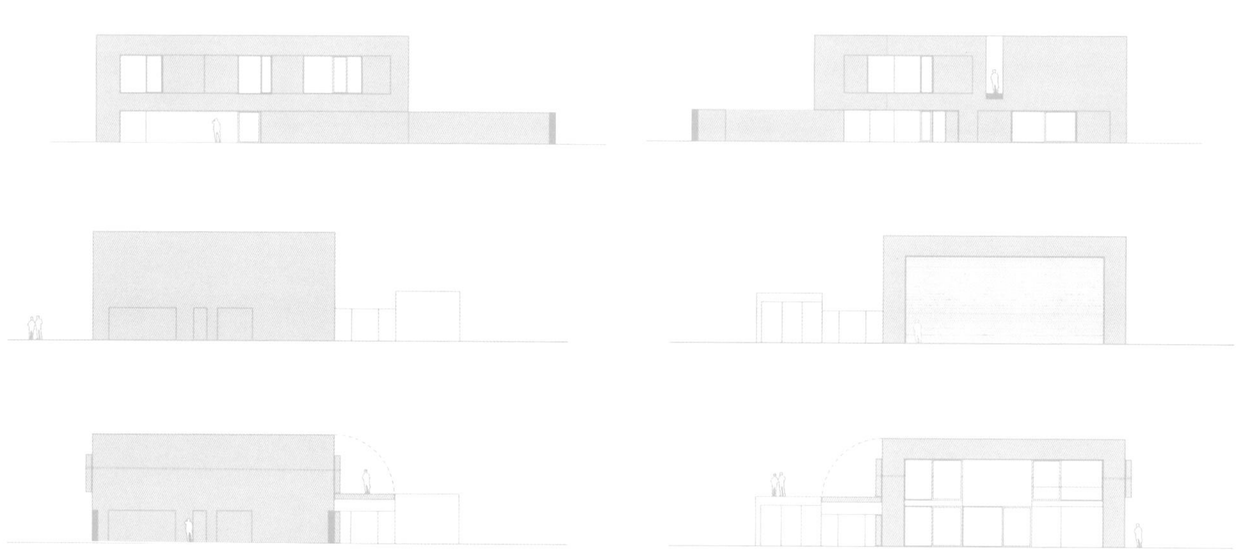

The house is both massive and intentionally closed in appearance (and in reality). From some angles, it seems to have no openings at all (right).

Das Haus wirkt ebenso massiv wie bewusst geschlossen (und ist es tatsächlich). Aus bestimmten Blickwinkeln betrachtet scheint es keinerlei Fassadenöffnungen zu haben (rechts).

La maison est à la fois massive et d'aspect volontairement clos. Sous certains angles, elle semble même complètement fermée.

OUTRIAL HOUSE

Ksiazenice, Poland, 2005–08

Area: 180 m². Client: not disclosed. Cost: not disclosed.
Collaboration: Marcin Jojko

Seen from the angle above, the OUTrial House seems quite ordinary, with its interior seemingly carved out of the strong white walls.

Aus der oben gezeigten Perspektive wirkt das OUTrial House eher konventionell, der Innenraum scheint aus den massiven weißen Mauern herausgeschnitten zu sein.

Vue du jardin (ci-dessus), la maison OUTrial pourrait sembler presque conventionnelle, même si ses volumes semblent creusés dans les épais murs blancs.

Again located near Warsaw, this residence sits on a 1440-square-meter site in a green clearing near the forest. As this natural setting was the only context with which the architect could relate, he decided to "carve out a piece of the grass-covered site, move it up and treat it as the roofing to arrange all the required functions underneath." The client requested an additional recording studio when the project was quite far along, which led the architect to make an "incision" in the grass roof. He explains: "This procedure turned the roof into an atrium, as the only way to reach it was through the interior of the house. As opposed, however, to a typical atrium, the newly created space has all the advantages of an outer garden while remaining a safe, internal zone within the building." The name "OUTrial" is meant to convey the fact that the atrium is at once part of the interior and the exterior of the house.

Auch dieses Anwesen befindet sich in der Nähe von Warschau, auf einem 1440 m² großen neben einem Wald gelegenen Grundstück. Da dies der einzige Kontext war, auf den der Architekt Bezug nehmen konnte, entschied er sich, „einen Teil der Rasenfläche aus- und anzuheben und als Dach zu nutzen, unter dem die erforderlichen Funktionen untergebracht werden sollten". Als das Projekt schon recht weit fortgeschritten war, bat der Bauherr um ein zusätzliches Aufnahmestudio, sodass der Architekt beschloss, einen „Einschnitt" in das Grasdach vorzunehmen. „Durch diesen Eingriff", so erläutert er, „wurde das Dach zu einem Lichthof; der Zugang ist ausschließlich durch das Innere des Hauses möglich. Anders jedoch als bei einem typischen Atrium hat dieser neu geschaffene Bereich alle Vorteile eines Gartens und bleibt dabei doch eine sichere Zone im Innern des Gebäudes." Der Name „OUTrial" soll signalisieren, dass das Atrium ebenso Teil des Innen- wie des Außenraums dieses Hauses ist.

Située elle aussi près de Varsovie, cette résidence occupe un terrain de 1440 m² dans une vaste clairière en forêt. Comme ce cadre naturel était le seul contexte auquel il pouvait se relier, l'architecte a décidé de « découper un morceau de terrain planté d'herbe, de le soulever, de le traiter comme une toiture, puis de loger en dessous les diverses fonctions de la maison. » Le client avait également souhaité disposer d'un studio d'enregistrement, alors que le projet était déjà assez avancé, ce qui a conduit à pratiquer une « incision » dans le toit : « Cette intervention transformait le toit en atrium, puisque la seule façon de l'atteindre était par l'intérieur de la maison. Cependant, par contraste avec un atrium classique, ce nouvel espace possède tous les avantages d'un jardin, tout en restant une zone intérieure et sûre au cœur de la maison même. » Le nom de « OUTrial » traduit le fait que l'atrium fait à la fois partie de l'intérieur et de l'extérieur de la maison.

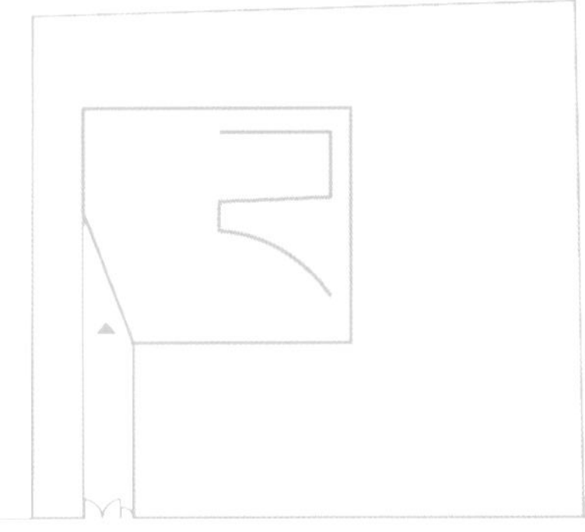

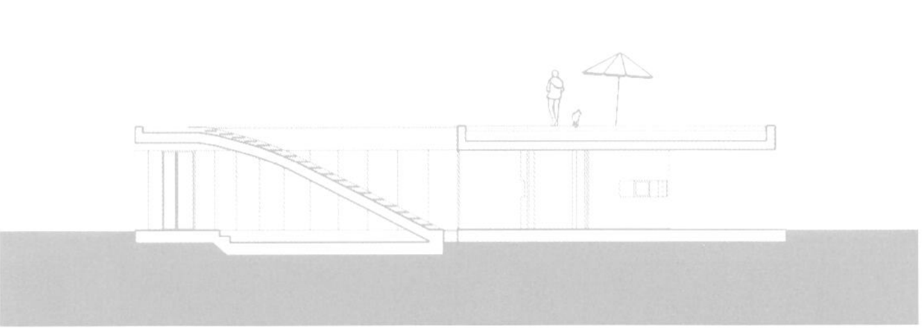

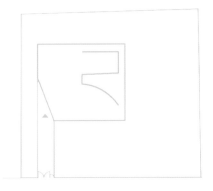

Essentially square in plan, the house opens in a sweeping curve that rises from the base of the house to its ceiling, creating the living space visible below.

Das im Grundriss annähernd quadratische Haus öffnet sich mit einem ausgreifenden Schwung vom Sockel des Hauses bis hinauf zur Decke; dieser Schwung definiert zugleich den Wohnraum (unten im Bild).

De plan presque carré, la maison s'ouvre par une ample courbe qui part de sa base et rejoint le plafond en découpant le volume du séjour (ci-dessous).

A curving staircase rises from the living area up to the grass-covered roof of the house.

Eine geschwungene Treppe führt vom Wohnraum hinauf zum begrünten Dach des Hauses.

Un escalier incurvé part du séjour pour accéder à la toiture végétalisée.

Seen from roof level, the house appears to be sunken into its site, which is not entirely the case. It does blend into the countryside particularly well, though, as seen from this angle.

Vom Dach aus wirkt es, als sei das Haus im Boden versenkt, was nicht der Fall ist. Dennoch fügt es sich aus dieser Perspektive besonders gut in die landschaftliche Umgebung.

Vue du toit, la maison semble enfoncée dans le sol, ce qui n'est pas vraiment le cas. Elle se fond avec le paysage, en particulier vue sous cet angle.

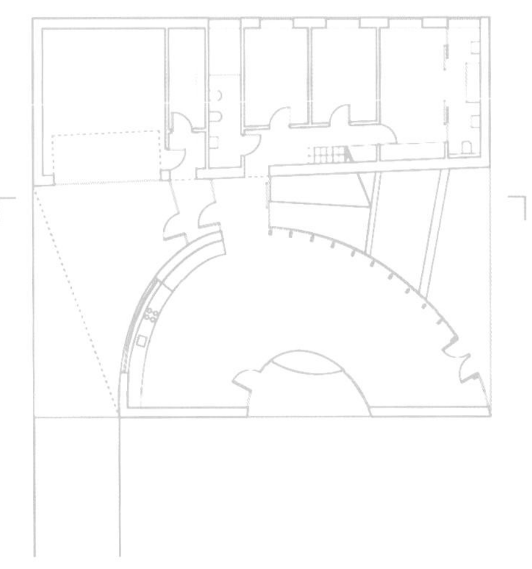

J. MAYER H.

J. MAYER H.
Bleibtreustr. 54
10623 Berlin
Germany

Tel: +49 30 644 90 77 00
Fax: +49 30 644 90 77 11
E-mail: contact@jmayerh.de
Web: www.jmayerh.de

Jürgen Mayer-Hermann was born in Stuttgart in 1965. He studied at University of Stuttgart (Architecture and Town Planning, 1986–92), the Cooper Union (1990–91), and Princeton University (M.Arch, 1992–94). He created his firm **J. MAYER H.** Architekten in Berlin in 1996. Jürgen Mayer-Hermann has taught at Princeton University, University of the Arts Berlin, Harvard University, Kunsthochschule Berlin, Architectural Association (London), Columbia University (New York), and the University of Toronto. Recent projects include the Town Hall in Ostfildern (2001); the canteen at Karlsruhe University of Applied Sciences (2006); the redevelopment of the Plaza de la Encarnacion in Seville (Spain, 2004–); and the Dupli.Casa (near Ludwigsburg, 2006–08, published here), all in Germany unless stated otherwise.

Jürgen Mayer-Hermann wurde 1965 in Stuttgart geboren. Sein Studium absolvierte er an der Universität Stuttgart (Architektur und Stadtplanung, 1986–92), der Cooper Union (New York, 1990–91) und der Princeton University (M.Arch., 1992–94). 1996 gründete er sein Büro **J. MAYER H.** Architekten in Berlin. Jürgen Mayer-Hermann lehrte u. a. an der Princeton University, der Universität der Künste Berlin, der Harvard University, der Kunsthochschule Berlin, der Architectural Association (London), der Columbia University (New York) sowie an der University of Toronto. Neuere Projekte sind u. a. das Stadthaus in Ostfildern (2001), die Mensa der Hochschule Karlsruhe (2006), die Neugestaltung der Plaza de la Encarnacion in Sevilla (Spanien, 2004–) sowie die Dupli.Casa (bei Ludwigsburg, 2006–08, hier vorgestellt), alle in Deutschland soweit nicht anders angegeben.

Jürgen Mayer-Hermann, né à Stuttgart en 1965, a étudié à l'université de cette ville (architecture et urbanisme, 1986–92), à Cooper Union (1990–91), et à l'université de Princeton (M.Arch, 1992–94). Il a créé son agence, **J. MAYER H.** Architekten, à Berlin en 1996. Jürgen Mayer-Hermann a enseigné à l'université de Princeton, à l'Université des Arts à Berlin, à l'université Harvard, à la Kunsthochschule de Berlin, à l'Architectural Association (Londres), à l'université Columbia (New York) et à l'université de Toronto. Parmi ses récents projets : l'hôtel de ville d'Ostfildern (2001) ; le restaurant universitaire à l'École supérieure de Karlsruhe (2006) ; la rénovation de la Plaza de la Encarnacion à Séville (Espagne, 2004–) ; et la Dupli.Casa (près de Ludwigsburg, 2006–08, publiée ici), le tout en Allemagne, sauf mention contraire.

DUPLI.CASA

near Ludwigsburg, Germany, 2006–08

Area: 1190 m². Client: not disclosed.
Cost: not disclosed

The concept of this house takes into account the family house built on the site in 1984, and subsequently extended and modified it. Thus, according to the architect, the new structure "echoes the 'family archeology' by duplication and rotation." The openings of the house offer views of the old town of Marbach, and the German National Literature Archives, located in this city, which is the birthplace of Friedrich Schiller. A semi-public space is created at ground level, where the house is lifted up. The architect's diagrams show the careful attention that has gone into circulation patterns and the separation of public and private areas. The way that this remarkable house flows down its slightly sloped site makes this emphasis on movement and views quite clear.

Integriert in das Konzept des Hauses wurde das 1984 auf dem Grundstück erbaute Eigenheim der Familie, das aus- und umgebaut wurde. Dementsprechend „lässt der Neubau", so der Architekt, „die ‚Familienarchäologie' durch Duplizierung und Rotation anklingen". Die Fassadenöffnungen ermöglichen Ausblicke in Richtung Marbacher Altstadt, Schillers Geburtsstadt, und zum Deutschen Literaturarchiv. Durch die Aufständerung des Hauses entsteht im Erdgeschoss ein halböffentlicher Bereich. Zeichnungen des Architekten veranschaulichen, mit welcher Sorgfalt die Wege durch das Haus analysiert und öffentliche und private Bereich voneinander getrennt wurden. Wie entscheidend Dynamik und Ausblicke hier waren, wird deutlich, wenn man sieht, wie dieses außergewöhnliche Haus das sanft geneigte Hanggrundstück hinabzufließen scheint.

Le concept de cette maison prend en compte une précédente maison familiale construite au même endroit en 1984, puis agrandie et modifiée par la suite. Ainsi, comme l'explique l'architecte, la nouvelle structure « fait écho à "l'archéologie familiale" par duplication et rotation ». Les ouvertures offrent des vues sur les quartiers anciens de Marbach, ville natale de Friedrich Schiller, et le bâtiment des Archives nationales de la littérature allemande. La maison se soulève pour créer un espace semi-public au rez-de-chaussée. Les plans montrent l'attention soignée portée aux circulations et à la séparation entre les zones privées et de réception. La façon dont cette remarquable maison se pose sur son terrain légèrement incliné met en valeur les perspectives et fait naître un sentiment de mouvement.

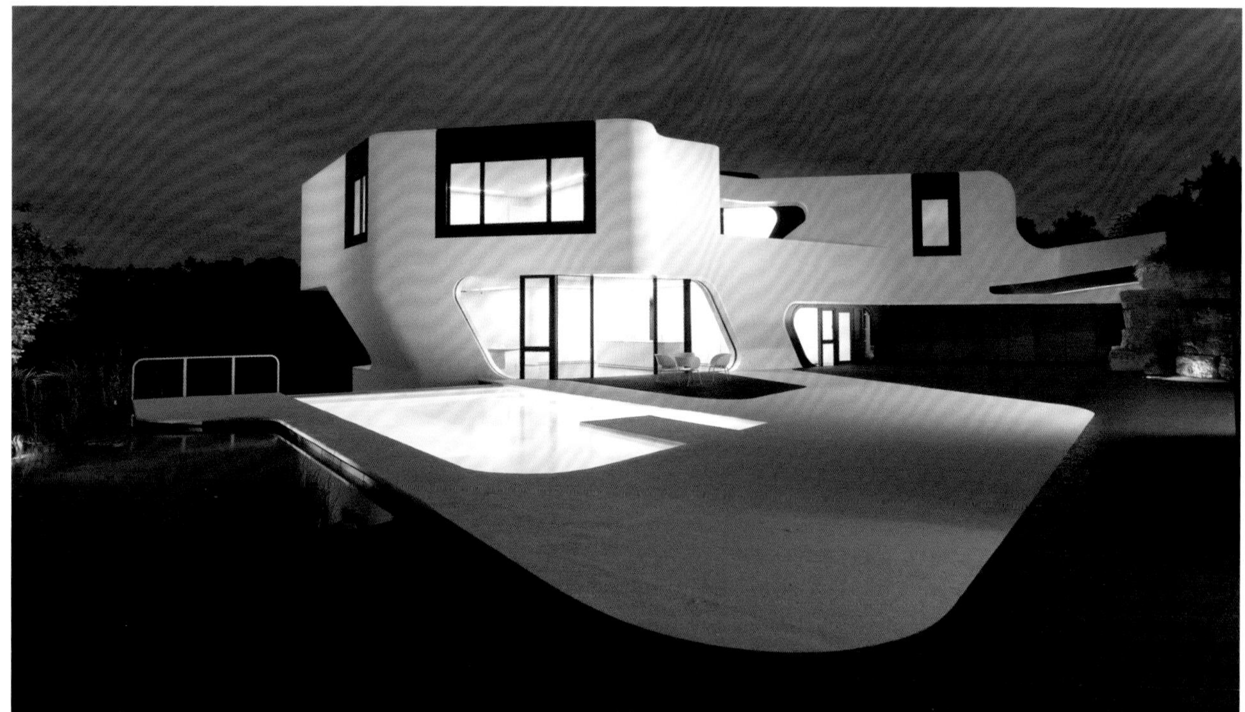

The areas around the house, such as the swimming pool seen above, appear to be an integral part of the design, with terraces flowing out of the main structure.

Auch die an das Haus angrenzenden Bereiche wie der Pool (oben) wirken wie integrale Bestandteile des Entwurfs. Die Terrassen scheinen geradezu aus dem Hauptbaukörper herauszufließen.

Les aménagements autour de la maison, comme la piscine (ci-dessus), font partie intégrante du plan. Les terrasses semblent vouloir s'échapper de la structure.

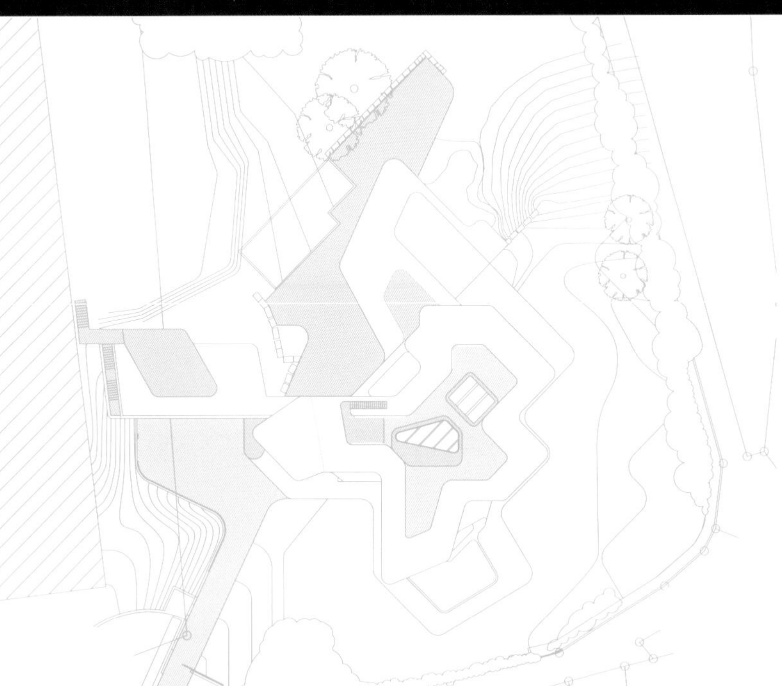

A plan shows the complexity of the design of this residence, which is one of the more spectacular and unusual houses to be built in Germany in recent years.

Der Lageplan belegt die Komplexität des Entwurfs. Der Bau zählt zu den spektakulärsten und ungewöhnlichsten Häusern, die in den vergangenen Jahren in Deutschland realisiert wurden.

Le plan montre la complexité de conception de cette résidence, l'une des plus spectaculaires et surprenantes construites en Allemagne au cours des années récentes.

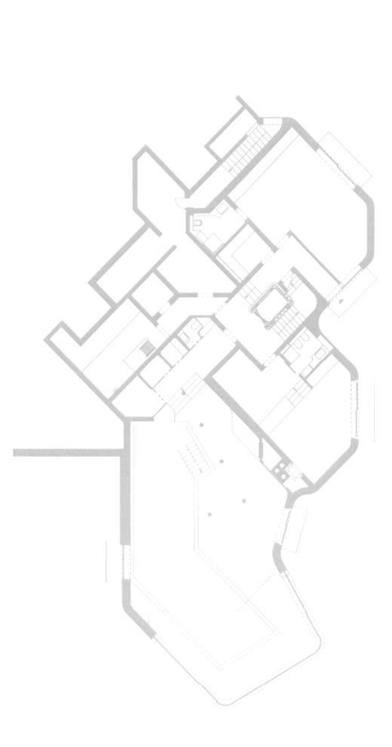

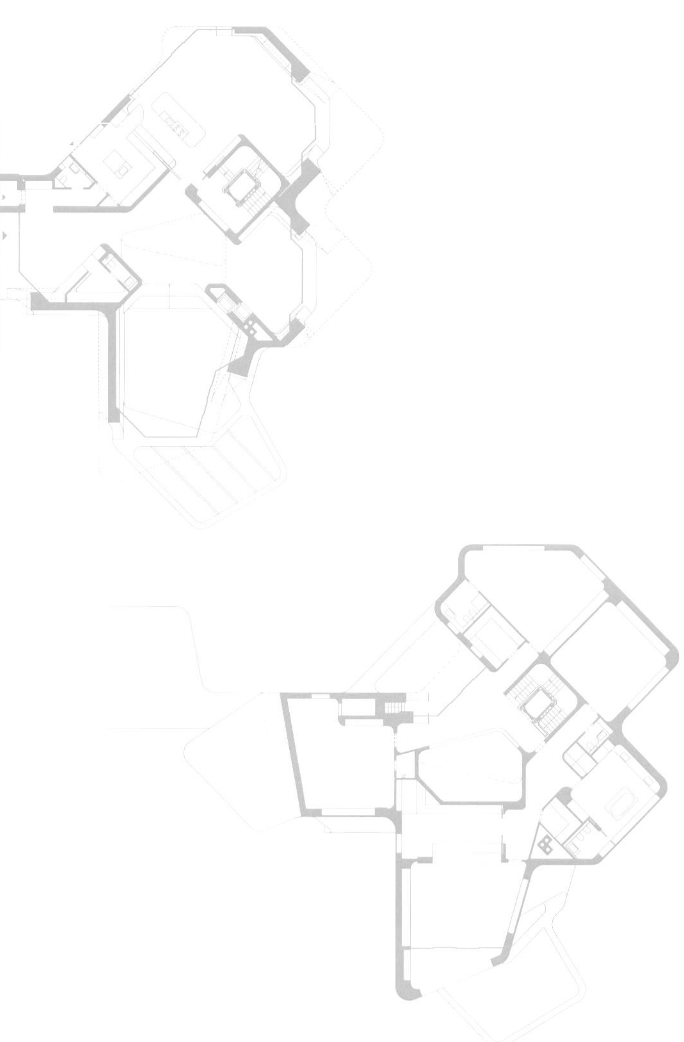

Sparsely furnished in these images, the house has soaring open spaces and dramatic curves, with generous openings giving an impression of a close connection to the exterior.

Das auf diesen Ansichten sparsam möblierte Haus zeichnet sich durch hohe, offene Räume und dramatisch geschwungene Linien aus. Großzügige Fassadenöffnungen schaffen eine enge Verbindung zum Außenraum.

À peine meublée dans ces images, la maison présente des volumes ouverts presque vertigineux et des courbes spectaculaires. La générosité des ouvertures donne l'impression d'un lien étroit avec la nature.

MCBRIDE CHARLES RYAN

McBride Charles Ryan
4/21 Wynnstay Road
Prahran, Victoria 3181
Australia

Tel: +61 3 9510 1006
Fax: +61 3 9510 0205
E-mail: mail@mcbridecharlesryan.com.au
Web: www.mcbridecharlesryan.com.au

Robert McBride was born in Tarnworth, NSW, Australia, in 1960. He received his B.Arch degree from RMIT (Melbourne) in 1985 and his M.Arch degree from the same institution in 1994. **MCBRIDE CHARLES RYAN** was founded in 1988. Debbie Ryan studied interior design at RMIT, arts at Monash University, and interior decoration at the Melbourne College of Decoration. Robert McBride's and Debbie Ryan's significant works include Kent Court Residence (Toorak, VIC, 2005); Narveno Court Residence (Hawthorn, VIC, 2005); Pine Street Residence (Camberwell, VIC, 2007); Klein Bottle House (Rye, VIC, 2007, published here); Mondaco House (Melbourne, VIC, 2007); and Letterbox House (Blairgowrie, VIC, 2006–08, also published here), all in Australia. The Klein Bottle House won the 2008 Robyn Boyd Award for New Residential Architecture (AIA National Annual Award) and the 2009 World Architecture Award for house design.

Robert McBride wurde 1960 in Tarnworth, NSW, Australien, geboren. Am RMIT in Melbourne erwarb er 1985 zunächst seinen B.Arch., 1994 dann seinen M.Arch. Die Gründung von **MCBRIDE CHARLES RYAN** erfolgte 1988. Debbie Ryan studierte Design am RMIT, Kunst an der Monash University sowie Innenausstattung am Melbourne College of Decoration. Zu Robert McBrides und Debbie Ryans bedeutendsten Arbeiten zählen die Kent Court Residence (Toorak, VIC, 2005), die Narveno Court Residence (Hawthorn, VIC, 2005), die Pine Street Residence (Camberwell, VIC, 2007), das Klein Bottle House (Rye, VIC, 2007, hier vorgestellt), das Mondaco House (Melbourne, VIC, 2007) sowie das Letterbox House (Blairgowrie, VIC, 2006–08, ebenfalls hier vorgestellt), alle in Australien. Das Klein Bottle House wurde 2008 mit dem Robyn Boyd Award für neue Wohnarchitektur ausgezeichnet (Nationaler Jahrespreis der AIA) sowie 2009 mit dem World Architecture Award für Wohnbauten.

Robert McBride est né à Tarnworth (NGS), en Australie, en 1960. Il a obtenu son B.Arch du RMIT (Melbourne, 1985) et son M.Arch de la même institution en 1994. L'agence **MCBRIDE CHARLES RYAN** a été fondée en 1988. Debbie Ryan a étudié l'architecture intérieure au RMIT, les arts à l'université Monash, et la décoration intérieure au Melbourne College of Decoration. Parmi leurs réalisations notables : la résidence de Kent Court (Toorak, VIC, 2005) ; la résidence de Narveno Court (Hawthorn, VIC, 2005) ; la résidence de Pine Street (Camberwell, VIC, 2007) ; la maison Bouteille de Klein (Klein Bottle House, Rye, VIC, 2007, publiée ici) ; la maison Mondaco (Melbourne, VIC, 2007) ; et la Maison Boîte aux lettres (Letterbox House, Blairgowrie, VIC, 2006–08, également publiée ici), le tout en Australie. La maison Bouteille de Klein a remporté le prix Robyn Boyd 2008 pour une nouvelle architecture résidentielle (AIA National Annual Award) ; et le 2009 World Architecture Award pour les maisons individuelles.

LETTERBOX HOUSE

Blairgowrie, Victoria, Australia, 2006–08

Area: 290 m². Client: Heather Ryan. Cost: $836 000.
Collaboration: Adam Pustola, Meredith Dufour, Angela Woda

"We like the buildings that make you smile (not laugh)," say the architects. "It makes people smile, a building with the smallest façade on the peninsula—the building begins as a letterbox and unfurls to become this healthy scaled verandah; to some it is an upturned boat, to others it is a wave or a cliff." This house won the Australian Institute of Architects (AIA)—Victorian Chapter—Harold Desbrowe-Annear Award for Residential Architecture. It is indeed the copper letterbox of this house situated at its very tip that appears to be the point from which the entire design develops. The ground floor contains the garage, three bedrooms, a hall and lounge, courtyard, living and dining areas, a children's room, and a laundry area, with an ample exterior terrace. On the top level, just the master bedroom and a smaller deck complete the design.

„Wir mögen Häuser, die Menschen zum Lächeln (nicht etwa zum Lachen) bringen", meinen die Architekten. „Ein Haus mit der kleinsten Fassade auf der gesamten Halbinsel bringt die Leute zum Lächeln – das Gebäude beginnt als Briefkasten und entwickelt sich hin zu einer recht großzügig dimensionierten Veranda. Für manche ist es ein umgedrehtes Boot, für andere eine Welle oder ein Kliff." Ausgezeichnet wurde das Haus mit dem Harold Desbrowe-Annear Award für Wohnarchitektur, einem Preis des Australian Institute of Architects (AIA – Regionalverband Victoria). Tatsächlich scheint sich der gesamte Entwurf aus dem kupfernen Briefkasten an der äußersten Spitze des Hauses zu entwickeln. Im Erdgeschoss befinden sich die Garage, drei Schlafzimmer, eine Diele und eine Lounge, ein Hof, Wohn- und Essbereich, ein Kinderzimmer und eine Waschküche sowie eine großzügige Terrasse. Im Obergeschoss wird der Entwurf mit einem Elternschlafzimmer und einer kleineren Terrasse abgerundet.

« Nous aimons les constructions qui font sourire (pas rire) », précise l'architecte. « Elle fait sourire, en effet, cette maison qui possède la plus petite façade de la péninsule. Elle commence par une boîte aux lettres et se déploie en véranda de bonnes dimensions. Pour certains, c'est un bateau à l'envers, pour d'autres, une vague ou une falaise. » Cette maison a remporté le prix Harold Desbrowe-Annear de l'architecture résidentielle décerné par l'Australian Institute of Architectes (AIA, section du Victoria). C'est bien en effet une boîte aux lettres en cuivre posée à son extrémité qui semble être le point à partir duquel le projet tout entier se développe. Le rez-de-chaussée contient le garage, trois chambres, un hall et un salon, une cour, le séjour-salle à manger, une pièce pour les enfants, une lingerie, ainsi qu'une vaste terrasse. L'étage n'est occupé que par la chambre principale et une petite terrasse.

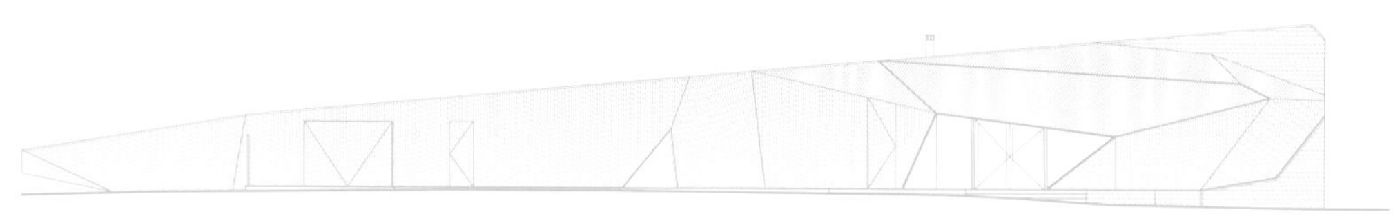

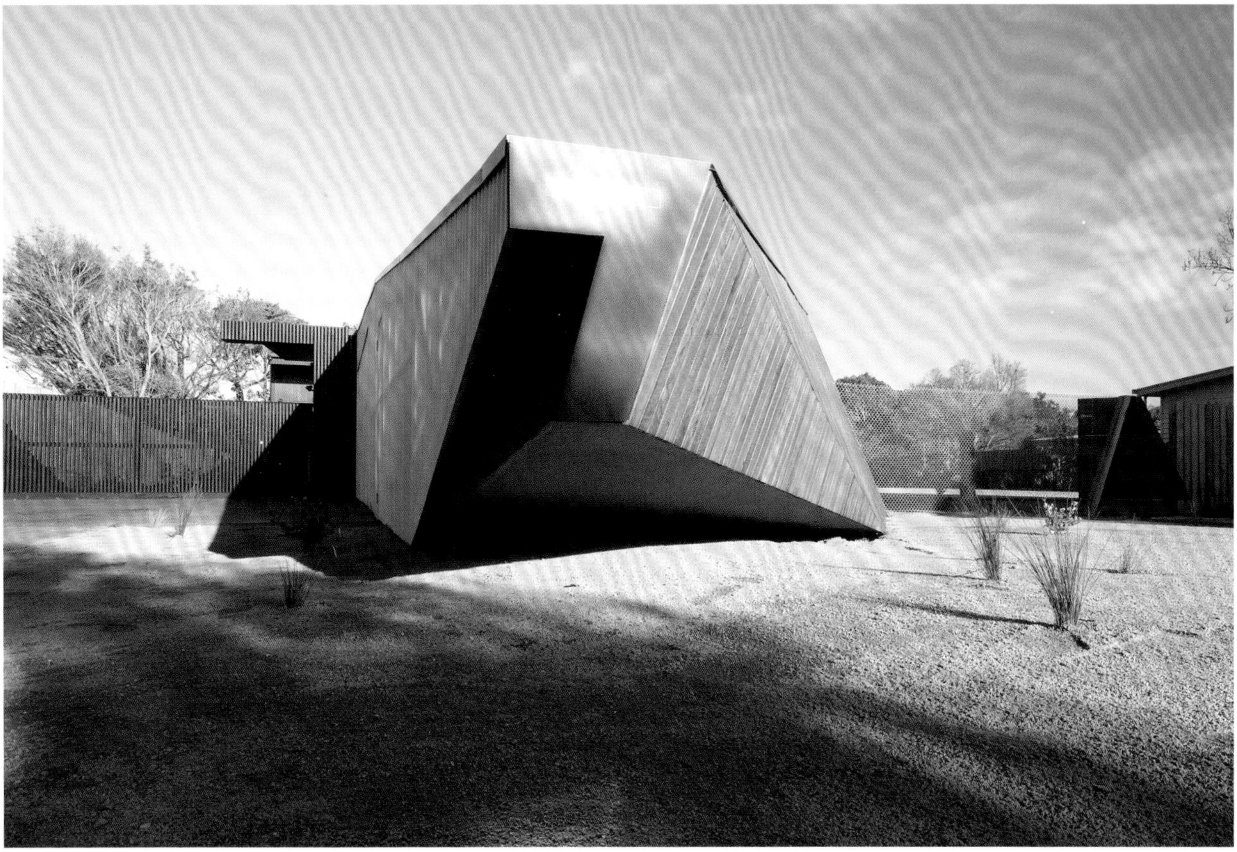

The surprising wedge-like form of the house is articulated in timber with few openings on this side, but an integrated terrace visible in the image below.

Die überraschende Keilform des Hauses artikuliert sich in Holz und in wenigen Öffnungen zur einen Seite. Im Foto unten ist die in den Baukörper integrierte Terrasse zu sehen.

L'étonnante forme de cale de cette maison de bois s'articule dans une sorte de continuité. Elle ne possède que peu d'ouvertures de ce côté mais une terrasse intégrée, visible ci-dessous.

The red, structuring elements visible in these images provide a marked contrast with the more continuous lines of the wooden exterior.

Die tragenden roten Bauteile bilden einen markanten Kontrast zu den eher fließenden Linien der holzverkleideten äußeren Hülle.

Les éléments structurants rouges contrastent fortement avec les lignes continues de la façade en bois.

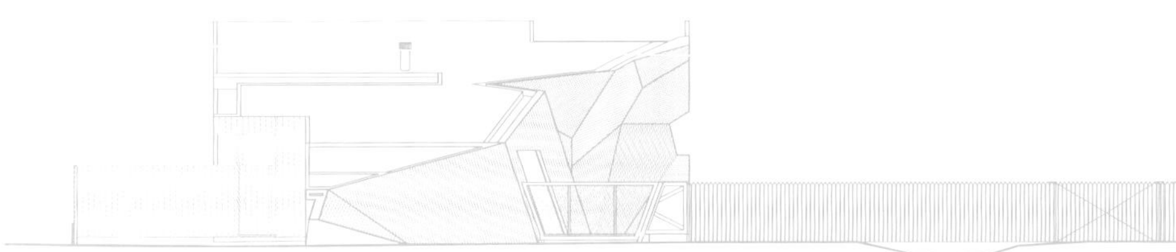

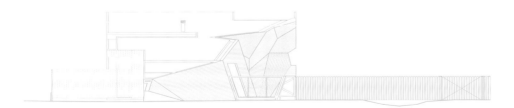

Plans show the long outside terrace visible on the previous double page, as well as the interior spaces of the ground floor.

Die Grundrisse zeigen die lange Terrasse, zu sehen auf der vorhergehenden Seite, sowie die Räume im Erd- und Obergeschoss.

Plans montrant le rez-de-chaussée et la terrasse allongée vue sur la double page précédente.

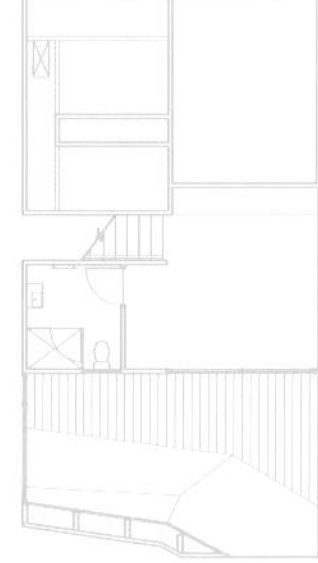

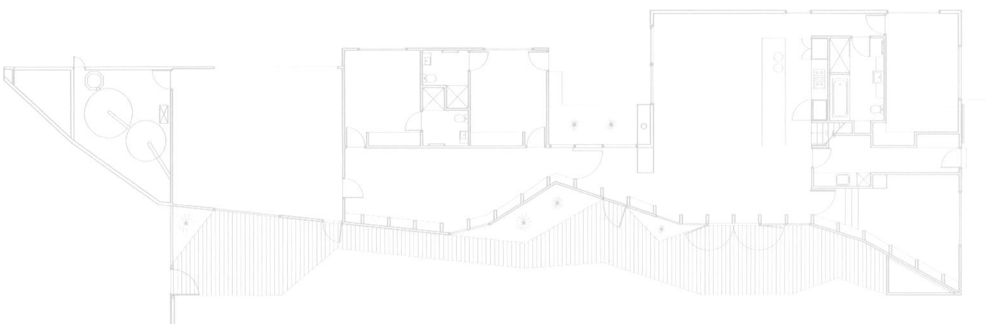

KLEIN BOTTLE HOUSE

Rye, Victoria, Australia, 2005–07

Area: 350 m². Clients: Donna and Mark Howlett. Cost: not disclosed.
Collaboration: Drew Williamson, Fang Cheah

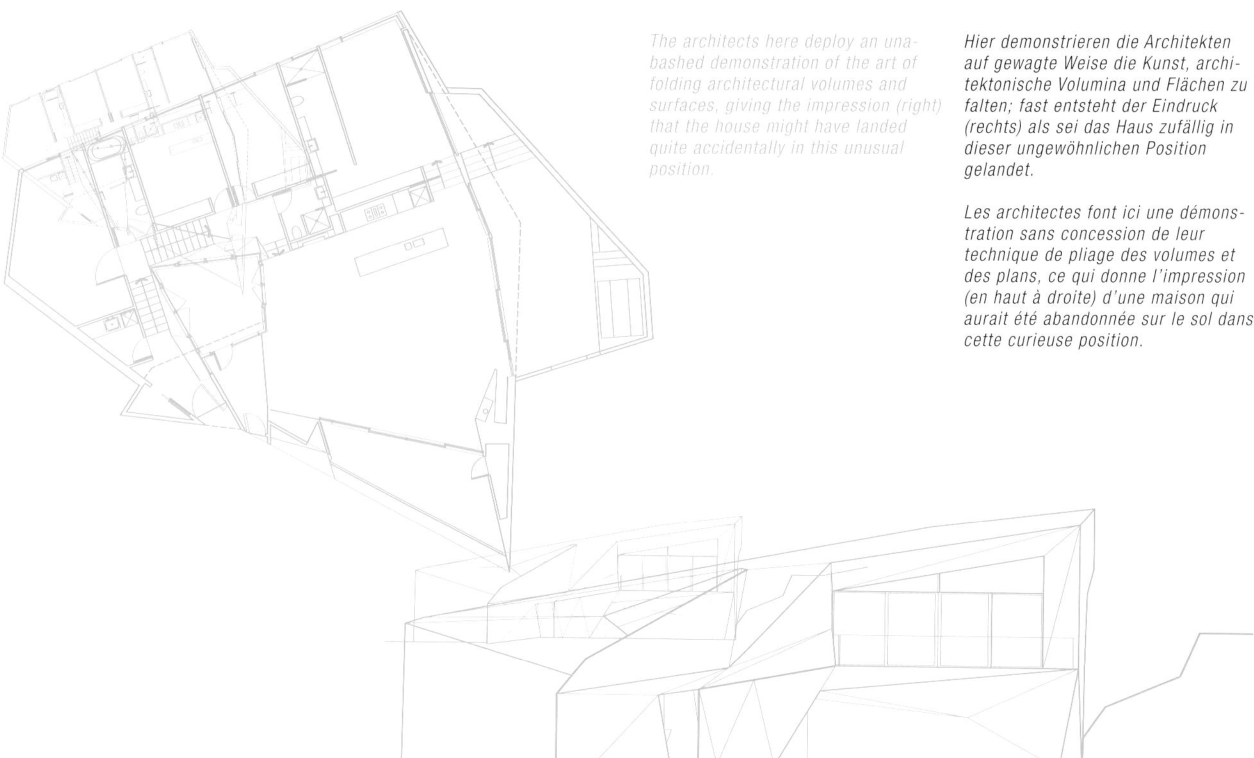

The architects here deploy an unabashed demonstration of the art of folding architectural volumes and surfaces, giving the impression (right) that the house might have landed quite accidentally in this unusual position.

Hier demonstrieren die Architekten auf gewagte Weise die Kunst, architektonische Volumina und Flächen zu falten; fast entsteht der Eindruck (rechts) als sei das Haus zufällig in dieser ungewöhnlichen Position gelandet.

Les architectes font ici une démonstration sans concession de leur technique de pliage des volumes et des plans, ce qui donne l'impression (en haut à droite) d'une maison qui aurait été abandonnée sur le sol dans cette curieuse position.

This house is located on the Mornington Peninsula about one and a half hours from Melbourne, near dunes and the beach. Although the architects allowed themselves to be inspired by the Klein bottle, which they define as a "descriptive model of a surface developed by topological mathematicians," they were, of course, determined to make the design "function as a home." They refer to the project as an "origami version" of the original topological figure, but find that the result looks much like "the Aussie cement-sheet beach house." The house has a central courtyard and a "grand regal" stairway connecting the levels. "The building," conclude the architects, "is within that tradition of the use of an experimental geometry that could be adapted to more suitably meet contemporary needs, and desires. In that sense it is within the heroic tradition of invigorating the very nature of the home; most notable of this tradition would be the great experimental heroic houses by Melbourne architects in the 1950s (McIntyre and Boyd in particular)."

Das Haus liegt auf der Halbinsel Mornington, rund eineinhalb Stunden von Melbourne entfernt, nicht weit von Dünen und Strand. Obwohl sich die Architekten von der Klein'schen Flasche inspirieren ließen, die sie als ein „von topologischen Mathematikern entworfenes, deskriptives Flächenmodell" bezeichnen, ging es ihnen natürlich darum, dass der Entwurf „als Haus funktioniert". Sie beschreiben das Projekt als „Origamiversion" der topologischen Ausgangsfigur. Dennoch finden sie, das Resultat sehe im Grunde wie ein „australisches Strandhäuschen aus Betonplatten" aus. Das Haus verfügt über einen zentralen Innenhof und eine „repräsentative Freitreppe", die die verschiedenen Ebenen erschließt. „Das Gebäude", fassen die Architekten zusammen, „ist einer Tradition verpflichtet, die experimentelle Geometrien nutzt, um sie sinnvoll an zeitgenössische Anforderungen und Wünsche anzupassen. In diesem Sinn steht es in einer lobenswerten Tradition, die das Zuhause von Grund auf neu zu beleben versuchte – und in der insbesondere Melbourner Architekten der 1950er Jahre (speziell McIntyre und Boyd) großartige experimentelle, heroische Häuser realisierten."

Cette maison est située sur la péninsule de Mornington a environ une heure et demie de voiture de Melbourne, dans les dunes, en bordure de la plage. Bien que les architectes se soient inspirés de la bouteille de Klein, « un modèle descriptif de surface développé par les mathématiciens topologistes », ils voulaient évidemment que ce projet fonctionne réellement « comme une maison ». Ils parlent de « version origami » de la figure topologique d'origine, mais pensent que le résultat fait davantage penser à « la maison de plage typique en plaques de ciment ». La maison possède une cour centrale et un escalier « de prestige » qui relie les niveaux. « Cette construction », concluent les architectes, « se rattache à une tradition de mise en pratique de recherches de géométrie expérimentale adaptées pour répondre plus précisément aux besoins et aux désirs contemporains. En ce sens, elle appartient à une tradition héroïque, celle de retourner à la nature même du foyer ; les exemples les plus notables de cette tradition ont été de superbes maisons d'architectes de Melbourne construites dans les années 1950 (par McIntyre et Boyd en particulier). »

Wooden decks and sliding glass windows allow the house to be very open to the exterior. Simple furnishings enable the architecture to speak for itself.

Terrassen aus Holz und Glasschiebetüren öffnen das Haus weit zum Außenraum. Schlichtes Mobiliar lässt die Architektur für sich sprechen.

Les baies coulissantes qui donnent sur des balcons-terrasses en bois créent un sentiment de grande ouverture sur l'extérieur. Le mobilier aux lignes simples laisse l'architecture s'exprimer.

Again contrasting a red interior surface with the more sober exterior colors, the architects clearly enjoy surprises. Below, a section shows how the house steps down its sloped site.

Auch hier arbeiten die Architekten mit dem Kontrast zwischen einem roten Innenraum und nüchterneren Farben außen; ganz offensichtlich sind sie für Überraschungen zu haben. Unten ein Schnitt, der zeigt, wie das Haus dem Hanggrundstück folgt.

Dans ce contraste entre l'intérieur rouge et les couleurs plus sobres de la façade, les architectes montrent qu'ils aiment créer des surprises. Ci-dessous, une élévation montrant l'implantation de la maison au flanc de la colline.

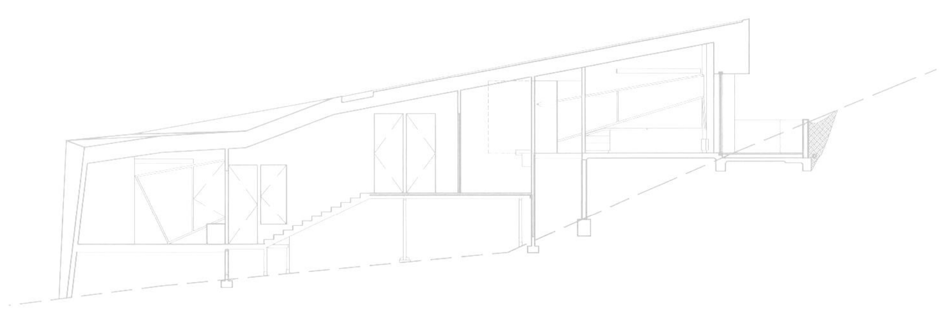

RICHARD MEIER

Richard Meier & Partners
475 Tenth Avenue
New York, NY 10018
USA

Tel: +1 212 967 6060
Fax: +1 212 967 3207
E-mail: mail@richardmeier.com
Web: www.richardmeier.com

RICHARD MEIER was born in Newark, New Jersey, in 1934. He received his architectural training at Cornell University, and worked in the office of Marcel Breuer (1960–63), before establishing his own practice in 1963. In 1984, he became the youngest winner of the Pritzker Prize, and he received the 1988 RIBA Gold Medal. His notable buildings include the Atheneum (New Harmony, Indiana 1975–79); High Museum of Art (Atlanta, Georgia, 1980–83); Museum of Decorative Arts (Frankfurt, Germany, 1979–84); Canal Plus Headquarters (Paris, France, 1988–91); Barcelona Museum of Contemporary Art (Barcelona, Spain, 1988–95); City Hall and Library (The Hague, The Netherlands, 1990–95); and the Getty Center (Los Angeles, California, 1984–97). Recent work includes the US Courthouse and Federal Building (Phoenix, Arizona, 1995–2000); Yale University History of Art and Arts Library (New Haven, Connecticut, 2001); Jubilee Church (Rome, Italy, 1996–2003); Crystal Cathedral International Center for Possibility Thinking (Garden Grove, California, 1998–2003); 66 Restaurant in New York (New York, 2002–03); Ara Pacis Museum (Rome, Italy, 1995–2006); 165 Charles Street (New York, New York, 2003–06); and Arp Museum (Rolandseck, Germany, 1997–2007). More recent and current work includes the ECM City Tower (Pankrác, Prague, Czech Republic, 2001–08); Rickmers Residence (Hamburg, Germany, 2005–08, published here); and On Prospect Park (Brooklyn, New York, USA, 2003–09).

RICHARD MEIER wurde 1934 in Newark, New Jersey, geboren. Seine Ausbildung zum Architekten erhielt er an der Cornell University und arbeitete anschließend bei Marcel Breuer (1960–63), ehe er 1963 sein eigenes Büro gründete. 1984 wurde er als jüngster Preisträger mit dem Pritzker-Preis ausgezeichnet und erhielt 1988 die RIBA-Goldmedaille. Zu seinen bekanntesten Bauten gehören das Atheneum (New Harmony, Indiana, 1975–79), das High Museum of Art (Atlanta, Georgia, 1980–83), das Museum für Angewandte Kunst (Frankfurt am Main, 1979–84), die Hauptverwaltung von Canal Plus (Paris, 1988–91), das Museum für Zeitgenössische Kunst in Barcelona (1988–95), Stadthaus und Bibliothek in Den Haag (1990–95) sowie das Getty Center (Los Angeles, 1984–97). Zu seinen jüngeren Projekten zählen das Bundesgerichtsgebäude in Phoenix (Arizona, 1995–2000), die Bibliothek für Kunst und Kunstgeschichte der Universität Yale (New Haven, Connecticut, 2001), die Kirche Dio Padre Misericordioso in Rom (1996–2003), das Crystal Cathedral International Center for Possibility Thinking (Garden Grove, Kalifornien, 1998–2003), das Restaurant 66 in New York (2002–03), das Museum Ara Pacis (Rom, 1995–2006), 165 Charles Street (New York, 2003–06) sowie das Arp-Museum (Rolandseck, Deutschland, 1997–2007). Aktuellere Projekte sind u. a. der ECM City Tower (Pankrác, Prag, 2001–08), das Haus Rickmers (Hamburg, 2005–08, hier vorgestellt) und das Haus On Prospect Park (Brooklyn, New York, USA, 2003–09).

RICHARD MEIER, né à Newark (New Jersey) en 1934, a fait ses études à l'université Cornell, puis a travaillé dans l'agence de Marcel Breuer (1960–63), avant de fonder sa propre structure en 1963. En 1984, il a été le plus jeune titulaire du prix Pritzker, et a reçu en 1988 la médaille d'or du RIBA. Parmi ses réalisations les plus connues : l'Atheneum (New Harmony, Indiana 1975–79) ; le High Museum of Art (Atlanta, Georgie, 1980–83) ; le Musée des arts décoratifs (Francfort, Allemagne, 1979–84) ; le siège de Canal Plus (Paris, 1988–91) ; Le Musée d'art contemporain de Barcelone (MACBA, Barcelone, Espagne, 1988–95) ; l'hôtel de ville et bibliothèque municipale de La Haye (Pays-Bas, 1990–95) ; et le Getty Center (Los Angeles, 1984–97). Parmi ses réalisations récentes : le tribunal et immeuble fédéral (Phoenix, Arizona, 1995–2000) ; la bibliothèque des arts et d'histoire de l'art de l'université Yale (New Haven, Connecticut, 2001) ; l'église du Jubilé (Rome, 1996–2003) ; la cathédrale de cristal, l'International Center for Possibility Thinking (Garden Grove, Californie, 1998–2003) ; le Restaurant 66 à New York (2002–03) ; le musée de l'Ara Pacis (Rome, 1995–2006) ; l'immeuble d'appartements du 165 Charles Street (New York, 2003–06) ; le Arp Museum (Rolandseck, Allemagne, 1997–2007) ; la City Tower ECM (Pankrác, Prague, République tchèque, 2001–08) ; la résidence Rickmers (Hambourg, 2005–08, publiée ici) ; et l'immeuble d'appartements On Prospect Park (Brooklyn, New York, 2003–09).

RICKMERS RESIDENCE

Hamburg, Germany, 2005–08

Area: 848 m² (including garage). Client: Bertram R. C. Rickmers.
Cost: not disclosed. Collaboration: Bernhard Karpf, Ringo Offermann

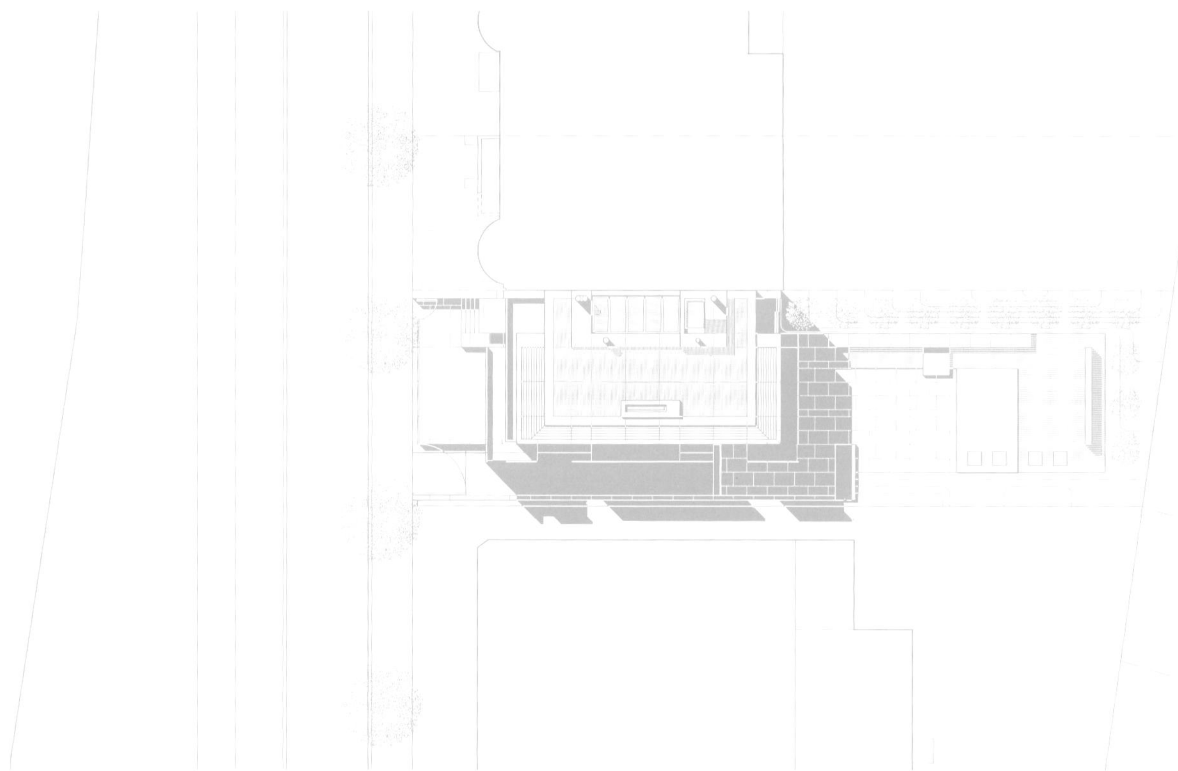

This terraced townhouse is located in the center of the northern German city of Hamburg and overlooks a lake. Five stories high, it includes living space on the ground floor, a children's room, guest room and study on the second floor, master bedroom on the third floor, an exercise suite on the fourth level, and a penthouse and roof terrace. The bedroom areas have sliding walls that allow some flexibility in the definition of the spaces. A top-lit stair and elevator hallmarks the ground-floor entrance. An opaque panel is hung on the façade of the east elevation and continues onto the north elevation of the building, participating in Meier's complex rhythm of transparency, light, and shadow. Essentially rectangular in form, the house has paved garden courts on the southern and northern sides, and a rear court with a lawn and trees. The Rickmers Residence is a more urban exercise than many Meier houses, seeking to fit into the four-story alignment of the roofs of its far more traditional neighbors.

Dieses Stadthaus steht im Zentrum Hamburgs und bietet einen Ausblick auf die Alster. Der Bau mit insgesamt fünf Geschossen hat einen Wohnraum im Erdgeschoss, Kinderzimmer, Gästezimmer und Arbeitszimmer im ersten Obergeschoss, Hauptschlafzimmer im zweiten, einen Fitnessraum im dritten Obergeschoss sowie ein Penthouse mit Terrasse. Die Schlafbereiche sind mit Schiebetüren ausgestattet, was die Raumaufteilung flexibler gestaltet. Der Eingangsbereich mit Treppenhaus und Aufzug im Erdgeschoss wird durch ein Oberlicht erhellt. Der Ostfassade ist eine opake Platte vorgehängt, die sich um die Nordfassade des Hauses zieht und zu dem für Meier typischen, komplexen Rhythmus aus Transparenz, Licht und Schatten beiträgt. An der Süd- und Nordseite des im Grunde rechteckigen Gebäudes liegen gepflasterte Bereiche, in einem rückwärtiger Hof gibt es eine Rasenfläche und Bäume. Das Haus Rickmers wirkt urbaner als viele andere Wohnbauten Meiers und passt sich an die Traufhöhe der wesentlich traditionelleren, viergeschossigen Nachbarbauten an.

Cette résidence urbaine, qui fait partie d'un alignement de maisons, est située au centre de Hambourg, et donne sur un lac. Sur cinq niveaux, elle comprend un séjour au rez-de-chaussée, une chambre d'enfant, une chambre d'amis et un bureau au premier étage, la chambre principale au deuxième, une salle de fitness au quatrième et enfin une penthouse et sa terrasse. Les chambres sont dotées de parois coulissantes qui permettent une certaine souplesse dans la définition des espaces. Un escalier à éclairage zénithal et une cage d'ascenseur occupent une partie du hall d'entrée. Le panneau opaque suspendu sur la façade est se poursuit sur la façade nord, et participe au rythme complexe de transparences, d'ombre et de lumière créé par Meier. De forme rectangulaire, la maison est bordée de cours pavées au nord et au sud, et d'une cour gazonnée plantée d'arbres à l'arrière. Cette résidence est davantage un exercice urbain que bien d'autres maisons de Meier, et s'efforce de s'adapter à l'alignement des toits de ses voisines beaucoup plus traditionnelles.

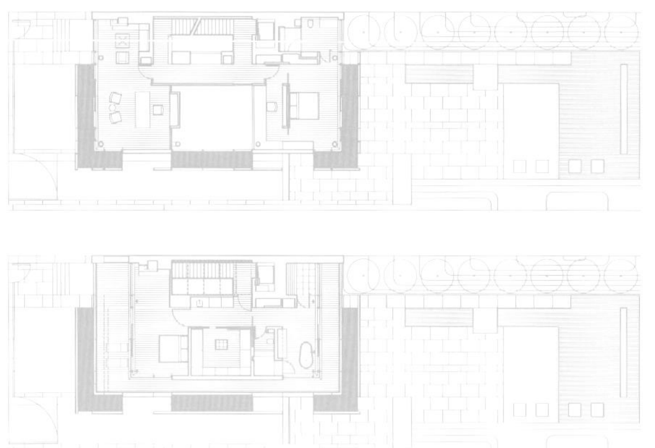

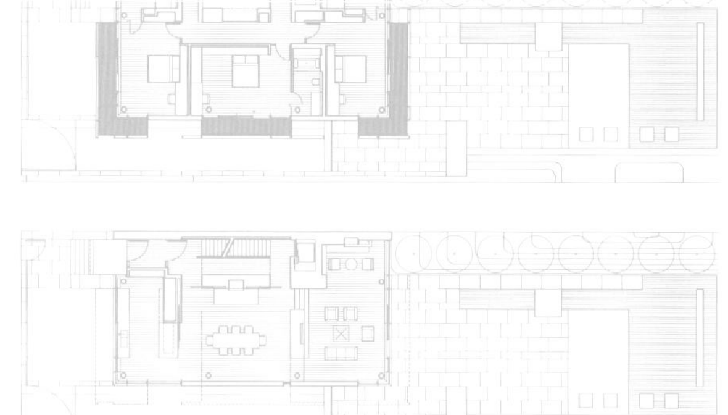

Though Richard Meier has built many houses, most of them have spectacular views, which is not the case here. Screens are used to offer privacy to this kitchen space.

Richard Meier hat zahlreiche Häuser gebaut, die meisten von ihnen mit einer spektakulären Aussicht, was hier nicht der Fall ist. Jalousien verhelfen der Küche zu einer Privatsphäre.

Richard Meier a construit de nombreuses résidences privées aux vues spectaculaires, ce qui n'est pas le cas ici. Des stores vénitiens protègent l'intimité de cette cuisine.

Plans (above left) show all the rigor and willful complexity of a Richard Meier design. The architect plays on openings and ceiling heights to give the interior a musical variety.

Die Grundrisse (oben links) illustrieren die typische Strenge und Komplexität eines Richard-Meier-Entwurfs. Der Architekt spielt mit Fassadenöffnungen und Deckenhöhen, um dem Innenraum eine geradezu musikalische Vielfalt zu verleihen.

Les plans (ci-dessus à gauche) montrent la rigueur et la complexité calculée du projet de Richard Meier. L'architecte joue sur les ouvertures et les hauteurs de plafond pour élaborer des rapports de nature quasi musicale.

JOEB MOORE

Joeb + Partners Architects, LLC
20 Bruce Park Avenue
Greenwich, CT 06830
USA

Tel: +1 203 769 5828
Fax: +1 203 629 0717
E-mail: office@joebmoore.com
Web: www.joebmoore.com

JOEB MOORE received his B.S. in Architectural Design (1983) and his M.Arch. (1985) degrees from Clemson University (Clemson, South Carolina). He did postgraduate studies in architectural theory and history at Yale (1989–91). He worked for Shope Reno Wharton (1986–93) and was a principal of Kaehler Moore (1993–), both in Greenwich, Connecticut, before creating Joeb + Partners Architects, LLC, in 2008. He is a Professor at both Yale and Columbia, teaching design studios and history/theory courses. His built work includes the Riverbank Residence (Stamford, Connecticut, 2005); Broad Street Residence (Greenwich, Connecticut, 2006); ReDa Residence (Guilford, Connecticut, 2006); 44PL House (Greenwich, Connecticut, 2006–08, published here); and Bridge House (Kent, Connecticut, under construction), all in the USA.

JOEB MOORE erwarb seinen B.S. in Entwurf (1983) und seinen M. Arch. (1985) an der Clemson University (Clemson, South Carolina). Als Postgraduate studierte er Architekturtheorie und -geschichte in Yale (1989–91). Er arbeitete für Shope Reno Wharton (1986–93) und war leitender Architekt bei Kaehler Moore (1993–), beide in Greenwich, Connecticut, ehe er 2008 sein Büro Joeb + Partners Architects, LLC, gründete. Er ist Professor an den Universitäten Yale und Columbia, wo er Entwurf sowie Geschichte und Theorie unterrichtet. Zu seinen realisierten Bauten zählen die Riverbank Residence (Stamford, Connecticut, 2005), die Broad Street Residence (Greenwich, Connecticut, 2006), die ReDa Residence (Guilford, Connecticut, 2006), das 44PL House (Greenwich, Connecticut, 2006–08, hier vorgestellt) und das Bridge House (Kent, Connecticut, in Bau), alle in den USA.

JOEB MOORE a obtenu son B.S. en conception architecturale (1983) et son M.Arch. (1985) de l'université Clemson (Clemson, Caroline du Sud). Il a effectué des études supérieures en théorie et histoire de l'architecture à Yale (1989–91). Il a travaillé chez Shope Reno Wharton (1986–93) et a été l'un des associés de Kaehler Moore (1993–), deux agences de Greenwich (Connecticut), avant de fonder Joeb + Partners Architects, LLC, en 2008. Il est professeur à Yale et Columbia, enseignant dans des ateliers de conception et donnant des cours d'histoire et de théorie. Parmi ses réalisations : la résidence Riverbank (Stamford, Connecticut, 2005) ; la résidence de Broad Street (Greenwich, Connecticut, 2006) ; la résidence ReDa (Guilford, Connecticut, 2006) ; la maison 44PL (Greenwich, Connecticut, 2006–08, publiée ici) ; et la maison Pont (Bridge House, Kent, Connecticut, en construction).

44PL HOUSE

Greenwich, Connecticut, USA, 2006–08

Area: 1068 m². Client: not disclosed. Cost: not disclosed.
Collaboration: Jake Watkins, Thalassa Curtis

The architect plays on the form of the typical double-slope roof house (image below) and introduces wood siding that gives this large residence a more residential feeling than it might otherwise have.

Der Architekt spielt mit der Form des traditionellen Satteldachhauses (Bild unten) und versieht es mit einer Außenwandverschalung aus Holz. So verleiht er dem großen Haus ein wohnlicheres Gesicht, als es es sonst gehabt hätte.

L'architecte joue sur la forme de toiture classique à double pente (cidessous) mais y introduit des parements en bois qui renforcent l'atmosphère chaleureuse de cette grande résidence.

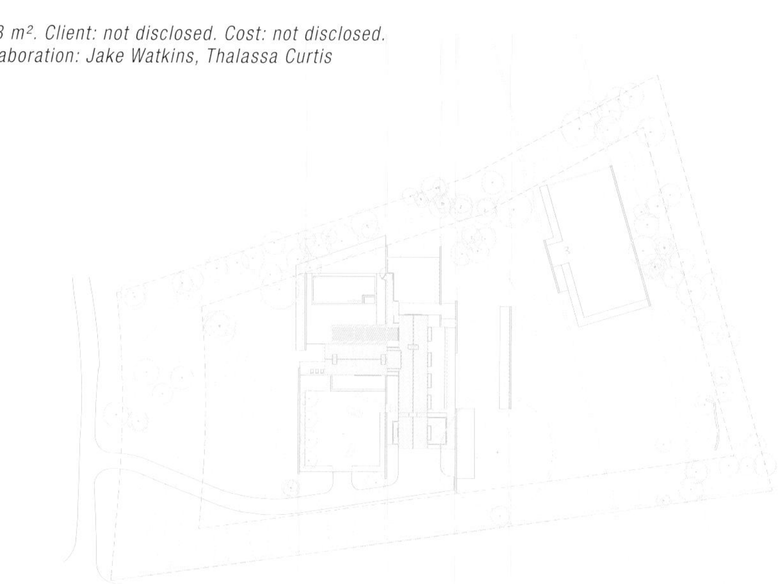

The steeply sloped site of this house is 183 meters long and 61 meters wide. A series of concrete retaining walls is used to manage the nine-meter difference in height from one side of the plot to the other. The residence is described as a "geometric house primitive" that hovers above and is anchored to these retaining walls. The actual design of the house is termed by the architect "strongly iconic, if not nostalgic (but not sentimental)." The "container-box" forms of the house are rotated according to their location, with a first element on the street side, and, above it, a second perpendicular box. A waterfall and canal bring reflected light and sound into the house, which seeks to allow the exterior environment to penetrate the architecture. An open wood-slat exterior cladding on the upper volume of the house allows it to glow from within at night. A willful, modern sleekness is contrasted with the "primitive" aspect of the wooden hut aspects of the design.

Das steil abfallende Hanggrundstück des Hauses ist 183 m lang und 61 m breit. Mehrere Betonstützmauern dienen dazu, den Höhenunterschied von 9 m zwischen einem Ende des Grundstücks und dem anderen zu überbrücken. Das Haus selbst nennt der Architekt einen „geometrischen Primitivbau", der über den Stützmauern zu schweben scheint und in ihnen verankert ist. Seinen Entwurf beschreibt er als „eigentümlich ikonisch, wenn nicht gar nostalgisch (jedoch nicht sentimental)". Die boxartigen Formen des Hauses sind gemäß ihres Standorts gedreht: ein erster Baukörper ist zur Straße hin gelegt, darüber steht eine zweite Box aufrecht. Ein Wasserfall und ein kleiner Kanal holen Lichtreflexe und Geräusche in das Haus; so darf das äußere Umfeld die Architektur durchdringen. Nachts leuchtet das Haus hinter den Holzlatten, mit denen das Obergeschoss verkleidet ist. Hier wird ein Kontrast geschaffen zwischen dem „primitiven" Aspekt einer Holzhütte und einem gewollt modernen, glatten Design.

Le terrain en forte pente mesure 183 m de long par 61 m de large. Une série de murs de soutènement gèrent le dénivelé de 9 m entre les deux extrémités de la parcelle. La résidence, décrite comme une « maison primitive de style géométrique », est suspendue au-dessus des murs auxquels elle s'ancre à certains points. Son style est qualifié par l'architecte de « fortement iconique, si ce n'est nostalgique (mais non sentimental) ». Les formes de « conteneur » des différentes parties pivotent en fonction de leur localisation, avec un premier élément côté rue au-dessus duquel vient se poser une boîte perpendiculaire. Une cascade bruissante et un canal réfléchissent la lumière naturelle dans la maison, qui se laisse pénétrer par l'environnement extérieur. Le parement de façade en lattes de bois en partie supérieure crée des transparences lumineuses la nuit. Le caractère lisse, volontaire et moderne du traitement de l'ensemble contraste avec l'aspect « primitif » de « hutte de bois » du projet.

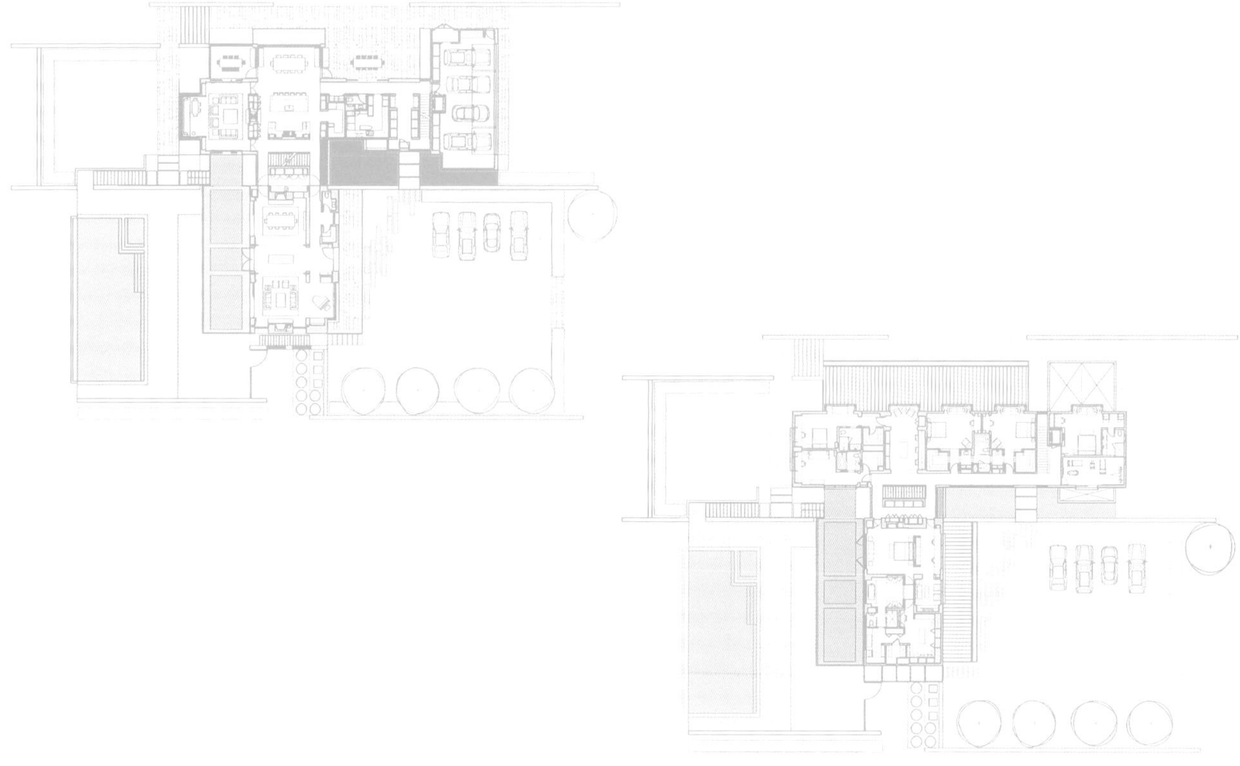

The size and complexity of the L-shaped house are visible in the plans above. Right, water and the natural environment contrast with the hard edges of the architectural forms.

Größe und Komplexität des L-förmigen Gebäudes sind an den Grundrissen oben abzulesen. Wasser und landschaftliche Umgebung bilden einen Kontrast zu den scharfen Linien der Architektur (rechts).

Les dimensions et la complexité de cette maison en forme de L sont illustrés par les plans ci-dessus. À droite, la présence de l'eau et de l'environnement naturel contraste avec la rigueur géométrique des éléments architecturaux.

OLSON KUNDIG ARCHITECTS

Olson Kundig Architects
159 South Jackson Street, Suite 600
Seattle, WA 98104
USA

Tel: +1 206 624 5670
Fax: +1 206 624 3730
E-mail: newinquiry@olsonkundigarchitects.com
Web: www.olsonkundigarchitects.com

Tom Kundig received his B.A. in Environmental Design (1977) and his M.Arch (1981) from the University of Washington. He was a Principal of Jochman/Kundig (1983–84) before becoming a Principal of **OLSON KUNDIG ARCHITECTS** (since 1986). Tom Kundig is the recipient of the 2008 National Design Award in Architecture Design, awarded by the Smithsonian's Cooper-Hewitt National Design Museum. Olson Sundberg Kundig Allen Architects received the 2009 National AIA Architecture Firm Award. Aside from the Montecito Residence (Montecito, California, 2006–08) and Rolling Huts (Mazama, Washington, 2007, both published here), the firm's work includes Chicken Point Cabin (Northern Idaho, 2002); the widely published Delta Shelter (Mazama, Washington, 2005); and the Hong Kong Villa (Shek-O, China, lead architect Jim Olson, 2008). Current projects include the 1900 First Avenue Hotel and Apartments (Seattle, Washington, in progress) and the T. Bailey Offices (Anacortes, Washington, in progress), all in the USA unless stated otherwise.

Tom Kundig erhielt seinen B. A. in Umweltplanung (1977) ebenso wie seinen M. Arch. (1981) an der University of Washington. Er war leitender Architekt bei Jochman/Kundig (1983–84) und ist seit 1986 Chefarchitekt bei **OLSON KUNDIG ARCHITECTS**. Tom Kundig wurde 2008 mit dem National Design Award für Architektur ausgezeichnet, der vom zur Smithsonian Institution gehörenden Cooper-Hewitt National Design Museum verliehen wird. 2009 wurde das Team mit dem Preis der AIA für Architekturbüros ausgezeichnet. Projekte des Büros sind neben der Montecito Residence (Montecito, Kalifornien, 2006–08) und den Rolling Huts (Mazama, Washington, 2007, beide hier vorgestellt) auch die Chicken Point Cabin (Northern Idaho, 2002), das vielfach publizierte Delta Shelter (Mazama, Washington, 2005) sowie die Hong Kong Villa (Shek-O, China, leitender Architekt Jim Olson, 2008). Zu den aktuellen Projekten zählen u. a. 1900 First Avenue Hotel and Apartments (Seattle, Washington, in Bau) sowie Büros für T. Bailey (Anacortes, Washington, in Arbeit), alle in den USA soweit nicht anders angegeben.

Tom Kundig a obtenu son B.A. en conception environnementale (1977) et son M.Arch (1981) de l'université de Washington. Il a été associé et dirigeant de Jochman/Kundig (1983–84), avant de devenir le dirigeant d'**OLSON KUNDIG ARCHITECTS** (depuis 1986). Tom Kundig a reçu le Prix national de conception architecturale 2008 du Smithsonian's Cooper-Hewitt National Design Museum. Olson Sundberg Kundig Allen Architects a reçu en 2009 le Prix national de l'agence d'architecture de l'année de l'AIA. En dehors de la résidence de Montecito (Montecito, Californie, 2006–08) et des huttes roulantes (Rolling Huts, Mazama, Washington, 2007, toutes deux publiées ici), l'agence a également construit, entre autres, le chalet de Chicken Point (Chicken Point Cabin, nord de l'Idaho, 2002) ; le très publié abri du Delta (Delta Shelter, Mazama, Washington, 2005) ; et une villa à Hong-Kong (Shek-O, Chine, architecte de projet : Jim Olson, 2008). Parmi leurs projets actuels figurent le 1900 First Avenue Hotel and Apartments (Seattle, Washington, en chantier) et les bureaux T. Bailey (Anacortes, Washington, en chantier).

MONTECITO RESIDENCE

Montecito, California, USA, 2006–08

Area: 316 m². Client: not disclosed. Cost: not disclosed.
Collaboration: Elizabeth Bianchi Conklin, Huyen Hoang, Debbie Kennedy

This house is located in Toro Canyon, which is prone to fires. A raised roof shields the broadly glazed residence from the sun while allowing generous views of the ocean. A central hallway encourages natural ventilation, while very low or almost non-existent vegetation around the house would seem to offer some protection from approaching fires. The same hallway marks the division between the private and public spaces of the house. A public entrance and garage are set to the east, while a garden, pool and guest rooms are located on the west side. The architect states: "The house is made of simple, fire-resistant materials. Steel will be allowed to oxidize and concrete is toned to allow the house to blend into the landscape."

Dieses Haus liegt im Toro Canyon, der häufig von Bränden heimgesucht wird. Das angehobene Dach schützt das großzügig verglaste Haus vor Sonnenlicht und ermöglicht zugleich einen offenen Blick aufs Meer. Ein mittig verlaufender Flur fördert die natürliche Belüftung. Die sehr niedrige, fast gänzlich fehlende Vegetation um das Haus dürfte zumindest etwas Schutz vor Feuern bieten. Der Flur markiert zugleich die Gliederung des Hauses in private und öffentliche Bereiche. Der öffentliche Eingangsbereich und die Garage sind nach Osten ausgerichtet, während Garten, Pool und Gästezimmer an der Westseite liegen. „Das Haus", berichtet der Architekt, „wurde aus einfachen, feuerfesten Materialien gebaut. Der Stahl wird im Lauf der Zeit oxidieren; der Beton wurde abgetönt, um sich in die Landschaft einzufügen."

Cette maison est située dans le Toro Canyon, dans un environnement naturel soumis à de hauts risques d'incendies. Le toit surélevé protège du soleil la résidence largement vitrée qui bénéficie de vues généreuses sur l'océan. Un corridor central facilite la ventilation naturelle. La végétation très basse, voire presque inexistante, autour de la maison pourrait apporter une certaine protection contre le feu. Le même corridor sépare les espaces de réception et privés. L'entrée et le garage sont implantés à l'est, tandis qu'un jardin, une piscine et les chambres d'invités sont positionnés à l'ouest. « La maison est réalisée en matériaux simples, résistant au feu. L'acier se patinera avec le temps et le béton est teinté pour permettre à la maison de se fondre dans le paysage », précise l'architecte.

As seen in the image above, the house takes on the appearance of a glass box enclosed in a protective steel frame. The ample glazing allows for full views of the spectacular site.

Wie oben zu sehen, wirkt das Haus wie eine Glasbox, die von einem schützenden Stahlrahmen umfangen wird. Die großzügige Verglasung erlaubt einen weiten Blick in die spektakuläre Landschaft.

Ci-dessus, la maison, une boîte de verre protégée par une structure d'acier. Les immenses baies vitrées offrent une vue dégagée sur un panorama extraordinaire.

The surprising cantilevered roof of the entrance corridor (left and previous page) sets the tone for the house, which blends the relatively understated simplicity seen in the views below with an astonishing site.

Das überraschende, auskragende Dach über dem Eingang (links und vorhergehende Seite) prägt das Haus, das sich mit seiner unaufdringlichen Schlichtheit in die atemberaubende Umgebung einfügt.

Le surprenant auvent en porte-à-faux du corridor de l'entrée (à gauche et page précédente) donne le ton, celui de la fusion d'une architecture relativement simple et d'un site étonnant.

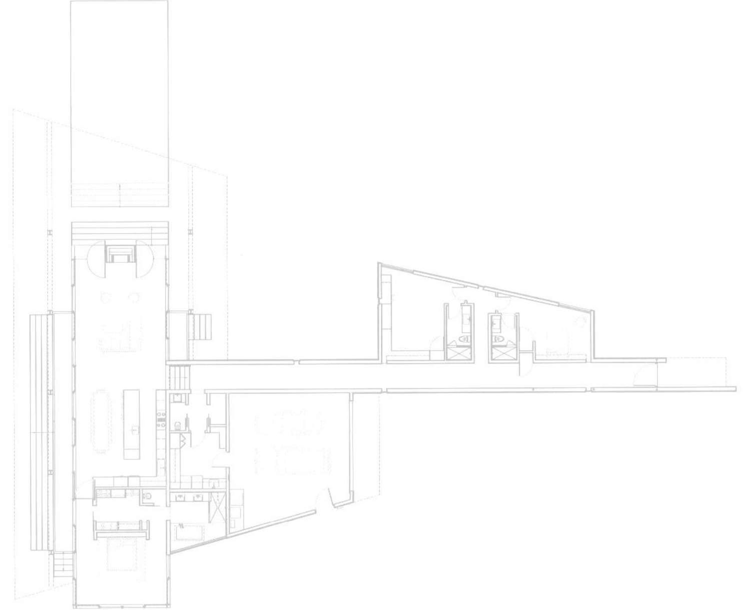

A bedroom is fully glazed, allowing residents to take full advantage of the hilltop site. Left, a basic plan that shows the long entrance corridor at right angles to the main volume of the residence.

Ein deckenhoch verglastes Schlafzimmer erlaubt den Bewohnern, den Ausblick vom Hügelgrundstück zu genießen. Links der einfache Grundriss, auf dem der lange Eingangsflur im rechten Winkel zum Hauptbaukörper zu erkennen ist.

La chambre entièrement vitrée permet à ses occupants de profiter d'une vue plongeante sur le paysage. À gauche, plan au sol montrant le long corridor d'entrée perpendiculaire au volume principal.

ROLLING HUTS

Mazama, Washington, USA, 2007

Area: 19 m² (interior); 41 m² (interior plus deck).
Client: Michal Friedrich. Cost: not disclosed

A number of the Rolling Huts set in a former Washington camping ground. With their slanted roofs and light structures, these rolling residences address numerous ecological concerns.

Eine Gruppe von Rolling Huts auf einem ehemaligen Campingplatz im Staat Washington. Mit ihren geneigten Dächern und der leichten Konstruktion werden die rollenden Domizile gleich mehreren ökologischen Anliegen gerecht.

Quelques huttes roulantes dans un ancien terrain de camping de l'État de Washington. Ces maisonnettes sur roues de structure légère et toiture à simple pente répondent à de nombreuses préoccupations écologiques.

Intended as guest housing for friends and family, these structures are described by the architect as being "several steps above camping, while remaining low-tech and low-impact in their design." Installed on a former camping site, the **ROLLING HUTS** are meant to allow the mountain meadow where they are located to return to its natural state. Raised up on wheels, the structures are little more than steel-clad boxes set on steel and wood platforms. Double-paned sliding glass doors provided access to the small interior space where cork and plywood are the main materials. Facilities such as showers and parking space are located in a nearby barn. Tom Kundig states: "The huts evoke Thoreau's simple cabin in the woods; the structures take second place to nature."

Die als Gästehäuser für Freunde und Verwandte gedachten Hütten liegen laut Architekt „ein paar Klassen über Campingniveau, sind aber dennoch mit nur minimaler Technik ausgestattet und auf minimalen Umwelteingriff ausgelegt". Die **ROLLING HUTS** (rollende Hütten) befinden sich auf einem ehemaligen Campingplatz und sollen sicherstellen, dass sich die Bergwiese, auf der sie stehen, in ihren ursprünglichen Zustand zurückentwickeln kann. Die auf Rädern montierten Hütten sind kaum mehr als stahlverkleidete Boxen und ruhen auf einer Plattform aus Stahl und Holz. Schiebetüren mit Isolierverglasung bieten Zugang zum kleinen Innenraum, der überwiegend mit Kork und Sperrholz ausgebaut wurde. Einrichtungen wie Duschen und Parkplätze befinden sich in einer nahe gelegenen Scheune. Tom Kundig erklärt: „Die Hütten lassen an Thoreaus schlichte Hütte im Wald denken; diese Bauten ordnen sich der Natur unter."

Prévues pour des amis ou la famille du client, ces petites constructions sont présentées par les architectes comme « plusieurs niveaux au-dessus d'un camping, mais techniquement simples et sans beaucoup d'impact sur l'environnement grâce à leur conception ». Implantées sur un ancien terrain de camping, ces « huttes » devraient permettre le retour de la prairie à son état naturel si elles devaient être déplacées. Ce sont essentiellement des boîtes habillées de tôle d'acier, reposant sur des plates-formes en bois et acier montées sur roues. Des portes à double vitrage coulissantes donnent accès au volume intérieur où règnent le contreplaqué et le liège. Les installations comme les douches ou les emplacements de parking sont regroupées dans une grange voisine. « Ces huttes évoquent la cabane dans les bois de Thoreau. La construction vient en second plan par rapport à la nature », explique Tom Kundig.

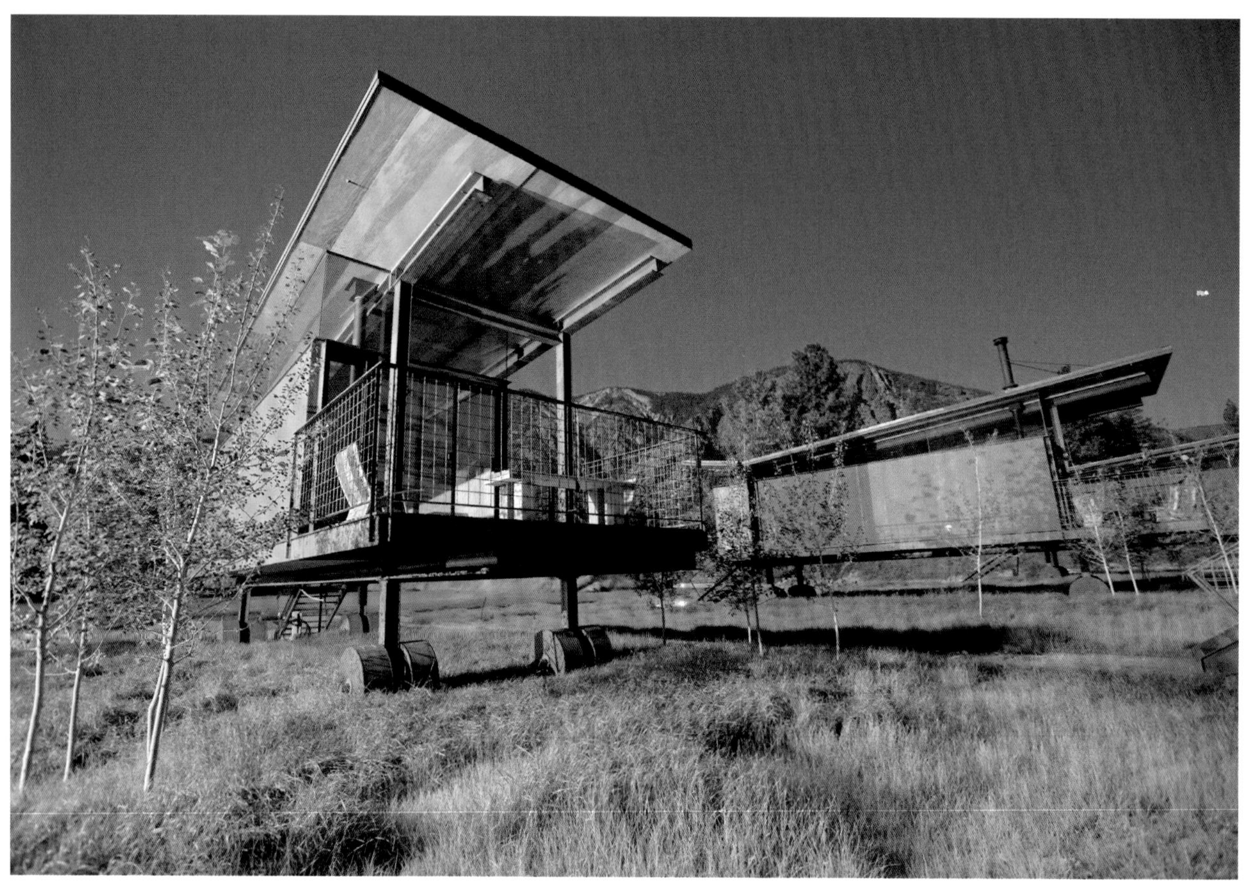

In a summer setting, the wheels of the Rolling Huts are visible, making clear their minimal impact on the site.

Im Sommer sind auch die Räder der Rolling Huts zu sehen, anhand derer der minimale Eingriff in die Landschaft deutlich wird.

Dispersées dans un cadre estival, les huttes roulantes dévoilent leurs roues, qui limitent leur impact sur le sol.

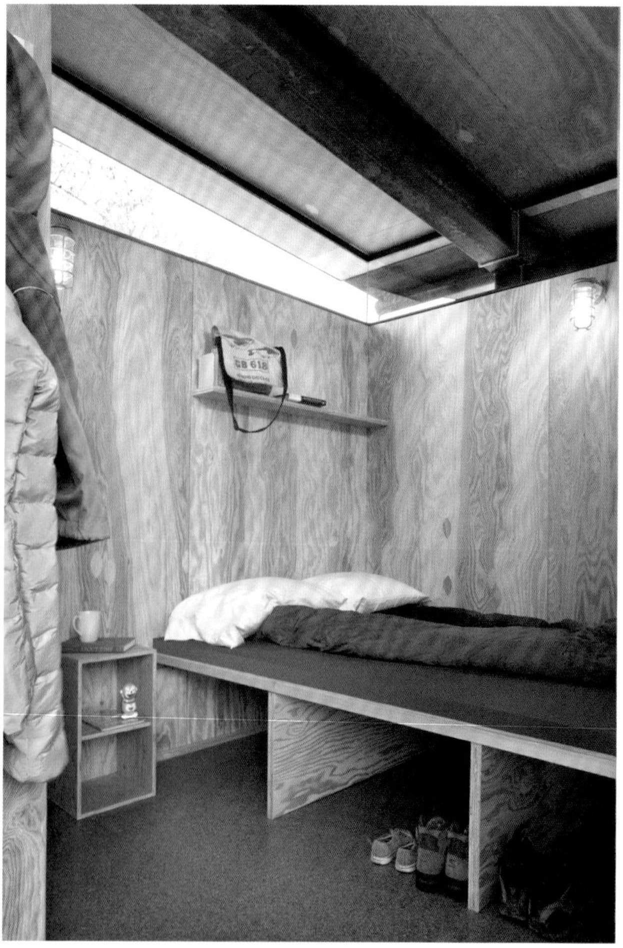

The Rolling Huts have a rather sophisticated, mountain cabin feeling about them inside, with large, glazed surfaces and a wood-burning stove, as seen in the image above.

Der Innenraum einer Rolling Hut mit seinen großen Glasfronten und einem Holzofen lässt an eine eher anspruchsvolle Berghütte denken (Foto oben).

L'intérieur bénéficie d'une atmosphère assez sophistiquée de chalet de montagne. Elles sont équipées de grandes baies vitrées et d'un poêle à bois (ci-dessus).

PALERM & TABARES DE NAVA

Palerm & Tabares de Nava Arquitectos
Calle 25 de Julio, n. 48
38004 Santa Cruz de Tenerife
Canary Islands
Spain

Tel: +34 922 24 75 70
E-mail: paltab@paltab.com
Web: www.paltab.com

JUAN MANUEL PALERM SALAZAR was born in Santa Cruz de Tenerife in 1957. **LEOPOLDO TABARES DE NAVA Y MARÍN** was born in La Laguna in 1958. They have been working together since 1986 and formed their current partnership in 1996. They place a particular emphasis on location and territory, with an interest in landscape and urban morphology. They have worked mainly in the Canary Islands, although they have also undertaken projects in Argentina, Costa Rica, Mexico, and the United States (Los Angeles), as well as in the cities of Gerona (Spain), and Trento and Venice (Italy). Their work includes the Public Library of Estado (Las Palmas de Gran Canaria, Grand Canary Island, 1996–2002); Espacio Expositivo-Taller Fundación César Manrique (Teguise, Lanzerote, 1996–2004); the García Sanabria Park (Santa Cruz de Tenerife, Tenerife, 2004–06); the Space in La Laguna (San Cristóbal de La Laguna, 2004–07, published here); a Theater, Service Center, and Sports Palace (Trento, Italy, 2007); and Barranco de Santos (Santa Cruz de Tenerife, Tenerife, 1997–2010).

JUAN MANUEL PALERM SALAZAR wurde 1957 in Santa Cruz de Tenerife geboren, **LEOPOLDO TABARES DE NAVA Y MARÍN** 1958 in La Laguna. Seit 1986 arbeiten die Architekten zusammen; ihre Partnerschaft begründeten sie 1996. Besonderen Wert legt das Team auf Standort und Geländebeschaffenheit, außerdem gilt ihr Interesse der Landschafts- und Stadtmorphologie. Ihre Projekte realisierten sie in erster Linie auf den Kanarischen Inseln, jedoch auch in Argentinien, Costa Rica, Mexiko und den USA (Los Angeles) sowie den Städten Gerona (Spanien), Trento und Venedig (Italien). Zu ihren Arbeiten zählen die Stadtbibliothek von Estado (Las Palmas de Gran Canaria, Gran Canaria, 1996–2002), der Espacio Expositivo-Taller Fundación César Manrique (Teguise, Lanzarote, 1996–2004), der Park García Sanabria (Santa Cruz de Tenerife, Teneriffa, 2004–06), ein Haus in La Laguna (San Cristóbal de La Laguna, 2004–07, hier vorgestellt), ein Theater, Service- und Sportcenter (Trient, Italien, 2007) und der Barranco de Santos (Santa Cruz de Tenerife, Teneriffa, 1997–2010).

JUAN MANUEL PALERM SALAZAR est né à Santa Cruz de Tenerife en 1957. **LEOPOLDO TABARES DE NAVA Y MARÍN** est né à La Laguna en 1958. Ils travaillent ensemble depuis 1986 et se sont associés sous la forme actuelle en 1996. Ils mettent particulièrement l'accent sur la situation et le territoire et s'intéressent à la morphologie de la ville et du paysage. Ils interviennent principalement dans les Îles Canaries, mais ont aussi travaillé en Argentine, au Costa Rica, au Mexique et aux États-Unis (Los Angeles) ainsi qu'à Gérone (Espagne), Trente et Venise (Italie). Parmi leurs réalisations : la bibliothèque publique d'Estado (Las Palmas de Gran Canaria, Grande Canarie, 1996–2002) ; l'Espacio Expositivo-Taller Fundación César Manrique (Teguise, Lanzerote, 1996–2004) ; le parc García Sanabria (Santa Cruz de Tenerife, Tenerife, 2004–06) ; le Space à La Laguna (San Cristóbal de La Laguna, 2004–07, publié ici) ; un théâtre, palais des sports et centre de services à Trente (Italie, 2007) ; et le Barranco de Santos (Santa Cruz de Tenerife, Tenerife, 1997–2010).

SPACE IN LA LAGUNA

San Cristóbal de La Laguna, Spain, 2004–07

Area: 297 m². Client: not disclosed.
Cost: not disclosed

Above, an exterior and garden view of the house showing the use of wood alternating with steel and glass.

Oben ein Blick auf die Fassade und den Garten des Hauses. Hier zeigt sich der abwechslungsreiche Einsatz von Holz, Stahl und Glas.

Ci-dessus, vue extérieure de la maison prise du jardin montrant l'utilisation du bois en alternance avec les baies vitrées et les éléments structurels en acier.

The project involved the renovation and expansion of an existing house. Only the first two bays of the original house remain, while the architects created a new corridor and patio that separates the public and private areas of the residence. Access to the house is gained through an alleyway that provides for both pedestrian and vehicular entry. Service areas and bathrooms are located along one side of the structure, while storage spaces have been created near the garage. The ample use of wood in the house offsets more modern materials and gives warmth to the entire design.

Dieses Projekt umfasste die Sanierung und Erweiterung eines bestehenden Hauses. Nur zwei Fassadenfelder des Altbaus blieben bestehen, zugleich fügten die Architekten einen neuen Korridor und eine Terrasse hinzu, die öffentliche und private Bereiche des Hauses voneinander trennt. Fußgänger und Fahrzeuge erreichen das Haus über einen schmalen Zufahrtsweg. Betriebsflächen und Bäder liegen auf einer Seite des Hauses; neben der Garage wurden Abstellräume eingerichtet. Der großzügige Einsatz von Holz im Haus bildet einen Kontrast zu den moderneren Baumaterialien und verleiht dem gesamten Entwurf Wärme.

Ce projet portait sur la rénovation et l'extension d'une maison existante. Seules ont été conservées les deux premières travées de la construction d'origine. Un nouveau corridor et un patio séparent maintenant les parties privées et de réception. L'accès se fait par une allée empruntée aussi bien par les piétons que par les voitures. Les services et les salles de bains sont regroupés d'un même côté, et des espaces de rangement ont été aménagés près du garage. La forte présence du bois dans la maison prend le pas sur des matériaux plus modernes et génère une chaleureuse ambiance d'ensemble.

Inside, wood floors or wall cladding alternate with generous glazed walls, bringing natural light and outdoor views into the residence.

Im Innern des Hauses wechseln sich Holzböden und -verkleidungen mit großzügigen Glasfronten ab. Diese lassen Tageslicht ein und bieten Ausblicke nach draußen.

À l'intérieur, les sols et les habillages muraux en bois alternent avec de généreuses parois vitrées qui laissent pénétrer une abondante lumière naturelle et offrent de multiples perspectives sur l'extérieur.

CLAUDIO & SARA PELLEGRINI

Studio Architetti Pellegrini & Partners SA
Via A. di Sacco 4
6500 Bellinzona
Switzerland

Tel: +41 91 820 24 50
Fax: +41 91 820 24 59
E-mail: cfp.arch@bluewin.ch
Web: www.arch-cfp.ch

CLAUDIO PELLEGRINI was born in Mendrisio in 1939. He was educated at the ETH in Zurich (1966), and opened his own office in 1970. He has worked on a scheme involving the construction of 90 villas in the Canton of Ticino (1968–2008). **SARA PELLEGRINI** was born in Lugano in 1968. She received her degree in architecture from the École Polytechnique Fédérale in Lausanne (EPFL, 1995). She worked in the office of Stankovic & Bonnen (Berlin, 1997) and with the lighting designers L'Observatoire International (New York, 1997–98). Since 2000, she has worked with her father, the architect Claudio Pellegrini, in Bellinzona, becoming one of the directors of the firm in 2008. Their work includes the House with a Patio 2 (Manno, Ticino, 2006, published here); an artist's studio (Verscio, 2008); the restructuring and addition of a new floor to a 1938 house in Casiano (Lugano, 2008); restructuring and expansion of San Giovanni Hospital (Bellinzona, 1970–2009); restructuring and expansion of the Beata Vergine Hospital (Mendrisio, 2009); and Stella Maris home for the elderly (Bedano, 2009), all in Switzerland.

CLAUDIO PELLEGRINI wurde 1939 in Mendrisio geboren. Seine Ausbildung erhielt er an der ETH Zürich (1966), 1970 gründete er sein eigenes Büro. Eines seiner Projekte war der Bau von 90 freistehenden Wohnhäusern im Kanton Tessin (1968–2008). **SARA PELLEGRINI** wurde 1968 in Lugano geboren und schloss ihr Architekturstudium an der École Polytechnique Fédérale in Lausanne (EPFL, 1995) ab. Sie arbeitete für Stankovic & Bonnen (Berlin, 1997) sowie die Leuchtenfirma L'Observatoire International (New York, 1997–98). Seit 2000 ist sie in Bellinzona für ihren Vater Claudio Pellegrini tätig und wechselte 2008 in die Geschäftsleitung des Büros. Zu ihren Projekten zählen das Haus mit Patio 2 (Manno, Tessin, 2006, hier vorgestellt), ein Künstleratelier (Verscio, 2008), Umbau und Aufstockung eines 1938 gebauten Hauses in Casiano (Lugano, 2008), Umbau und Erweiterung des Krankenhauses San Giovanni (Bellinzona, 1970–2009), Umbau und Erweiterung des Krankenhauses Beata Vergine (Mendrisio, 2009) sowie das Seniorenheim Stella Maris (Bedano, 2009), alle in der Schweiz.

CLAUDIO PELLEGRINI, né à Mendrisio en 1939, a étudié à l'ETH à Zurich (1966) et créé son agence en 1970. Il a travaillé sur un programme de construction de 90 villas dans le canton du Tessin (1968–2008). **SARA PELLEGRINI**, née à Lugano en 1968, est diplômée en architecture de l'École polytechnique fédérale de Lausanne (EPFL, 1995). Elle a travaillé chez Stankovic & Bonnen (Berlin, 1997) et avec les concepteurs de luminaires de l'Observatoire international (New York, 1997–98). Depuis 2000, elle collabore avec son père, Claudio Pellegrini, à Bellinzona, et fait partie de la direction de l'agence depuis 2008. Parmi leurs réalisations, toutes en Suisse : la maison avec patio 2 (Manno, Ticino, 2006, publiée ici) ; un atelier d'artiste (Verscio, 2008) ; la restructuration et l'ajout d'un étage à une maison datant de 1938 à Casiano (Lugano, 2008) ; la restructuration et l'agrandissement de l'hôpital San Giovanni (Bellinzona, 1970–2009) ; la restructuration et l'agrandissement de l'hôpital de la Beata Vergine (Mendrisio, 2009) ; et la maison de retraite pour personnes âgées Stella Maris (Bedano, 2009).

HOUSE WITH A PATIO 2

Manno, Ticino, Switzerland, 2006

Area: 367 m². Client: Claudio Pellegrini.
Cost: € 1.316 million. Collaboration: Fabrizio Falcone

Designed by Claudio and Sara Pellegrini in 2003, this house was built in 2006. The site area is 1295 square meters. A first villa was built on the site between 1993 and 1998. Both are oriented toward the south and are separated by a green space. Claudio Pellegrini also built apartments and public facilities nearby in the 1970s and 1980s. The two neighboring houses are conceived along similar architectural lines, with a patio, fountain, pergola, bridge, and stairway. A reinforced-concrete volume links the houses and contains parking as well as service areas. According to the architects, the houses "resemble each other but are fundamentally different." Furniture in lacquered wood was conceived for the house, while interior floors are in epoxy resin.

Das 2003 von Claudio und Sara Pellegrini entworfene Haus wurde 2006 gebaut. Das Grundstück ist 1295 m² groß. Zwischen 1993 und 1998 wurde ein erstes freistehendes Haus auf dem Grundstück gebaut. Beide Bauten sind nach Süden orientiert und durch eine Grünfläche voneinander getrennt. Bereits in den 1970er- und 1980er Jahren hatte Claudio Pellegrini in der Nähe Wohnungen und öffentlichen Einrichtungen realisiert. Die nebeneinanderstehenden Häuser wurden in ähnlicher architektonischer Formensprache entworfen – mit Patio, Brunnen, Pergola, Brücke und Treppe. Ein Baukörper aus Stahlbeton, in dem auch Garagen und Betriebsflächen untergebracht sind, verbindet die beiden Häuser. Den Architekten zufolge „ähneln die Häuser einander, sind jedoch fundamental verschieden". Für das Haus wurden eigens Lackmöbel entworfen; die Böden sind aus Epoxidharz.

Cette maison a été conçue par Claudio et Sara Pellegrini en 2003 et édifiée en 2006. La surface du terrain s'élève à 1295 m². Une première villa avait été construite au même endroit entre 1993 et 1998. Les deux constructions sont orientées vers le sud et séparées par un espace vert. Dans les années 1970 et 1980, Claudio Pellegrini avait également réalisé des immeubles d'appartements et des bâtiments public à proximité. Les deux maisons voisines sont conçues sur des principes architecturaux similaires, avec un patio, une fontaine, une pergola, une passerelle et des escaliers. Le volume en béton armé qui les réunit contient à la fois le garage et diverses installations techniques. Pour l'architecte, les maisons « se ressemblent, mais sont fondamentalement différentes ». Le mobilier en bois laqué a été spécialement dessiné pour la maison. Les sols intérieurs sont en résine époxy.

While glass block walls may bring to mind some of the origins of modern architecture, the house also has a rather industrial feel about it, as evidenced in the external smokestack and the visible metal beams.

Die Wände aus Glasbausteinen erinnern an die frühe Moderne, zugleich wirkt das Haus industriell. Dies zeigt sich am außen angebrachten Rauchabzug des Kamins und den sichtbaren Stahlträgern.

Si les murs en pavés de verre rappellent l'architecture moderne des origines, la maison n'en présente pas moins un certain aspect industriel, comme le montrent le conduit de cheminée extérieur ou les poutres métalliques apparentes.

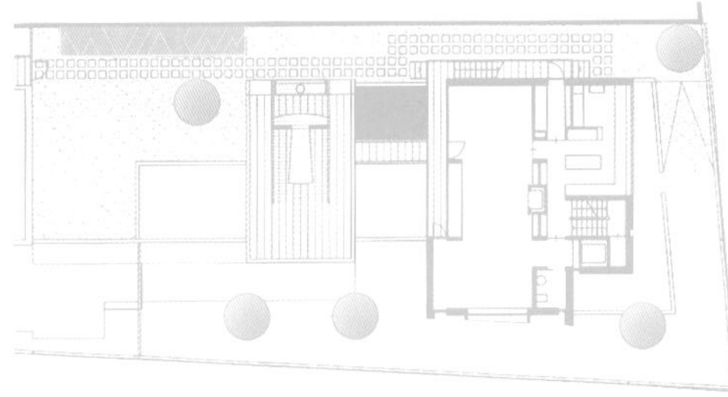

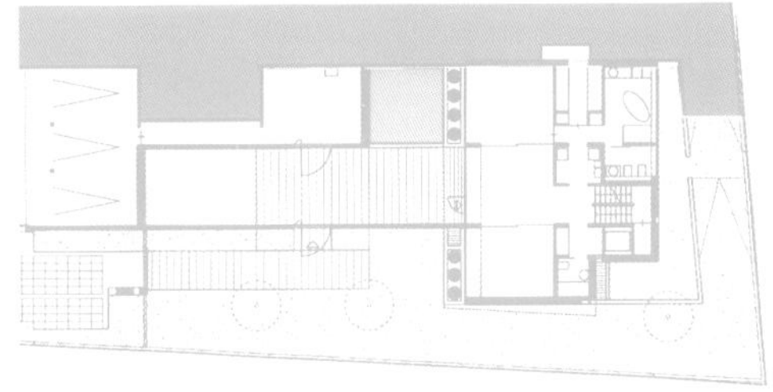

An external bridge passes over a pool (seen both left and right). Plans and a section drawing emphasize the strongly rectilinear design.

Außen führt eine Brücke über den Pool (links und rechts im Bild). Grundrisse und ein Schnitt veranschaulichen die ausgeprägte Geradlinigkeit des Entwurfs.

Une passerelle extérieure franchit un bassin (à gauche et à droite). Plans et coupe illustrent la conception géométrique rigoureuse du projet.

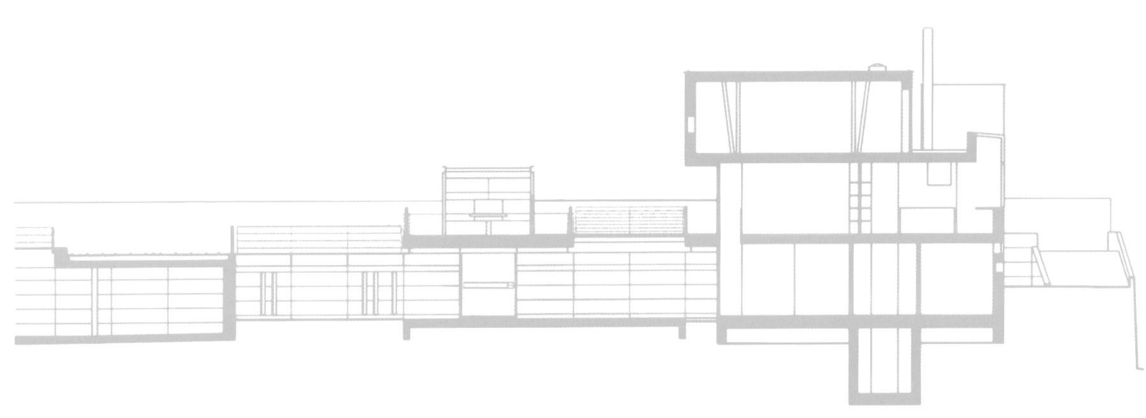

PEZO VON ELLRICHSHAUSEN ARCHITECTS

Pezo Von Ellrichshausen Arquitectos
Lo Pequén 502 / Concepción / Chile

Tel: +56 41 221 0281 / E-mail: info@pezo.cl
Web: www.pezo.cl

PEZO VON ELLRICHSHAUSEN ARCHITECTS was founded in Buenos Aires in 2001 by Mauricio Pezo and Sofía Von Ellrichshausen. Mauricio Pezo was born in Chile in 1973 and completed his M.Arch degree at the Universidad Católica de Chile (Santiago, 1998). He graduated from the University of Bío-Bío (Concepción, 1999). He is a visual artist and director of the Movimiento Artista del Sur (MAS). He teaches at the School of Architecture of Bío-Bío University, Talca University, and has been Visiting Critic at AAP Cornell University in New York. Pezo was awarded the Young Chilean Architect Prize 2006. Sofía Von Ellrichshausen was born in Argentina in 1976. She holds a degree in Architecture from the University of Buenos Aires (Buenos Aires, 2002). She teaches at the School of Architecture of Talca University and has been Visiting Critic at AAP Cornell University in New York. They were awarded the Commended Prize at the AR Awards for Emerging Architecture (London, 2005) and the Best Work by Young Architects Prize at the 5th Iberoamerican Architecture Biennial (Montevideo, 2006). Their built work includes XYZ Pavilions (Concepción, 2001); Rivo House (Valdivia, 2003); 120 Doors Pavilion (Concepción, 2003); Poli House (Coliumo, 2005); Wolf House (Andalue, 2006–07); Parr House (Chiguayante, 2008); Fosc House (San Pedro, 2008–09, published here); and several public art projects. Projects under construction are R15 Building in Zaragoza (Spain); Hema Studio in Buenos Aires (Argentina); and Gold Building, Cien House, and Pael House in Concepción, all in Chile unless stated otherwise.

PEZO VON ELLRICHSHAUSEN ARCHITECTS wurde 2001 von Mauricio Pezo und Sofía von Ellrichshausen in Buenos Aires gegründet. Mauricio Pezo wurde 1973 in Chile geboren, erhielt seinen M. Arch. an der Universidad Católica de Chile (Santiago, 1998) und schloss sein Studium an der Universidad del Bío-Bío (Concepción, 1999) ab. Er ist bildender Künstler und Direktor der Movimiento Artista del Sur (MAS). Er lehrt an der Fakultät für Architektur der Universidad del Bío-Bío sowie der Universidad de Talca und war Gastkritiker am College für Architektur, Kunst und Planung (AAP) der Cornell University in New York. 2006 wurde Pezo mit dem Preis für junge chilenische Architekten ausgezeichnet. Sofía von Ellrichshausen wurde 1976 in Argentinien geboren. Ihr Architekturstudium schloss sie an der Universität Buenos Aires ab (2002). Sie lehrt an der Fakultät für Architektur der Universidad de Talca und war Gastkritikerin am AAP der Cornell University in New York. Bei den AR Awards for Emerging Architecture (London, 2005) wurden ihre Arbeiten besonders hervorgehoben sowie als bestes Projekt von jungen Architekten auf der 5. Iberoamerikanischen Architekturbiennale (Montevideo, 2006) ausgezeichnet. Zu ihren realisierten Bauten zählen: XYZ-Pavillons (Concepción, 2001), Rivo House (Valdivia, 2003), 120 Doors Pavilion (Concepción, 2003), Poli House (Coliumo, 2005), Wolf House (Andalue, 2006–07), Parr House (Chiguayante, 2008), Fosc House (San Pedro, 2008–09, hier vorgestellt) sowie verschiedene öffentliche Kunstprojekte. Im Bau befinden sich derzeit R15 in Saragossa (Spanien), Hema Studio in Buenos Aires (Argentinien) sowie Gold Building, Cien House und Pael House in Concepción, alle in Chile soweit nicht anders vermerkt.

L'agence **PEZO VON ELLRICHSHAUSEN ARCHITECTS** a été fondée à Buenos Aires en 2001 par Mauricio Pezo et Sofía Von Ellrichshausen. Mauricio Pezo, né au Chili en 1973, a obtenu son M.Arch de l'Université catholique du Chili (Santiago, 1998) et est diplômé de l'université de Bío-Bío (Concepción, 1999). Artiste plasticien, il est directeur du Movimiento Artista del Sur (MAS). Il enseigne à l'École d'architecture de l'université Bío-Bío, à l'université de Talca, et a été critique invité à l'université Cornell à New York. Il a reçu le prix des jeunes architectes chiliens en 2006. Sofía von Ellrichshausen, née en Argentine en 1976, est diplômée en architecture de l'université de Buenos Aires (2002). Elle enseigne à l'École d'architecture de l'université de Talca et a été également critique invitée à l'université Cornell (NY). Ils ont reçu un prix de l'Architectural Review pour l'architecture émergente (Londres, 2005) et le prix de la meilleure œuvre de jeunes architectes à la Ve Biennale d'architecture ibéro-américaine (Montevideo, 2006). Parmi leurs réalisations : les pavillons XYZ (Concepción, 2001) ; la maison Rivo (Valdivia, 2003) ; le pavillon des cent vingt portes (Concepción, 2003) ; la maison Poli (Coliumo, 2005) ; la maison Wolf (Andalue, 2006–07) ; la maison Parr (Chiguayante, 2008) ; la maison Fosc (San Pedro, 2008–09, publiée ici) ; et plusieurs projets artistiques publics. Ils ont en chantier l'immeuble R15 à Zaragoza (Espagne) ; le studio Hema à Buenos Aires (Argentine) ; l'immeuble Gold, la maison Cien et la maison Pael à Concepción, le tout au Chili, sauf mention contraire.

FOSC HOUSE

San Pedro, Chile, 2008–09

Area: 160 m². Client: not disclosed. Cost: not disclosed

Located on a 597-square-meter site, this is a reinforced-concrete structure with aluminum window frames. Interiors are finished in painted concrete, or wood, with wood and stone floors. Intended for a family with four children (five bedrooms, three bathrooms, family room, studio, etc), the house has three levels. Bedrooms are located on the ground and top floors. The public spaces are set on the intermediate level. A thin, folded-steel sheet, vertical circulation shaft with wooden steps links the spaces. The poured-in-place concrete walls are dyed green and coated with copper oxide. The architects state: "The owners of the house, involved in contemporary art, once showed us the rusted and aged pedestals of monuments found in local squares. The oxide drippings, we thought, imprint the surfaces with an elusive natural quality, always halfway between mineral and vegetal."

Der Stahlbetonbau mit Aluminiumfenstern liegt auf einem 597 m² großen Grundstück. Materialien in den Innenräumen sind gestrichener Beton bzw. Holz sowie Holz- und Steinböden. Das für eine Familie mit vier Kindern geplante Haus (fünf Schlafzimmer, drei Bäder, Wohnzimmer, Atelier etc.) hat drei Ebenen. Die Schlafzimmer liegen im Erdgeschoss und im obersten Geschoss, während die öffentlichen Bereiche im mittleren Geschoss untergebracht sind. Ein schmaler Treppenschacht aus dünnen gefalteten Metallplatten und Holzstufen verbindet die Ebenen. Die Wände aus Ortbeton wurden grün eingefärbt und mit Kupferoxid überzogen. Die Architekten erklären: „Die im Bereich zeitgenössischer Kunst tätigen Bauherren zeigten uns einmal verrostete und verwitterte Denkmalsockel, die man auf manchen Dorfplätzen findet. Uns schien es, als würde die Oberfläche durch die Tropfspuren des oxidierenden Metalls eine schwer zu beschreibende Natürlichkeit gewinnen, die irgendwo zwischen mineralisch und pflanzlich liegt."

Implantée sur un terrain de 597 m², cette maison en béton armé à châssis de fenêtres en aluminium est de construction simple. L'intérieur est en béton peint ou en bois, les sols en bois ou en pierre. Prévue pour une famille de quatre enfants (cinq chambres, trois salles de bains, un séjour familial, un atelier, etc.), l'ensemble s'étend sur trois niveaux. Les chambres sont au rez-de-chaussée et au dernier étage. Les espaces communs sont au niveau intermédiaire. Un puits de circulation vertical est occupé par un escalier en bois entouré d'une cage en tôle d'acier qui relie les différents volumes. Les murs en béton coulé en place sont teints en vert et enduits d'oxyde de cuivre. « Les propriétaires de la maison, qui s'intéressent à l'art contemporain, nous avaient montré un jour les piédestaux patinés et rouillés issus de monuments publics. Nous avons pensé que les coulures d'oxyde donneraient aux surfaces une qualité presque naturelle, entre le minéral et le végétal », expliquent les architectes.

The exterior of the house has a patinated and fairly closed appearance. Its rectilinear structure is punctuated in an irregular way by windows and an angled door.

Die patinierte Fassade des Hauses wirkt eher geschlossen. Der geradlinige Bau ist unregelmäßig mit Fensteröffnungen und einer schräg in die Fassade gesetzten Tür punktiert.

L'extérieur de la maison présente un aspect patiné et un caractère d'une certaine opacité. La structure rectiligne est irrégulièrement ponctuée de fenêtres et d'une porte d'angle.

An interior view shows how the openings are articulated in a way that allows ample light to penetrate the space and gives residents broad views to the outside.

Die Innenansicht zeigt, dass die Fassadenöffnungen so artikuliert wurden, dass Tageslicht großzügig einfallen kann und die Bewohner einen weiten Ausblick nach draußen genießen.

Une vue de l'intérieur montre comment les ouvertures s'articulent pour faciliter la pénétration de la lumière et offrir d'amples perspectives sur l'extérieur.

POWERHOUSE COMPANY

Powerhouse Company
Westzeedijk 399 / EK Rotterdam / The Netherlands
Tel: +31 10 404 67 89

Yderlandsvej 1 / 2300 Copenhagen / Denmark
Tel: +45 50 59 14 54

E-mail: office@powerhouse-company.com
Web: www.powerhouse-company.com

POWERHOUSE COMPANY was founded in 2005 simultaneously in Rotterdam and in Copenhagen by Charles Bessard and Nanne de Ru. The firm works on furniture design, architecture, planning, and research, and presently employs seven people, including the founding partners. Charles Bessard was born in 1971 in France and received his degrees from the École Speciale d'Architecture (Paris, 1993) and the Berlage Institute (Amsterdam, 2002). He worked for Bodin & Associates (Paris, 1993), Sheppard Robson Architects (London, 1997–2000), and Atelier Jean Nouvel (Paris, 2002–04). Nanne de Ru was born in 1976 in the Netherlands and also graduated from the Berlage Institute (2002) after attending the Hogeschool van Amsterdam (1998). From 1998 to 1999, Nanne de Ru worked as a project leader at One Architecture in Amsterdam, before joining Rem Koolhaas' AMO/OMA in 2002 (Rotterdam). In 2008, Powerhouse Company was granted the Dutch Design Award 2008 for the category of Best Private Interior Design and the biannual AM/NAi prize for the best building by architects under 40. Their recent and current work includes Villa 1 (Ede, 2006–08, published here); Spiral House (Burgundy, France, 2007–08, also published here); an Ambulance Post with offices (Dordrecht, 2009); an office building in Almere (Olympia, 2009, with MVRDV); Villa L (Utrecht, 2008–), all in the Netherlands unless stated otherwise.

Charles Bessard und Nanne de Ru gründeten ihr Büro **POWERHOUSE COMPANY** 2005 gleichzeitig in Rotterdam und Kopenhagen. Das Team ist in den Bereichen Möbeldesign, Architektur, Stadtplanung und Forschung tätig und beschäftigt derzeit sieben Mitarbeiter, darunter vier Partner. Charles Bessard wurde 1971 in Frankreich geboren und schloss sein Studium an der École Speciale d'Architecture (Paris, 1993) und am Berlage Institute (Amsterdam, 2002) ab. Er arbeitete für Bodin & Associates (Paris, 1993), Sheppard Robson Architects (London, 1997–2000) und das Atelier Jean Nouvel (Paris, 2002–04). Nanne de Ru wurde 1976 in den Niederlanden geboren und schloss ihr Studium ebenfalls am Berlage Institute (2002) ab, nachdem sie zuvor die Hogeschool van Amsterdam (1998) besucht hatte. Von 1998 bis 1999 arbeitete Nanne de Ru als Projektleiterin für One Architecture in Amsterdam, ehe sie sich 2002 Rem Koolhaas' Büro AMO/OMA in Rotterdam anschloss. 2008 wurde Powerhouse Company mit dem Niederländischen Designpreis in der Kategorie Beste Innenarchitektur für Privatbauten ausgezeichnet, darüber hinaus mit dem alle zwei Jahre vergebenen AM/NAI-Preis für das beste Gebäude von Architekten unter 40. Jüngere und aktuelle Projekte sind u. a. Villa 1 (Ede, 2006–08, hier vorgestellt), Spiral House (Burgund, Frankreich, 2007–08), eine Ambulanz mit Büros (Dordrecht, 2009), ein Bürogebäude in Almere (Olympia, 2009, mit MVRDV) sowie die Villa L (Utrecht, seit 2008), alle in den Niederlanden, soweit nicht anders angegeben.

L'agence **POWERHOUSE COMPANY** a été fondée en 2005, simultanément à Rotterdam et Copenhague par Charles Bessard et Nanne de Ru. Elle intervient dans les domaines du design de mobilier, de l'architecture, de l'urbanisme et de la recherche, et emploie actuellement sept personnes, y compris ses fondateurs. Charles Bessard, né en 1971 en France, est diplômé de l'École spéciale d'architecture (Paris, 1993) et de l'Institut Berlage (Amsterdam, 2002). Il a travaillé pour Bodin & Associates (Paris, 1993), Sheppard Robson Architects (Londres, 1997–2000) et l'Atelier Jean Nouvel (Paris, 2002–04). Nanne de Ru, née en 1976 aux Pays-Bas, est également diplômée de l'Institut Berlage (2002), après avoir suivi des études à la Hogeschool van Amsterdam (1998). De 1998 à 1999, elle a été chef de projet à One Architecture à Amsterdam, avant d'entrer chez Rem Koolhaas et son agence AMO/OMA (Office for Metropolitan Architecture, Rotterdam) en 2002. En 2008, la Powerhouse Company a reçu le prix du Design néerlandais dans la catégorie du meilleur aménagement intérieur et le prix biannuel AM/NAi pour le meilleur projet réalisé d'architectes de moins de 40 ans. Parmi leurs réalisations récentes ou actuelles : la Villa 1 (Ede, 2006–08, publiée ici) ; la maison Spirale (Bourgogne, France, 2007–08) ; un centre pour ambulances et ses bureaux (Dordrecht, 2009) ; un immeuble de bureaux à Almere (Olympia, 2009, avec MVRDV) ; et la Villa L (Utrecht, 2008–), le tout aux Pays-Bas, sauf mention contraire.

VILLA 1

Ede, The Netherlands, 2006–08

Area: 480 m². Client: not disclosed. Cost: not disclosed. Collaboration: Gilbert van der Lee (Structural Engineering)

Although the house does dip into the terrain, it is essentially constituted by a continuous external band and full-height glazing.

Obwohl das Haus teilweise im Boden versenkt ist, besteht es im Grunde aus einem umlaufenden Fassadenband und einer raumhohen Verglasung.

Bien que la maison soit en partie enterrée, elle se présente essentiellement sous la forme d'un bandeau extérieur continu, vitré sur toute sa hauteur.

This was the first commission granted to Powerhouse Company, just two months after the firm was created. The site is a clearing in a pine forest, requiring half of the program to be located below grade because of local zoning restrictions. The glass box above ground contrasts with the "medieval" atmosphere of the spaces under ground. The Y-shape of the plan is derived from the architects' analysis of views and the movement of the sun. There is one wing for work, study, and music, one for cooking and eating, and the third for living and painting. The point where the wings meet is the entrance hall, dining room, bar, and music room. Below grade, one wing is occupied by the master bedroom, another one by parking, and the third by guest rooms and storage. According to the architects, below ground, the "scarcity of daylight is complemented by a richness in spatial effects." Two covered decks are situated on the east and south sides at ground level. Large pieces of furniture were designed for the house by the architects. The cantilevered steel roof was designed with the assistance of the structural engineer Gilbert van der Lee.

Dieses Projekt war der erste Auftrag für die Powerhouse Company, nur zwei Monate nach Gründung der Firma. Das Grundstück liegt auf einer Kiefernwaldlichtung. Aufgrund der Bebauungsvorschriften wurde die Hälfte des Raumprogramms unter die Geländeoberfläche verlegt. Die oberirdische Glasbox steht im Kontrast zur geradezu „mittelalterlichen" Atmosphäre der unterirdischen Räume. Nachdem die Architekten Blickbeziehungen und Sonnenlauf analysiert hatten, entschieden sie sich für einen Y-förmigen Grundriss. Dementsprechend gibt es einen Flügel für Arbeit, Studium und Musik, einen für Kochen und Essen und einen dritten zum Wohnen und Malen. Am Schnittpunkt der Flügel liegen Eingangsbereich, Esszimmer, Bar und Musikzimmer. Im Untergeschoss sind in einem der Flügel das Hauptschlafzimmer untergebracht, im zweiten die Garage sowie im dritten Gästezimmer und Abstellräume. Den Architekten zufolge wird „die Lichtknappheit" im Untergeschoss „durch den Reichtum an räumlichen Effekten aufgewogen". Im Erdgeschoss befinden sich an der Ost- und Südseite je eine überdachte Terrasse. Zudem entwarfen die Architekten große Möbelstücke speziell für das Haus. Das auskragende Stahldach wurde unter Mitarbeit des Bauingenieurs Gilbert van der Lee geplant.

Il s'agit de la première commande reçue par la Powerhouse Company, deux mois seulement après sa création. Le site est une clairière au milieu des pins, avec une réglementation locale de zonage nécessitant que la moitié du programme soit en sous-sol. La boîte de verre contraste avec l'atmosphère « médiévale » des espaces souterrains. Le plan en « Y » vient de l'analyse des vues et des déplacements du soleil. Une aile est réservée au travail, à l'étude et à la musique, l'autre aux repas et la troisième au séjour et à la peinture. Ces trois ailes se rejoignent dans un volume faisant à la fois entrée, salle à manger, bar et salon de musique. En sous-sol, une partie est réservée à la chambre principale, une autre au parking et la troisième aux chambres d'amis et rangements. Selon les architectes, « la faiblesse de l'éclairage naturel [en sous-sol] est compensée par la richesse des effets spatiaux ». Deux terrasses couvertes ont été prévues à l'est, et au sud du rez-de-chaussée. De grands meubles ont été spécialement dessinés par les architectes. Le toit en acier en porte-à-faux a été mis au point avec l'assistance de l'ingénieur structurel Gilbert van Lee.

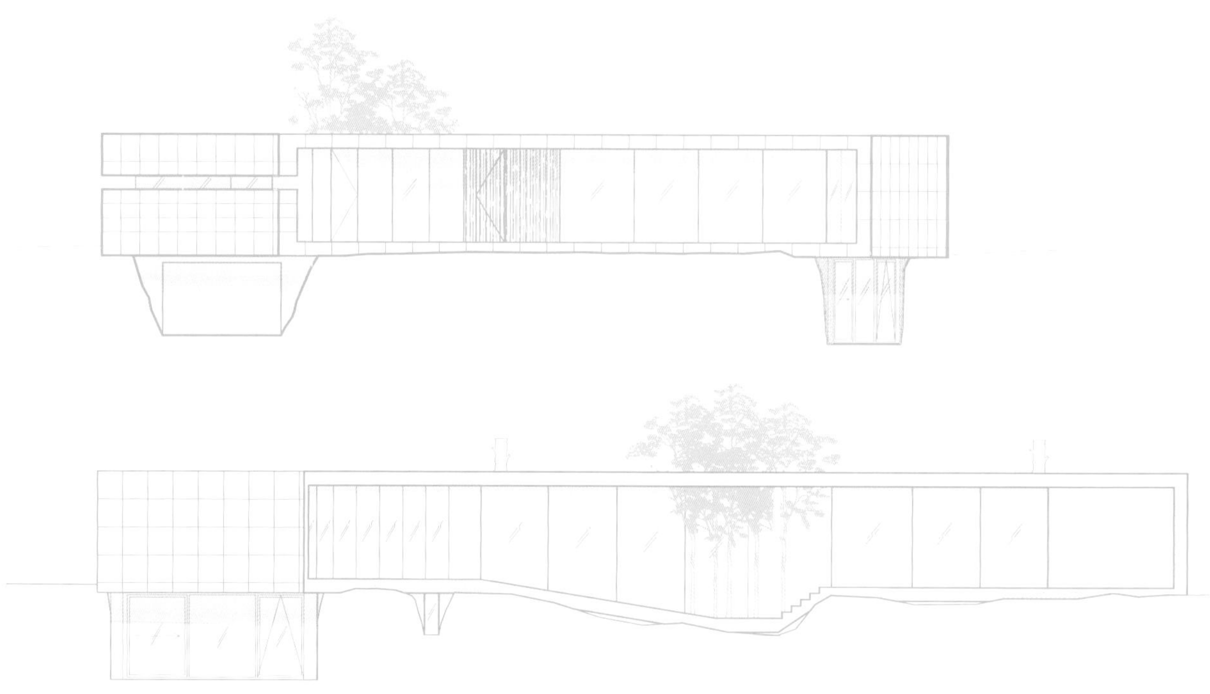

The full glazing makes the house particularly open to its environment. Flowing recessed areas (right page) create both unusual interior space and a covered outdoor patio area.

Die raumhohe Verglasung öffnet das Haus in besonderem Maße zu seiner Umgebung. Fließende Einbuchtungen (rechte Seite) schaffen sowohl ungewöhnliche Innenräume als auch einen überdachten Terrassenbereich.

Le vitrage intégral rend la maison particulièrement perméable à son environnement. Des retraits et des avancées dans cette paroi transparente créent des volumes intérieurs intéressants et un patio couvert.

PRODUCTORA

PRODUCTORA
Av. Insurgentes Sur 348, penthouse (piso 10)
Colonia Roma Sur
Delegación Cuauhtémoc
06760 Mexico City
Mexico

Tel: +52 55 5584 1278
E-mail: info@productora-df.com.mx
Web: www.productora-df.com.mx

PRODUCTORA is a Mexico City-based office founded in 2006. Its founding members are Abel Perles, born in Argentina in 1972 (Universidad de Buenos Aires (UBA), Buenos Aires, 1999); Carlos Bedoya, born in 1973 in Mexico (Universidad Iberoamericana, Mexico City, 1998; M.Arch, ETSAB, Barcelona, 2000); Victor Jaime, born in 1978 in Mexico (Universidad Iberoamericana, Mexico City, 2001); and Wonne Ickx, born in 1974 in Belgium (Civil Engineer – Architect, University of Gent, 1998; Master's in Urbanism and Development, University of Guadalajara, 2001). The name PRODUCTORA, which is Spanish for producer or production company, indicates continuous production as a testing method. The office is realizing a variety of projects in Mexico—among which the House in Chihuahua, 2008, published here—and abroad (Asia, South America), ranging from single-family dwellings to office or public buildings. They were winners of the Young Architect's Forum organized by the Architectural League in New York (2007) and their work was presented in the context of the 2nd Architectural Biennale in Beijing (2006), and the Venice Architecture Biennale in Italy (2008). PRODUCTORA was selected by Herzog & de Meuron as one of the architectural studios to build a villa for the Ordos 100 Project in Inner Mongolia, China (see p. 12 of the main text), and won the International Competition for the CAF Headquarters in Caracas, Venezuela, in collaboration with Lucio Muniain (2008).

PRODUCTORA ist ein 2006 gegründetes Büro mit Sitz in Mexiko-Stadt. Gründungsmitglieder sind Abel Perles, geboren 1972 in Argentinien (Universidad de Buenos Aires (UBA), 1999), Carlos Bedoya, geboren 1973 in Mexiko (Universidad Iberoamericana, Mexiko-Stadt, 1998, M. Arch., ETSAB, Barcelona, 2000), Victor Jaime, geboren 1978 in Mexiko (Universidad Iberoamericana, Mexico-Stadt, 2001) und Wonne Ickx, geboren 1974 in Belgien (Bauingenieur und Architekt, Universität Gent, 1998, Master in Urbanistik und Stadtentwicklung, Universidad de Guadalajara, 2001). Der Name PRODUCTORA, Spanisch für Produzent bzw. Produktionsgesellschaft, steht für kontinuierliche Produktion als Testverfahren. Das Büro realisiert eine ganze Bandbreite von Projekten in Mexiko – darunter das hier vorgestellte Haus in Chihuahua, 2008 – ebenso wie im Ausland (Asien, Südamerika), von Einfamilienhäusern bis hin zu Bürohäusern und öffentlichen Bauten. Das Team gewann das von der Architectural League in New York organisierte Young Architects Forum (2007). Darüber hinaus wurde sein Werk auf der 2. Architekturbiennale in Peking (2006) und der Architekturbiennale in Venedig (2008) präsentiert. PRODUCTORA war zudem eines der von Herzog & de Meuron ausgewählten Büros, um ein freistehendes Haus für das Projekt Ordos 100 in der Inneren Mongolei in China (siehe Haupttext Seite 22) zu entwerfen. Gemeinsam mit Lucio Muniain gewann das Team den internationalen Wettbewerb für die CAF-Zentrale in Caracas in Venezuela (2008).

PRODUCTORA est une agence de Mexico créée en 2006. Ses fondateurs sont Abel Perles, né en Argentine en 1972, diplômé de l'université de Buenos Aires (UBA, 1999) ; Carlos Bedoya, né en 1973, diplômé de l'Université ibéro-américaine (Mexico, 1998) et ayant un M.Arch de l'ETSAB (Barcelone, 2000) ; Victor Jaime, né en 1978 au Mexique, diplômé de l'Université ibéro-américaine (Mexico, 2001) ; et Wonne Ickx, né en 1974 en Belgique, ingénieur civil-architecte, diplômé de l'université de Gand (1998) et master en urbanisme et développement de l'université de Guadalajara (2001). Le nom de PRODUCTORA (producteur ou société de production en espagnol) traduit une approche de production continue considérée comme une forme de test. L'agence travaille sur divers projets au Mexique, dont la maison à Chihuahua (2008, publiée ici), et à l'étranger (Asie, Amérique du Sud), allant de la conception de maisons individuelles à celle d'immeubles de bureaux ou de bâtiments publics. Elle a remporté le prix du Forum des jeunes architectes, organisé par l'Architectural League à New York (2007), et était présente dans le contexte de la IIe Biennale d'architecture de Pékin (2006) et à la Biennale de Venise (2008). PRODUCTORA a été sélectionnée par Herzog & de Meuron avec plusieurs autres agences pour construire une villa dans le cadre du Projet Ordos 100 en Mongolie intérieure (Chine, voir p. 33), et a remporté le concours international pour le siège social de la CAF à Caracas (Venezuela, en collaboration avec Lucio Muniain, 2008).

HOUSE IN CHIHUAHUA

Chihuahua, Mexico, 2008

Area: 360 m^2. Client: Granados family. Cost: not disclosed

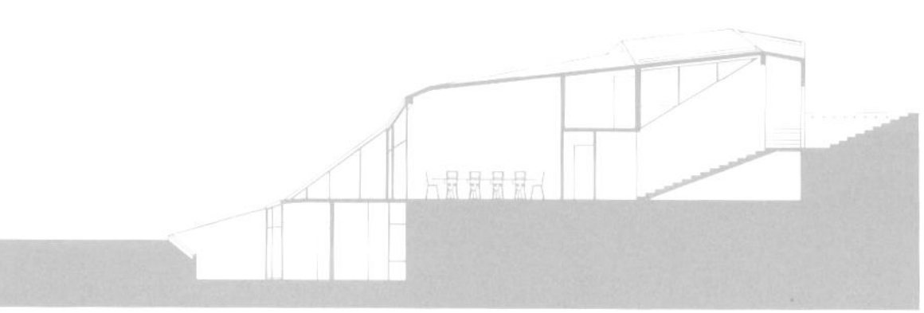

As the section drawings above demonstrate, the house rises up from the sloped site and is set partially into the hillside.

Die Schnitte oben zeigen, wie sich das Haus über das abschüssige Grundstück erhebt und teilweise in den Hang integriert ist.

Comme le montrent les coupes ci-dessus, la maison s'élève au flanc d'une pente à laquelle elle s'est partiellement intégrée.

With the earth rising up to cover parts of the house, the design allows for terraces that overlook the surrounding countryside.

Durch die den Entwurf, bei dem der Erdboden Teile des Hauses bedeckt, entstehen Terrassen, die Ausblick auf die landschaftliche Umgebung bieten.

La terre recouvre certaines parties de la maison tandis que des terrasses étagées offrent des vues sur le paysage.

The exterior façade of this house is made of concrete blocks, covered with white-painted stucco. It has timber floors and interior walls also made of concrete blocks, plastered and painted white. The site is in a golf club community in northern Mexico. Summer temperatures get up to 40° centigrade, while in the winter they may fall to -10°. To help deal with these temperature extremes, the architects decided to partially bury the residence. Patios and polygonal roof openings provide natural ventilation, while the sloped roof acts as a new topography that blurs the boundaries between the constructed area and the surrounding landscape. The continuous roof allowed construction without beams or special reinforcement.

Die Fassade des Hauses besteht aus Betonformsteinen, die verputzt und weiß gestrichen wurden. Auch die Wände im Innenraum, der mit Holzböden ausgestattet ist, sind aus Betonformstein gefertigt, verputzt und weiß gestrichen. Das Baugrundstück liegt auf dem Gelände einer zu einem Golfclub gehörenden Siedlung in Nordmexiko. Die Temperaturen steigen im Sommer bis auf 40 °C, fallen im Winter jedoch mitunter bis auf -10 °C. Um diesen extremen Witterungsverhältnissen gerecht zu werden, beschlossen die Architekten, den Bau teilweise im Boden zu versenken. Patios und polygonale Öffnungen im Dach sorgen für eine natürliche Belüftung. Das Dach selbst wird zur Topografie, die die Grenze zwischen bebauter Fläche und Landschaft verschwimmen lässt. Dank der durchgängigen Dachfläche war es möglich, ohne Träger und spezielle Bewehrung zu bauen.

La façade extérieure de cette maison en bordure d'un terrain de golf dans le nord du Mexique est en blocs de béton enduit de stuc blanc. À l'intérieur, les sols sont en bois, les murs en blocs de béton plâtré et peints en blanc. Dans cette région, les températures estivales peuvent monter jusqu'à 40°C et descendre à -10°C en hiver. Pour répondre à ces températures extrêmes, les architectes ont décidé d'enterrer en partie la construction. Des patios et des ouvertures découpés dans la toiture polygonale facilitent la ventilation naturelle. La pente du toit crée une topographie nouvelle qui gomme les frontières entre le bâti et le paysage. Le toit continu a permis de construire sans poutres ni renforts particuliers.

Interior spaces, such as the living and dining area (above), are animated by a sharply angled ceiling and equally angular windows.

Die Innenräume, etwa der Wohn- und Essbereich (oben), werden durch die auffällige Deckenschräge und entsprechend schiefwinklige Fenster belebt.

Les espaces intérieurs comme la pièce de séjour et des repas (ci-dessus) sont animés par la forte inclinaison du plafond et la découpe des baies qui suivent son profil.

The living and dining space seen from another angle (above, left). Right, above, an interior balcony looks out to a triangular window.

Der Wohn- und Essbereich aus einem anderen Blickwinkel (oben, links). Von der Galerie (oben) hat man einen Ausblick durch ein dreieckiges Fenster.

La même pièce de séjour et de repas vue sous un autre angle (ci-dessus à gauche). À droite, ci-dessus, un balcon intérieur donne sur une baie triangulaire.

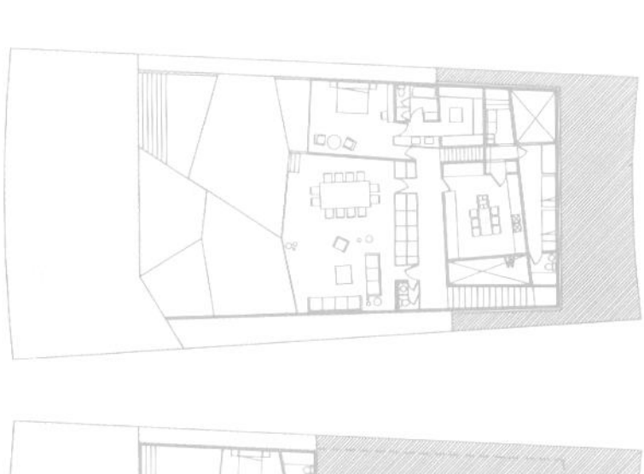

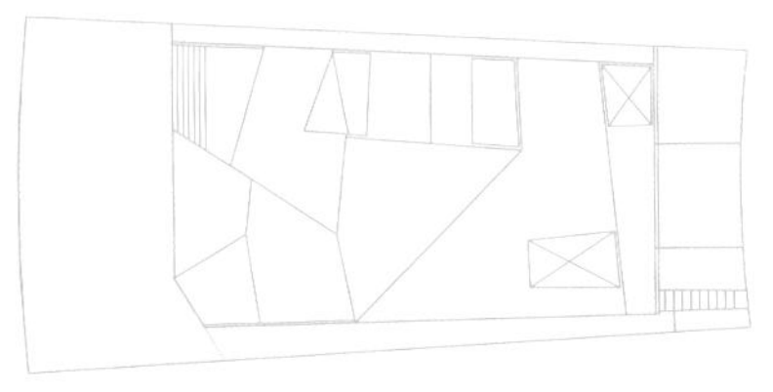

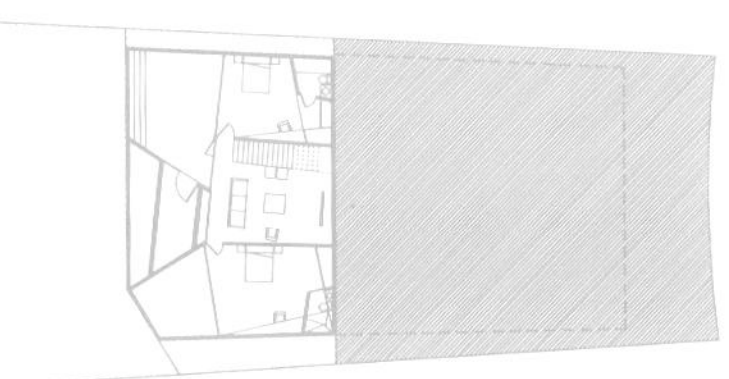

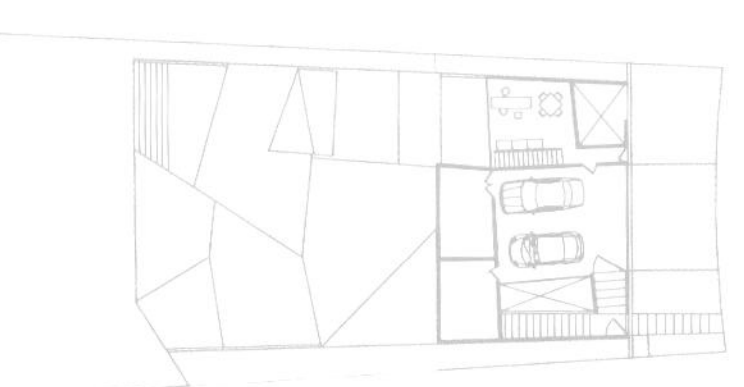

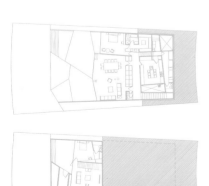

RCR

RCR Aranda Pigem Vilalta Arquitectes
Fontanella 26
17800 Olot (Girona)
Spain

Tel: +34 972 26 91 05
Fax: +34 972 27 22 67
E-mail: rcr@rcrarquitectes.es

Rafael Aranda, Carme Pigem, and Ramon Vilalta completed their studies in architecture at the ETSA of Vallès in 1987, and the following year created their own studio, **RCR** Arquitectes, in Olot, the city where they were born. Since 1989, they have been Consultant Architects for the Natural Park in the Volcanic Zone of La Garrotxa. They have taught urbanism (1989–2001, Vilalta) and studio projects (1992–2003, Pigem) at ETSAV. Pigem was a guest lecturer at the Department of Architecture at ETH in Zurich. They have won a number of competitions, ranging from a Lighthouse in Punta Aldea in 1988 to the Crematorium of Hofheide (Belgium), and most recently the very ambitious project for The Edge in Dubai (2007–). Built work includes the M-Lidia House (Montagut, Girona, 2001–02); Els Colors Kindergarten (Manlleu, Barcelona, 2003–04); the surprising Rough Rock Park (Les Preses, Girona, 2003–04); and House for a Carpenter (Olot, Girona, 2005–07, published here), all in Spain.

Rafael Aranda, Carme Pigem und Ramon Vilalta schlossen ihr Architekturstudium 1987 an der ETSA in Vallès ab und gründeten im darauffolgenden Jahr ihr Büro **RCR** Arquitectes in Olot, ihrer Geburtsstadt. Seit 1989 sind die Architekten als Berater des Naturschutzparks des Vulkangebiets La Garrotxa tätig. An der ETSAV unterrichteten sie Urbanistik (1989–2001, Vilalta) und leiteten Studioprojekte (1992–2003, Pigem). Pigem war zudem Gastdozent an der Fakultät für Architektur an der ETH Zürich. Das Team gewann zahlreiche Wettbewerbe, etwa 1988 für den Leuchtturm in Punta Aldea oder für das Krematorium in Hofheide (Belgien) sowie vor kurzem für das ambitionierte Projekt The Edge in Dubai (ab 2007). Zu ihren gebauten Projekten zählen das Haus M-Lidia (Montagut, Girona, 2001–02), der Kindergarten Els Colors (Manlleu, Barcelona, 2003–04), der erstaunliche Rough Rock Park (Les Preses, Girona, 2003–04) sowie das Haus für einen Schreiner (Olot, Girona, 2005–07, hier vorgestellt), alle in Spanien.

Rafael Aranda, Carme Pigem et Ramon Vilalta ont achevé leurs études d'architecture à l'ETSA de Vallès en 1987, et ont créé l'année suivante l'agence **RCR** Arquitectes à Olot, leur ville natale. Depuis 1989, ils sont architectes consultants pour le parc naturel de la zone volcanique de la Garrotxa. Ils ont enseigné l'urbanisme (1989–2001, Vilalta) et dans un atelier de projets (1992–2003, Pigem) à l'ETSAV. Pigem a été conférencier invité au département d'architecture de l'ETH à Zurich. Ils ont remporté ensemble un certain nombre de concours allant d'un phare à Punta Aldea (Catalogne) en 1988 au crématorium de Hofheide (Belgique), et, plus récemment celui du très ambitieux projet réalisé à Dubaï, « The Edge » (2007–). Ils ont réalisé la maison M-Lidia (Montagut, Girona, 2001–02) ; le jardin d'enfants Els Colors (Manlleu, Barcelone, 2003–04) ; le suprenant parc de Pedra Tosca (Les Preses, Girona, 2003–04) ; et la maison pour un Menuisier (Olot, Girona, 2005–07, publiée ici), tous en Espagne.

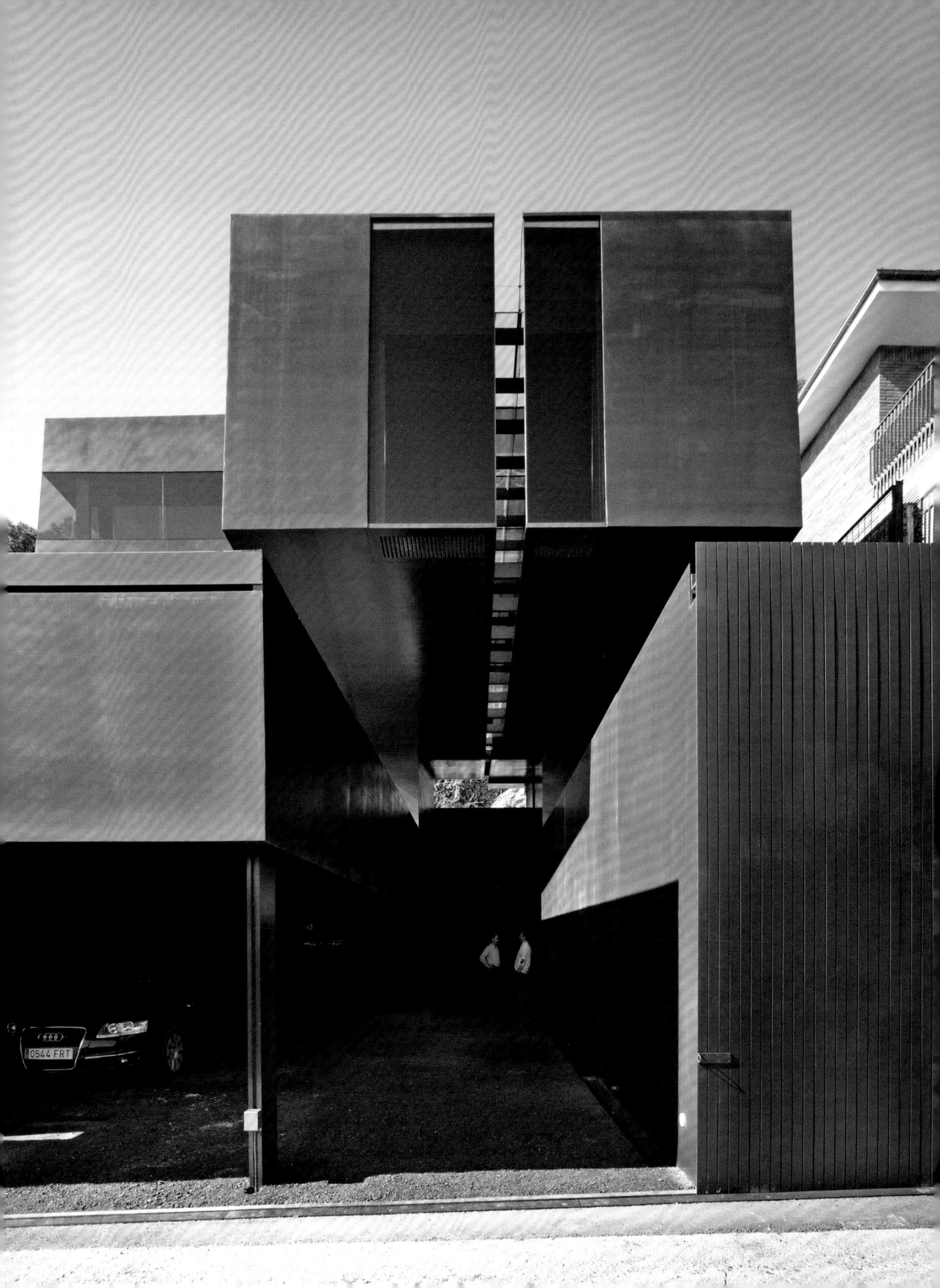
0544 FRT

HOUSE FOR A CARPENTER

Olot, Girona, Spain, 2005–07

Area: 284 m^2. Client: not disclosed. Cost: not disclosed.
Collaboration: RCR: M. Subiràs, M. Venâncio. M. Ortega (Quantity Surveyor); Blázquez-Guanter (structure)

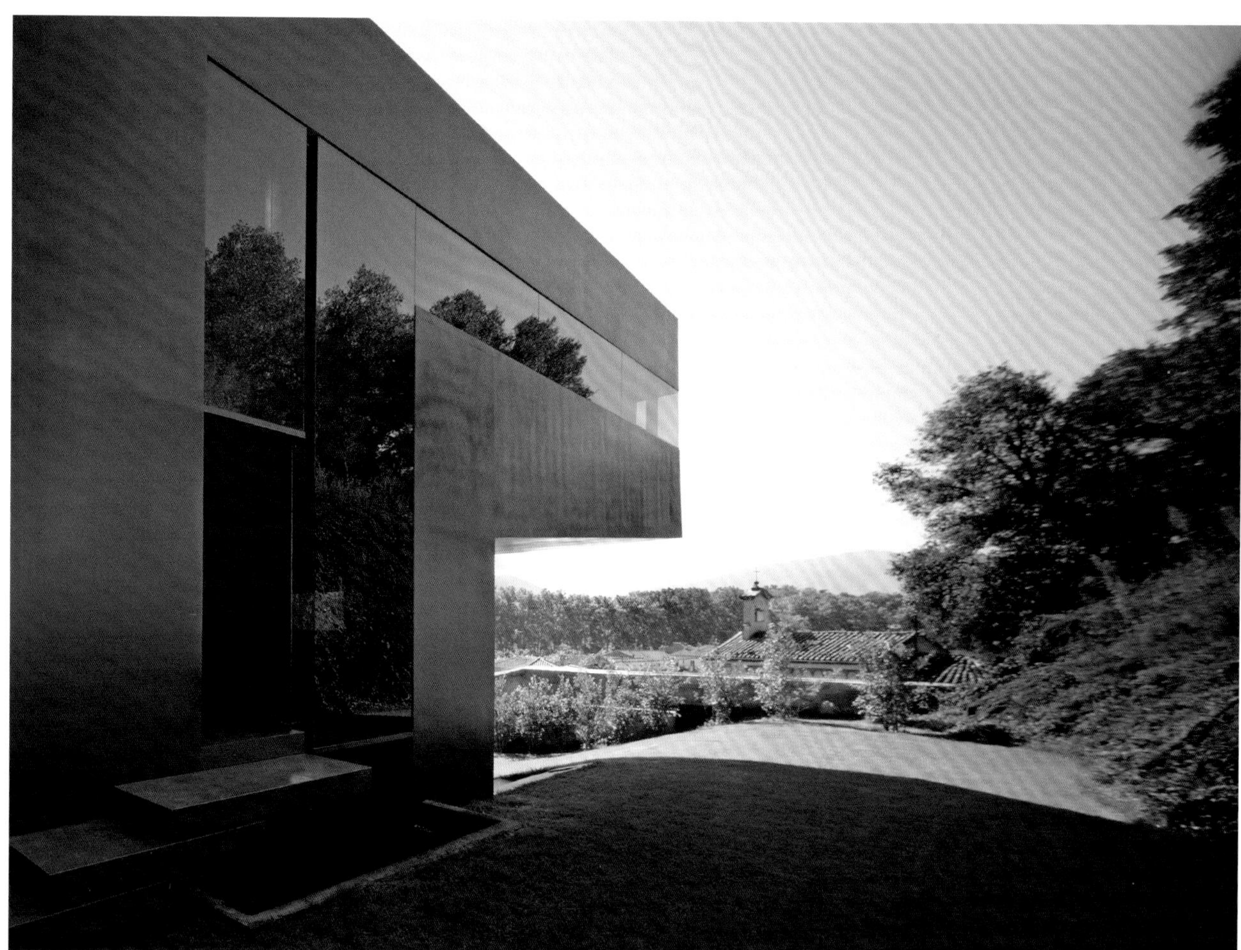

This house is built on the steep slope of an extinct volcano. The architects state, in rather poetic terms: "The largest possible amount of land is reserved for the enjoyment of a garden or a forest, where the urban-natural divisions disappear. Shelter by, amidst, through and under all, appears and disappears, but it is also exchanged with the view of a distant world that spreads out at its feet." The plan of the house is a strict rectangle, but it reserves such surprises as a substantial cantilevered overhang. The name of the house, which refers to a "carpenter," makes the dark, metallic appearance of the residence all the more surprising.

Das Haus wurde an den steilen Hang eines erloschenen Vukans gebaut. Die Erläuterung der Architekten ist geradezu poetisch: „Der größtmögliche Teil des Grundstücks wurde dafür reserviert, den Garten oder Wald genießen zu können, dort, wo die Grenzen zwischen Stadt und Natur verschwimmen. Schutz an, in und unter dem Gebäude zeigt sich und verschwindet wieder und wechselt sich ab mit dem Blick in eine ferne Welt, die sich zu seinen Füßen ausbreitet." Der Grundriss des Hauses ist ein strenges Rechteck, das dennoch Überraschungen bereithält wie etwa den markanten Überhang des auskragenden Baukörpers. Der dunkle, metallische Eindruck des Gebäudes ist umso überraschender, als der Name des Hauses auf einen Schreiner verweist.

Cette maison se dresse sur le flanc d'un cratère de volcan. Les architectes s'expliquent en termes assez poétiques : « Nous avons réservé la plus grande partie possible du terrain aux plaisirs du jardin ou de la forêt, là où disparaissent les divisions entre ville et nature. L'abri apparaît et disparaît, dans, parmi, à travers, par-dessous, mais dialogue aussi avec la vue d'un monde distant qui se déploie à ses pieds. » Si le plan est strictement rectangulaire, il réserve néanmoins quelques surprises, comme un porte-à-faux substantiel. Le nom de la maison, qui se réfère à un « charpentier », surprend à la vue de l'aspect sombre et métallique de cette résidence.

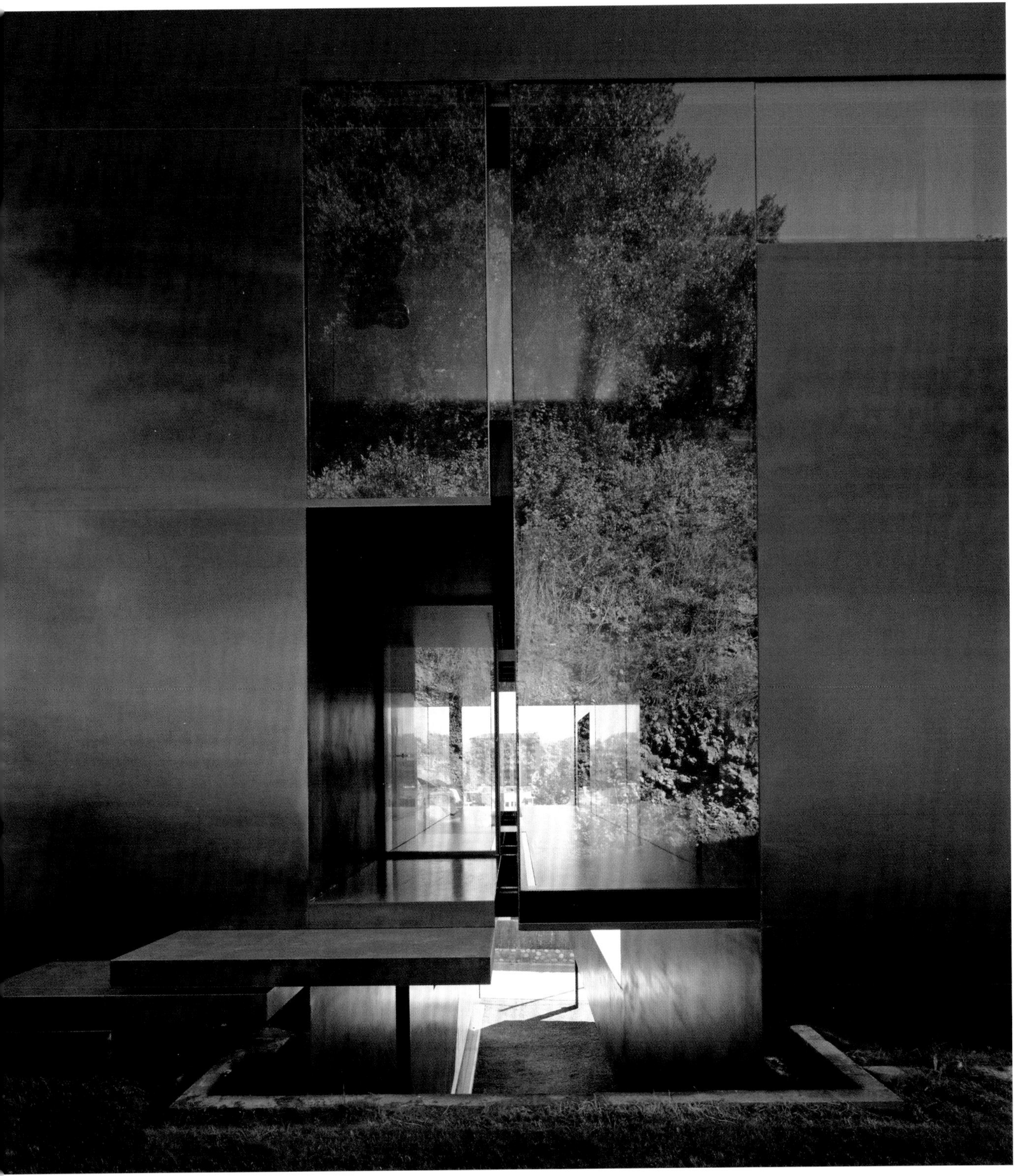

The dark, seemingly closed appearance of the house allows for willful contrasts with the garden, and, also, a certain amount of ambiguity in the spaces and views (above).

Die dunkle, geschlossen wirkende Erscheinung des Hauses schafft einen gewollten Kontrast zum Garten und zudem eine gewisse Mehrdeutigkeit in den Räumen und Blickbeziehungen (oben).

L'aspect sombre et apparemment fermé de la maison suscite des contrastes calculés avec le jardin, mais aussi une certaine ambiguïté dans les volumes et les perspectives (ci-dessus).

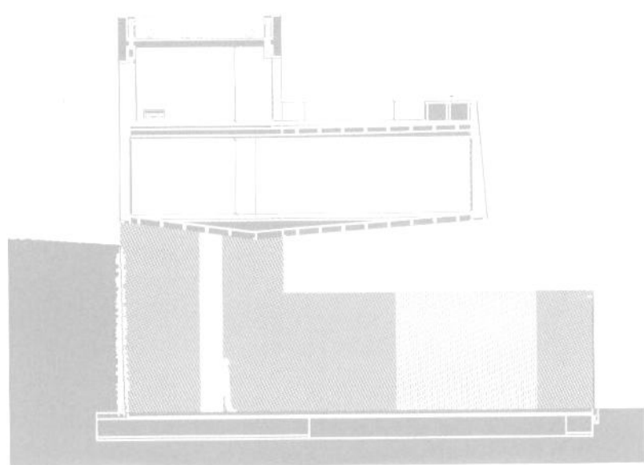

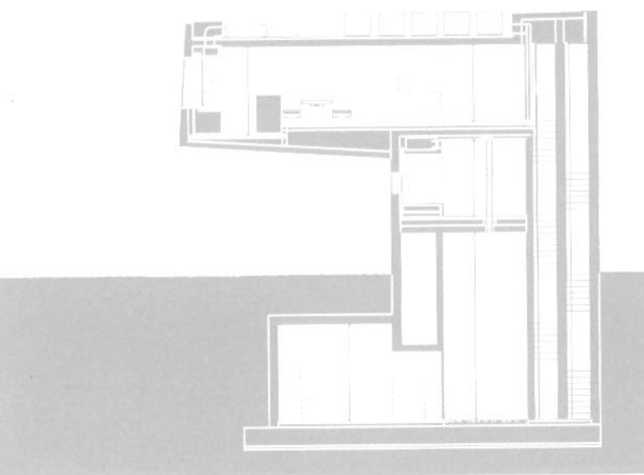

Broad, glazed bands and occasional full-height glazing make the dark interior vibrate with outside light and views. At the top of this page, watercolor sketches by the architects.

Breite gläserne Bänder und eine teilweise deckenhohe Verglasung lassen die dunklen Innenräume im einfallenden Licht und durch die Ausblicke geradezu vibrieren. Oben auf dieser Seite Aquarellskizzen des Architekten.

De larges bandeaux vitrés, parfois toute hauteur, entrent en vibration avec la lumière et les vues sur l'extérieur. En haut, croquis à l'aquarelle réalisés par les architectes.

ROCHA TOMBAL

Rocha Tombal Architecten
Nieuwpoortkade 2A-110
1055 RX Amsterdam
Netherlands

Tel: +31 20 606 07 72
Fax: +31 20 606 07 78
E-mail: info@rocha.tombal.nl
Web: www.rocha.tombal.nl

ANA ROCHA was born in 1972. She graduated from FAUP (Porto, 1996). She worked with Mecanoo Architects (Rotterdam, 1997–2005), where she was responsible for the design of the "Heilige Maria der Engelen" Chapel in Rotterdam, amongst other projects. She has given lectures and coordinated groups in workshops, such as "Archiprix-international," in Holland and abroad. She has been a member of judging committees and a guest teacher at the TU Delft. **MICHEL TOMBAL** was born in 1963 and graduated from the TU Delft in 1989. As a board member at Mecanoo Architects (1991–2005), he was responsible for the design of the Cultural center in Alkmaar and the Open-Air Museum in Arnhem. He has been a guest teacher at the AvB, Amsterdam. Ana Rocha and Michel Tombal founded Rocha Tombal Architecten in February 2006. Their work includes the refurbishment of a Water Tower (Delft, 2006–07); a House in Ijburg (Amsterdam, 2006–07); Galjoenschool Aletrinoplantsoen (The Hague, 2006–08); and Bierings-De Haas House (Leidsche Rijn, 2008–09, published here), all in the Netherlands.

ANA ROCHA wurde 1972 geboren. Ihr Studium schloss sie an der FAUP (Porto, 1996) ab. Sie arbeitete für Mecanoo Architects (Rotterdam, 1997–2005), wo sie neben anderen Projekten auch für den Entwurf der Kapelle „Heilige Maria der Engelen" in Rotterdam verantwortlich zeichnete. Sie hielt verschiedene Vorträge und koordinierte Gruppen in Workshops, z. B. dem „Archiprix-international", in den Niederlanden und im Ausland. An der TU Delft war sie sowohl als Jurymitglied als auch als Gastdozentin tätig. **MICHEL TOMBAL** wurde 1963 geboren und schloss sein Studium 1989 an der TU Delft ab. Als Vorstandsmitglied bei Mecanoo Architects (1991–2005) war er für den Entwurf des Kulturzentrums in Alkmaar und das Freilichtmuseum in Arnheim verantwortlich. Er lehrte als Gastdozent an der AvB in Amsterdam. Ana Rocha und Michel Tombal gründeten Rocha Tombal Architecten im Februar 2006. Zu ihren Projekten zählen die Sanierung eines Wasserturms (Delft, 2006–07), ein Haus in Ijburg (Amsterdam, 2006–07), die Galjoenschool Aletrinoplantsoen (Den Haag, 2006–08) sowie das Haus Bierings-De Haas (Leidsche Rijn, 2008–09, hier vorgestellt), alle in den Niederlanden.

ANA ROCHA, née en 1972, est diplômée de la Faculté d'archtecture de l'université de Porto (FAUP, Porto, 1996). Elle a travaillé avec Mecanoo Architects (Rotterdam, 1997–2005), où elle a été responsable de la conception de la chapelle de Sainte-Marie-des-Anges à Rotterdam, entre autres projets. Elle a donné des conférences et coordonné des ateliers comme « Archiprix-international », aux Pays-Bas et ailleurs. Elle a été membre de jury et enseignante invitée à l'Université de technologie (TU) de Delft. **MICHEL TOMBAL**, né en 1963, est diplômé de la TU de Delft (1989). Membre du comité de direction de Mecanoo Architects (1991–2005), il a été responsable de la conception du Centre culturel d'Alkmaar et de l'Open-Air Museum à Arnhem. Il a été enseignant invité à l'AvB (Amsterdam). Ana Rocha et Michel Tombal ont fondé Rocha Tombal Architecten en février 2006. Parmi leurs travaux : la rénovation d'un château d'eau (Delft, 2006–07) ; une maison à Ijburg (Amsterdam, 2006–07) ; l'école Galjoenschool Aletrinoplantsoen (La Haye, 2006–08) ; et la maison Bierings-De Haas (Leidsche Rijn, 2008–09, publiée ici), le tout aux Pays-Bas.

BIERINGS-DE HAAS HOUSE

Leidsche Rijn, The Netherlands, 2008–09

Area: 237 m² (excluding kitchen and garden). Client: Bierings-De Haas family.
Cost: € 410 000

This house assumes a very "normal" shape (defined by a municipal urban plan), but from its cladding to its glazing or its interiors, it is quickly apparent that the architects have built anything but a normal house. The openings avoid visual contact with neighboring residences, and bring what the architects call "fingers of light" into the house. The main door is very large and pivots. An over-scale window looks out from the kitchen, termed the "heart of the house" by the designers, while a small, high stairway up gives an impression of "walking in a medieval street." Green areas around the house are viewed through the upper level living space "like a framed painting."

Mit seiner Form, die vom Bebauungsplan der Stadt vorgegeben ist, mag dieses Haus zunächst „normal" wirken, doch von der Verkleidung über die Fenster bis zur Innenraumgestaltung wird schnell deutlich, dass die Architekten alles andere als ein normales Haus gebaut haben. Die Fassadenöffnungen vermeiden direkten Sichtkontakt zu den Nachbarhäusern und lassen, so die Architekten, „Lichtfinger" in das Haus einfallen. Die Haustür, eine Schwenktür, ist ungewöhnlich groß. Während die Küche, die die Architekten „Herz des Hauses" nennen, ein überdimensioniertes Fenster hat, vermittelt der schmale, hohe Treppenraum den Eindruck, „durch eine mittelalterliche Gasse zu laufen". Aus der oberen Wohnebene sind die Fenster mit Blick auf angrenzende Grünflächen wie „ein gerahmte Bilder" angeordnet.

Cette maison se présente sous une forme très « normale » (définie par le plan d'urbanisme municipal), mais il est rapidement décelable par les choix de son parement, de ses vitrages ou de son intérieur que les architectes n'ont pas conçu une résidence banale. Les ouvertures évitent soigneusement toutes vues sur les maisons voisines et attirent vers l'intérieur ce que les architectes appellent des « doigts de lumière ». La porte principale, très large, est montée sur pivots. Une fenêtre surdimensionnée se projette de la façade à partir de la cuisine, « le cœur de la maison » d'après les concepteurs, tandis qu'un petit escalier à marches hautes donne l'impression de « marcher dans une ruelle médiévale ». Les espaces verts autour de la maison se contemplent du séjour situé à l'étage, comme jouant le rôle « d'une peinture encadrée ».

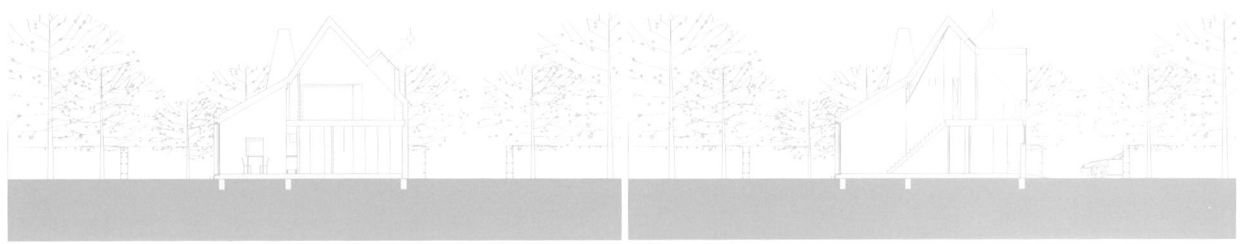

Although a cursory look at the elevations of the house (above) might imply a rather common suburban house type, views of the exterior and interior on this double page show that the architects have gone far beyond the ordinary.

Obwohl ein flüchtiger Blick auf die Aufrisse (oben) ein eher durchschnittliches Vorstadthäuschen vermuten lassen würde, belegen die Außen- und Innenansichten auf dieser Doppelseite, dass die Architekten den Durchschnitt tatsächlich weit hinter sich gelassen haben.

Si un regard rapide sur les coupes de la maison (ci-dessus) peut faire penser à une maison de banlieue assez banale, les vues de l'extérieur et de l'intérieur montrent que les architectes sont allés beaucoup plus loin dans leurs recherches.

Windows in unusual places (above) and a white stairway that appears to flow directly out of a wall are amongst the spatial surprises in this residence.

Die ungewöhnlich platzierten Fenster (oben) und eine weiße Treppe, die direkt aus den Wand zu fließen scheint, zählen zu den räumlichen Überraschungen in diesem Haus.

Les fenêtres curieusement disposées (ci-dessus) ou l'escalier blanc qui semble jaillir d'un mur font partie des surprises spatiales que réserve cette résidence.

Villa Storingavika

TODD SAUNDERS

Saunders Architecture
Vestre Torggaten 22
5015 Bergen
Norway

Tel: +47 97 52 57 61
E-mail: post@saunders.no
Web: www.saunders.no

TODD SAUNDERS was born in 1969 in Gander, Newfoundland, Canada. He obtained his M.Arch from McGill University (Montreal, Canada, 1993–95) after receiving a Bachelor of Environmental Planning from the Nova Scotia College of Art and Design (1988–92). He has worked in Austria, Germany, Russia, Latvia, and Norway (since 1997). He teaches part-time at the Bergen School of Architecture. His work includes Villa Storingavika (Bergen, 2004–07, published here); Aurland Look-Out (Aurland, 2006, with Tommie Wilhelmsen); Villa G (Hjellestad, Bergen, 2007–09, also published here); the nearly completed Villa Hjermann (Hjellestad); and Villa Morild (Gulen), all in Norway. He is currently designing a house on Salt Spring Island (British Columbia), and a series of artist studios for an artist-in-residence program on Fogo Island (Newfoundland), both in Canada.

TODD SAUNDERS wurde 1969 in Gander, Neufundland, Kanada, geboren. Er absolvierte seinen M.Arch. an der McGill University (Montreal, Kanada, 1993–95) sowie einen Bachelor in Umweltplanung am Nova Scotia College of Art and Design (1988–92). Er hat in Österreich, Deutschland, Russland, Lettland und Norwegen gearbeitet (ab 1997). Saunders lehrt neben seiner Tätigkeit als Architekt an der norwegischen Bergen Arkitekt Skole. Zu seinen Projekten zählen die Villa Storingavika (Bergen, 2004–07, hier vorgestellt), Aurland Look-Out (Aurland, 2006, mit Tommie Wilhelmsen), die Villa G (Hjellestad, Bergen, 2007–09, ebenfalls hier vorgestellt) sowie die nahezu fertiggestellte Villa Hjermann (Hjellestad) und die Villa Morild (Gulen), alle in Norwegen. Aktuell entwirft er ein Haus auf Salt Spring Island (British Columbia) sowie mehrere Künstlerateliers für ein Artist-in-Residence-Programm auf Fogo Island (Neufundland), beide in Kanada.

TODD SAUNDERS, né en 1969 à Gander, Terre-Neuve (Canada), a un M.Arch de l'université McGill (Montréal, 1993–95) et un Bachelor of Environmental Planning du Nova Scotia College of Art and Design (1988–92). Il a travaillé en Autriche, Allemagne, Russie, Lettonie et Norvège (depuis 1997). Il enseigne à temps partiel à l'École d'architecture de Bergen. Parmi ses réalisations, toutes en Norvège : la villa Storingavika (Bergen, 2004–07, publiée ici) ; la plate-forme d'observation d'Aurland (Aurland Look-Out, 2006, avec Tommie Wilhelmsen) ; la Villa G (Hjellestad, Bergen, 2007–09, également publiée ici) ; la villa Hjermann presque achevée (Hjellestad) ; et la Villa Morild (Gulen). Il conçoit actuellement une maison sur l'île de Salt Spring (Colombie-Britannique) et des ateliers d'artistes pour un programme d'artistes en résidence sur l'île de Fogo (Terre-Neuve), au Canada.

VILLA STORINGAVIKA

Bergen, Norway, 2004–07

Area: 304 m². Clients: Jan Sem Olsen, Eli Bakka. Cost: not disclosed. Collaboration: Node AS (Structural Engineers), and Ove Hannisdal (General Contractor)

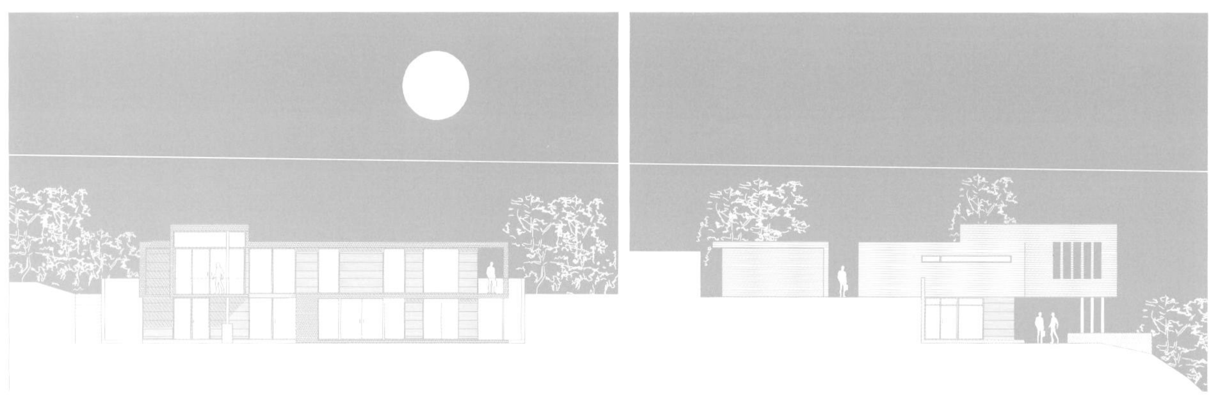

A dark wood shell overlaps the lighter wood of the main part of the house. Large windows and a balcony held up by thin pilotis further distinguish the house.

Ein Rahmen aus dunklem Holz umfängt die hellere Holzverschalung des Hauptbaukörpers. Große Fenster und ein auf schlanken pilotis ruhender Balkon sind weitere Besonderheiten des Baus.

Une sorte de coque de bois sombre enveloppe le cœur de la maison habillé de bois clair. De grandes baies et un balcon-loggia soutenu par de fins pilotis personnalisent ce projet.

Outdoor wooden terraces offer residents a water view during warmer months. Right, a terrace sheltered by the upper level of the house.

Holzterrassen bieten den Bewohnern in den warmen Monaten einen Ausblick aufs Wasser. Rechts eine vom Obergeschoss des Hauses geschützte Terrasse.

Les terrasses en bois offrent aux occupants de la maison une vue sur l'eau à la belle saison. À droite, une terrasse à l'abri de l'étage supérieur.

This house overlooks the fjords of Norway's western coast. The architect explains: "It is a pale timber volume enrobed in a crisp, 'pleated' dark timber exterior." The property had belonged to the client's mother and had a small cottage on it that was razed. The clients asked for an upper level with an open-plan living area and master suite, with an apartment for their children below. The clients also stipulated that they wanted to "wake up in the morning and see the ocean." The architect used the rocky-outcrop site to its utmost, seeking to increase the available exterior area as much as possible. A six-meter-long cantilevered balcony recalls other work by Saunders. A low, six-meter-long window is also part of the design. "A balcony is pierced by three circular steel columns that are 'threaded' from the ground to the roof." The main materials are glass, black-stained fir, and oiled Canadian cedar.

Dieses Haus liegt oberhalb der Fjorde an der Westküste Norwegens. Der Architekt erklärt: „Es ist ein heller Holzbau, der von einer klaren, dunklen, ‚in Falten gelegten' Holzhülle umfasst wird." Auf dem Grundstück, das der Mutter des Bauherrn gehörte, hatte ursprünglich ein kleines Häuschen gestanden, das abgerissen wurde. Die Auftraggeber hatten sich ein Obergeschoss mit einem offenen Wohnbereich und Elternschlafzimmer gewünscht; unten sollten die Kinder ein Apartment haben. Die Bauherren hatten außerdem den Wunsch geäußert, „morgens beim Aufwachen das Meer zu sehen". Der Architekt nutzte den Felshang als Baugrund, um so viel Außenraum zu gewinnen wie möglich. Ein 6 m langer Balkon erinnert an andere Projekte des Architekten. Auch ein niedriges, 6 m langes Fenster ist Teil des Entwurfs. „Ein Balkon wird von drei runden Stahlstützen durchstoßen, die vom Boden bis zum Dach ‚gefädelt' sind." Die dominierenden Materialien sind Glas, schwarz gebeizte Fichte und geöltes kanadisches Zedernholz.

Cette maison surplombe la côte ouest de Norvège aux nombreux fjords. « C'est un volume de bois clair enrobé d'un habillage extérieur "plissé" en bois sombre », explique l'architecte. Le terrain appartenait à la mère du client et le petit cottage qui s'y trouvait a été rasé. Les clients souhaitaient un séjour de plan ouvert et leur chambre à l'étage supérieur, ainsi qu'un appartement pour leurs enfants au rez-de-chaussée. Ils voulaient « voir l'océan en se réveillant le matin ». L'architecte a tiré un parti maximum du terrain rocheux, en cherchant à multiplier autant que possible les aménagements extérieurs. Le balcon en porte-à-faux de 6 m de long rappelle une autre intervention de Saunders. Une longue et basse grande baie de 6 m de long éclaire la façade. « Le balcon est percé de trois colonnes cylindriques en acier qui sont "enfilées" du sol au toit. » Les principaux matériaux utilisés sont le verre, le bouleau noirci et le cèdre du Canada huilé.

A fully glazed wall looking toward the water gives an impression of unity between interior and exterior, which may be difficult to generate in the cold climate of Bergen.

Eine raumhoch verglaste Wand mit Blick aufs Wasser vermittelt eine Einheit von Innen- und Außenraum, etwas, das im kühlen Klima von Bergen nur schwer zu erzielen ist.

Une paroi vitrée donnant sur l'eau crée un sentiment d'unité entre l'intérieur et l'extérieur, ce qui semble difficile dans le climat plutôt froid de Bergen.

The sharp geometric lines of the architecture and its interior contrast with the natural views that surround the house.

Die scharf gezeichneten, geometrischen Linien der Architektur und der Innenräume kontrastieren mit den Ausblicken in die landschaftliche Umgebung.

La stricte géométrie de l'architecture et des aménagements intérieurs contraste avec les vues sur la nature qui entoure la maison.

VILLA G

Hjellestad, Bergen, Norway, 2007–09

Area: 368 m². Client: not disclosed. Cost: not disclosed
Collaboration: Node AS (Structural Engineers),
and Bygg AS (General Contractor)

Three different sizes of wood cladding are used in a random pattern for this house. A stairway made of one-centimeter-thick galvanized steel that is folded into a very simple form was the result of close discussions with the client. An eight-meter-long kitchen bench is another feature that developed during these discussions. The client was also interested in the latest technology, such as hidden light plugs and central controls for the house being concentrated in the kitchen. The sweeping lines and bright spaces of this house make it decidedly modern, although the architect has taken into account numerous aspects of traditional Norwegian residential architecture.

Dieses Haus wurde mit Holzbrettern in drei verschiedenen Abmessungen und einem unregelmäßigen Muster verschalt. Nach intensiven Gesprächen mit dem Bauherrn entschied man sich, für die Treppe eine schlichte Form aus 1 cm starkem feuerverzinktem Stahl falten zu lassen. Auch der 8 m lange Küchentresen war ein Resultat dieser Gespräche. Der Auftraggeber war an technischen Details wie verdeckt eingebauten Steckdosen und der in der Küche angeordneten Zentralsteuerung für das Haus interessiert. Dank der großzügigen Linien und hellen Räume wirkt das Haus entschieden modern; dennoch berücksichtigte der Architekt zahlreiche Aspekte traditioneller norwegischer Wohnarchitektur.

Cette maison est habillée de trois types de parements de bois de dimensions différentes posés de manière aléatoire. L'escalier en tôle d'acier galvanisé plié de 1 cm d'épaisseur a fait l'objet de discussions serrées avec le client, de même que le comptoir de la cuisine qui mesure 8 m de long. Le client s'intéresse à la technologie comme le montrent les prises dissimulées et la commande centrale des diverses fonctions de la maison à partir de la cuisine. Les lignes enveloppantes et les volumes lumineux de cette maison sont résolument modernes, même si l'architecte a pris en compte de nombreux aspects du style résidentiel traditionnel norvégien.

In this house, Todd Saunders uses an overhanging roof and the very design of the structure to generate terraces and protected areas.

Bei diesem Haus nutzt Todd Saunders ein auskragendes Dach und den Baukörper selbst, um Terrassen und geschützte Bereiche zu definieren.

Dans cette maison, Todd Saunders utilise le surplomb du toit et du dessin des façades pour créer des terrasses et des zones protégées.

Bright, open interior spaces are characterized by a certain contrast in materials, ranging from tiles to wood or large glazed areas, such as the one seen on the right.

Die hellen, offenen Innenräume sind von verschiedenen Materialkontrasten gopprägt – von Fliesen über Holz bis hin zu großen Glasflächen, wie rechts zu sehen.

Les volumes intérieurs ouverts et lumineux se caractérisent par une recherche de contrastes entre les matériaux comme les carrelages, le bois ou les vastes panneaux de verre, comme ici à droite.

HARTWIG N. SCHNEIDER

Hartwig N. Schneider
Birkenwaldstr. 54
70191 Stuttgart
Germany

Tel: +49 711 901 14 70
Fax: +49 711 90 11 47 11
E-mail: info@hartwigschneider.de
Web: www.hartwigschneider.de

HARTWIG N. SCHNEIDER was born in Stuttgart, Germany, in 1957, and studied architecture at the University of Stuttgart and at the Illinois Institute of Technology in Chicago (1977–84). He worked in the offices of Peter C. von Seidlein in Munich (1985–86) and Norman Foster in London (1986–87). He created his own office in Stuttgart with Gabriele Schneider in 1990 and since 1999 has been Professor of Building Construction and Design at the RWTH Aachen. Their work includes Birkenwaldstrasse House (Stuttgart, 2003, published here); the Lude-Hopf House (Kornwestheim, 2003, also published here), Stihl Art Gallery and Art School (Waiblingen, 2008); Kunsthalle Ernst-Sachs-Bad (Schweinfurt, 2009); an office and restaurant for the Stihl Art Gallery (Waiblingen, 2009), and Hegger House (Aachen, 2008–10), all in Germany.

HARTWIG N. SCHNEIDER wurde 1957 in Stuttgart geboren und studierte Architektur an der Universität Stuttgart sowie dem Illinois Institute of Technology in Chicago (1977–84). Von 1985 bis 1986 war er für Peter C. von Seidlein in München und von 1986 bis 1988 für Norman Foster in London tätig. 1990 gründete er mit Gabriele Schneider ein eigenes Büro in Stuttgart und ist seit 1999 Professor für Baukonstruktion und Entwurf an der RWTH Aachen. Zu den Projekten des Büros zählen das Haus Birkenwaldstraße (Stuttgart, 2003, hier vorgestellt), das Haus Lude-Hopf (Kornwestheim, 2003, ebenfalls hier vorgestellt), die Galerie Stihl und Kunstschule Waiblingen (2008), die Kunsthalle Ernst-Sachs-Bad (Schweinfurt, 2009), ein Büro und Restaurant für die Galerie Stihl (Waiblingen, 2009) sowie das Haus Hegger (Aachen, 2008–10), alle in Deutschland.

HARTWIG N. SCHNEIDER, né à Stuttgart, Allemagne, en 1957, a étudié l'architecture à l'université de Stuttgart et à l'Illinois Institute of Technology à Chicago (1977–84). Il a travaillé chez Norman Foster à Londres (1986–87). Il a fondé son agence à Stuttgart avec Gabriele Schneider en 1990 et, depuis 1999, est professeur de construction et de conception au RWTH à Aix-la-Chapelle. Parmi leurs réalisations : la Maison Lude-Hopf (Kornwestheim, 2001–2003, publiée ici) ; la maison de Birkenwaldstrasse (Stuttgart, 2003, également publiée ici) ; la galerie et école d'art Stihl (Waiblingen, 2005–2008) ; la Kunsthalle Ernst-Sachs-Bad (Schweinfurt, 2006–09) ; un bureau et un restaurant pour la galerie d'art Stihl (Waiblingen, 2009) ; et la Maison Hegger (Aix-la-Chapelle, 2008–10), tous en Allemagne.

LUDE-HOPF HOUSE

Kornwestheim, Germany, 2003

Area: 320 m². Clients: Sybille and Ralf Lude-Hopf.
Cost: not disclosed

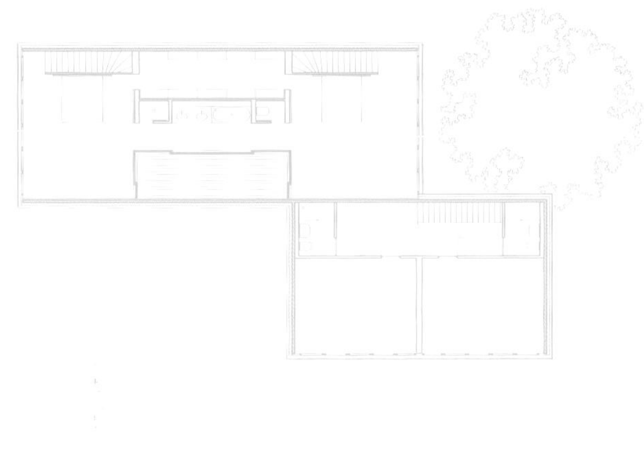

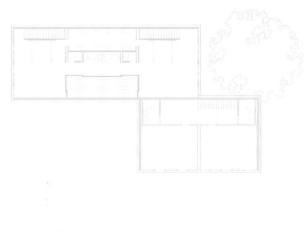

Compromising a series of rectangular volumes, the house makes ample use of wooden screens, giving rise to the unexpected exterior appearance seen on the right page when screens are closed.

Das aus zwei rechteckigen Volumina zusammengesetzte Haus ist großflächig mit Fensterläden aus Holz versehen. Sind die Läden geschlossen, ergibt sich die ungewöhnliche Außenansicht auf der rechten Seite.

Composée d'une série de volumes rectangulaires, la maison utilise beaucoup le principe de volets-écrans en bois, qui lui confèrent un aspect étrange une fois fermés (page de droite).

A century-old maple tree to be preserved and a five-meter-level difference between the road and the actual building site were two factors influencing this design. The architects were further required not to have an impact on the privacy of two houses that already existed on this former factory site. The house is made up of two volumes that are staggered along a central spine, allowing for a private terrace to be created. The spine also divides the upper level into two distinct areas—for the children and for the parents. An atrium provides a median space between interior and exterior. A sloping tunnel leads to garages set at the level of the reinforced-concrete basement.

Ein 100-jähriger Ahorn, den es zu erhalten galt, und ein Höhenunterschied von 5 m zwischen Straße und eigentlichem Baugrundstück waren zwei der Faktoren des Außenraumes, die den Entwurf beeinflussten. Darüber hinaus wurden die Architekten gebeten, die Privatsphäre der zwei Wohnhäuser zu wahren, die bereits auf diesem ehemaligen Fabrikgrundstück stehen. Das Haus besteht aus zwei Volumina, die entlang einer zentralen Achse gegeneinander verschoben wurden, wodurch eine geschützte Terrasse möglich wurde. Die zentrale Achse gliedert auch das Obergeschoss in zwei klar getrennte Bereiche für die Kinder und die Eltern. Eine Loggia dient als Übergang zwischen innen und außen. Ein Tunnel mit Gefälle führt zu den Garagen, die auf einer Ebene mit dem Stahlbetonfundament liegen.

Un érable centenaire à préserver et une différence de niveau de 5 m entre la route et le terrain à bâtir expliquent en partie ce projet. Par ailleurs, il avait été demandé aux architectes de ne pas gêner l'intimité des deux habitations existant déjà sur cet ancien site d'usine. La maison se compose de deux volumes décalés en quinconce, ce qui permet de créer une terrasse. À l'étage, ce décalage sépare la zone réservée aux parents de celle des enfants. Un atrium offre un espace médian entre l'intérieur et l'extérieur. Un tunnel en pente conduit aux garages aménagés au niveau de la route dans le sous-sol en béton armé.

In its unfurnished state (below), living spaces open broadly onto the terrace and garden through use of sliding glass walls.

Im unmöblierten Zustand (unten) öffnen sich die Wohnräume dank der Schiebewände aus Glas großzügig zur Terrasse und zum Garten.

Non encore meublés (ci-dessous), les volumes du séjour s'ouvrent largement vers la terrasse et le jardin par des baies de verre coulissantes.

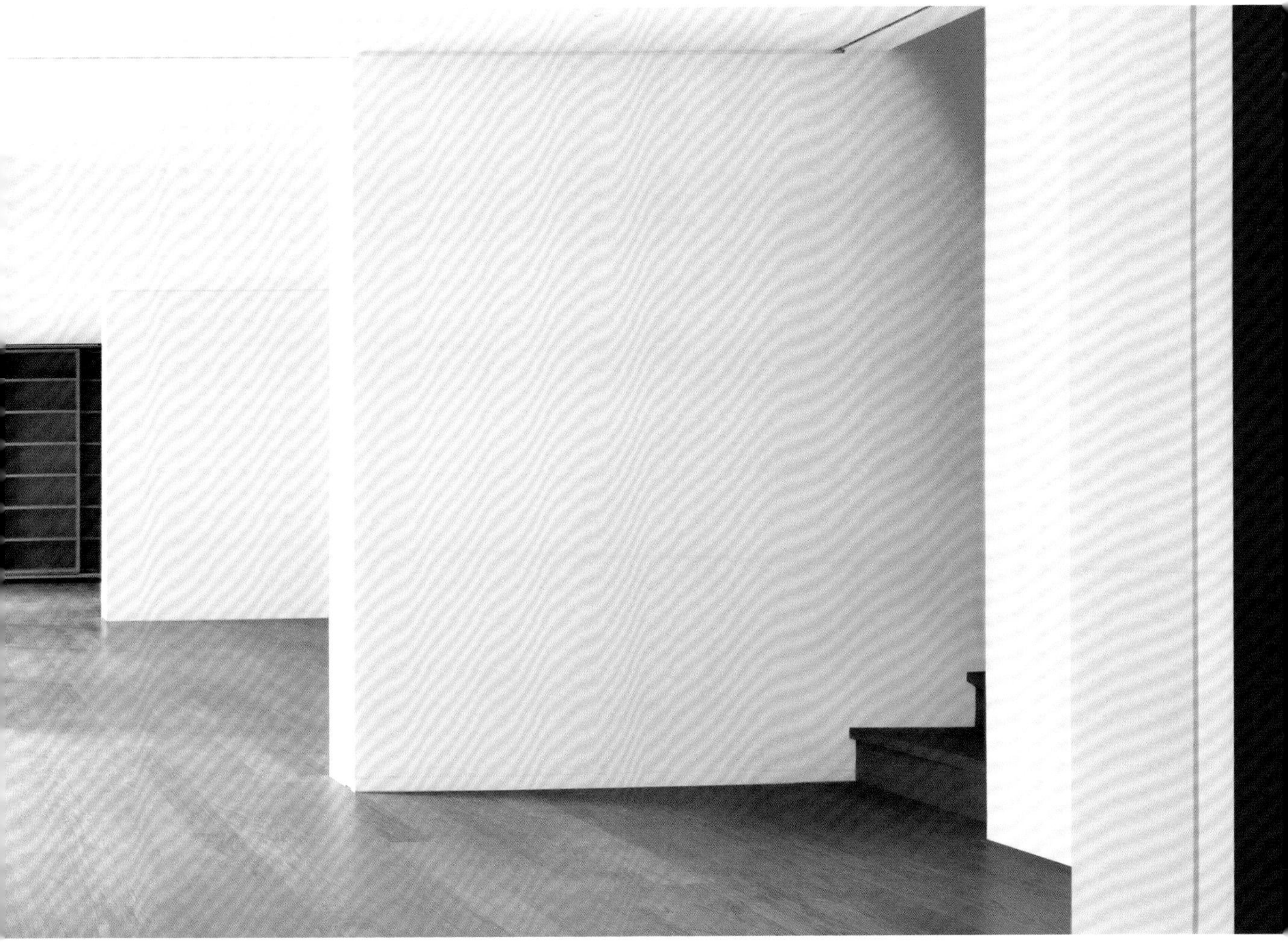

BIRKENWALD HOUSE

Stuttgart, Germany, 2003

*Area: 185 m² (penthouse); 280 m² (office). Clients: Gabriele and Hartwig Schneider.
Cost: not disclosed*

This house is in fact a penthouse built over a small 1950s apartment building. Given the nature of the existing structure, the architects were obliged to pay careful attention to the weight of the new elements, which include a terrace. The earlier building was renovated and resurfaced as a result of the new construction. The ground floor of the building has been maintained as independent apartments, while the existing first and second floors have been incorporated into the penthouse structure for use as an office. A new, external, spiral staircase provides access to both these upper levels. Full-height all-around glazing gives the upper level a feeling of openness, accentuated by the use of six 1.9-meter sliding doors.

Dieses Haus ist im Grunde ein Penthouse, das auf ein kleines Mehrfamilienhaus aus den 1950er Jahren aufgesetzt wurde. Angesichts des vorhandenen Tragwerks mussten die Architekten besonders auf das Gewicht der neuen Elemente, zu denen auch eine Terrasse gehört, achten. Im Zuge des Neubaus wurde der Altbau saniert und neu verputzt. Während das Erdgeschoss des Gebäudes als unabhängige Wohnungen beibehalten wurde, koppelte man das bestehende erste und zweite Obergeschoss, in dem sich Büroräume befinden, mit dem Penthouse. Eine neue, nach außen verlegte Wendeltreppe verbindet die beiden oberen Ebenen. Die deckenhohe Rundumverglasung verleiht der obersten Ebene eine Offenheit, die von den sechs 1,9 m breiten Schiebetüren noch unterstrichen wird.

Cette maison est en fait une penthouse édifiée au sommet d'un petit immeuble d'appartements datant des années 1950. Étant donnée la nature de la construction existante, les architectes ont été obligés de faire très attention au poids de cette adjonction et de sa terrasse. Le bâtiment ancien a été rénové à l'occasion du chantier. Le rez-de-chaussée a conservé ses appartements indépendants, tandis que le premier et le second étage ont été incorporés dans le projet de la penthouse et servent de bureaux. Un nouvel escalier extérieur en spirale assure l'accès à ces niveaux. L'étage supérieur est vitré to ute hauteur, ce qui crée un sentiment de grande ouverture, accentué par la présence de six portes coulissantes de 1,9 m de large.

With its wooden deck and glass-box design, the house contrasts with other architecture around it. Section drawings (left page) show the apartment building on top of which the house is built.

Durch seine hölzernen Terrassen und die Glasbox präsentiert sich das Haus als Kontrast zur benachbarten Architektur. Schnitte (linke Seite) zeigen das Mehrfamilienhaus, auf das das Wohnhaus aufgesetzt wurde.

Conçue comme une boîte en verre à terrasses de bois, la maison contraste avec les constructions voisines. Les coupes de la page de gauche montrent l'immeuble d'appartements sur lequel elle a été édifiée.

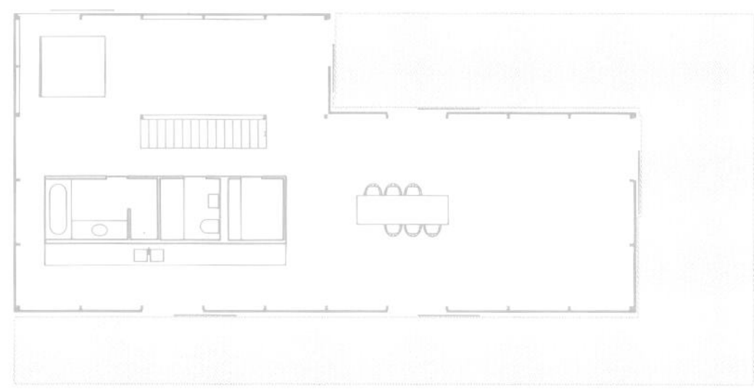

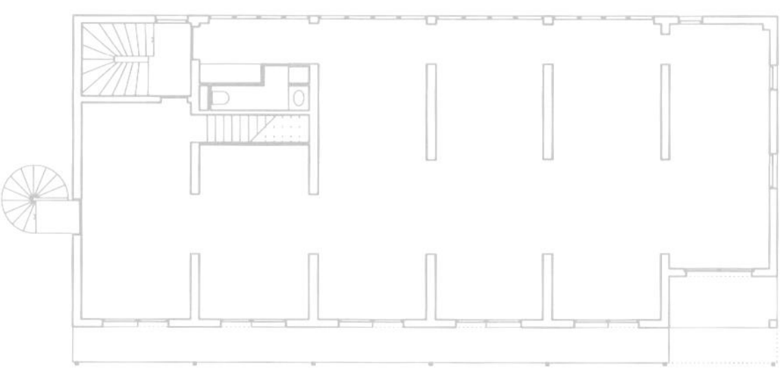

The architects have privileged the extremely pure and simple lines of a minimal modernism that allows the view and the life within to develop fully.

Die Architekten bevorzugen die extrem puristischen und schlichten Linien eines minimalistischen Modernismus, der Ausblicken und Entfaltung uneingeschränkten Raum gibt.

Les architectes ont privilégié des lignes extrêmement pures et simples d'un modernisme minimaliste qui laisse toute leur place aux espaces de vie et aux perspectives.

Fully rectilinear and glazed from floor to ceiling, the house is essentially a glass box sitting on top of a preexisting building.

Das konsequent geradlinige und vom Boden bis zur Decke verglaste Wohnhaus ist im Grunde eine Glasbox, die auf ein bestehendes Gebäude aufgesetzt wurde.

De plan entièrement rectiligne, vitrée du sol au plafond, la maison est une boîte de verre posée sur un immeuble existant.

House in the Berkshires

SCHWARTZ/SILVER

Schwartz/Silver Architects, Inc.
75 Kneeland Street
Boston, MA 02111
USA

Tel: +1 617 542 6650
Fax: +1 617 951 0779
E-mail: arch@schwartzsilver.com
Web: www.schwartzsilver.com

Warren Schwartz and Robert Silver founded their firm in Boston in 1980. Schwartz was educated at Cornell (1966) and Harvard, where he received his M.Arch degree in Urban Design in 1967. Silver attended Queens College CUNY, Cambridge University, and Harvard, where he received his M.Arch in 1970. **SCHWARTZ/SILVER** has received the AIA National Honor Award five times, and they pride themselves on being a "middle-sized firm… organized as an open design studio." Recent work includes the Farnsworth Art Museum and Wyeth Study Center (Rockland, Maine, 1998); Abbe Museum (Bar Harbor, Maine, 2001); a renovation and expansion of the Boston Atheneum (2002); Belmont Hill School Prenatt Music Center (Belmont, Massachusetts, 2004); Princeton University Anglinger Center for the Humanities (Princeton, New Jersey, 2004); and the Shaw Center for the Arts (Baton Rouge, Louisiana, 2003–05). More recent projects include work for the Maine Historical Society; a master plan for the University of Vermont; the Studio Arts Building for the University of Virginia (Charlottesville, Virginia); the Massachusetts Institute of Technology Rotch Library (Cambridge, Massachusetts); and the Burke High School and Combined Library (Dorchester, Massachusetts), all in the USA.

Warren Schwartz und Robert Silver gründeten ihr Büro 1980 in Boston. Schwartz hatte an den Universitäten Cornell (1966) und Harvard studiert, wo er 1967 seinen M. Arch. in Stadtplanung erhielt. Silver hatte das Queens College CUNY sowie die Universitäten Cambridge und Harvard besucht, wo er 1970 seinen M.Arch. machte. **SCHWARTZ/SILVER** wurde bereits fünf Mal der AIA National Honor Award verliehen. Sie sind stolz darauf, „ein mittelständisches Unternehmen zu sein, das ... wie ein offenes Designstudio organisiert ist". Zu ihren jüngeren Projekten zählen das Farnsworth Art Museum und Wyeth Study Center (Rockland, Maine, 1998), das Abbe Museum (Bar Harbor, Maine, 2001), die Sanierung und Erweiterung des Boston Atheneum (2002), das Prenatt Music Center an der Belmont Hill School (Belmont, Massachusetts, 2004), das Anglinger Center für Geisteswissenschaften der Universität Princeton (Princeton, New Jersey, 2004) und das Shaw Center for the Arts (Baton Rouge, Louisiana, 2003–05). Aktuellere Projekte sind u. a. Aufträge für die Maine Historical Society, ein Masterplan für die Universität Vermont, ein Gebäude mit Ateliers für die Universität Virginia (Charlottesville, Virginia), die Rotch Library am Massachusetts Institute of Technology (Cambridge, Massachusetts) sowie die Burke High School mit Bibliothek (Dorchester, Massachusetts), alle in den USA.

Warren Schwartz et Robert Silver ont créé leur agence à Boston en 1980. Schwartz a étudié à Cornell (1966) et Harvard, dont il est M.Arch en urbanisme (1967). Silver a étudié au Queens College CUNY, aux universités de Cambridge et Harvard, où il a passé son M.Arch (1970). **SCHWARTZ/SILVER** a reçu cinq fois le Prix d'honneur national de l'AIA, et se présente comme « une agence de taille moyenne… organisée comme un studio ouvert ». Parmi leurs réalisations récentes : le Musée d'art Farnsworth et le Wyeth Study Center (Rockland, Maine 1998) ; le Abbe Museum (Bar Harbor, Maine, 2001) ; la rénovation et l'expansion du Boston Atheneum (2002) ; le Centre de musique Prenatt de l'École de Belmont (Belmont, Massachusetts, 2004) ; le Centre Anglinger pour les humanités de l'université de Princeton (Princeton, New Jersey, 2004) ; et le Shaw Center for the Arts (Baton Rouge, Louisiane, 2003–05). Plus récemment, ils ont été chargés de travaux pour la Maine Historical Society ; ont réalisé un plan directeur pour l'université du Vermont ; le bâtiment des ateliers d'art de l'université de Virginie (Charlottesville, Virginie) ; la bibliothèque Rotch de l'Institut de technologie du Massachusetts (Cambridge, Massachusetts) ; et la Burke High School et sa bibliothèque (Dorchester, Massachusetts), le tout aux États-Unis.

HOUSE IN THE BERKSHIRES

Massachusetts, USA, 2006–08

*Area: 223 m². Clients: Sheila Fiekowsky, Warren Schwartz. Cost: $1.075 million.
Collaboration: Robert Silver, Christopher Ingersoll,
Sarkis Zerounian (Structural Engineer)*

The architect makes clear that the house has little in common with the typical houses of the region. It makes extensive use of glass and industrial materials. The living area opens out onto spectacular views at the end of a 13.7-meter-long cantilever. Warren Schwartz writes: "In January 2006, I began to sketch a house that projected out from the hillside where my then-present house stood. My wife and I had been talking about replacing our house because it was weathering poorly, and in the following weeks I developed images of a new house that was derived from a dream. The earlier house was vertical; the new house would be horizontal. The earlier house was mostly wall with framed views; the new house would be mostly glass with panoramic views. The earlier house was made of wood; the new house would be made of steel, concrete, and glass. The 50% cantilever would be a structural challenge, but I wanted to see if the house could appear to take flight."

Dieses Haus hat wenig gemein mit den typischen Häusern der Region, wie der Architekt betont. Überwiegend kamen Glas und industrielle Baumaterialien zum Einsatz. An der Spitze eines 13,7 m langen Auslegers öffnet sich der Wohnbereich zu einem spektakulären Panoramablick. Warren Schwartz schreibt: „Im Januar 2006 begann ich Skizzen für ein Haus anzufertigen, das über den Hang des Hügels, auf dem mein damaliges Haus stand, auskragte. Meine Frau und ich hatten darüber gesprochen, unser Haus durch einen Neubau zu ersetzen, weil es der Witterung nicht befriedigend standhielt. In den darauffolgenden Wochen machte ich Skizzen für ein neues Haus, das von einem Traum inspiriert war. Das alte Haus war vertikal, das neue sollte horizontal sein. Das frühere Haus war primär Wand und gerahmte Ausblicke, das neue Haus sollte aus Stahl, Beton und Glas bestehen. Der Ausleger, der 50 % des Baus ausmacht, würde eine technische Herausforderung sein, aber ich wollte sehen, ob es gelingen würde ein Haus zu bauen, das abzuheben scheint."

Les architectes ne font pas mystère de ce que leur maison n'a pas grand chose à voir avec les résidences typiques de la région. Elle utilise pour une bonne part le verre et les matériaux industriels. Le séjour ouvre sur de spectaculaires perspectives à l'extrémité d'un porte-à-faux de 13,7 m. Warren Schwartz a écrit : « En janvier 2006, j'ai commencé à tracer des croquis pour une maison qui se projetait du flanc de la colline, là où se dresse la construction actuelle. Mon épouse et moi avions pensé la remplacer parce qu'elle vieillissait mal et, dans les semaines qui suivirent, j'ai mis au point les images d'une maison issue d'un rêve. La précédente était verticale, la nouvelle serait horizontale. L'ancienne était tout en murs avec des vues cadrées, la nouvelle serait essentiellement en verre avec des vues panoramiques. L'ancienne était en bois, la nouvelle serait en acier, en béton et en verre. Les 50 % du plan en porte-à-faux allaient être un défi, mais je voulais voir si cette maison pouvait donner l'impression de s'envoler. »

The angled, cantilevered nature of the house allows it to serve as a kind of balcony looking out to the scenery of the site. It is in willful contrast to the setting.

Das Haus, im Grunde ein schräger Ausleger, erlaubt wie ein Balkon die Aussicht auf die umliegende Landschaft und bildet einen gewollten Kontrast zur Umgebung.

L'inclinaison et l'important porte-à-faux en font une sorte de balcon ouvert sur le paysage qui cultive le contraste avec la nature.

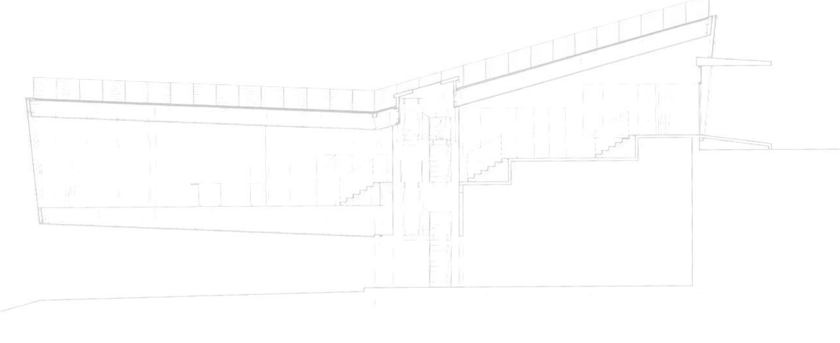

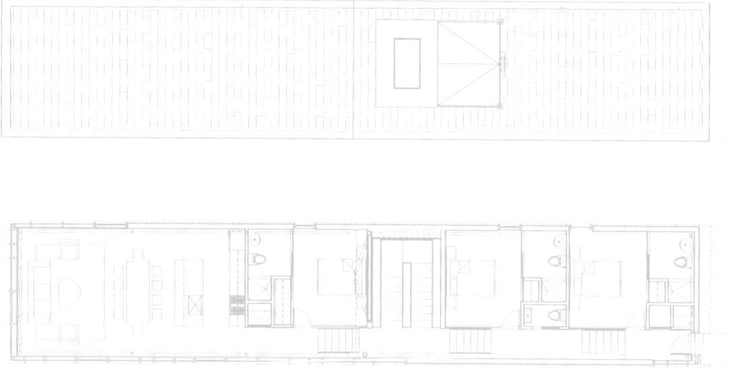

The architecture of the house demonstrates that rigorous geometric forms can be audacious and spectacular.

Die Architektur des Hauses belegt, dass strenge geometrische Formen gewagt und spektakulär sein können.

L'architecture de la maison démontre à quel point des formes géométriques rigoureuses peuvent se révéler spectaculairement audacieuses.

The dining area is located at the fully glazed end of the cantilevered section of the house, allowing residents to sit suspended above the view.

Der Essbereich liegt an der voll verglasten Stirnseite des Auslegers und gestattet den Bewohnern, schwebend über dem Panorama Platz zu nehmen.

La partie salle à manger est située à l'extrémité entièrement vitrée de la section en porte-à-faux : on y déjeune suspendu dans le paysage.

SeARCH & CMA

SeARCH
Hamerstraat 3
1021 JT Amsterdam
The Netherlands

Tel: +31 20 788 99 00
Fax: +31 20 788 99 11
E-mail: info@search.nl
Web: www.search.nl

CMA / Christian Müller Architects
Delftseplein 36
3013 AA Rotterdam
The Netherlands

Tel: +31 10 213 67 63
E-mail: mail@christian-muller.com
www.christian-muller.com

SeARCH is an architecture office, established in Amsterdam in 2002 by Bjarne Mastenbroek and Ad Bogerman. Bjarne Mastenbroek was born in 1964, attended the TU Delft Faculty of Architecture (1982–89) and then worked in the Van Gameren Mastenbroek project team that was part of architectengroep in Amsterdam from 1993. SeARCH currently employs 20 people. Christian Müller was born in 1963 in Switzerland, and graduated from the ETH in Zurich in 1989. He is the Principal of Christian Müller Architects (**CMA**, Rotterdam) and is currently collaborating with SeARCH, Kraaijvanger, Urbis, and GGAU on a number of projects. SeARCH has worked on the Dutch Embassy in Addis Ababa (1998–); Triade, the conversion and extension of a cultural education center (Den Helder, 1997–2001); Bredero College, extension to a trade school (Amsterdam Noord, 1998–2001); and buildings in Lelystad and Alemere. They also completed the Posbank Tea Pavilion (National Park Veluwe Zoom, Rheden, 1998–2002); the TwentseWelle museum in Enschede (2003–08); a watchtower in Putten (2004–09); and Villa Vals (Vals, Switzerland, 2005–09, published here), which is the work of SeARCH (Bjarne Mastenbroek) and Christian Müller Architects (Christian Müller), all in the Netherlands unless stated otherwise. Current projects are a new synagogue (2005–10) in Amsterdam; a conference and activity center in Hillerød (Denmark (2007–11); large-scale mixed-use projects in Leuven (Belgium, 2003–12); and several projects in Bahrain.

Das Architekturbüro **SEARCH** wurde 2002 von Bjarne Mastenbroek und Ad Bogerman in Amsterdam gegründet. Bjarne Mastenbroek wurde 1964 geboren, studierte an der Fakultät für Architektur der TU Delft (1982–89) und arbeitete anschließend im Projektteam Van Gameren Mastenbroek, das ab 1993 Teil der architectengroep in Amsterdam war. Derzeit beschäftigt SeARCH 20 Mitarbeiter. Christian Müller wurde 1963 in der Schweiz geboren und schloss sein Studium 1989 an der ETH Zürich ab. Er leitet Christian Müller Architects (**CMA**, Rotterdam) und arbeitet zurzeit an verschiedenen Projekten mit SeARCH, Kraaijvanger, Urbis und GGAU zusammen. SeARCH arbeitete an der niederländischen Botschaft in Addis Abeba (ab 1998), und hat Triade, den Umbau und die Erweiterung eines Kulturbildungszentrums (Den Helder, 1997–2001), die Erweiterung einer Handelsschule am Bredero College (Amsterdam Noord, 1998–2001) sowie Bauten in Lelystad und Alemere geplant. Realisieren konnten sie außerdem den Posbank Teepavillon (Nationalpark Veluwe Zoom, Rheden, 1998–2002), das Museum TwentseWelle in Enschede (2003–08), die Villa Vals (Vals, Schweiz, 2005–09, hier vorgestellt) – eine Kooperation von SeARCH (Bjarne Mastenbroek) und Christian Müller Architects (Christian Müller) – sowie einen Wachturm in Putten (2004–09), alle in den Niederlanden sofern nicht anders angegeben. Aktuelle Projekte sind eine neue Synagoge in Amsterdam (2005–10), ein Konferenz- und Fitnesszentrum in Hillerød (Dänemark, 2007–11), ein Großprojekt mit gemischter Nutzung in Löwen (Belgien, 2003–12) und verschiedene Projekte in Bahrain.

SEARCH est une agence créée à Amsterdam en 2002 par Bjarne Mastenbroek et Ad Bogerman. Bjarne Mastenbroek, né en 1964, a étudié à la Faculté d'architecture de la TU de Delft (1982–89), puis dans l'équipe de projet de Van Gameren Mastenbroek faisant partie de l'architectengroep d'Amsterdam à partir de 1993. SeARCH emploie actuellement vingt personnes. Christian Müller, né en 1963 en Suisse, est diplômé de l'ETH de Zurich (1989). Il dirige Christian Müller Architects (**CMA**, Rotterdam) et collabore actuellement avec SeARCH, Kraaijvanger, Urbis et GGAU sur un certain nombre de projets. SeARCH a réalisé l'ambassade néerlandaise à Addis Abeba (1998–) ; Triade, conversion et extension d'un centre éducatif culturel (Den Helder, 1997–2001) ; le Bredero College, extension d'une école de commerce (Amsterdam Noord, 1998–2001) ; et des immeubles à Lelystad et Alemere. Ils ont également réalisé le pavillon de thé de la Posbank (Parc national Veluwe Zoom, Rheden, 1998–2002) ; le musée TwentseWelle à Enschede (2003–08) ; une tour de guet à Putten (2004–09) ; et la villa Vals (Vals, Suisse, 2005–09, publiée ici), œuvre de SeARCH (Bjarne Mastenbroek) et de Christian Müller Architects (Christian Müller), le tout aux Pays-Bas, sauf mention contraire. Parmi leurs projets actuels : une nouvelle synagogue (2005–10) à Amsterdam ; un centre de conférences et d'activités à Hillerød (Danemark, 2007–11) ; des projets d'immeubles mixtes de grandes dimensions à Louvain (Belgique, 2003–12) ; et plusieurs projets au Bahreïn.

VILLA VALS

Vals, Grisons, Switzerland, 2005–09

Area: 285 m². Client: not disclosed.
Cost: not disclosed

In the rather enclosed and remote valley of Vals, known mainly for the Thermal Baths by Peter Zumthor located there, the new house is set into the hillside, not far from the green stone structure by the Swiss master.

Im abgelegenen Tal von Vals, bekannt in erster Linie für die von Peter Zumthor gestaltete Therme, liegt das Haus eingebettet in den Hang, nicht weit vom grünlichen Steinbau des Schweizer Meisters.

Dans cette vallée assez isolée et fermée, la maison s'insère dans le flanc d'une montagne, non loin de l'établissement thermal en pierre verte édifié par Peter Zumthor, qui a fait la célébrité de Vals.

Until the completion of this house, the mountain village of Vals was best known for its mineral water and the Thermal Baths (1996) designed there by Peter Zumthor. Villa Vals is located close to the site of Zumthor's building, but it is largely below grade. "Shouldn't it be possible to conceal a house in an Alpine slope while still exploiting the wonderful views and allowing light to enter the building?", ask the architects. A central patio with a steep angle emphasizes and enlarges the views from the house, without challenging those of Zumthor's Baths. Local authorities approved the design of this house despite their reputation for conservative rulings. The placement of a typical old barn near the entrance to the house and the fact that access is through a tunnel seems to have swayed the authorities. The architects explain: "Switzerland's planning laws in this region dictate that it is only possible to grant a definitive planning permission after a timber model of the building's volume has first been constructed on site. This can then be accurately appraised by the local community and objected to if considered unsuitable. For this proposal, logic prevailed and this part of the process was deemed to be unnecessary."

Bis zur Fertigstellung dieses Hauses war das Bergdorf Vals am ehesten für sein Mineralwasser und die von Peter Zumthor entworfene Therme Vals (1996) bekannt. Die Villa Vals liegt nicht weit von Zumthors Bau, jedoch weitgehend unter der Geländeoberfläche. „Sollte es nicht möglich sein," fragen die Architekten, „ein Haus in einem Alpenhang zu verbergen und dabei trotzdem die wunderbare Aussicht zu nutzen und Licht in den Bau zu lassen?" Ein zentraler Innenhof mit steiler Neigung unterstreicht den Blick, den das Haus bietet, und lässt ihn noch spektakulärer wirken, ohne den Ausblick von Zumthors Therme zu beeinträchtigen. Die örtlichen Behörden genehmigten den Bau trotz ihres Rufs, äußerst konservativ zu sein. Dass in der Nähe des Eingangs eine traditionelle alte Scheune steht und man den Bau durch einen Tunnel betritt, scheint die Behörden positiv gestimmt zu haben. Die Architekten erklären: „Die schweizerischen Bauvorschriften dieser Region sehen vor, dass eine verbindliche Baugenehmigung nur erteilt werden kann, wenn zuvor ein Holzmodell des Baukörpers vor Ort errichtet wurde. Dies erlaubt es den Anwohnern, das Gebäude genau zu beurteilen und Einspruch zu erheben, falls es unpassend erscheint. Bei diesem Entwurf jedoch war es ein Gebot der Logik, dass dieser Teil des Procederes für unnötig befunden wurde."

Jusqu'à l'achèvement de cette maison, le village de montagne de Vals était surtout connu pour son eau et ses thermes conçus par Peter Zumthor (1996). La villa Vals se trouve non loin de ce bâtiment mais est en grande partie enterrée. « Ne serait-il pas possible de dissimuler une maison dans une pente d'alpage, tout en bénéficiant de vues magnifiques et en permettant au soleil d'éclairer cette construction ? », se sont demandés les architectes. Un patio central découpé dans la pente exploite la vue splendide, sans gêner celle de l'établissement de bains de Zumthor. Les autorités locales ont approuvé ce projet malgré leur réputation de conservatisme. L'implantation d'une vieille grange typique près de l'entrée de la maison et son accès par un tunnel les ont sans doute rassurées. « La réglementation de la construction suisse dans cette région dit que l'on ne peut obtenir de permis de construire définitif qu'après l'édification d'une maquette en bois du volume du bâtiment sur le site, ce qui permet à la communauté de juger du projet et de faire ses observations. Pour notre proposition, la logique a prévalu et cette partie du processus d'autorisation a été jugée inutile. »

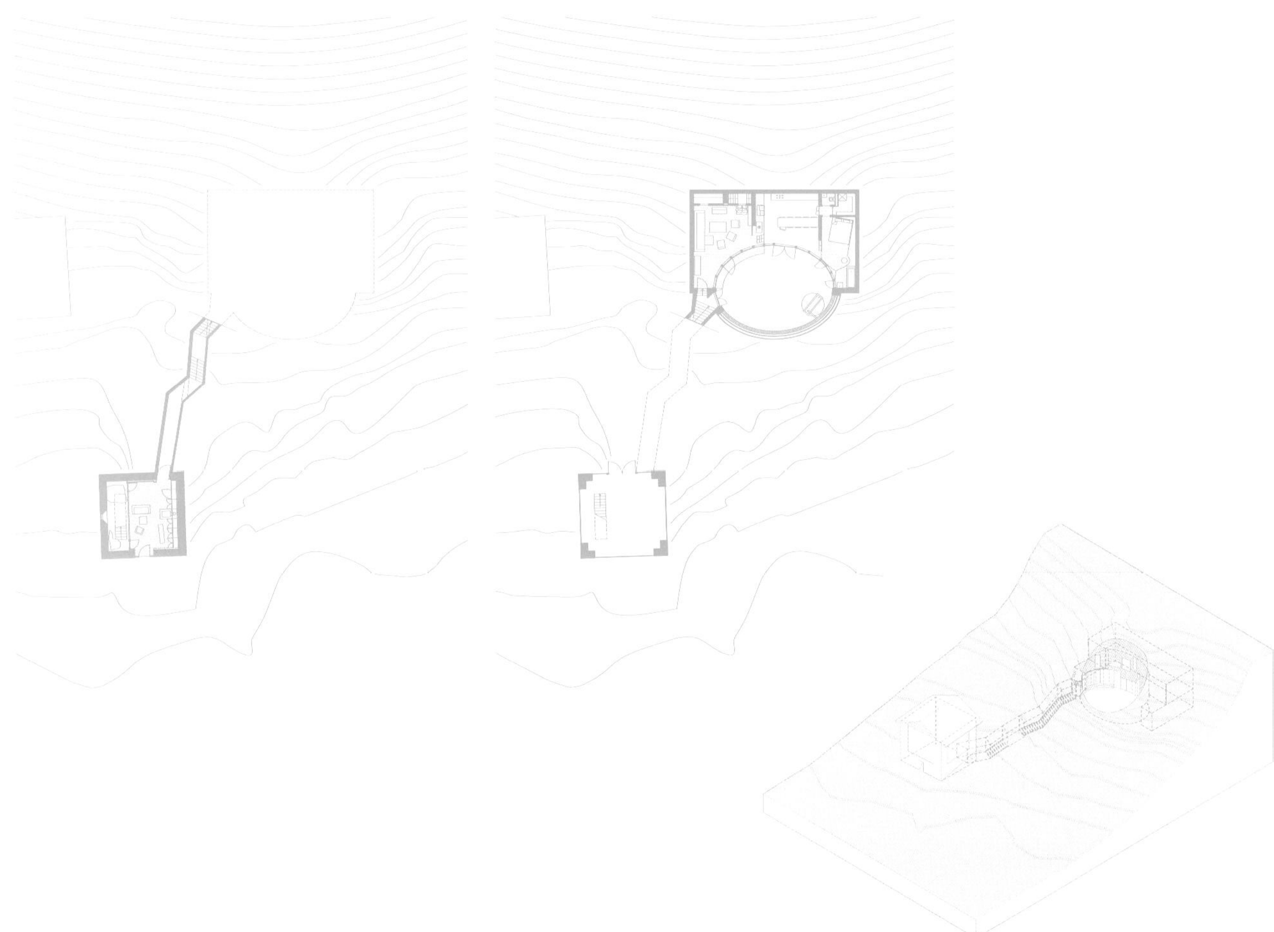

The oval form of the house, visible in the plans to the left, is echoed in the curious emergent part of the largely buried structure.

Die ovale Form des Hauses, zu sehen an den Grundrissen links, wird formal im eigentümlich aufragenden Teil des überwiegend versenkten Baus aufgegriffen.

La forme de la section semi-ovale de la maison en partie enterrée (plans de gauche) se retrouve dans la curieuse découpe du terrain par laquelle elle s'ouvre sur l'extérieur.

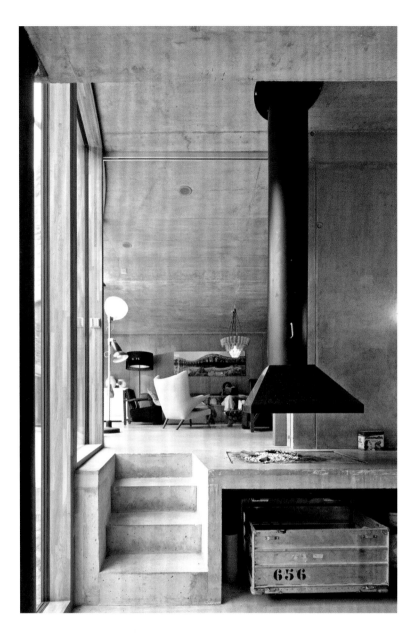

The concrete surfaces of the house are rough like the mountain terrain into which it is embedded.

Die Betonoberflächen des Hauses sind ebenso rau wie das Felsterrain, in das das Domizil eingebettet wurde.

À l'intérieur, les murs sont restés en béton brut, en rappel de la nature du terrain environnant.

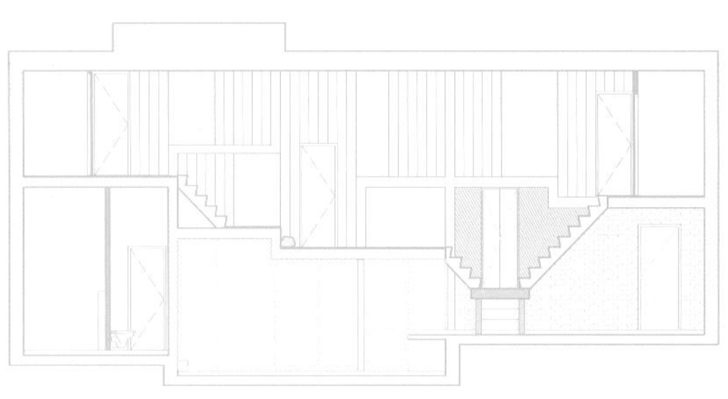

Concrete alternates with stone and furniture that may be more "cozy" than the architects would have imagined.

Beton im Wechselspiel mit Stein und einem Mobiliar, das möglicherweise „gemütlicher" ist, als es sich die Architekten vorgestellt haben.

Le béton alterne avec des parties en pierre mais aussi des meubles de style peut-être plus cosy que les architectes ne l'auraient souhaité.

As the drawing to the right demonstrates, the house is largely underground, with its concrete surfaces in some sense echoing the stone of the mountain itself.

Wie die Zeichnung rechts veranschaulicht, liegt das Haus überwiegend unter der Geländeoberfläche. In gewisser Weise antworten die Betonflächen auf den Fels des Berges.

Comme le montre l'élévation de sa « façade » à droite, la maison est en grande partie enterrée. Le béton omniprésent fait écho au sol caillouteux de la montagne.

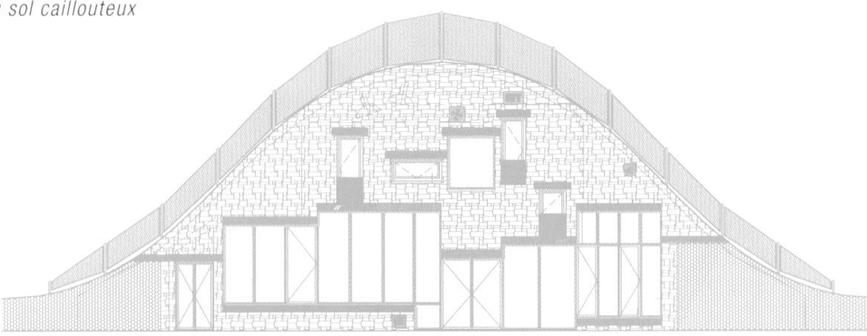

ROBERT STONE

RSd
Robert Stone
1507 Scott Avenue
Los Angeles, CA 90026
USA

Tel: +1 323 481 3934
E-mail: rs@robertstonedesign.com
Web: www.robertstonedesign.com

ROBERT STONE was born in 1968 in Palm Springs, California. He obteined his Bachelor's degree from the University of California at Berkeley (1992) and his M.Arch degree from the same institution in 1995. He is licensed as an architect, but also as a general contractor. His work includes the Vacancy Motel (Palm Springs, California, 2001); Echo Night Club (Los Angeles, 2002); a design for the exhibition "Beyond Geometry" (Los Angeles County Museum of Art, Los Angeles, 2004); Rosa Muerta House (Joshua Tree, California, 2006–09, published here); and currently Acido Dorado House (Joshua Tree, California, 2010), all in the USA. His work usually includes the design of many custom elements that are then fabricated by Stone himself. Both the Rosa Muerta House and the Acido Dorado House are intended as vacation rentals.

ROBERT STONE wurde 1968 in Palm Springs, Kalifornien, geboren. Nach seinem Bachelor (1992) erwarb er auch seinen M.Arch. an der University of California in Berkeley (1995). Er ist eingetragener Architekt und Bauunternehmer. Zu seinen Projekten zählen das Vacancy Motel (Palm Springs, Kalifornien, 2001), der Echo Night Club (Los Angeles, 2002), ein Entwurf für die Ausstellung „Beyond Geometry" (Los Angeles County Museum of Art, Los Angeles, 2004), das Haus Rosa Muerta (Joshua Tree, Kalifornien, 2006–09, hier vorgestellt) sowie aktuell das Haus Acido Dorado (Joshua Tree, Kalifornien, 2010), alle in den USA. In der Regel integriert Stone in seine Entwürfe zahlreiche Sonderwünsche, die er dann selbst anfertigt. Sowohl das Haus Rosa Muerta als auch das Haus Acido Dorado sind als Ferienhäuser gedacht, die vermietet werden.

ROBERT STONE, né en 1968 à Palm Springs (Californie), a un B.Arch. de l'université de Californie à Berkeley (1992), et un M.Arch de la même institution, obtenu en 1995. Il intervient à la fois comme architecte licencié et entreprise générale. Parmi ses réalisations : le Vacancy Motel (Palm Springs, Californie, 2001) ; le Night-Club Echo (Los Angeles, 2002) ; la conception de l'exposition « Beyond Geometry » (Los Angeles County Museum of Art, Los Angeles, 2004) ; la maison Rosa Muerta (Joshua Tree, Californie, 2006–09, publiée ici) ; la maison Acido Dorado (Joshua Tree, Californie, 2010). Ses interventions incluent généralement le dessin de nombreux éléments sur mesure fabriqués par Stone lui-même. La maison Rosa Muerta et la maison Acido Dorado sont destinées à la location de vacances.

ROSA MUERTA

Joshua Tree, California, USA, 2006–09

Area: 124 m². Client: Pretty Vacant Properties.
Cost: not disclosed

In the words of Robert Stone: "**ROSA MUERTA** is a sparse pavilion in the open desert of southern California. It was built as an exploration of new architectural aesthetics developed out of a personal, subcultural, and local vocabulary rather than the ubiquitous universal and abstract approaches of international modernism. This is essentially an underground architecture made for a specific time, place, and culture." The house is located on a one-hectare site in the open desert. The structure uses shade control, thermal mass, solar absorption, and breeze flow to regulate temperatures. Partially set into the ground, the house rises to a maximum of 2.4 meters above grade, appearing to be difficult to inhabit, but in fact it has three-meter-high ceiling inside. Many of the materials are custom made, including concrete blocks, lighting and plumbing fixtures, hardware, wrought iron, cabinets, and furniture. Stone declares: "Imagine critical regionalism that works with the real beautiful and fucked-up cultural context rather than idealized archetypes. Imagine modernism that displays rather than hides the beautiful scars accrued over a century of cultural use and abuse. Somewhere in the middle of all of that, I have found a lot of possibilities for new architecture."

Robert Stone formuliert es so: „**ROSA MUERTA** ist ein karger Pavillon in der offenen Wüste Südkaliforniens. Gebaut wurde er als Auseinandersetzung mit einer neuartigen architektonischen Ästhetik, die aus einer persönlichen, subkulturellen und lokalen Formensprache entwickelt wurde und weniger aus jener allgegenwärtigen, universellen und abstrakten Herangehensweise der internationalen Moderne. Im Grunde ist es eine Underground-Architektur, die für einen spezifischen Augenblick, Ort und eine spezielle Kultur entworfen wurde." Das Haus liegt auf einem 1 ha großen Grundstück mitten in der Wüste. Die Temperaturkontrolle wird durch Beschattungssteuerung, Wärmespeicherfähigkeit, Solarabsorption und natürliche Belüftung gewährleistet. Der teilweise in den Boden versenkte Bau erhebt sich maximal 2,4 m über die Geländeoberfläche und wirkt auf den ersten Blick schwer bewohnbar, hat im Innern jedoch 3 m hohe Räume. Viele der Bauteile sind Sonderanfertigungen, darunter die Betonformsteine, die Beleuchtungskörper und Armaturen, Beschläge, schmiedeeiserne Elemente, Einbauschränke und sonstiges Mobiliar. Stone erklärt: „Stellen Sie sich einen kritischen Regionalismus vor, der mit dem wirklich schönen und kaputten kulturellen Kontext arbeitet statt mit idealisierten Klischees. Stellen Sie sich eine Moderne vor, die die wunderbaren Narben herausstreicht, die ein über ein Jahrhundert währender kultureller Gebrauch und Missbrauch hinterlassen haben, statt sie zu kaschieren. Irgendwo dazwischen habe ich für mich zahlreiche Möglichkeiten für eine neue Architektur entdeckt."

Pour Robert Stone : « **ROSA MUERTA** est un pavillon perdu dans l'immensité désertique de la Californie du Sud. Il a été construit dans l'esprit d'une exploration d'une esthétique architecturale développée à partir d'un vocabulaire personnel, subculturel et local, plutôt qu'à partir de l'approche omniprésente, universelle et abstraite du modernisme international. C'est essentiellement une architecture souterraine, étudiée pour un moment, un lieu et une culture spécifiques. » La maison est située sur un terrain d'un hectare en plein désert. Elle fait appel à des principes de réduction du gain solaire, de masse thermique, d'absorption solaire et de ventilation naturelle pour réguler les températures. En partie enterrée, elle s'élève à un maximum de 2,40 m au-dessus du sol. Si elle semble difficilement habitable à première vue, elle possède en réalité des plafonds de 3 m de haut à l'intérieur. Beaucoup de matériaux et d'équipements ont été spécialement réalisés pour ce chantier comme les blocs de béton, les appareils d'éclairage et de plomberie, la quincaillerie, des éléments en fer forgé et divers meubles. « Imaginer un régionalisme critique qui opère en dialogue avec le contexte culturel vraiment superbe mais très problématique plutôt que des archétypes idéalisés. Imaginer un modernisme qui montre plutôt que cache les magnifiques cicatrices laissées par un siècle d'us et d'abus culturels. Quelque part au milieu de tout cela, j'ai trouvé de multiples possibilités pour une architecture nouvelle », a également écrit Stone.

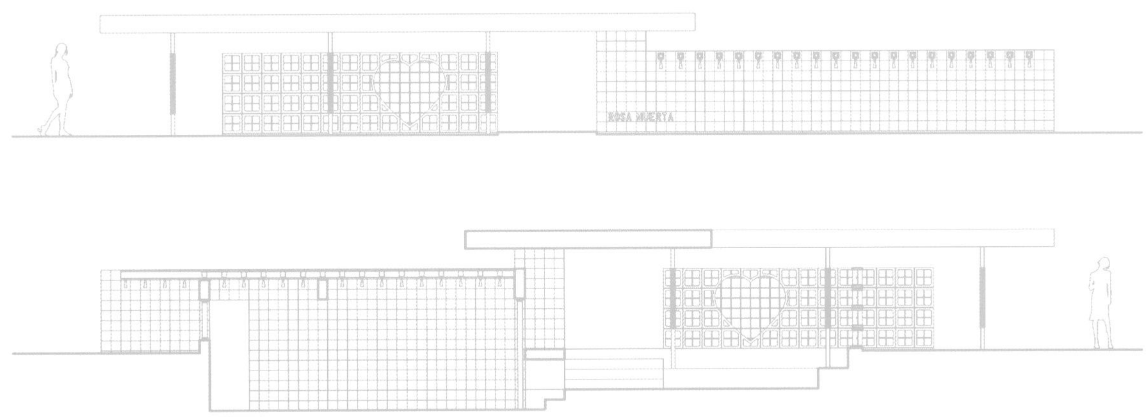

The extreme simplicity of the house, with its cantilevered slab roof and low-lying rectangular volumes, makes it seem to emerge from its arid setting like an alien presence that somehow has legitimacy here.

Durch die extreme Schlichtheit des Hauses mit der auskragenden Dachplatte und den niedrigen, geradlinigen Baukörpern entsteht der Eindruck, als tauche das Haus inmitten des unwirtlichen Terrains wie ein außerirdisches Wesen auf, das seine Rechte geltend macht.

La simplicité extrême de la maison – toit plat en porte-à-faux et volumes rectangulaires surbaissés – donne l'impression qu'elle émerge de ce cadre aride comme un objet extraterrestre mais néanmoins légitime.

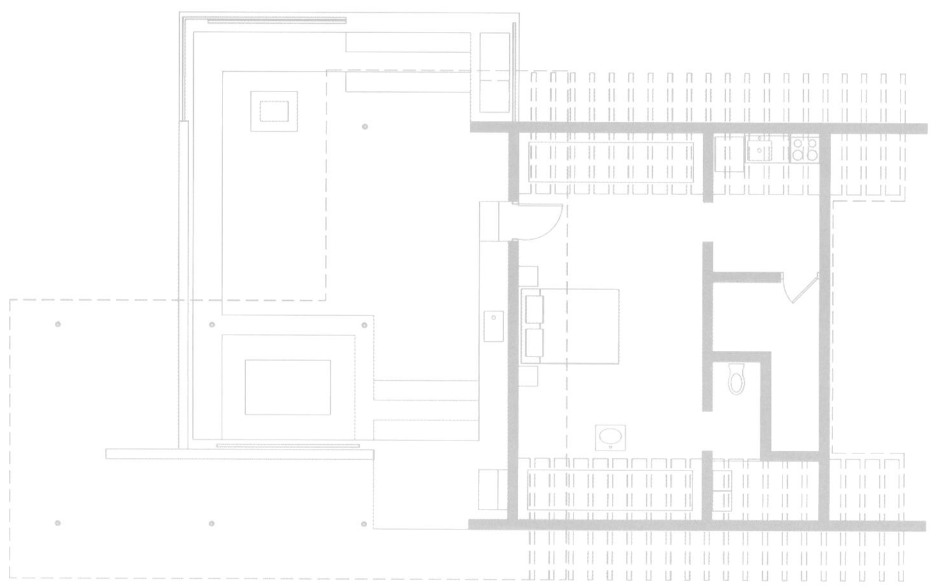

Screens echo the grid of the house itself, providing a limit between the zone of the residence and the much vaster one of the site and the natural environment.

Die Wandschirme greifen das Grundraster des Hauses auf und markieren zugleich eine Grenze zwischen dem Areal des Hauses und dem ungleich größeren Bereich des Grundstücks und der landschaftlichen Umgebung.

Les écrans qui rappellent la trame du plan de la maison marquent la limite entre la résidence, le terrain qui l'entoure et son immense environnement naturel.

Strong natural light penetrates the house but does not disturb the essential darkness generated by the architecture.

Helles Tageslicht fällt in den Bau, stört jedoch nicht die dominierende Dunkelheit der Architektur.

L'éclairage naturel puissant qui pénètre à certains moments dans la maison, ne lui fait pas perdre pour autant l'atmosphère sombre voulue par l'architecte.

STUDIO PEI-ZHU

Studio Pei Zhu
B-618 Tian Hai Business Center
107 North Dongsi Street
Beijing 100007
China

Tel: +86 10 6401 6657
Fax: +86 10 6403 8967
E-mail: office@studiozp.com

Pei Zhu was born in Beijing in 1962. He received his M.Arch degree from Tsinghua University, and Master of Architecture and Urban Design degree from the University of California at Berkeley. He has worked with the large American firm RTKL Associates, and as an Associate Professor at Tsinghua University. He is the Principal Architect and founder of **STUDIO PEI ZHU** (which he views as a platform for researching the relationship between traditional Chinese philosophy and contemporary architecture) and, prior to opening this office in 2005 in Beijing, he was a founding partner and Design Principal of URBANUS (2001–04). He has been involved in major projects in the United States, as well as in China, such as Shanghai Science Land, a science museum; Cai Guo-Qiang Courtyard House Renovation (Beijing, 2007, published here); Guggenheim Art Pavilion in Abu Dhabi (design 2006–07); the Guggenheim Museum in Beijing (design 2007); Digital Beijing, Control Center for the 2008 Olympics (Beijing, 2005–08); and Blur Hotel, a design hotel in the center of Beijing.

Pei Zhu kam 1962 in Peking zur Welt. Er erlangte seinen M.Arch. an der Universität Tsinghua sowie einen Master in Architektur und Stadtplanung an der University of California in Berkeley. Anschließend war er für das große amerikanische Büro RTKL Associates tätig und war Lehrbeauftragter an der Universität Tsinghua. Pei Zhu ist Chefarchitekt und Gründer des **STUDIO PEI-ZHU**, das er als Grundlage betrachtet, um die Beziehung zwischen traditioneller chinesischer Philosophie und zeitgenössischer Architektur zu erforschen. Vor der Eröffnung seines Büros in Peking (2005) war er Gründungspartner und leitender Architekt für Entwurf bei URBANUS (2001–04). Er war an zahlreichen Großprojekten in den USA und an Projekten in China beteiligt, darunter dem Shanghai Science Land, einem Wissenschaftsmuseum, der Sanierung des Wohnhofs von Cai Guo-Qiang (Peking, 2007, hier vorgestellt), dem Guggenheim-Kunstpavillon in Abu Dhabi (Entwurf 2006–07), dem Guggenheim-Museum in Peking (Entwurf 2007), Digital Beijing, dem Kontrollzentrum für die Olympischen Spiele 2008 (Peking, 2005–08) sowie dem Blur Hotel, einem Designhotel im Herzen Pekings.

Pei-Zhu, né à Pékin en 1962, a obtenu son M.Arch. de l'université de Tsinghua, Chine, son M.Arch. et son diplôme d'urbanisme de l'université de Californie à Berkeley. Il a travaillé dans la grande agence américaine RTKL Associates et a été professeur associé à l'université de Tsinghua. Il a fondé, en 2005 à Pékin, le **STUDIO PEI-ZHU** (qu'il voit comme une plate-forme de recherches sur les relations entre la philosophie traditionnelle chinoise et l'architecture contemporaine), mais avait précédemment participé à la création de l'agence URBANUS (2001–04), dont il était responsable des projets. Il est intervenu sur de grands projets aux États-Unis et en Chine, comme le musée des Sciences de Shanghaï, Science Land ; la rénovation de la maison à cour de l'artiste Cai Guo-Qiang (Pékin, 2007, publiée ici) ; le pavillon d'art Guggenheim à Abou Dhabi (conception 2006–07) ; Digital Beijing, centre de contrôle des Jeux olympiques de 2008 à Pékin, ainsi que le Blur Hotel, un hôtel design au centre de Pékin.

CAI GUO-QIANG COURTYARD HOUSE RENOVATION

Beijing, China, 2007

Area: 413 m². Client: Cai Guo-Qiang. Cost: not disclosed.
Collaboration: Tong Wu, Wentian Liu

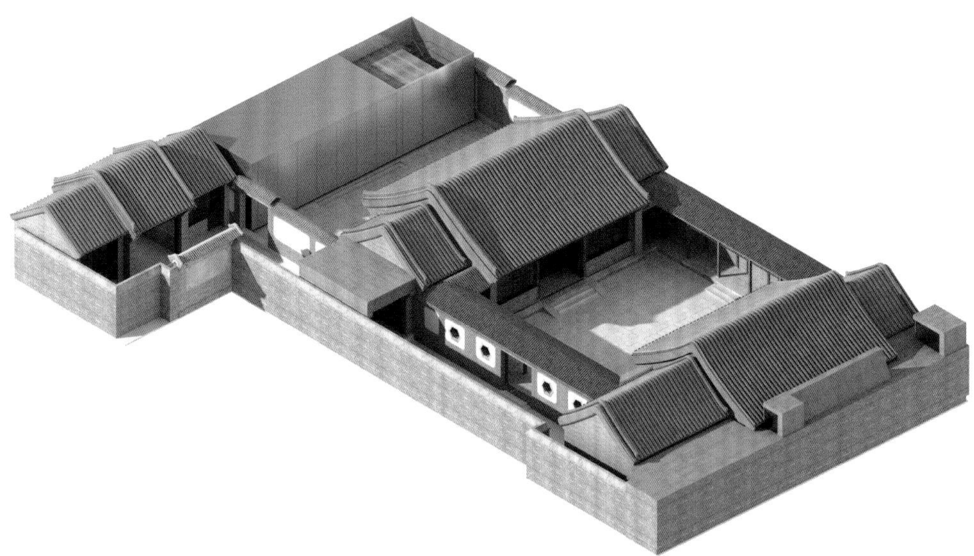

Cai Guo-Qiang, born in 1957 in Quanzhou City (Fujian, China), is one of the best-known contemporary Chinese artists, and was the client of this project. The architect sought to "reinforce the old, introduce the new," as he restored an existing courtyard house and added a titanium-aluminum alloy façade. Through collaboration with the artist-client, the house's three courtyards are expressed and organized by "spatial themes" that have resonance with Chinese philosophy and the role of contemporary art in China. The architect explains that the north "compartment" was defined as a "three-dimensional installation." The old wood structure in this space was exposed in order to express its strength. The middle compartment was defined as "two-dimensional Chinese painting." Here, white walls dominate the interior, expressing a "sense of relaxation and grace." The south room was defined as "futuristic space." Pei Zhu states that the old and new architecture both conflict and converse with each other: "The visual and spatial penetration between the courtyards forms a symphony of tradition and the future."

Cai Guo-Qiang, geboren 1957 in Quanzhou (Fujian, China), ist einer der bekanntesten zeitgenössischen Künstler Chinas und Auftraggeber dieses Projekts. Bei der Sanierung eines alten Wohnhofs, bei der ein Gebäude eine Fassade aus Titan-Aluminium-Legierung erhielt, ging es dem Architekten darum, „das Alte zu stärken und Neues hinzuzufügen". Zusammen mit seinem künstlerisch tätigen Auftraggeber entwickelte er ein Konzept, das die drei Höfe nach „räumlichen Themen" gestaltet und organisiert, die sowohl die chinesische Philosophie als auch die Rolle zeitgenössischer Kunst in China widerspiegeln. Wie der Architekt erklärt, wurde die nördliche „Abteilung" als „dreidimensionale Installation" definiert. In diesem Bereich legte man die alte Holzkonstruktion frei, um ihre Kraft herauszustreichen. Der mittlere Bereich wurde als „zweidimensionale chinesische Malerei" gestaltet. Hier prägen weiße Wände den Innenraum und schaffen eine Atmosphäre von „Entspanntheit und Eleganz". Der südliche Bereich wurde als „futuristischer Raum" interpretiert. Pei Zhu betont, dass sich alte und neue Architektur sowohl aneinander reiben als auch miteinander kommunizieren: „Das visuelle und räumliche Ineinandergreifen der einzelnen Höfe schafft eine Symphonie aus Tradition und Zukunft."

Cai Guo-Qiang, né en 1957 à Quanzhou (Fujian, Chine), est l'un des plus célèbres artistes chinois contemporains et le destinataire de ce projet. L'architecte a cherché « à renforcer l'ancien, introduire le nouveau », en restaurant une maison à cour existante, et en ajoutant une façade en alliage de titane et d'aluminium. La collaboration avec le client artiste a conduit à exprimer et organiser les trois cours en « thèmes spatiaux » qui viennent en résonance à la philosophie chinoise et au rôle de l'art contemporain en Chine. L'architecte explique que le « compartiment » nord se définit comme « une installation tridimensionnelle ». La vieille structure en bois a été laissée apparente pour exprimer sa solidité. Le compartiment central se définit comme « une peinture chinoise bidimensionnelle ». Ici, l'intérieur est dominé par des murs blancs qui expriment un « sentiment de relaxation et de grâce ». La salle sud est décrite comme un « espace futuriste ». Pei Zhu fait remarquer que l'ancienne et la nouvelle architecture sont à la fois en conflit et en dialogue: « La pénétration visuelle et spatiale entre les cours forme une symphonie de tradition et de futur. »

Within the environment of a typical Chinese house, the architect has generated modern volumes that remain in harmony with the setting.

Innerhalb der Anlage eines traditionellen chinesischen Wohnhauses realisierte der Architekt moderne Baukörper, die sich harmonisch in ihre Umgebung einfügen.

Dans le cadre d'une maison chinoise traditionnelle, l'architecte a créé des volumes modernes qui restent en harmonie avec son esprit.

A brick wall with the outline of a filled window appears like the pentimenti *of Old Master paintings. Wood floors and walls contrast with this rougher surface.*

Eine Backsteinmauer mit den Spuren eines zugemauerten Fensters erinnert an die pentimenti *in den Gemälden Alter Meister. Holzböden und -wandverkleidungen bilden einen Kontrast zu den raueren Oberflächen.*

Un mur de brique marqué de traces de fenêtres murées qui font penser aux repentirs des peintures de maîtres anciens. Les planchers et les murs en bois contrastent avec la surface plus brute de la brique.

A view through the volumes of the house shows the kind of interpenetration of interior courtyards and interior architectural spaces that are frequently seen in the traditional houses of China.

Ein Blick durch die verschiedenen Baukörper hindurch verdeutlicht die Durchdringung von Innenhöfen und Innenräumen, die in traditionellen chinesischen Häusern oft zu finden ist.

Une perspective à travers la maison montre cette interpénétration des cours intérieures et des volumes intérieurs que l'on observe fréquemment dans les maisons traditionnelles chinoises.

Pei Zhu has alternated and contrasted modern and traditional elements in this house, much in the way that Cai Guo-Qiang does in his own works of art.

Pei Zhu gestaltet in diesem Haus ein Wechselspiel zwischen modernen und traditionellen Elementen – auf ähnliche Weise wie Cai Guo-Qiang in seinen künstlerischen Arbeiten.

Pei Zhu a fait alterner des éléments modernes et traditionnels, comme le fait d'ailleurs l'artiste Cai Guo Qiang dans ses œuvres.

MAKIKO TSUKADA

Makiko Tsukada Architects
6–12–15 Shimosyakujii
Nerima-ku
Tokyo 177–0042
Japan

Tel: +81 3 5372 7584
Fax: +81 3 5372 7862
E-mail: tsukada@plala.to
Web: www15.plala.or.jp/maaa

MAKIKO TSUKADA was born in 1961 in Hokkaido. In 1986, she graduated from Hokkaido University. In 1986, she began to work with the Obayashi Corporation (until 1989). She then took a position with the architect Minoru Takeyama (1989–93), and finally worked with Shigeru Ban Architects in Tokyo (1993–94), before creating her own firm, Makiko Tsukada Architects, in 1995. Her current work includes Kondo House (Tokyo, 2007–08, published here); S&S House (Yokohama, 2007–08); Shakuji Pleats (Tokyo, 2010); and Kozuki House (Tokyo, 2010), all in Japan.

MAKIKO TSUKADA kam 1961 in Hokkaido zur Welt. 1986 schloss sie ihr Studium an der Universität Hokkaido ab und nahm eine Tätigkeit bei der Obayashi Corporation auf (bis 1989). Anschließend war sie im Architekturbüro von Minoru Takeyama (1989–93) tätig und arbeitete schließlich für Shigeru Ban Architects in Tokio (1993–94), ehe sie 1995 ihr eigenes Büro, Makiko Tsukada Architects, gründete. Aktuelle Projekte sind u. a. das Haus Kondo (Tokio, 2007–08, hier vorgestellt), das Haus S&S (Yokohama, 2007–08), Shakuji Pleats (Tokio, 2010) sowie das Haus Kozuki (Tokio, 2010), alle in Japan.

MAKIKO TSUKADA est née en 1961 à Hokkaido. Elle est diplômée de l'université d'Hokkaido (1986). La même année, elle a commencé à travailler pour la Obayashi Corporation (jusqu'en 1989), puis pour l'architecte Minoru Takeyama (1989–93), et finalement Shigeru Ban Architects à Tokyo (1993–94), avant de créer sa propre structure, Makiko Tsukada Architects, en 1995. Parmi ses travaux actuels : la maison Kondo (Tokyo, 2007–08, publiée ici) ; la maison S&S (Yokohama, 2007–08) ; Shakuji Pleats (Tokyo, 2010) ; et la maison Kozuki (Tokyo, 2010). tous au Japon.

KONDO HOUSE

Tokyo, Japan, 2007–08

Area: 78 m². Client: Yuji Kondo. Cost: not disclosed

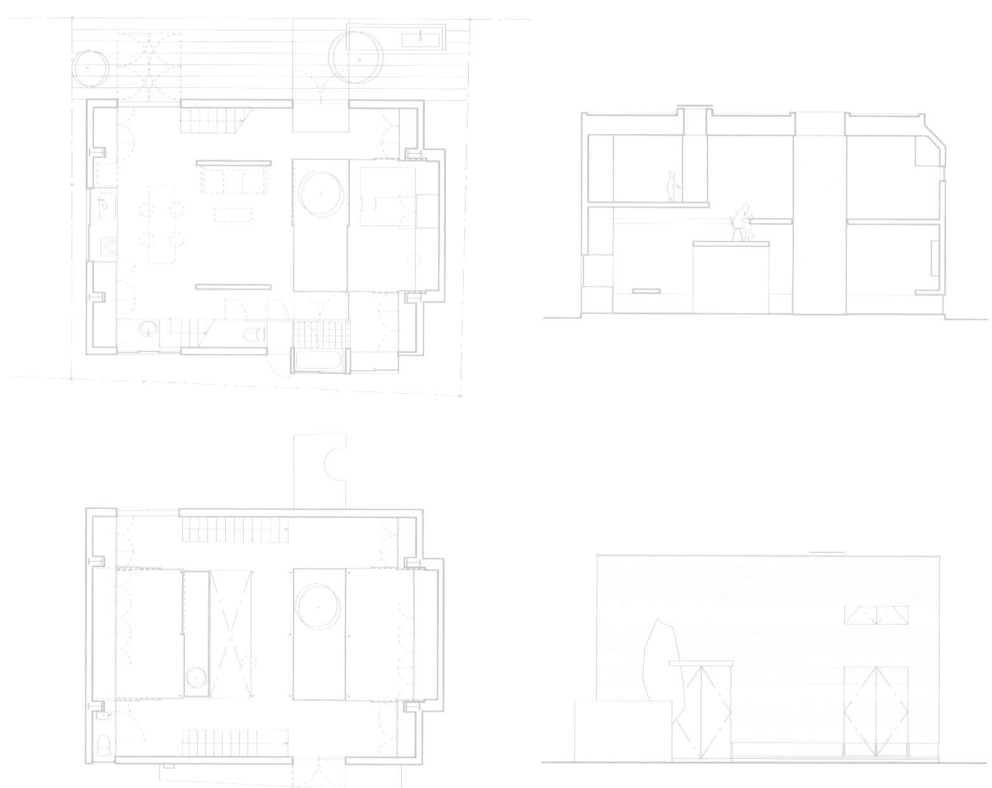

This house was designed for a young couple, their small child, and the father of the man. Both of the owners are graphic designers. The small site with poor natural light required unusual architectural solutions. The family also wanted to avoid views into the busy street on which the house is located. Further, they wished to have internal courtyards, as is often the case of Japanese urban homes. The double steel-frame design with a reinforced foundation allows the external wall and the second floor to hang from this framework. The architect managed to create column-free space within this context. Two glass-enclosed courtyards are part of the scheme. The ground floor contains the kitchen, dining area, and the grandfather's bedroom, as well as storage space around one of the external courtyards. Despite the urban context, light, air, and views of the sky are an integral part of this design.

Dieses Haus wurde für ein junges Paar, ihr kleines Kind und den Vater des Mannes entworfen. Beide Auftraggeber sind Grafikdesigner. Das kleine Grundstück erhält nur wenig Tageslicht und erforderte ungewöhnliche architektonische Lösungen. Außerdem wollte die Familie vermeiden, auf die stark befahrene Straße zu blicken, an der das Haus liegt. Darüber hinaus wünschten sie sich Innenhöfe, wie sie oft in japanischen Stadthäusern zu finden sind. Die doppelte Stahlrahmenkonstruktion mit einem Stahlbetonfundament ermöglicht es, die Außenwand und das Obergeschoss an diesen Rahmen zu hängen. So gelang es der Architektin, einen stützenfreien Innenraum zu schaffen. Zwei verglaste Innenhöfe sind in den Entwurf integriert. Im Erdgeschoss befinden sich Küche, Essbereich und das Schlafzimmer des Großvaters sowie Abstellflächen um einen der äußeren Höfe herum. Trotz der Lage in der Stadt sind Licht, Luft und die Aussicht auf den Himmel integrale Bestandteile dieses Entwurfs.

Cette maison a été conçue pour un jeune couple, leur enfant et le père du client. Les deux propriétaires sont graphistes. Le terrain très réduit, mal éclairé, nécessitait des solutions architecturales inhabituelles. La famille souhaitait également éviter toutes vues sur la rue très fréquentée, et disposer de cours intérieures, comme c'est souvent le cas dans les maisons de ville japonaises. Le principe à double ossature en acier sur fondations renforcées a permis de suspendre le mur et l'étage à ce cadre. L'architecte a ainsi réussi à créer un volume sans colonnes. Deux « cours » dans une cage de verre font partie du projet. Le rez-de-chaussée contient la cuisine, le coin des repas et la chambre du grand-père, ainsi qu'un espace de rangement autour des cours externes. Malgré son contexte urbain, ce projet réussit à donner une impression de lumière, d'air, avec des vues sur le ciel.

Within apparently blank rectilinear volumes, the architect has inserted fully glazed volumes that draw the light into the house from above.

In den vermeintlich nichtssagenden, rechtwinkligen Baukörper integrierte die Architektin voll verglaste Volumina, die von oben Licht in das Haus lassen.

Dans des espaces rectilignes neutres, l'architecte a inséré des volumes entièrement vitrés qui attirent la lumière dans la maison.

With some walls made only of glass, the house offers strong contrasts, such as the protective wooden shell seen around the sitting area in the image above.

Einige Wände bestehen vollständig aus Glas. Doch das Haus bietet starke Kontraste, etwa die schützende Hülle aus Holz, die einen Sitzbereich umfängt (oben im Bild).

Divisée intérieurement par des murs de verre, la maison multiplie les contrastes, comme par exemple dans la construction en bois qui isole une partie du séjour.

Metamorphosis House ►

ULLOA + DING

Ulloa + Ding
Rosal 377 C
8320000 Santiago
Chile

Tel: +56 2 632 5244
E-mail: ulloadavet@yahoo.com
Web: www.jud-arq.blogspot.com

DELPHINE DING was born in Switzerland in 1978 and graduated from the École Polytechnique Fédérale de Lausanne (EPFL) in 2005, assisting with teaching in the Geometry Department there (2003–04). She studied Architecture at the Universitat Politécnica de Catalunya (UPC, Barcelona, 2003) before beginning her professional career. **JOSÉ ULLOA DAVET** was born in Chile in 1977. He graduated as an architect from the Universidad Católica de Chile in 2002. Between 1999 and 2000, he studied at the Universitat Politécnica de Catalunya (UPC, Barcelona). Ding and Ulloa Davet have been collaborating on projects in Barcelona and Chile since 2005: Metamorphosis House (Casablanca, Tunquén, Chile, 2008, published here) is an example.

DELPHINE DING wurde 1978 in der Schweiz geboren und schloss ihr Studium 2005 an der École Polytechnique Fédérale de Lausanne (EPFL) ab, wo sie als Assistentin am Lehrstuhl für Geometrie unterrichtete (2003–04). Sie studierte Architektur an der Universitat Politècnica de Catalunya (UPC, Barcelona, 2003), bevor sie ihre berufliche Laufbahn begann. **JOSÉ ULLOA DAVET** wurde 1977 in Chile geboren. Sein Architekturstudium schloss er 2002 an der Universidad Católica de Chile ab. Von 1999 bis 2000 studierte er an der Universitat Politècnica de Catalunya (UPC, Barcelona). Delphine Ding und Ulloa Davet arbeiten seit 2005 gemeinsam an Projekten in Barcelona und Chile – ihr Haus Metamorphosis (Casablanca, Tunquén, Chile, 2008, hier vorgestellt) ist ein Beispiel.

DELPHINE DING, née en Suisse en 1978, est diplômée de l'École polytechnique fédérale de Lausanne (EPFL, 2005), où elle a été assistante au département de géométrie (2003–04). Elle a étudié l'architecture à l'Université polytechnique de Catalogne (UPC, Barcelone, 2003), avant d'entamer sa carrière professionnelle. **JOSÉ ULLOA DAVET**, né au Chili en 1977, est diplômé de l'Université catholique du Chili (2002). De 1999 à 2000, il a également étudié à l'UPC à Barcelone. Ding et Ulloa Davet collaborent, depuis 2005, à des projets à Barcelone et au Chili : la maison Metamorphosis (Casablanca, Tunquén, Chili, 2008, publiée ici) est un exemple de leurs réalisations.

METAMORPHOSIS HOUSE

Casablanca, Tunquén, Chile, 2008

Area: 180 m². Client: not disclosed. Cost: $70 000

Because the architects undertook a reworking of an existing (1990) wooden house in this instance, they called the house "Metamorphosis." The roof of the old house was made into a panoramic deck with an independent access. A new room was cantilevered over the entrance without the use of any visible columns. Although the south façade was enlarged to give a sea view to the new living area, the original layout of the house was otherwise maintained. A "ventilated wooden skin" provides greater thermal stability for the house. With its outside decks and framed views, the house seems nothing if not thoroughly modern and integrated with its site—a substantial achievement for this renovation.

Bei diesem Projekt integrierten die Architekten ein bestehendes Holzhaus (1990), weshalb sie den Bau „Metamorphosis" nannten. Was früher das Dach des älteren Gebäudes war, wurde zu einer Panoramaterrasse mit separatem Zugang. Über dem Eingang wurde ein neuer Raum geschaffen, der in einem Ausleger ohne sichtbare Stützen untergebracht ist. Zwar wurde die Südfassade vergrößert, damit der neue Wohnraum einen Blick aufs Meer hat, ansonsten jedoch wurde der ursprüngliche Grundriss beibehalten. Eine „hinterlüftete Holzhaut" sorgt für einen Temperaturausgleich im Haus. Mit seinen Terrassen und gerahmten Ausblicken wirkt das Haus uneingeschränkt modern und in sein Umfeld integriert – eine beträchtliche Leistung dieser Sanierung.

C'est parce que ce projet consistait à retravailler une maison en bois datant de 1900 que les architectes l'ont appelé « Metamorphosis ». L'ancienne toiture a été transformée en terrasse panoramique à accès indépendant. Une pièce nouvelle a été créée en porte-à-faux au-dessus de l'entrée sans colonnes apparentes. Le plan d'origine de la maison a été maintenu, même si la façade sud a été élargie pour donner une vue sur la mer au nouveau séjour. Une « peau de bois ventilée » apporte une plus grande stabilité thermique à l'ensemble. Par ses terrasses et ses vues cadrées, la maison semble résolument moderne et intégrée à son site, une réussite particulièrement bienvenue pour cette rénovation.

The slope of the wood-clad house follows that of the site, with a rooftop terrace offering unobstructed views of the ocean.

Die Schräge der holzverblendeten Fassade entspricht dem Gefälle des Grundstücks. Eine Dachterrasse erlaubt einen unverstellten Ausblick aufs Meer.

Le plan de la maison, entièrement habillée de bois, suit la pente du terrain. Le toit-terrasse offre une vue illimitée sur l'océan.

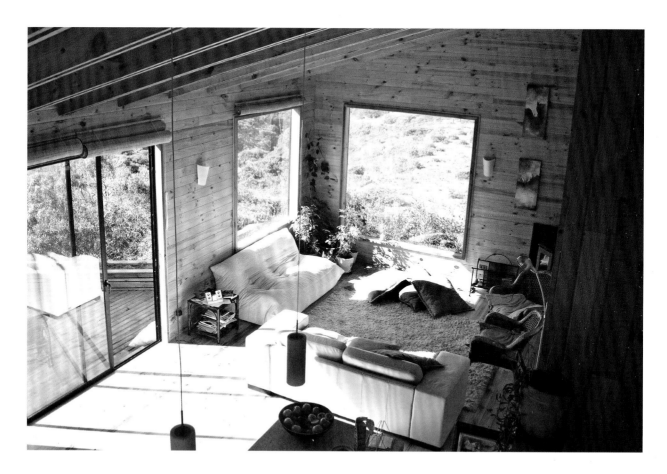

Wood and glass are the most evident materials employed in the interior of the house. Outdoor terraces emphasize the connection between the site and the architecture.

Holz und Glas sind die dominierenden Materialien im Innern des Hauses. Terrassen betonen die Verbindung von Umgebung und Architektur.

Les matériaux utilisés à l'intérieur sont essentiellement le bois et le verre. Les terrasses mettent en évidence le lien entre le site et l'architecture.

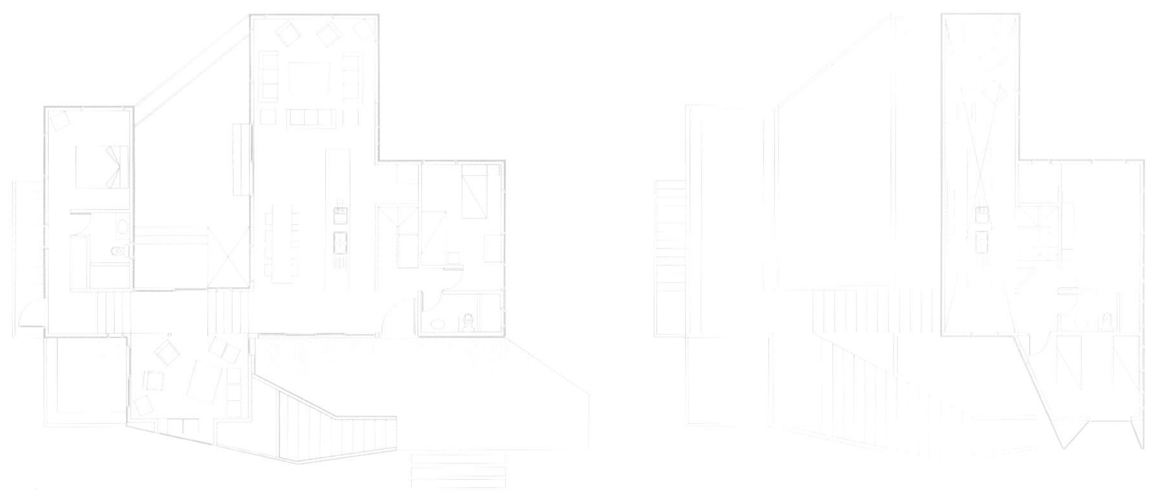

House BB ►

WM + ASSOCIATES

WM + Associates
884–8 Tomitake
Nagano-shi
Nagano 381–0006
Japan

Tel: +81 90 5755 3612
Fax: +81 262 95 0958
E-mail: wm@wm-associates.jp
Web: www.d.hatena.ne.jp/wm_associates/

WM was created in 2007 by Norihisa Kawashima, Wataru Tanaka, Yoshiyuki Hiraiwa, and Kozo Takase. Kawashima was born in 1982 in Kanagawa and graduated from the University of Tokyo in 2007 (M.Arch). He has worked since 2007 with thc large firm Nikken Sekkei. Wataru Tanaka was born in 1983 in Tokyo, and also graduated from the University of Tokyo with an M.Arch degree in 2007. He has worked with the architectural office B.I.G., Copenhagen (2005–06), and with Nikken Sekkei since 2007. Yoshiyuki Hiraiwa is a structural engineer, born in Nara in 1982. He received an M.Arch degree from the University of Tokyo (2007). He works with Sasaki Structural Consultants (2007–). Kozo Takase is an environmental engineer born in Kanagawa in 1983. He graduated with an M.Arch degree from the University of Tokyo in 2009 and is studying to obtain a doctorate in Environmental Engineering. Their only completed work to date is House BB in Nagano (Japan, 2009, published here).

WM wurde 2007 von Norihisa Kawashima, Wataru Tanaka, Yoshiyuki Hiraiwa und Kozo Takase gegründet. Kawashima wurde 1982 in Kanagawa geboren und schloss sein Studium 2007 an der Universität Tokio ab (M.Arch.). Seit 2007 arbeitet er für das große Architekturbüro Nikken Sekkei. Wataru Tanaka wurde 1983 in Tokio geboren und beendete sein Studium ebenfalls 2007 mit einem M.Arch. an der Universität Tokio. Er war für B.I.G. in Kopenhagen tätig (2005–06) und arbeitet seit 2007 ebenfalls für Nikken Sekkei. Yoshiyuki Hiraiwa ist Baustatiker und wurde 1982 in Nara geboren. 2007 erlangte auch er seinen M. Arch. an der Universität Tokio. Er ist für Sasaki Structural Consultants (ab 2007) tätig. Kozo Takase ist Umweltingenieur und wurde 1983 in Kanagawa geboren. 2009 schloss er sein Studium an der Universität Tokio mit dem M. Arch. ab und arbeitet derzeit an seiner Dissertation. Das bisher einzige realisierte Projekt des Büros ist das Haus BB in Nagano (Japan, 2009, hier vorgestellt).

L'agence **WM** a été créée en 2007 par Norihisa Kawashima, Wataru Tanaka, Yoshiyuki Hiraiwa et Kozo Takase. Kawashima, né en 1982 à Kanagawa, sort diplômé d'un M.Arch de l'université de Tokyo en 2007. Il a travaillé ensuite pour l'importante agence Nikken Sekkei. Wataru Tanaka, né en 1983 à Tokyo, a également un M.Arch de l'université de Tokyo (2007). Il a travaillé à l'agence B.I.G. à Copenhague (2005–06) et travaille avec Nikken Sekkei depuis 2007. Yoshiyuki Hiraiwa est un ingénieur structurel né à Nara en 1982, et détient un M.Arch de l'université de Tokyo (2007). Il travaille chez Sasaki Structural Consultants (2007–). Kozo Takase, également ingénieur structurel, est né à Kanagawa en 1983. Ayant obtenu un M.Arch de l'université de Tokyo en 2009, il prépare un doctorat en ingénierie environnementale. Leur seule réalisation achevée à cette date est la Maison BB à Nagano (Japon, 2009, publiée ici).

HOUSE BB

Nagano, Japan, 2009

Area: 73 m². Client: Takashi Baba. Cost: ¥24 million

The architects explain that this house consists of three layers—a first porch with eight timber frames, a "white floating doughnut" above that, and a rooftop that they call a "floating ground with a shaggy penthouse." It is the "doughnut," lifted three meters off the ground, that makes this house stand out from its more traditional neighbors. The surprising timber structure at the base was specifically studied for earthquake resistance. The 21 openings of the house were also designed with ecological concerns in mind, creating a solar collector or a Venturi effect of wind cooling. The outside of the house is wrapped in waterproof urethane and has no gutters. Rainwater drips off the slated roof and into a pebbled courtyard. The architects also emphasize the "ambiguity" of empty space left in the site.

Den Architekten zufolge besteht das Haus aus drei Schichten – einem Unterbau mit acht Holzrahmen, einem „weißen, schwebenden Donut" darüber und einem Dach, das sie als „schwebenden Boden mit einer schäbigen Dachhütte" beschreiben. Gerade durch den 3 m über den Boden aufgeständerten „Donut" hebt sich das Haus von seinen eher traditionellen Nachbarn ab. Die erstaunliche Tragkonstruktion aus Holz wurde speziell im Hinblick auf Erdbebenresistenz entwickelt. Die 21 Fassadenöffnungen des Hauses sind nach ökologischen Gesichtspunkten geplant und haben den Effekt eines Sonnenkollektors bzw. einer Venturi-Düse, die für Luftkühlung sorgt. Von außen ist das Haus mit wasserfestem Urethan ummantelt und hat keine Regenrinnen. Das Regenwasser tropft direkt vom Dach in den kiesbedeckten Innenhof. Besonderen Wert legen die Architekten auch auf die „Mehrdeutigkeit" des offenen Raums auf dem Grundstück.

Cette maison se compose de trois strates, un porche à huit arcs de bois, un « *doughnut* flottant blanc » au-dessus, et une toiture qu'ils qualifient de « sol flottant avec une petite penthouse amusante ». C'est précisément le *doughnut* à 3 m du sol qui fait que cette maison semble se détacher de ses voisines plus conventionnelles. L'étonnante structure en bois de la base a été spécifiquement étudiée pour résister aux tremblements de terre. Les 21 ouvertures de la maison ont été disposées en fonction de critères écologiques et créent un collecteur solaire à effet Venturi qui facilite le rafraîchissement de l'air. L'extérieur de la maison est enveloppé d'une membrane d'uréthane étanche, sans gouttières. Les tuyaux de récupération des eaux pluviales dirigent celles-ci vers une cour de graviers. Les architectes insistent également sur « l'ambiguïté » de l'espace vide sous la maison.

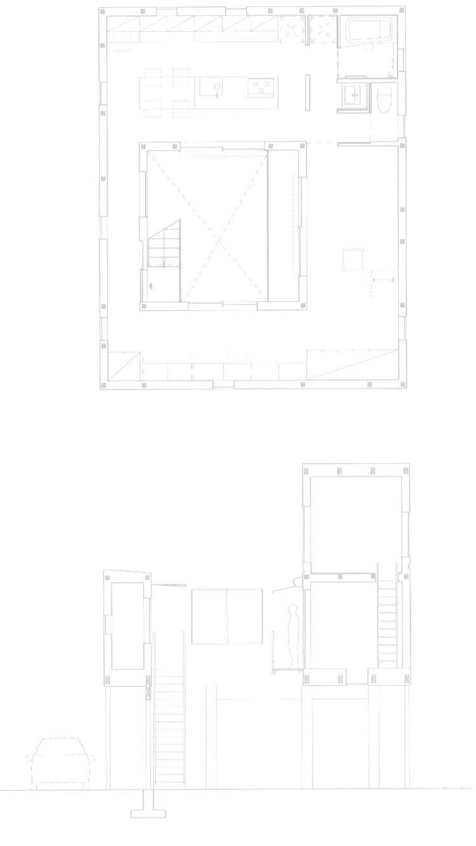

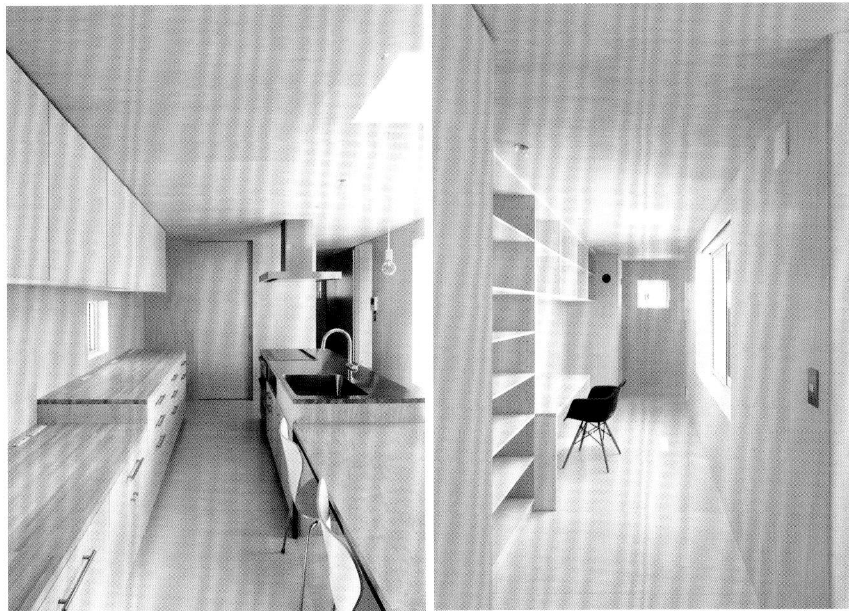

Plan and section of the house (above) show its square shape and the stairway leading from the empty ground level up.

Der Grundriss des Hauses (oben links) ist nahezu quadratisch. Der Querschnitt sowie die Ansicht (oben) zeigen die Treppe, die von der offenen unteren Ebene nach oben führt.

Le plan carré et la coupe de la maison (ci-dessus) montrent l'escalier qui part du volume vide de sa base.

Putney Mountain House ►

KYU SUNG WOO

Kyu Sung Woo Architects
488 Green Street
Cambridge, MA 02139
USA

Tel: +1 617 547 0128
E-mail: kswa@kswa.com
Web: www.kswa.com

KYU SUNG WOO was born in Seoul, Korea, and received B.Sc. and M.Sc. degrees in Architectural Engineering at Seoul National University. He moved to the United States to continue his architectural studies, receiving Master's degrees in Architecture from Columbia University (New York, 1968) and in Urban Design from Harvard (Cambridge, Massachusetts,1970). He worked in the office of José Luis Sert at Sert, Jackson & Associates (Cambridge, Massachusetts, 1970–74), and as an urban designer for a new town development in South Carolina. He was senior Urban Designer for the Mayor's office Midtown Planning and Development (New York, 1975), and then founded his own practice in Cambridge, Massachusetts, in 1978 initially as Woo Associates, and since 1990, as Kyu Sung Woo Architects. Recent significant projects include the Heller School for Social Policy and Management at Brandeis University (Waltham, Massachusetts, 2006); Putney Mountain House (Putney, Vermont, 2005–07), published here); Nerman Museum for Contemporary Art (Overland Park, Kansas, 2007); Harvard Graduate Student Housing (Cambridge, Massachusetts, 2008); Northeastern University Student Housing (Boston, Massachusetts, 2009), all in the USA; and the Asian Culture Complex (Gwangju, South Korea, 2012).

KYU SUNG WOO kam im koreanischen Seoul zur Welt und erlangte einen B.Sc. und einen M.Sc. in Bauingenieurwesen an der Nationaluniversität Seoul. Zur Fortsetzung seines Architekturstudiums zog er in die USA, wo er mit einem Master in Architektur an der Columbia University (New York, 1968) sowie in Stadtplanung in Harvard (Cambridge, Massachusetts, 1970) seine Studien abschloss. Er arbeitete für José Luis Sert bei Sert, Jackson & Associates (Cambridge, Massachusetts, 1970–74) sowie als Stadtplaner an einem Neubaugebiet in South Carolina. Er war leitender Stadtplaner im Büro des Bürgermeisters für die Planung und Entwicklung von Midtown (New York, 1975) und gründete 1978 sein eigenes Büro in Cambridge, Massachusetts, zunächst als Woo Associates. Seit 1990 firmiert das Büro unter dem Namen Kyu Sung Woo Architects. Bedeutende jüngere Projekte sind die Heller School for Social Policy and Management an der Brandeis University (Waltham, Massachusetts, 2006), das Putney Mountain House (Putney, Vermont, 2005–07, hier vorgestellt), das Nerman Museum for Contemporary Art (Overland Park, Kansas, 2007), ein Graduiertenwohnheim in Harvard (Cambridge, Massachusetts, 2008), ein Studentenwohnheim an der Northeastern University (Boston, Massachusetts, 2009), alle in den USA, sowie der Asian Culture Complex (Gwangju, Südkorea, 2012).

KYU SUNG WOO, né à Séoul (Corée), a obtenu son B.Sc. et son M.Sc. en ingénierie architecturale de l'Université nationale de Séoul. Parti poursuivre ses études aux États-Unis, il a obtenu un M.Arch de l'université Columbia (New York, 1968) et un second en urbanisme d'Harvard (Cambridge, Massachusetts,1970). Il a travaillé dans l'agence de José Luis Sert – Sert, Jackson & Associates (Cambridge, Massachusetts, 1970–74) – et comme urbaniste sur un projet de ville nouvelle en Caroline du Sud. Il a été urbaniste senior au Bureau du maire pour l'urbanisme et le développement de Midtown à New York (1975), puis a fondé sa propre agence à Cambridge (Massachusetts) en 1978, initialement sous le nom de Woo Associates et, depuis 1990, de Kyu Sung Woo Architects. Parmi ses projets récents les plus importants : Heller School for Social Policy and Management à l'université Brandeis (Waltham, Massachusetts, 2006) ; la maison de Putney Mountain (Putney, Vermont, 2005–07, publiée ici) ; le Nerman Museum for Contemporary Art (Overland Park, Kansas, 2007) ; des logements pour étudiants à Harvard (Cambridge, Massachusetts, 2008) et à Northeastern University (Boston, Massachusetts, 2009) ; et le complexe de la culture asiatique (Gwangju, Corée du Sud, 2012).

PUTNEY MOUNTAIN HOUSE

Putney, Vermont, USA, 2005–07

Area: 372 m². Client: Kyu Sung Woo. Cost: not disclosed. Collaboration: Brett Bentson (Project Architect), Waclaw Zalewski (Structural Concept), Reed Hilderbrand Associates Inc. (Landscape)

This is the architect's own vacation residence. It has a concrete foundation and was built with standard dimensional lumber and a single long-span wood truss. Western red cedar, corrugated, galvanized steel, Vermont granite, maple, and mahogany are the main building materials. Views of the Green Mountains are framed by the composition through large aluminum-frame windows. According to the architect, the house seeks to reinterpret "the simple volumes of Vermont rural architecture." Organized in three elements around a rock outcropping, the house is intended to provide shelter in the harsh winters, while allowing a maximum amount of contact with the exterior. One volume contains a workshop and storage area, while the two main, connected elements respectively contain private family living space for three generations, and a public studio and meditation space. High-performance insulation and photovoltaic panels reduce energy consumption. Wood stoves and radiant heat floors are also part of the energy scheme of the residence.

Dieses Haus ist das Ferienhaus des Architekten. Gebaut wurde es auf einem Betonfundament mit Bauholz in Standardmaßen und einem einzigen Weitspannträger aus Holz. Hauptmaterialien sind Holz vom Riesen-Lebensbaum, feuerverzinktes Wellblech, Granit aus Vermont, Ahorn und Mahagoni. Große Aluminiumfenster wurden so positioniert, dass sie Ausblicke auf den Green Mountain rahmen. Dem Architekten zufolge ist das Haus der Versuch, „die schlichten Baukörper der ländlichen Architektur Vermonts“ neu zu interpretieren. Das in drei Elementen um einen Felsvorsprung gruppierte Haus soll während der harten Winter Zuflucht bieten und dennoch maximalen Kontakt nach außen gewähren. In einem der Baukörper sind eine Werkstatt und Abstellräume untergebracht, während sich in den beiden anderen, miteinander verbundenen Volumina private Wohnräume für die drei Generationen der Familie sowie ein öffentlich zugängliches Atelier und ein Meditationsraum befinden. Eine leistungsstarke Dämmung und Solarpanele senken den Energieverbrauch. Auch Holzöfen und eine Fußbodenheizung sind in das Energiekonzept des Hauses integriert.

Cette maison est la résidence de vacances de l'architecte. Elle repose sur des fondations en béton et la construction fait appel à des éléments de bois de dimensions standard, et à une ferme préfabriquée de longue portée. Ses principaux matériaux sont le cèdre rouge, la tôle ondulée d'acier, le granit du Vermont, l'érable et l'acajou. Les vues sur les Green Mountains sont cadrées par de grandes fenêtres à châssis en aluminium. Selon l'architecte : la maison cherche à réinterpréter « les volumes simples de l'architecture rurale du Vermont ». Organisée en trois éléments autour d'un affleurement rocheux, la maison devait résister aux hivers rudes de cette région, tout en permettant le maximum de contacts avec l'extérieur. Un volume contient un atelier et un espace de rangement, tandis que les deux éléments principaux, reliés entre eux, abritent les diverses pièces nécessaires à trois générations, un atelier et un espace de méditation. Une isolation haute performance et des panneaux photovoltaïques permettent de réduire la consommation d'énergie. La stratégie énergétique déployée comprend également des poêles à bois et des sols chauffants.

With its steep single sloped roofs and generous glazing (right, bottom), the house exudes a combination of structural simplicity and sophistication that allows residents to take in the setting in comfort.

Mit seinen steilen Pultdächern und der großflächigen Verglasung (rechts unten) wirkt das Haus konstruktiv ebenso schlicht wie anspruchsvoll. So können die Bewohner die Umgebung des Hauses in allem Komfort genießen.

À travers ses toits fortement inclinés et ses généreux vitrages (en bas à droite), la maison exprime à la fois une simplicité structurelle et une sophistication qui permettent à ses occupants de profiter confortablement de son cadre.

Left, plans of the house show its angled design, made up of attached, rectangular boxes. Above, a living room interior, with large glazed surfaces, wood floors, and an overall, elegant simplicity.

Links: Die Grundrisse des Hauses zeigen die winklige Anordnung der kastenförmigen Elemente. Oben: Der Wohnbereich mit großflächigen Verglasungen und Holzboden in seiner schlichten Eleganz.

À gauche, les plans de la maison illustrent sa composition d'ensemble, faite de boîtes rectangulaires reliées entre elles. Ci-dessus, un séjour aux grandes ouvertures vitrées et à plancher de bois d'une élégante simplicité.

Angled surfaces and numerous openings animate the interior spaces, which have been decorated in a sober, attractive way that corresponds well to the architecture.

Winklige Flächen und zahlreiche Öffnungen beleben die Innenräume, welche in nüchterner, ansprechender Weise eingerichtet wurden, die gut mit der Architektur harmoniert.

Les plafonds inclinés et de nombreuses ouvertures animent des volumes intérieurs décorés de manière sobre et séduisante, dans l'esprit de l'architecture.

INDEX OF ARCHITECTS, BUILDINGS, AND PLACES

CREDITS

PHOTO CREDITS — 2 © Iwan Baan / **7** © Tim Bies/Olson Kundig Architects / **8** © Iwan Baan / **10–11** © John Gollings / **12** © GRAFT / **13** © Jeroen Musch / **14** © Timothy Hursley / **15** © davidfranck.de / **17** © Gary Tarleton Photograhy / **19** © Karin Kohlberg / **20** © Iwan Baan / **21** © Christóbal Palma / **22** © P. Hyatt/fabpics / **24** © HHF architects / **25** © Ulloa + Ding / **26–31** © Iwan Baan / **32** © Leonardo Finotti / **33** © Patrick Reynolds/ **34** © Zhenning Fang / **37** © Juliusz Sokolowski / **38** © Amarterrance / **39–43** © Yutaka Suzuki / **44** © Arkpabi / **45–49** © Roland Halbe / **50** © Eduardo Arroyo – NO.MAD Arquitectos / **51–55** © Roland Halbe / **56** © Atelier Bow-Wow / **57–61** © Alessio Guarino / **62–67** © Iwan Baan / **68** © Bellemo & Cat / **69–73** © P. Hyatt/fabpics / **74** © Bernardes + Jacobsen Arquitetura / **75–79** © Leonardo Finotti / **80** © Estudio Arquitectura Campo Baeza / **81–87** © Javier Callejas / **88** © Casey Brown Architecture / **89–93** © Penny Clay / **94** © Gina Kwon / **95–99** © Iwan Baan / **100** © Celula Arquitectura / **101–105** © Paúl Rivera – archphoto / **106** © Estudio de Arquitectura José Cruz Ovalle / **107–109** © Roland Halbe / **110** © Andreas Sterzing / **111–115** © Alex de Rijke / **116** © dRN Architects / **117–125** © Felipe Camus / **126** © Thomas Fabrinsky / **127–131** © K. Ortmeyer/ fabpics / **132** © Fearon Hay Architects Ltd. / **133–137** © Patrick Reynolds **138** © Carlos Ferrater Partnership / **139–143** © Alejo Bagué / **144** © Susan Detroy / **145–151** © Gary Tarleton Photograhy / **152** © FOVEA / **153–157** © Thomas Jantscher / **158** © David Vintiner Photography / **159–167** © Iwan Baan / **168** © Alexander Gorlin Architects / **169–175** © Michael Moran / **176** © Jorge Gracia Studio / **177–179** © Sandra Muñoz / **180** © Ricky Ridecós / **181–182** © Graft Gesellschaft von Architekten GmbH / **186–191** © Hangar Design Group / **192, 200–203** © HHF architects / **193–199** © Iwan Baan / **204** © Jun Igarashi Associates / **205–209** © Iwan Baan / **210** © Yosuke Inoue Architect & Associates / **211–215** © Yutaka Suzuki / **216** © Toyo Ito & Associates, Architects / David Vintiner Photography / Terunobu Fujimori / Taira Nishizawa Architects / **217–227** © Iwan Baan / **228** © Michael Jantzen / **232** © Johnston & Marklee / **233–237** © Leonardo Finotti / **238** © Katarina Nimmervoll / **239–243** © Jeff Goldberg/Esto / **244** © Kanner Architects / **245–249** © Benny Chan/Fotoworks / **250** © Taiji Kawano Architects / **251–255** © Alessio Guarino / **256** © KWK PROMES / **257–263** © Juliusz Sokolowski / **264** © Oliver Helbig / **265–269** © davidfranck.de / **270** © McBride Charles Ryan / **271–279** © John Gollings / **280** © Richard Meier & Partners / **281, 283–285** © Klaus Frahm/Artur / **286** © Joeb + Partners Architects / **287–289, 291** © David Sundberg/Esto / **292** © Olson Kundig Architects / **293–297** © Nikolas Koenig/trunkarchive / **298–303** © Tim Bies/Olson Kundig Architects / **304** © Palerm & Tabares de Nava Arquitectos / **305–307** © Roland Halbe / **308–313** © Studio Architetti Pellegrini & Partners / **314** © Pezo Von Ellrichshausen Architects / **315–317** © Christóbal Palma / **318** © Powerhouse Company / **319–323** © Bas Princen / **324** © PRODUCTORA / **325–329** © Iwan Baan / **330** © RCR Aranda Pigem Vilalta Arquitectes / **331–335** © Hisao Suzuki / **336** © Rocha Tombal Architecten / **337–341** © Christian Richters / **342** © Saunders Architecture / **343–344 top, 348–349** © Jan M. Lillebø, Bergens Tidende / **345 bottom–347** © Michael Perlmutter / **350–351** © Bent Renè Synnevåg / **352–361** © Hartwig N. Schneider Architects / **362** © Schwartz/Silver Architects, Inc. / **363–367** © Undine Pröhl / **368** © Frank Hanswijk / **369–377** © Iwan Baan / **378** © RSd Robert Stone / **379–383** © Brad Lansill / **384** © Studio Pei Zhu / **385–389** © Zhenning Fang / **390** © Makiko Tsukada Architects / **391–395** © K. Suzuki / **396–401** © Ulloa + Ding / **402** © WM + Associates / **403–405** © Yutaka Suzuki / **406** © Lucy Cobos Photography / **407–411** © Timothy Hursley

CREDITS FOR PLANS / DRAWINGS / CAD DOCUMENTS — 41 © Amarterrance / **46, 49** © Arkpabi / **52, 55** © Eduardo Arroyo – NO.MAD Arquitectos / **64** © Atelier Bow-Wow / **70, 72** © Bellemo & Cat / **79** © Bernardes + Jacobsen Arquitetura / **83, 87** © Estudio Arquitectura Campo Baeza / **91, 92** © Casey Brown Architecture / **96–98** © Padraic Cassidy Architect / **102–103, 105** © Celula Arquitectura / **108–109** © Estudio de Arquitectura José Cruz Ovalle / **113, 115** © dRMM / **118–119, 121, 123** © dRN Architects / **128, 130** © Thomas Fabrinsky / **135, 136** © Fearon Hay Architects Ltd. / **141** © Carlos Ferrater Partnership / **147** © FLOAT / **155, 157** © FOVEA / **161, 163, 167** © Sou Fujimoto Architects / **170, 174–175** © Alexander Gorlin Architects / **178** © Jorge Gracia Studio / **182–185** © Graft Gesellschaft von Architekten GmbH / **189–191** © Hangar Design Group / **195–196, 199, 201, 203** © HHF architects / **207–208** © Jun Igarashi Associates / **215** © Yosuke Inoue Architect & Associates / **219** © Toyo Ito & Associates, Architects / **221** © Sou Fujimoto Architects / **224–225** © Terunobu Fujimori / **229–231** © Michael Jantzen / **234–235, 237** © Johnston Marklee / **241–243** © Rick Joy Architects / **246, 248** © Kanner Architects / **252, 255** © Taiji Kawano Architects / **258, 261, 263** © KWK PROMES / **267–268** © J. MAYER H. / **272, 274–276, 279** © McBride Charles Ryan / **282, 284** © Richard Meier & Partners / **288, 290** © Joeb + Partners Architects / **297, 302** © Olson Kundig Architects / **307** © Palerm & Tabares de Nava Arquitectos / **313** © Studio Architetti Pellegrini & Partners / **322** © Powerhouse Company / **326, 329** © PRODUCTORA / **335** © RCR Aranda Pigem Vilalta Arquitectes / **339–340** © Rocha Tombal Architecten / **344** © Saunders Architecture / **354–355, 358, 360** © Hartwig N. Schneider Architects / **365–366** © Schwartz/Silver Architects, Inc. / **372, 374, 376** © SeARCH & CMA / **381–382** © RSd Robert Stone / **386** © Studio Pei Zhu / **392** © Makiko Tsukada Architects / **399, 401** © Ulloa + Ding / **405** © WM + Associates / **408, 410** © Kyu Sung Woo Architects